THE
CHARACTER
OF
NATIONS

Also by Angelo M. Codevilla

Informing Statecraft: Intelligence for a New Century

Modern France

War: Ends and Means (with Paul Seabury)

Machiavelli's Prince

No Victory, No Peace

Between the Alps and a Hard Place

Advice to War Presidents:
A Remedial Course in Statecraft

THE CHARACTER OF NATIONS

HOW POLITICS MAKES AND BREAKS PROSPERITY, FAMILY, AND CIVILITY

Revised Edition

ANGELO M. CODEVILLA

BASIC
BOOKS

A Member of the Perseus Books Group
New York

Typeset in 11 point Garamond

Library of Congress Cataloging-in-Publication Data
Codevilla, Angelo, 1943–
The character of nations : how politics makes and breaks prosperity, family, and
civility / Angelo M. Codevilla. — Rev. ed.
p. cm.
Includes bibliographical references and index.
ISBN 978-0-465-02800-9 (alk. paper)
1. Political culture. 2. Moral conditions. 3. Social values.
JA75.7 .C63 2009
306.2—dc22
2009000660

10 9 8 7 6 5 4 3 2 1

What the Prince does then do many
for upon the Prince are the eyes of all.
—LORENZO DE' MEDICI

CONTENTS

III OUR CHARACTER

PREFACE

As an adolescent Italian immigrant to the New York of the 1950s, I adapted to a way of life I had not imagined. A half century later, the American way of life that I learned then has changed in ways that neither I nor those who taught it to me imagined. How might it change yet again?

The Greek classics teach us that habits make for very different ways of life, and that habits are subject to change. Plato and Aristotle's descriptions of how Lycurgus's laws made the Spartans dogged while Solon's laws made the Athenians expansive make sense. So does Thucydides' account of the Macedonian barbarians adopting Greek ways while any number of Greeks were degenerating into barbarism. And what is Roman history if not the tale of human character and political institutions rising and falling intertwined? The more we live and travel—and the more deeply we reflect about faraway times and places—the more we wonder what it would take for us to live like others, and for our country to change into yet something else. While the lesson that peoples really are different, and that they can change, is as old as Herodotus, fooling ourselves into thinking that all the neighborhoods in the global village are alike, that they will remain as they are and always were, is all too human.

We are interested in how habits change peoples because the character of the American way of life is up for grabs perhaps more than ever before, and because our government and the sectors of society associated with it—our regime—affects our character arguably more than it did generations ago, when it was smaller. Even as our regime is bringing about vast changes in how we live, liberals and conservatives are trumpeting ideas for social engineering. This book is intended to give pause to all social engineers by making the case that the powerful levers they want to pull really are connected to living tissue, that each scheme for reform has reasonably well-known effects.

As a student, as a naval officer, and as a professor, as a civilian fulfilling various assignments within the U.S. government, and as a consultant, researcher, lecturer, and curious tourist, I have been privileged to poke into almost every corner of the world, to read about it, and to talk about it with interesting people. This has strengthened my awe for the countervailing powers of habit and contingency. By and large, people live as they do primarily by following old patterns. Nevertheless, ways of life change because everywhere some make themselves champions of "new modes and orders," which Machiavelli says is the hardest thing in the world, but the most powerful.

I confess to sympathy with John Adams's *A Defense of the American Constitutions* and *Discourse on Avila,* which surveyed the world's political systems. Adams found it easy to imagine the world's peoples digging themselves deeper into misery, despotism, depravity, and superstition, but more difficult to imagine them raising themselves to the prosperity, civility, decency, and piety in which the American people of his time found themselves. Indeed, thought Adams, the Americans should realize how precarious is their hold on the virtues responsible for their happiness, how "strait is the gate." Along with Adams, I see new modes and orders as not so likely to improve human character as they are to worsen it.

Political science, as founded by Aristotle, had as its principal object understanding the human consequences of certain forms and acts of government. The great tyrannies of our time challenge political science to explain how so many peoples have changed so much. Walking around the last of the rubble of postwar Germany as a college student, I found it difficult to understand how the solid burghers I met could have been party to the Holocaust. What could have led such nice folks to do that? My political science courses hardly gave a clue. But Hannah Arendt explained, much as Aristotle would have, how their regime had made evil banal. I read that the Soviet Union had murdered on an even grosser scale. Arthur Koestler and Aleksandr Solzhenitsyn—not political scientists—explained the effects of living by lies. How could the superpolite Japanese people, who are filling the world with Sonys, have wreaked unspeakable cruelties around the Pacific? General Douglas MacArthur explained how one facet of this people's character gave way to another. The Japanologists were otherwise occupied. This is why I have preferred the old political science to the new, and from the outset of my career wanted to write in the style of Aristotle and Montesquieu, of Alexis de Tocqueville, Walter Bagehot, Lord Bryce, and Ferdinand A. Hermens. I wanted to grasp the meaning of our time's regimes by looking at their effects, the better to understand how America's regime is shaping us.

Since the following is political science in the old style, it does not mean to prove anything. It is an essay that musters facts because the author thinks they point to interesting phenomena. Notes are provided to help the reader check quotes, to provide the sources of statistics, to indulge some tangential thoughts, and to thank authors from whom I have learned. This book contains no facts previously unknown. It does bring the experiences of faraway places and times to bear on choices very close to us.

I began this book during my decade as a senior research fellow at Stanford's Hoover Institution (1985–1995) and am indebted to a number of colleagues there whose wisdom enriched and delighted me: to the late Lewis Gann for his wisdom on Africa, Germany, and the English language; to Mikhail Bernstam and Robert Conquest for years of discussions on Soviet and post-Soviet Russia; to Hilton Root for insights on economics in China and the Third World; and to Thomas Metzger and Ramon Myers for introducing me to the interaction of Confucianism and the West. I am also indebted to Thomas West of the University of Dallas, and to the Claremont Institute in general, for discussions on the character of the American founding; as well as to the late Hernan Cubillos for countless conversations on the Chilean revolution of 1973–1990. I thank also graduate students David Corbin and Matt Parks and undergraduate Meredith Wilson, all of whom were at Boston University in the late 1990s, for helping with the original research. I alone am responsible for all interpretations and errors.

Since the first edition of this book was published in 1997, the regimes it described have evolved, and my reflections on them have deepened. This second edition draws from the ensuing decade's events and includes illustrations of our topic that are more familiar and lively. It also considers some aspects of the topic in greater depth and detail.

This book is about the logic of modern regimes and how that logic affects America. That is why, after explaining what regimes are, it focuses on how the legacy of the Soviet Union—the twentieth-century regime in which all of the elements of modernity were concentrated most heavily, the one in which modernity's logic unfolded most fully—affected the prosperity and civility, the families and souls, and the capacity for national survival of the people who lived under it. While we can be grateful that nowhere on earth, least of all in Russia, are any of that monstrosity's elements as virulent today as they were between 1917 and 1991, nevertheless some version of them tempts regimes pretty much everywhere. That is important, because the logic of modern regimes exposes all of them to modernity's temptations. Because modern regimes administer much, the number of prominent persons who constitute them tends to be large. Few, if any, sectors or aspects of society are beyond their reach. To keep from wrecking prosperity, civility, family, and spiritual life, modern regimes would need powerful reasons. They seldom seek them.

Though production is the key to prosperity, redistribution is the economic logic of modern regimes. Whether in Russia, Asia, Europe, or increasingly in America, government itself or association with it is the likeliest path to plenteous, pleasant living. It matters less whether the government owns businesses, as in Cuba; mandates detailed operations, as in Europe; or permits economic activity as a privilege, as in China. The rulers' degree of discretion is key. Modern regimes determine prices, and it matters less whether it is by taxes, by regulations, by management of trade, or by manipulating credit and the value of money. Economic modernity—as it exists, for example, in the European Union—consists less of high tax rates than of exquisitely detailed choices of the categories and even the individuals who benefit, and at whose expense. By subsidies or rules, modern regimes make valuable things that would be worthless, and vice versa. Because regimes can make you a hot commodity, bankrupt you, or save you from bankruptcy regardless of your stupidity, the most economically profitable thing you can do, whether in Europe or Argentina, or China or Chicago, is to worry less about producing than about building a profitable relationship with the regime. Because exchanging economic privilege for political support is the essence of modern government, access to economic opportunities and enjoyment of the fruits of one's labor depends increasingly on what part you play in holding up the regime.

Economic life in America has become inexorably more modern as more and more people at the top, bottom, and even the middle of society have found it increasingly normal to stake their prosperity on the state. Whereas by the late 1990s, even as state power over the economy was growing, there was superficial consensus that it should not, and the subsequent decade saw America's upper socioeconomic end increasingly behaving as if it were entitled to having government cover its bets. The financial panic of 2008 became the occasion for the government authorizing itself to spend $700 billion on top of some $300 billion, and otherwise assuming responsibility for over

$8 *trillion* in private liabilities. The point was to save from bankruptcy whatever businesses it thought worthiest. Not surprisingly, industry after industry argued that it deserved public financing. The winner of the 2008 presidential election, for his part, said that "the middle class" (itself the source and repository of the nation's productive energies and wealth) needed to be "rescued." Who would rescue whom? To whose profit?

The Republican administration of President George W. Bush initiated, and the administration of his Democratic successor expanded, the practice of "rebating" taxes to people who do not pay them—that is, of transferring money from those who pay taxes to those who do not. Composed of interchangeable people, they patronized the lowest strata with "compassionate" programs that they administered. In short, the regime punished the prudent and productive to patronize the imprudent.

The notion that any regime could distribute society's wealth, pick winners and losers while abstracting from its own interests, that it would treat political supporters and opponents equally, is not worth a second thought. In sum, our regime, with the American people in tow, seemed to have accepted the premise that all are *entitled to expect* the government to guarantee their dreams—the very premise that led Argentina, wealthy in the 1920s, to food riots in the 1960s.

Citizenship and the rule of law are even rarer than economic prosperity. Our Declaration of Independence's statement that "all men are created equal," and its exposition of the logic that proceeds from it, sound even stranger to modern ears than to those of the late eighteenth century. That is because modern thought developed antibodies to the notion of God-given human equality. Whether through paths traced by Rousseau, or by Hegel, or by V. I. Lenin, Fidel Castro, John Rawls, or Valéry Giscard d'Estaing, the former French president, who authored the European Union's constitution, the conclusion is the same: Ordinary people are equal only in their duty to meld into large organizations in which the rules are made for the good of all by those who know best.

In the most recent decades, however, in America as elsewhere in the Western world, regimes have added a new twist to old arguments about why ordinary humans are unfit to rule themselves—namely, that government must depend on science, which dictates that peoples must surrender to their betters plenary powers over where and how they live, how much and what kind of energy or even food they consume, in order to "save the planet" from human habitation's effects. The details of such rules being purely scientific and technical, so goes the argument, it would be inappropriate to debate them and subject them to contending interests. Yet, given the existence of contrary interests, scientifically inspired government must harmonize them. Special sensitivity to especially important matters is also the main premise of the argument for why judges and bureaucrats should decide such matters rather than persons tainted by politics. Because this argument has gained so much traction, this second edition examines its roots and consequences in some detail.

Few peoples live under rules of their own making. While some modern regimes have chosen to apply their laws more regularly than others, the American people were well nigh alone (Switzerland excepted) until the late 1930s in making and administering the laws under which they lived, mostly at the local level. Later, as the United States joined the ranks of administrative states, U.S. laws became grants of power to administrative agencies to make the actual rules by which we live, and local autonomy withered.

The effects of modern regimes on family life have continued to develop along a simple logic: As much as it can, the state deals with men, women, and children as individuals with inalienable duties to itself, and with such relationships with one another as each individual may choose. While there have been vast differences in the actual "family policies" of the Soviet Union, Sweden, China, Europe, and the United States, the assumptions underlying them have varied less. The actual condition of families varies widely, from, say, Japan, where they seem most coherent; to Sweden, where they barely exist and few seem to miss them; to Russia, where at least the women seem to miss them terribly. Nevertheless, the result has been a general decline in the rate at which families form, in how long they last, and in what responsibilities they bear for their members. In America the overall (though slower) decline in the various indices of family health can be understood by paying attention to a peculiarly American habit, as old as the nation itself, namely, the tendency of the population to sort itself out according to habits and preferences. Thus there are some sectors—notably unchurched blacks—among which families have practically ceased to exist, and others—Orthodox Jews, Mormons, conservative Catholics, and evangelicals—in which families thrive.

Sorting out and secession are natural reactions to cultural and above all religious differences. Separation of religious communities was the twentieth century's dominant demographic fact. The Indian subcontinent saw Hindus and Muslims separate. Whereas in 1900 Christians, Jews, and Muslims lived side by side from the Caucasus to Morocco, a hundred years later the Christians had retreated to Armenia and Georgia or gone to the West, while the Jews were concentrated in Israel. No sooner had the Soviet empire's dissolution given the Orthodox and Catholic populations of the Balkans and Eastern Europe their freedom than they used it to push away from one another, if not to make war. The millennial strife between Sunni and Shia Muslims became arguably the force driving wars from Gaza to Baghdad.

No doubt, identity politics drive this strife and separation more than zeal over theological particulars does. Nevertheless, the non-Western world is alive with a lively life of the spirit. In China, that life includes perhaps 60 million who practice some kind of Christianity, as well as countless adepts of native cults. The government, eager to tap into what it perceives are the roots of Western civilization's strength, sponsors the teaching of Christianity in the universities. Seemingly understanding that spiritual emptiness is unsustainable, the Chinese regime approves unofficially of its people living spiritual lives as long as they do not threaten it politically.

By contrast, Western regimes have gone out of their way to deny their peoples' and polities' kinship with Christianity—the drafters of the European Union's constitution rejected references to it vehemently and repeatedly. In America, arguing that America is a Christian country endangers careers. Spiritual emptiness, the proposition that human life is qualitatively indistinguishable from animal life and hence meaningless, holds monopoly status in the schools. More important, acceptance of it is *de rigueur* for interacting with those who count. Moreover, Western regimes have tried to engender ersatz sentiments of reverence for "the planet," and for their own status as priests of the culture of liberating meaninglessness. Though this culture is entrenched in regimes, and though it has diminished or suppressed the West's Christianity, it has not engendered enthusiasm, even among its priests.

Whereas in cultural as in other matters Europeans are habituated to following their regimes—usually passively—or revolting, Americans typically tend to gather into subcultures, turning their backs on, and disengaging from, religious as well as secular leaders they dislike. In short, many Americans have reacted to our regime's cultural policy as they have to its family policy: by sorting themselves out into subcultures. Hence America's pluralism is a long-term challenge to its regime—and not just on matters of the spirit.

At all times, however, regimes depend for their survival on their armed forces' willingness and capacity to win battles. Ultimately, these depend on the population's identification of their lives and fortunes with the regime. Arguably (but seldom noted), modern regimes differ from their ancestors of a century ago most significantly in the diminished—often to the vanishing point—willingness of their peoples to defend them. The Soviet regime died in August 1991 when it could not find within its armed forces—the world's largest—a few hundred men to capture the rebellious Russian parliament. That regime, compared with its Russian successor—never mind the regimes of Western Europe—had devoted thought, resources, and brutality to ensuring its forces' responsiveness. They did not answer the call simply because the regime had long since lost the capacity to attract, or to compel, commitments of lives.

Note well, however, that the number of modern regimes that can inspire or compel men to lay down their lives for them is very small. Certainly it does not include any Western European regime. The world's tinpot tyrannies, from the Middle East to Africa and the rest of the Third World, generate plenty of violence through hired thugs. Sometimes, as in the Iran-Iraq war of 1981–1988, they can get people to kill one another by appeals to race, backed by police. Even China's regime trembled in 1989 as it scraped the bottom of its military barrel to find a unit willing to put down a student revolt in Tiananmen Square. In sum, most modern regimes are militarily fragile because their subjects do not see them as worthy of sacrifice.

In this as in other matters the American regime is exceptional, but becoming less so. If, as in Tocqueville's time, religion's pervasiveness is the first thing that foreigners notice in America, patriotism is surely the second. Although, like religion, willingness to fight for America is spread unevenly among American demographic groups, it is widespread enough to make of America probably the only country that can draw a large, reliable army from its population. But as that willingness and that participation in the armed forces becomes more and more peculiar to demographic groups that feel themselves less and less in tune with the regime, as America's regime becomes more and more like those of Europe, and as the regime's military ventures rack up one unsatisfactory end after the other, so is America's military losing its uniqueness.

The change began in the 1950s, as the social groups that make up the regime began to look down on their fellow citizens' revulsion to communism. During the Vietnam War, America's leaders revolted against those they had sent to fight it and withdrew from the armed forces. America's upper and upper-middle classes did not return, but imposed on the armed forces elements of their own culture: acceptance of homosexuals and restrictions on prayer. Our regime, absent in body and estranged in culture, especially scornful of the traditional military goal of victory, became accustomed to using the armed forces in ventures from the Balkans to Iraq that were neither war nor peace, that were more obviously related to regime goals than to American interests—but that got a lot of people killed nevertheless.

Alas, military incompetence is not the only drain on the sources of the American people's commitment to the regime. Increasingly, the regime has come to represent the opposite of the image that the American people have always had of our country. America, such is the image, is a place of bounty, which anyone may acquire without interference from one's presumed betters. Here, if nowhere else, "all men are created equal." Hence, if you live by the laws that you've had a hand in making, you need not suffer those who look down their noses at you. America is by, of, and for families; by, of, and for divine worship and thanksgiving. An equal among equals, you are familiar with weapons and are proud to defend a public realm that is very much your own.

In contrast with this vision, our increasingly Europeanizing administrative regime restricts opportunity. The grounds on which it does so— fairness, the environment—matter less than the fact that the restrictions on prosperity go along with an increase in the distance between the rulers and the ruled, between "authorized persons" and the herd. Americans are not used to such distinctions, or to being looked down upon for devotion to God and family. Add to this that our regime has not been successful as a manager of prosperity or as a healer of social maladies, that it has earned the reputation as a loser of wars.

In sum, different as the world's regimes are from one another, the modernity they share is affecting the peoples who live under them in ways that are comparable, and from the comparison, we may learn how our increasingly modern regime may affect us.

THE
CHARACTER
OF
NATIONS

INTRODUCTION

> Day by day, case by case [the Supreme Court] is busy designing a Constitution for a country I do not recognize.
> —JUSTICE ANTONIN SCALIA, *ROMER V. EVANS*

Americans have had reason to be nonchalant about government—at least until recently. We know that government cannot make us rich or wise—never mind good—and we would like to think that neither can government corrupt us into poverty and degeneracy. Our common sense tells us that people make their own poverty or prosperity, their own freedom or servitude. Moreover, until recently, Americans thought that the choices bearing on what kind of people we are had been made once and for all a long time ago, and we did not suspect that as we wrestled with the problems of the day we were changing our habits for the long run. Whereas once we were sure that the future would bring only more wealth, freedom, and happiness, now we realize that the range of possibilities is much broader.

Anyone over forty is tempted to think of the America in which we live as a different country from that in which we grew up. The changes in the ways we make our living, in how we raise children, and in what we expect from the future dwarf the physical and technological changes. And when we ask ourselves why so much has changed, we usually wind up talking about government. We then wonder how we might change further and how the things that our government does or does not do might make the

1

difference between our living in the land of our dreams or of our night-
mares. Agree as we might that our character makes the biggest difference in
how we live, we realize that government influences citizens' character, just
as the character of citizens shapes the government. Regardless of where we
begin, we are compelled to deal with the relationship between how we govern ourselves and how we live.

Consider a snapshot of life in New York City. In July 1994, after lengthy
deliberation, the city government decided that a person riding the subway
stark naked could be arrested—but only if the individual was smoking.
Whereas an earlier generation of city officials would not have hesitated to
protect the community against "indecent exposure," by 1994 it was difficult
to find an official who would explain that concept. But there was broad
agreement among officials that subway riders should be protected against
secondhand smoke, something unknown to these officials' parents. The
change from intolerance of public nudity to intolerance of public smoking
is just a whiff of what amounts to a revolution in American public life.

Or consider this: Until the late 1960s, on any Friday night in late spring,
the streets of New York were full of wandering prom couples in tuxes and long
gowns. These couples would close the bars, open the bakeries, and watch the
sunrise from the Staten Island ferry or from the city's big bridges. Few feared
for their safety any more than for their sobriety. Nowadays, serving beer to
eighteen-year-olds is a crime, and anyone wandering the streets of an American city until dawn would be suspected of having suicidal instincts.

Or think about this: Very occasionally, a teenage couple would generate a pregnancy, typically followed by a shotgun wedding—a lesson to one
and all that, as people sang then, "love and marriage go together like a
horse and carriage." Nowadays, the horse and carriage of sex (not to mention love) and marriage are increasingly uncoupled. Two-thirds of black children and one-fifth of whites are born out of wedlock.[1] If the young man
causing the pregnancy is lower class and if he sticks around, he may share the
girl's welfare payment. If he is above that, he normally joins in pressuring her
to have an abortion, regarding the baby as an intrusion on bigger agendas.
The very term "shotgun wedding" is hardly understood, and the compulsion to marital responsibility that gives it meaning is generally abhorred.

This revolution of mores is just as evident in public life. While in the
1960s, Nelson Rockefeller never got to first base as a presidential candidate
because his divorce shocked public morality, by the late 1970s cohabitation
had become so widespread that divorce and remarriage seemed conservative

by comparison. Thus, no one suggested that Ronald Reagan's divorce and remarriage disqualified him as the leader of American conservatism—never mind for the presidency. Then again, an American who graduated from college before the mid-1960s might well have come across the words of Creon in Sophocles' *Antigone: "He that is a righteous master of his house will be a righteous statesman."*[2] To later graduates, such sentiments are as foreign as the text.

Or reflect on this: In 1965, four-fifths of the members of Congress were veterans of the armed forces, and an exemplary military record was essential for men to advance in society.[3] In 1992, the country elected a president who had made no secret of his disdain for military service; and any young man trying to succeed in the corporate world, the media, or academe found that if military service did not disqualify him outright, it marked him as a social stranger with unsavory lower-class odors.

Nor will it do to describe the changes among us as a loosening of rules. No, the rules are as tight as ever, maybe tighter, as tight as anywhere. But they are different. Can one imagine an American television station today airing a drama about a repentant homosexual who confesses his sinful lifestyle to a priest? That is no more conceivable than a discussion of the sins of communism on Soviet television under Leonid Brezhnev. Modern America has its taboos no less than remotest New Guinea. But these taboos are ever changing. Some are brand new, while others are outright reversals of old ones. In our America, a single ethnic joke or even a remark merely susceptible of racial interpretation can cost a career. Thus, Howard Cosell's thirty years in sports broadcasting ended during a Monday night football game when he said of a great run by the Washington Redskins' Alvin Garrett: "Look at that little monkey go!" And although no law forbids the traditional English-language coverage of both sexes by masculine pronouns, nor has any law disestablished the words Miss and Mrs., editors importune authors to use gender-neutral language, as well as the appellation Ms.

Today, unlike a generation ago, one can do what one pleases to an American flag, anywhere. But no one is free to pray publicly in a public school. Students have been suspended for singing Christmas carols.[4] Police forces today must warn criminal suspects of procedural rights, but unlike in former years, police and other government agencies can now seize property without ever bringing criminal charges. More officials than ever have the discretion to subject individuals to onerous procedures. A fire chief in Massachusetts who relieved a small flood was fined his net worth for breaching a beaver dam without a permit, a Florida homeowner was fined $10,000 for killing a squirrel that was eating his garden, and an eighty-year-old New York woman was put through "the process," including a strip search, because a cop did not like her attitude. All that anyone needs to have his or her life wrecked in modern America is to become some bureaucrat's pet project or fit some agency's "profile." For example, people charged with sexual abuse of children can now get life in prison on the basis of testimony "recovered" from toddlers by experts, and a kindred expertise has turned spanking recalcitrant children, once the sign of dutiful parenting, into child abuse, about which the government solicits anonymous accusations. Above all, the list of things one can do today without some kind of permission from government is shorter than ever. So, not only does America "define deviancy down," in the words of Senator Daniel P. Moynihan, it also defines other kinds of behavior "up"—out of deficiency into normalcy—as well as creating wholly new categories of things that are praiseworthy or beyond the pale. In short, it will not do to describe our America simply as a place where "anything goes."

It is not necessary to protract the list of contrasts to see that our lives today differ more from those of Americans one generation ago than they do from those of our contemporaries in Western Europe. In short, we have changed enough to change countries. Some of us like the new country better than the old one. All will prefer some feature of the old or of the new. But that is not the point. Since we are continuing to change, a generation from now we might well live in yet another kind of country. For this reason, we should ask: What can become of us? What kind of people do we want to become? Another question, more immediately to the point, arises: What are the long-term consequences of our political choices on our capacity to be prosperous and civil, on our capacity to defend ourselves, and on the quality of our family lives and our spirit?

This book is about how, in various times and places, systems of government, or regimes, affect the economic, civic, familial, spiritual, and military habits of those who live under them. It does not attempt to give "the whole picture" of what is happening regarding any given set of habits in any given country, much less in the United States. The full picture includes the various forms of resistance to the regime by various parts of society, the struggles, and how they come out. But this book has the simpler task of describing what regimes do. Its premise is that governments and the leading elements of society—which together constitute what is variously called "the

Establishment" or "the regime"—have a lot to do with supporting ways of life, with tearing them down, or with building new ones.

CHOICES—RADICAL AND NOT SO

The America described by Alexis de Tocqueville in the 1830s, when John Marshall was chief justice, Andrew Jackson was president, and Daniel Webster was in the Senate, left a lively record of a kind of life fostered by its own kind of rules. That life, based on propositions self-evident at the time—a sovereign God and a very limited government—is remote enough from us to provide, if not a set of realistic options for political organization and economic and social policy in our own time, then an extreme pole by which to judge the direction in which we are moving. At the other extreme, and equally unlikely to be pursued wholeheartedly by the whole American people, is the life toward which much of mankind has been moving in our time. That life is based on the proposition, self-evident to many, that omnicompetent government as the executor of modern science can be the agent of unprecedented wealth, justice, and happiness. We err at our peril if, by focusing on the bloody show of totalitarian regimes, we imagine that they were wholly extraneous to the great trends of our time or to what is happening among us. In fact, the century's kindred spirits of secularism, of statism and radical individualism, most clearly manifest in the totalitarian regimes, as well as our century's peculiar combination of pacifism and disdain for human life, have affected in some measure the rules by which we live. This triad shapes the choices that face us in the future quite as much as our heritage from Tocqueville's America.

The twentieth century has retaught us the awesome power of governments to shape the character of the peoples living under them. The great totalitarian movements left a legacy even more fearsome and instructive than 100 million corpses, namely, the changes they wrought in the mentality and habits of the people who survived them, which they are passing down to new generations. The joy that greeted the collapse of communism was followed by the realization that it would be harder for whole nations to take socialism out of themselves than it had been to take themselves out of socialism. Whereas after the end of Nazism's twelve-year reign the German people quickly recovered the capacity to run a free, prosperous economy in civil peace, restoring eastern Germany to productive and happy life after forty-five years of communism is proving to be far more problematic. In Russia, which suffered for three generations, we see even more clearly how the atrophy of moral faculties mired able human beings in economic misery and crime, as if the Communist regime had killed something essential in the bodies it left standing and had created a spiritual Chernobyl.

Less dramatic, just as real, and perhaps more practically instructive are the effects of less polar forms of government—indeed, of individual policies by any government whatever. The histories of the Roman republic, for example, stress the litigiousness engendered by the redistributive "agrarian law." Well before our century, every kind of economic policy had compiled a record of its effects on wealth and on society, as had policies toward families and religion. Educated people have also long been acquainted with the effects on character of the various systems for organizing political competition. The debates surrounding the establishment of Germany's Federal Republic in 1949 were particularly replete with historical references to how government policy would affect the people's capacity to lead decent lives. All sides searched history for alternatives to the financial and political rules that had wrecked the Weimar Republic. But in their consideration of social policy, they sought different models. Konrad Adenauer sought to promote families in which the husband is the sole breadwinner, while Kurt Schumacher sought models of the good life based on the communal raising of children. America's founding fathers had not lived through the horrors of our century, nor even yet through those of the French Revolution. Nevertheless, led by George Washington (whose favorite phrase might well have been "we have a national character to establish"), they combed history for lessons about the possible long-term effects of the arrangements they were considering. America's founding generation saw in God's lengthy warning in the Old Testament against Israel's adoption of monarchy a "common-sense" historical argument for the principle of human equality and for the practical proposition that big government is inherently wasteful, as well as corruptive of mores.[5]

REGIMES AND CHARACTER

The first part of this book begins with the argument, strange to modern American minds but a staple of ancient thought, that regimes—governments and the Establishment associated with them—make big differences in how people live.

The diversity of human habits dwarfs the physical diversity of human beings. Not much travel or reading is needed to grasp that some peoples glory in labor while others shun it; that modesty is the rule of life in some places but exhibitionism rules in others; that in some places you can go out at night without fear, whereas in others daylight does not reassure; that among some peoples a handshake seals a deal but among others signatures are worthless; that some peoples will fight and others will not; that family ties bind some peoples more than others; that some peoples are more restrained by fear of God than by fear of man and others respond vice versa, along with a host of other contrasts. In short, while all men might well have been created equal, they regularly live lives that are obviously different. Moreover, the habits that enable us to live as we do disable us from living otherwise. And yet people's habits change—cumulatively. Social science, including economics, gives unsatisfactory single-cause explanations for such differences.

The ancients, however, realized that changes in political rules favor one set of habits over others and lay down new layers of habits. We have difficulty understanding this because we are the intellectual heirs of Western Christianity, which made society and individuals less dependent on government than ever before or since. The twentieth century, however, took sovereign government to its logical conclusion. Nowadays, few governments spend less than one-third of their people's wealth. Nearly all have become the chief makers and breakers of fortunes and reputation, even becoming the arbiters of truth. They create wholly new professions and sustain entire classes of people. In short, we now understand perhaps better than at any time since the fall of Rome what the ancients meant by "regime": an arrangement of offices and honors that fosters a peculiar complex of ideas, loves, hates, and fashions and that sets standards for adults and aspirations for children.

Attention to our surroundings leads to a practical grasp of the differences that regimes make in lives and how they go about making them. Well-traveled professionals, whether doctors, professional athletes, corporate or military officers, or journeymen mechanics, readily sense differences in the incentives and disincentives—the "climate"—established by those who dominate any given workplace. Indeed, most regimes—whether corporate or national—broadcast the tone they wish to set, for example, by requiring or banning certain items of clothing (the Muslim veil, the white shirt and tie that J. Edgar Hoover imposed on the FBI) or certain types of architecture, music, and art. Such outward signs are usually good indicators of the priorities that regimes press onto people. Often, governments leave the setting of the regime's tone to private elements. Sometimes they do this intentionally, as when the Chilean military let the country's free-market reformers set the tone of Chilean life between 1973 and 1989.

Particular regimes bring out some of the potential inherent in any given civilization while suppressing others. Civilizations so limit the influence of regimes that, for example, in civilizations where the God-given equality and worth of individuals is not self-evident, we may not properly use the term "democracy" to describe movements for spreading political power. Nor may we discuss the economic effects of regimes as if motivation to labor and allergy to corruption were spread equally throughout humanity. Because civilizations truly are different, talk of spreading capitalism to the ends of the earth is downright meaningless.

Within the bounds set by any given civilization, the various broad categories of regimes—tyranny, the several kinds of oligarchy, and democracy[6]—have peculiar effects on the capacity of peoples to be prosperous and civil and to live spiritually meaningful lives in families, free from foreign domination.

The hallmark of the politics and economics of tyranny is cronyism. Wealth is just another of the privileges that flow from connection to the tyrant. The differences between modern party dictatorships and ancient tyrannies lie primarily in the much greater size of the retinues that society is compelled to support and obey today, as well as in the modern dictatorship's intentional degradation of family and spiritual lives. In military matters, tyrannical regimes are marked by special units with privileges far superior to those of the (usually very large) regular armed forces. The loyalty of such units is both the arrow and the Achilles' heel of the regime. The differences between oligarchies, regimes built to enrich the rulers, lie in the attitudes of the rulers regarding the wealth of others. On one extreme are what we might call Mafia oligarchies such as post-Communist Russia, where the rulers regard others' prosperity as a threat to their own and where friendship is restricted to families. Religion is pressed into superstition, and armed force is something used to rub out rivals. Then there are defenseless free ports, like Singapore, where the rulers thrive within systems of law and low taxes that encourage large numbers of people to think of nothing but making money. At the other extreme are grand oligarchies such as those of nineteenth-century Britain, ancient Carthage, and medieval Venice, all of which hired armies, built empires, and spread refined manners along with wealth.

Because democracies have no character except that which their regimes and their peoples combine to give them at any particular time, they can exhibit any of the features of other regimes. And they can change rapidly. The history of the Roman and Athenian democracies, to name but two, is replete with swings between valor and cowardice, poverty and prosperity, freedom and tyranny, piety and sacrilege, harmony and civil war. While no people is ever spared the choices by which it defines its character, democratic peoples face those choices constantly. Alas, history teaches that when democracies find themselves astride the world, their enemies vanquished, they tend quickly to destroy the remnants of the habits that had made them great.

Few peoples have ever been in the position we are: to hope with some confidence to live with prosperity, limited only by our effort; to strive for government to be our servant rather than our master; to live in families undisturbed; and to overawe our enemies even as we walk humbly with our God. What can we do in our public lives to foster in ourselves the kinds of habits that make possible such an exalted wish list? What are the main choices through which we will create the character of our nation?

By deciding on the size of our government, we will decide to what extent we give in to the temptation to substitute power for voluntary relationships. Economic regulation affects civil society even more than the production of goods. To the extent that government squeezes civil society's autonomy over moral matters, it forces people to seek moral satisfaction through power. Governmental services provided to families tends to relieve them of their functions. In practical terms, the autonomy of civil society means chiefly the latitude of local government. But local discretion diminishes the power of society's most powerful, and tests everyone's tolerance of diversity.

We define ourselves by what we argue about and by how we structure our competition. Arguing about which interest group gets what is conducive neither to prosperity nor to civility. As Abraham Lincoln taught and as the contemporary controversy about abortion shows again, arguing about who shall be defined into and out of the human race is a recipe for civil war. Finally, whatever else we do, if we do not habituate the country's leading classes to sacrifice comfort and risk their lives in the country's defense, we will fall to the first serious military challenge.

THE DIFFERENCES REGIMES MAKE

The second part of the book describes the manifold ways in which governments have affected their peoples' capacity for prosperity, civility, family and spiritual life, as well as for military defense.

Mindful of the hallowed logical principle that the search for understanding of the good must begin with contemplation of the awful,[7] the section begins with consideration of the Soviet regime—whose destructiveness and failure are now more acknowledged than understood. The Soviet regime trained its people to waste labor and investments by teaching them through practice that political connections, rather than productivity, are the keys to the good things in life. The Soviet economy was a very efficient model of a pervasive patronage machine. Like the rest of society, the economy ran by one supreme law: The politically strong do what they can and the weak suffer what they must. The prevalence of officially sanctioned caprice accounted for much of the mutual spite that characterized life in the Soviet empire. The regime also tried to destroy families outright. Only the fear of a demographic crash in the 1930s stopped it. Nevertheless, the regime's conscription of female labor, its usurpation of men's duties as heads of households, and its use of abortion for birth control fostered in men the characteristics we associate with ghetto youths, sowed distrust between men and women, and built an unhappy matriarchy. By contrast, the regime's even more consistent campaign against religion failed utterly to destroy the people's longing for God. In the end, religious and nationalist symbols replaced those of communism. Longing and symbolism notwithstanding, post-Soviet life is characterized by religious ignorance and irreligious practice. Finally, no failure of the Soviet regime is more remarkable than that of its military, to which it had devoted the best of its material and moral resources. It failed mortally in what was supposed to have been its surest strength, the loyalty of the special units that were supposed to do its dirty work—and refused to.

Worldwide since World War II, crafting formulas for national prosperity has been almost as popular as selling financial advice to individuals. During the 1960s, the Third World model was in vogue, followed in the 1980s by the so-called Japanese-Asian model. But the flow of goods and money into the Third World has created classes of powerful parasites there, while in Japan, the mighty production of goods has left many people with Third World comforts. Quite simply, prosperity lies in producing more butter than guns, more widgets than lawsuits; in minimizing the "cut" that nonproducers take from producers; and, above all, in treating the economy's various participants equally under law. Yet regimes often place production far down on the scale of activities they reward, and they redistribute at will.

Note how different are the skills, attitudes, and lifestyles fostered by various countries that from time to time are held up as economically imitable. The Chinese government's occasionally permissive, consistently predatory, regulatory climate creates less prosperity than privilege. Business in China consists effectively of granting and using the privilege to hire labor for next to nothing. The system runs not on property rights secured by law but on the expectation that various officials will be content with the bribes they have received. Thus, the most talented Chinese will continue to prefer gatekeeping and rent seeking to the making of real prosperity. In Europe, dirigisme—the cozy relationship between government regulators and established business—and welfare jointly dominate economic life. Europe's welfare culture has grown fastest at the top as well as at the bottom of society in areas already inured to clientelism, as in eastern Germany and southern Italy. It grows alongside the tendency of workers to start careers later, to end them earlier, and to work ever-fewer hours. One reason that work is becoming less attractive than working the system is that dirigisme, plus high taxes, make favors and lottery likelier paths to wealth than work.

By contrast, Chile, under the government of General Augusto Pinochet, set out to separate political power from economic life as well as to replace habits of group competition with habits of individual responsibility. To wean people from seeking favors, Pinochet reduced the state's power to grant them while outlawing the simultaneous practice of politics and business. To foster habits of personal responsibility, he substituted consumer sovereignty for traditional state services while turning the state social security system into individual retirement accounts. In short, the Pinochet regime used economic means for political ends. Chile's subsequent economic and political well-being is less significant than the change in attitudes on which it is based.

Nothing so affects economic life, civic life, or, for that matter, family and spiritual life as whether the rulers are bound by law or rule by discretion. The rule of law—and citizenship—arise from the habitual belief that people have things and freedoms by right rather than by anyone's leave. This is problematic in modern governments that recognize none but positive law, where millions of unelected officials write and administer countless pages of rules, and where the broad scope of administration inevitably leads to arbitrary enforcement. The pretense that voting for national officials makes citizens out of people who in practice do nothing but obey and wheedle engenders nothing but cynicism. In practice, law and citizenship tend to grow or wither along with property rights and local prerogatives. The politics of redistribution has been destructive of citizenship precisely because it makes positive law—a thing without inherent limit—into a partisan tool. Some kinds of political parties engender more partisanship than others. Parties based on officials elected independently of one another have tended to be less destructive of law and citizenship, whereas parties that are controlled by their own apparatus have fostered the rule of men. The rule of law is a necessary but not sufficient condition of citizenship.

After 1949, the Communist Chinese regime largely succeeded in breaking down much of their people's Confucian respect for traditional virtues and order. But it has failed to inculcate any habitual respect for itself, never mind any of its ideals. Instead, it has trained ordinary people to imitate the leadership's use of power for personal satisfaction. As the regime has aged, it has granted to more and more people the franchise to take advantage of those below them—so long as they pay those above them for the privilege of doing so. In Taiwan, by contrast, the regime began by observing property rights and went on to build something like a civil society on Confucian foundations. The leaders of Singapore, the third regime within Chinese civilization, argue that the Taiwanese regime is doomed by the habits of indiscipline it has legitimized, while Singapore is nipping those habits in the bud. But while the future of citizenship in Taiwan may be shaky, few would argue that Singapore's inhabitants are any more than satisfied consumers of competent government.

The regimes of contemporary Europe, from North Cape to Crete, also present themselves as nonpolitical administrators of the only reasonable agenda—social security. Because Europeans largely accept that agenda, politics in Europe is dead. Although Scandinavians and Germans largely accept the government's good faith and Italians mostly do not, and although the currency of influence varies from north to south, all Europeans accept their roles as subjects—as entitled consumers of government services. The real citizens of Europe, from whom power and to whom privilege flow, are society's corporations, whether big business, unions, political parties, or the complex of bureaucrats and the interest groups they finance. Because of this, Europe's regimes differ only quantitatively from any number of non-European ones. The Mexican regime, for example, is not based on law but on what Mexicans call their national institution—the *mordida,* the "bribe." Like most modern regimes, Mexico claims socioeconomic expertise and co-opts the country's main private interests while ruling through informal networks. Mexico differs from most modern regimes not because its voters have so much less power over their lives or because the amount of favor brokering is so much greater than elsewhere, but rather because most Mexicans are wholly without illusion about law and citizenship.

Modern Western regimes are inherently enemies of families because their intellectual fashion dictates that all human relations (except those between sovereign government and each individual) are purely consensual. Marriage, the foundation of families, is everywhere a creature of law. Laws support the natural symbiosis of men and women when they protect the marriage contract and the party most faithful to it against the other party's evasion or abuse of responsibility. But when they favor the other party, laws tend to erase the essential difference between marriage and consensual relationships. By tilting to one side or the other, laws affect the character of men and women and families. Twentieth-century governments have also interposed themselves between parents and children, ostensibly to protect the latter but in fact diminishing habits of mutual responsibility between generations. To see radically different treatments in our time one must go outside the West—for example, to Japan or to Saudi Arabia.

Sweden shows the epitome of the tendency of Western regimes to atomize families into individuals whose primary recourse is to the state. The Swedish regime has achieved relations between the sexes similar to but less contested than those in the old Soviet Union. Its tax system makes sending women to work the most efficient way to raise a couple's income. Schools teach that marriage is just one of many lifestyles and encourage sexual uninhibitedness as the most socially acceptable expression of freedom. Government policy, implemented from day-care centers to the workplace and expressed even in the design of apartments, aims to feminize men and androgynize women while reducing intergenerational contact. One of the consequences of such social policies is that, by 1980, 63 percent of Stockholm's inhabitants lived alone.

Japan's government, by contrast, believes that the country's success and its very identity are due to the cohesion of its families. And so, Japanese tax laws encourage one-earner households, while the authorities back society's ostracism of cohabiting couples and unmarried parents. Japan's illegitimacy rate is one-fiftieth of Sweden's.[8] However, Japanese authorities have begun to pay at least lip service to modern European ideals of relations between the sexes, and Japanese public opinion tends to follow its leaders. The Saudi government, always under pressure by Muslim brotherhoods and various intellectuals to become more Islamic, is enforcing Islamic marriage laws that require equal treatment of multiple wives—something that is difficult even for the very rich and, some say, inherently impossible. Hence, as the government is being pushed ideologically, it is pulling its people toward practical monogamy.

The most contentious and consequential issues touch religion. Modern government's relationship with religion has been one of rivalry. Although there is not now and never has been a better predictor of prosperity, family, and civility than the practice of Judaism and Christianity, modern Western governments have used their power over education to teach secularism at first, followed by various antireligious dogmas and, most recently, lifestyles repugnant to religious morality. The fundamental Judeo-Christian teaching is that mankind lives under a single, objective set of laws equally binding on all. As governments drain Western societies of religious preferences, they introduce new beliefs based on relativism, that is, on power. Hence, nowadays nihilism does battle for Western souls with a thin, ill-fitting combination of self-worship and earth worship. The stark alternatives in the relationship between religion and political power have clear effects. Outright persecution (unless it is total) strengthens religion, while embrace usually suffocates it. More interesting are the effects of nuanced approaches.

Rome approached religion differently at various points in its long history. In early republican times, the city revered its gods and the oaths to them with a strictness greater than that of the Homeric Greeks. But since its focus was on the city's victory in war, the Roman religion never developed a complex philosophic or ethical component. Thus, it lent itself to becoming a mere motivational tool and quickly lost respect. During the Roman Empire, official religion became irrelevant, while each of the contending nonofficial cults fostered its own way of life. In modern northern Europe, established Protestant churches acquiesced first in the government's secularization of society and even in the teaching of official antireligion. In Catholic Europe, the Christian Democratic movement, the principal reaction to militant liberalism, gave up advocacy of Christian causes, refused to take clear stands on the major issues of the day, immersed itself in day-to-day administration, and died. Throughout the European continent, then, politics has trained people to forget the soul.

In Israel, the official religion is observed by perhaps one-fourth of the population. The most important part of Judaism's legal status is the autonomy it inherited from the laws of the Ottoman Empire. On behalf of a large majority of religiously indifferent Jews (and a substantial minority of antireligious ones), the Jewish state runs separate schools for the religious and accommodates some of their sensibilities about the Sabbath and marriage.

But as the religious increase in number and assertiveness, some secular Jews feel their irreligious Jewishness so outraged that they commit acts of mockery against their religious brethren. This helps neither Israeli souls nor Israel's chances of winning the next war.

The capacity to fight and win wars is the ultimate test of character, and nothing so characterizes a people or determines its fate as the way in which it draws military power from itself. In ancient republics, military service was synonymous with citizenship. The ultimate political question always and everywhere is which people will risk their lives to uphold the regime. Israel excuses its Arabs from military service, even as the South Africa of apartheid did not draft blacks: The regime could not expect to rely on them when it might need them most. Citizen soldiers and veterans have attitudes of ownership toward their regimes and are less likely to endure treatment as subjects. Regimes that purchase military service or compel it from subjects nevertheless have to ensure the loyalty of military cadres and satisfy their claims. Nothing so destroys any regime as soldiers' sentiment that their lives are being toyed with. A look at three regimes shows how their military establishments have shaped their very different characters.

Great Britain in the eighteenth and nineteenth centuries fashioned effective, reliable naval and ground forces out of men taken almost exclusively from the bottom of society for their entire useful lives. Officers from a gentry and bourgeoisie schooled severely in duty and in the glories of empire provided the forces' connection to the regime. In sum, the military functioned like the other parts of Britain's oligarchy and satisfied its measured aims. In Napoleonic France, by contrast, the military was the template of the regime. Just as the democratic nature of the armed forces enticed men to unlimited promotion by merit, the civil service and the educational system in general adopted exams as the key to advancement. The Napoleonic institution of schools of engineering, mines, and public works, and even the numbering of houses, was designed to facilitate the conscription of all of society's resources to serve the regime's unlimited thirst for glory. Charles de Gaulle noted that Napoleon ended up breaking France's sword by striking it senselessly. The Swiss, for their part, have marshaled their forces perhaps as fully as anyone ever has, though without striking, for 200 years. Male service is universal, as are high-quality weapons. Bank presidents are colonels. Training is fierce. Units are as local as their mission. Thus, today's Swiss are still as Niccolò Machiavelli described them half a millennium ago—"most armed and most free."

OUR CHARACTER

The third part of the book considers the struggles by which the American regime is reshaping itself and its people. In order to see how different the foundations of America's prosperity, civility, military defense, family, and religious life are from those of others and in order to see how new shoots are being grafted onto its stem, and how newer ones yet might be, we must begin by looking closely at the regime's point of departure—Tocqueville's time, when the sapling was young and most unique.

The economy of early America was not designed by anyone, and America's founders did not think of themselves as its managers. The vigor of the economy came from the freedom and equality of scattered farmers and artisans. Having been hurt by Britain's mercantilism, Americans were viscerally committed to free trade. In short, American capitalism was not a doctrine but rather the consequence of the country's religious, family, and civic institutions. Religion, wrote Tocqueville, was the first of America's political institutions. A kind of Judaized Christianity filled every nook and cranny of the public square and set the regime's tone, because both political and ecclesiastical authority was exercised by, of, and for a Bible-toting people. Clergymen, unlike today, were forbidden to hold office and taught that all men were equally under God's injunction to be virtuous—or else. The American people's love of liberty was anything but morally empty libertarianism. Tocqueville explained the American devotion to law and civic duty as a commitment to equality and to doing the right thing.

The old American regime's uniqueness may be grasped by the fact that the national Constitution does not even contain the most important word of modern government—"sovereignty"—meaning the prerogative to define one's own power. Habituated to making and respecting their own laws, to being their own police and their own militias, early Americans were wary of the notion that anyone, even the whole people, could exercise broad, ill-defined powers. The laws that principally shaped their private lives had to do with marriage. American laws punished adulterers and fornicators of either sex, as well as husbands who failed to support their families. Early Americans hanged rapists. Tocqueville reported that Americans also viewed marriage from the standpoint of the economic principle of the division of labor and distinguished the roles of men and women much more than

Europeans did. In sum, Americans saw their ways as part of the naturally and divinely ordained path to the good life.

In recent years, many Americans have adopted laws, customs, and habits that contrast sharply with those of America's founders. Others have sought to adhere to older ways. At any rate, today's America is substantially another country. The U.S. government and the regime it leads are not entirely responsible for this. But neither have they been spectators in the culture wars. On the contrary, they have lent growing force to those who have urged a rather coherent set of changes.

America's prosperity is being affected less by the kinds of forces mentioned in economics courses than by changes in the American people's economically relevant habits. Although there has been much talk of how the government expands irresponsibility among the poor by making acceptable the abandonment of responsibility, government-fostered changes in the habits of Americans in the middle and at the top of society are even more significant. As government imposes ever more rules and exceptions and gains greater power to endow and impoverish, it trains us to get ahead through official channels rather than through productive activities. It undermines middle-class responsibility through programs that promise more for less (alas, while delivering less). Above all, government corrupts America from the top by trading priceless access to power for the support of the wealthiest. Thus, the country is dividing between politically potent beneficiaries and the politically impotent who pay for them.

Big government is depriving Americans of self-rule by making unelected judges supreme over even referenda and by empowering them to legislate on whatever they choose. It is depriving us of the rule of law by multiplying bureaucrats who make, execute, and enforce rules. Bureaucrats and judges, along with well-connected labor unions, have well-nigh eliminated citizens' control over the education of their children. Having set out to right social wrongs by giving advantages to women and blacks, the government has spread habits of mutual recrimination. Having emasculated the police powers of localities, the government has curtailed citizens' capacity to protect themselves with firearms. Having made public places unpleasant, the leaders of the American regime have largely abandoned them. Not surprisingly, the country is filling up with people who like one another less—but who dislike the government most of all.

One reason for antigovernment sentiment is that government has become the main weapon of those who want to denigrate and diminish the role of family and religion in American life. This is not to say that government has campaigned directly to increase the rate of divorce or to decrease that of church attendance. But government did institute no-fault divorce, has mandated sex education that abstracts from families, has weakened parental control by spreading the presumption that families abuse children, has made abortion into the most absolute right in the land, and has campaigned for the proposition that all forms of human relationships are at least as valid as that of the natural family. Government has effectively driven religion out of America's public schools and indeed out of almost all public spaces. The odor of illegitimacy attached to public expressions of religiosity has largely caused the very word "Christmas" to be replaced with "holiday" on the airwaves and in public discourse. The government has established, at public expense and with a host of privileges, a secular priesthood of judges, social workers, psychologists, intellectuals, and artists, all of whom teach a contrary gospel. The result has been not only a host of social pathologies, including increased abuse of children and the elderly, but also a growing split between those who live in natural families and by biblical religion and those who live in alternative arrangements and by the regime's new gods.

Can the new American regime defend itself? Since the Vietnam War, the U.S. armed forces have stood on an ever-shakier social base. The leading elements of society, which opted out of the armed forces during the war, also rejected for themselves the whole complex of personal habits and attitudes involved with killing and being killed. They have consented to dispose of military forces composed of hired personnel who have that complex of habits. But the tensions between the U.S. armed forces (as well as the subculture from which they come) and the regime are sure to continue growing.

Our objective here is not to predict the outcome of the struggles over the habits of Americans. Rather, it is to note the directions in which the current regime is pushing those habits. Nevertheless, it is worthwhile to note two of America's deeply rooted habits that surely affect those struggles. First, America's very bones are pluralist. Americans tend to move away from people they cannot stand and to congregate with those whom they can. Thus, complete victory in the culture wars by any side is less likely than is the increasing separation of the people who worship the God of the Bible from those who worship the gods of the regime, of those whose views of marriage and child raising are anathema to one another, of those who march to different drummers. Of course, such growing separation will accelerate the trends that have thus far restricted civic life in America. And needless to say, all this casts a shadow over the country's capacity to face major challenges from abroad. Second, however, America is incorrigibly moralist. Not for nothing do historians point to the Civil War as the most telling event in our history. When two sets of Americans believe that their fundamental freedom to live righteously is being violated by the forces of darkness, they tend to the kinds of passion against which Abraham Lincoln warned—unsuccessfully.

PART I

REGIMES AND CHARACTER

1

REGIMES

How small, of all that human hearts endure
That part that laws or kings can cause or cure.
    —SAMUEL JOHNSON, IN OLIVER GOLDSMITH,
    "THE TRAVELLER"

Since the city is a partnership of citizens in a regime, when the
form of the government changes and becomes different, then it
may be supposed that the city is no longer the same, just as a
tragic differs from a comic chorus, although the members may be
identical. In the same manner . . . every union or compound is
different when the form of their composition changes.
    —ARISTOTLE, *POLITICS*

The oldest Germans alive in our time lived in five radically different countries without ever leaving their homes. Born under the Wilhelmine monarchy, among the most polite, orderly environments imaginable, they were young adults in the anything-goes, irreverent, inflationary Weimar

Republic. In their most vigorous years, these people lived by Nazi standards. They spent their middle age trying to approach the ideals of the Adenauer republic—bourgeois respectability, family, church, hard work, and hard money. Their old age has been passed in a country characterized by sex shops, welfare, and environmentalism, where the ways of the Adenauer republic are ridiculed. Their last impressions may be of Muslim neighbors whom it is dangerous to displease. By comparison, their contemporaries who emigrated to the German enclaves of southern Chile before World War I hardly moved at all. In sum, the character of nations is variable.

The range of human possibilities, of course, dwarfs the German experience. Travelers everywhere can hardly avoid asking themselves how the locals have come to live as they do, whether perhaps they, too, might wind up living like that, and if so, how. Yet few go further and ask how the locals can stand it. What would it be like to have to make my way here, among people like these, living by their rules and customs? Could I stand it? What do people like me have to do to keep living as we do rather than that way?

WHY THE DIFFERENCES?

The variety of human conditions is as striking today—and as baffling—as it was when Herodotus began to try to account for it. We see poverty of many types: clean, orderly, and striving in Turkey and Korea; in India, the striving and the hopeless kind mix; in West Africa, hopelessness mixes with violence. Wealth appears in clean, crime-free Japan or on trashy, crime-ridden U.S. college campuses, where children of privilege adopt the habits of skid row. We see rich Singaporeans whose parents were poor, and poor Argentineans whose parents were rich, poverty in the midst of Brazil's grand natural resources, and wealth on Japan's stingy land. We see peace in racially heterogeneous places and strife within the same race, as well as the opposite; clashes within civilizations even more than between them. Even within the same political boundary, some human beings grow up in families while others are raised by women whom men impregnate and leave. We see people living as if freedom were the most natural thing in the world, and we see others who put up with subjection to misery just as normally. And we ask: Why? What makes for the vast differences in the ways people live?

Academic disciplines do not help much because they consist of various sets of blinders. The cutting edge of modern social science presses convenient bits of reality into mathematical models and disregards the rest.[1] Older social science suffers from another kind of procrustean urge. Marxists teach a tripartite historical progression of human society—from slave through feudal to capitalist—based on different arrangements of the means of production. Freudians explain civilization as variations on the theme of repression of instincts. Some liberal theoreticians ascribe the differences among peoples to various stages of the progression of freedom, while others say it is equality that bears all other good things in its train. Most popular in academe nowadays is the mantra that everything follows from the inevitably clashing interests of sexes, races, and classes. But viewing complex realities through chosen lenses distorts them.

The most common error today is to believe that everything depends on how the economy is organized. And indeed we saw that the socialist countries' peculiar economic arrangements produced not just shoddy goods but also people whose motto was "They pretend to pay us and we pretend to work," people habituated to seeking and granting favors rather than producing, and inured to regarding positions of power as opportunities to take. In Hong Kong, by contrast, a population disciplined by a brutally free market developed characteristics very different from those of people living under socialism. Yet in the years when the shadow of Hong Kong's 1997 reversion to Chinese rule lengthened over its people, they began to exhibit many of the clientelistic ways of the mainland—the best apartment buildings were being bought up by bureaucrats from the mainland, and businessmen, mindful that the rule of law would go away, sought out patrons in the new power structure. In short, they adopted new habits. Meanwhile, however, new government policies encouraged millions of mainland Chinese to adopt habits reminiscent of Hong Kong. Still, because human beings are not mere bundles of incentives, merely changing economic policies—tariffs, tax policies, subsidies, and regulations—will not remake a people. History is full of government programs that crashed on the rocks of entrenched habits. But where do habits come from?

A common answer is that "it is all in the genes." Since race is the most obvious human characteristic, it makes superficial sense to associate how people live with what they look like. As Thomas Sowell has shown,[2] every people carries along its peculiar ways wherever it migrates. Germans, it seems, are inveterate engineers and military officers, whether they move to South America or to Russia. In Africa, Ibos are professionals and Zulus are fighters. Italians and Chinese are known for their skills in cooking and small business. Thus, few would be surprised if, when the first spaceship lands on Mars, it found Chinese and Italian restaurants already open for business. But there was a time when Roman cooking was, well, Spartan, and when Germans had to learn engineering from the British. Yet the British seem to have lost many of the skills they once taught to others. Then, of course, there is the fact that people who are equally Chinese live very differently in Taiwan, Singapore, and mainland China. Italians in Switzerland's Ticino are just as Italian as the Milanese who live just down the valley, but their attitude toward public life could not be more different. Since gene pools change over many centuries rather than in a few decades, and since they are quite unaltered by location, biology seems an insufficient explanation. We may therefore presume that the habits we correctly associate with ethnic groups are somehow acquired in particular circumstances. But how?

It is fashionable today to explain happiness and misery in the world according to the different ways in which various peoples come to grips with their environment. By this token, growth in population and depletion of natural resources bring all bad things, whereas the opposite brings good. This is the view of Robert D. Kaplan in his thoughtful 1994 article "The Coming Anarchy" and of Jared Diamond's 2005 *Collapse: How Societies Choose to Fail or Succeed*.[3] Kaplan draws scenes of hellish cities, where children drink from sewers, where disease is endemic, violence routine, and the vestiges of any civilization are dissolving. He concludes that it is all somehow due to populations exceeding the carrying capacity of the land. Diamond's argument, that the people of Easter Island ate up their resources and then died off, means to indict us all for using too many natural resources. Yet it is obvious that any land will carry fewer hunter-gatherers than farmers, fewer farmers than producers of computer software, and that no land at all can long carry a population that trashes it. Just as obviously, cities in Japan and the Netherlands are groomed gardens compared to the less-crowded Hobbesian plasma that Kaplan found in Africa. Because man makes his own environment, slums everywhere are sets of people rather than places. But how do people get to be destroyers or groomers of their surroundings?

Another explanation has to do with intelligence. Richard Herrnstein and Charles Murray have shown that all sorts of social pathologies are associated with lower test scores, while decent patterns of life are more often associated with higher scores.[4] The smarter you are, the healthier, wealthier, and happier you will be. Thus economists have long counted high levels of education as one of the principal assets any nation can possess—and rightly so. But Charles Murray has also pointed out that what he considers the mother of pathologies—namely, out-of-wedlock births—has tripled among American blacks and grown tenfold among American whites in recent decades. It is not unfair to note that while this pathology was gestating, test scores for whites were not falling tenfold, and those for blacks were increasing a bit. It is also true that between 1930 and 1960 Argentina slid from the First World to the Third World as its population's high educational level rose even further. Plato pointed out, knowledge and virtue are not identical. Neither are knowledge and wealth, or knowledge and happiness. But why do some peoples in particular times and places use knowledge to their advantage while others use it to their disadvantage? Could it be their upbringing?

Is it true, then, that "the two-parent family is the most successful health, education and welfare program ever invented"?[5] Was the prime minister of Japan correct when he predicted that his country would outcompete the United States in the long run because Japanese families are more cohesive than American ones?[6] A wealth of data stretching back to ancient Rome supports the contention, first argued by Xenophon[7] and later elaborated by Adam Smith, that the division of labor between man and woman is the foundation of economics, and hence that the two-parent, patriarchal family fosters in all its members the habits most conducive to their and the polity's happiness. But where do such families come from? And what weakens them?

Is society responsible for our behavior toward our families, our jobs, and everything else? No one would deny that society's strictures are important. Jonathan Rauch has argued persuasively that as societies age, they accrue layer upon layer of special privileges.[8] This progressively curtails the opportunity for talent and diminishes the return for effort. Growing rigidity engenders the selection of persons for top positions on the basis of their capacity to please those who are already there: This is negative selection. Rauch's point about societies reminds us of Seneca's observation about the human body: Advancing age is itself an illness. But how did Sparta and Venice beat this malady long enough to endure 800 years?

A similar line of reasoning proposes that societies live or die according to the flow of information through them. By this reckoning, the Soviet Union was killed by a flow of information that overwhelmed its structures.[9] Apparently believing something of this sort, the Islamic Republic of Iran outlawed TV satellite dishes, and China commissioned Google to build into its local search engine all of the regime's political predicates. During the

1996 campaign, President Bill Clinton promoted, as a safeguard for America's mores, a device by which parents could prevent television sets from receiving sexually explicit programs. But in subsequent years explicit messages became nearly impossible to avoid: Even the advertising for football games promoted drugs that enhance sexual performance. Nevertheless, none of this tells us how societies come to establish certain privileges and not others, and how some use the flow of information to improve themselves while others poison themselves with it. How can both occur?

One answer is so obviously true that it explains nothing at all: "It's the culture!" Well, of course it is. But what is a culture other than a way of life—T. S. Eliot's "all the characteristic activities and interests of a people"?[10] Eliot defined the English culture of his time in terms of Derby Day, the Henley Regatta, the music of Sir Edward Elgar, dartboards, and boiled cabbage. And no doubt contemporary American culture cannot be defined without football and Big Macs. Could anyone describe life in socialist countries without reference to hours spent in line at stores? Anyone who grew up in Japan would surely mention the stylized lunch boxes at school. The lists of such peculiarities are endless. But they say nothing about why one society is rich and another poor, self-governing or not, its people more self-restrained morally, or less. More telling in these regards would be a list of how specific habits correlate with peculiar attitudes.

The heart of any culture is a *forma mentis,* a set of attitudes expressed in life's most important behavior patterns. No Western visitor to Saudi Arabia or to Hindu India, for example, can help but be impressed by the prevailing contempt for labor and those who perform it. By the same token, the American underclass has been best described as a set of attitudes antithetical to the bourgeois virtues of discipline, fidelity, frugality, and so forth.[11] Travelers arriving at West African airports confronted by customs officials who demand bribes reach reasonable conclusions about what awaits them downtown. Visitors to Italy instantly notice that the locals circumvent laws ranging from traffic to taxes, while no visitor to Japan should be surprised to hear that narcotics are not a problem there, because they are against the law.

WE MAKE OUR DIFFERENCES

What then makes for the attitudes and patterns of behavior that make the crucial differences in how we live? Moses' conveyance of the Law from Mount Sinai is unique in that it sought to define the Israelites' entire way of life in one act. But, so the Bible says, even divine action could not remake a people who were already "stiff-necked" about their existing habits. Experience teaches that other peoples are pretty stiff-necked too. The birth, change, and death of cultures is gradual. Above all, most cultural norms do not come down from heaven to any extent. We ourselves make them, change them, and break them.

We choose for ourselves what we think and how we live. Surely, any choice at any given time is conditioned by previous choices. We are indeed creatures of habit. But human habit, as distinguished from animal instinct, is somehow tied to conscious choice. "In order to discover the character of any people," wrote St. Augustine, "we have only to observe what they love."[12] And to discover what they love, we must look at what they choose. Among the most important of the choices we humans make, among the most definitive ways that we show what we love and what we abhor, are the ways in which we govern ourselves. The Greek and Roman classics had no doubt that forms and acts of government are the clearest reflection and among the strongest influence on what people do and what they think, that they both reflect the souls of people and form them. Ethics, according to Aristotle, is a branch of politics. The Greek word *ethos* translates as "custom" or "habit." Thoughts and actions repeated become habits. In our time, an "ethos" has come to mean a culture. Aristotle would not have objected to the notion of culture as an accumulation of habits. But where do habits come from if not from *choices repeated and ingrained?*

Politics, thought Aristotle, is arguably the sovereign influence on our habits—but by no means the sole or omnipotent influence. No message of Aristotle's is clearer than that it is futile to try to govern barbarians as if they were Greeks. Habits make people, and any new act must inevitably contend with accumulated habits. In this vein, when the Jews asked Jesus why the law of Moses permits polygamy while he proposes monogamy, he answered that Moses could not have asked more of their sinful fathers. That answer makes Aristotelian sense. Culture, the accumulation of habits of heart and mind, sets limits to government. Those limits are sometimes so obvious as to lead one to conclude that government does not matter very much. Well, sometimes government matters little, and sometimes a lot.

THE IMPACT OF GOVERNMENT

The strongest argument for the point of view that government is of little consequence is that here and there in history one finds small governments ruling over strong, autonomous societies. But the bulk of history is full of big governments ruling over societies that either never had vigorous lives of their own or whose independence had long been crushed by the weight of rulers. As parochial westerners with short memories, we are wont to think that the natural state of mankind is to live under limited governments that treat everyone alike. But most of the world's peoples have no history of limited rule or of equality under the law. Their lot has been to be subjects of empire, with rulers who empower some subjects to take advantage of others. Only rarely and by much effort is government anything other than the manufacturer and enforcer of privileges. Because each ruler made a different world for his subjects, most of mankind has measured time from the beginning of the reign of particular rulers.

The proposition that government in our time does make a difference in people's lives becomes self-evident when we consider how very different from our own are the historical circumstances in which it made the least difference—the Christian Middle Ages. During this period, roughly between A.D. 800 and 1450, rulers were constrained as they had never been before and haven't been since.

In ancient times, no distinction had existed among religion, society, and government. With the partial exception of Israel in the age of the Judges, the rulers of each city or empire were also the most prominent men as well as the chief mediators with the gods. One set of rules, flowing from the same authority, commanded or forbade everything from the planting of crops to the sacrificing of human victims. When a city was conquered—assuming it was not annihilated—its gods were changed and its moral universe was refashioned. The attraction of the great ecumenical empires—of which the greatest was Rome's—was that they tried to leave the gods and lives of their subjects as untouched as possible. But they certainly imposed new bureaucracies, new taxes, and new mores that changed with each emperor. Alexander's empire seduced the educated classes of the East into Hellenic culture. After the Roman conquest, these same classes absorbed Roman ways, though often in Greek. Yet those ways changed substantially with each emperor. While Rome under the Antonines spread the habits of the rule of law, under Commodius and Maximus it forced people to live by the law of the jungle.

Plato and Aristotle thought that there was a direct, causal connection between any given form of government and the kind of human traits that flourished under it. Yet these philosophers—the twin fountainheads of our way of life—taught us to differentiate between the demands of rulers and the demands of nature. This distinction, which implies that rulers can be objectively unruly, theoretically diminished the scope of government to an extent previously unimaginable. Jesus' injunction to "render unto Caesar the things that are Caesar's and to God the things that are God's" removed any doubt that rulers could no longer lay claim to spiritual, moral, or intellectual authority by virtue of their offices. The Christian commentators combined Jesus' command with Platonic-Aristotelian natural law and gradually produced what might be called the social doctrine of the Christian Middle Ages—a set of ideas and practices that limited the consequences of government.

Medieval kings could ask for more or less money from their subjects, but they had no *right* to the property of their subjects. The different outcome of passionate struggles over the legality of royal financial requests in medieval England, France, and Spain eventually made the crucial difference between Anglo-Saxon societies ruled by law and European ones ruled by administrative edict. Nevertheless, the personal character of the kings, noblemen, and clergy surely affected the daily lives of ordinary people with whom they came in contact. Thus, Shakespeare's Henry V could say: "O Kate, nice customs court'sy to great kings. Dear Kate, you and I cannot be confined within the weak list of a country's fashion: we are the makers of manners, Kate."[13]

But in Kate's France as in Henry's England, kings and peasants were enmeshed in a network of canon law, civil law, and above all, customary law. At the base of all the rules and customs lay one principle: Only God is sovereign. Every family, every village, every contract, and indeed every human being and every human institution depends on Him. Consequently, every human association, every human being, is endowed by its Creator with its own particular place and purpose in the divine order. That is why Western societies thought it improper for kings to interfere with such institutions, much less to snuff them out. The notion that kings might issue rules on the conduct of farming or the raising of children, that they might require an annual act of financial confession of each and all, or that they might force people to fight in their armies, would have been regarded as both ridiculous and impious. And in fact, when radical movements seized political power in the thirteenth century, seeking to force the church and society in general to conform to virtuous models, society rose up and burned these movements' leaders at the stake.[14] In sum, powerful Christianity made for weak rulers and strong societies.

After the Reformation (caused in part by clashes between papal and princely temporal power), government became more powerful in both

Catholic and Protestant Europe. Hence, a change in rulers might mean either Catholic or Protestant dominance. In Ireland, dominion by another branch of Christianity went along with economically exploitative rule by another nationality. But this was the exception. In most of Europe, rulers cared little what languages their different subjects spoke, and their profession of transubstantiation or consubstantiation made no difference in the wealth or poverty, the decency or depravity, the vigor or the decadence of public life. The quality of public life differed widely, ranging from Spain's warrior regime to England's model feudalism, Venice's imperial republicanism, and the predatory monarchies of Naples. Yet nowhere in medieval and Renaissance Europe did government make the kind of difference in people's lives that it had in the ancient world or that it would later in the modern world.

Nevertheless, because examples from on high are always powerful, rulers always had an impact on society, even in the Middle Ages. Even trivial effects are instructive. Why do the French—except for some nonelites in the South—pronounce their "r's" gutturally instead of rolling them in the Latin manner? Because in the seventeenth century, France had a Danish queen who could not manage the Latin "r." Courtiers affected to speak as she did, noblemen affected court speech, and soon failure to growl one's "r's" became a sure sign of unsophistication. Four hundred years later, from the Boulevard Saint Germain to Tahiti, it still is. No historian would deny the importance of the sobering effects on the church and society of Pope Gregory VII's imposition of austerity on the worldly clergy of the eleventh century, any more than a scholar would contest the notion that the luxurious papal court at Avignon two centuries later helped spread corruption, and eventually revolution, in Europe. Nor did anyone ever deny the power of princely patronage. Cathedrals, and the priceless works of art in European museums, testify to the magnificent taste of Renaissance rulers—a taste that set standards for ours. The influence of patronage, however, depends in part on its size. To commission a handful of artists is one thing. But it is quite another, quite beyond the premodern imagination, to create whole classes of people who live by patronage. Finally, the Renaissance saw an outpouring of a genre of neoclassical literature called Mirror of Princes that pointed out the character traits that the prince should cultivate in himself and, by example, in his subjects. But in premodern times, the notion that princes should be partisans in what Bismarck called *kultur kampf* was incomprehensible.

The power of constitutional-legal incentive to spread ideas and habits was always well known. The grand political struggle of the Middle Ages between the pope and the emperor called forth the treatises of Marsilius of Padua and John of Paris, as well as commentaries by Thomas Aquinas and Dante. Both sides of the quarrel, though, accused the other of trying to wield power over matters that were not properly its own and thus of taking the first big step to rule over both temporal as well as spiritual matters— which all agreed was improper.[15] Similar arguments surrounded the big constitutional questions of the Renaissance—who should appoint bishops, and what should be the relationship between crown and nobles? Because all sides in these controversies ultimately founded their claims on God and natural law, all agreed that every part of society had its legitimate powers, none absolute, and that all were obliged to sustain the complex of customs of Christendom, the *Cristianitas.*

Following the Reformation, however, the struggles for power between Catholic and Protestant nobles, and the persecution of religious dissent, reintroduced the notion that culture and politics are linked. The first few years of the French Revolution, with its transformation of churches into temples to the fatherland, new calendars, and social purges not seen since the Roman civil wars, shocked the world. The rise of nation-states convinced millions that the cultural differences between the French, the Germans, the Russians, and so on were very important, and this development led to the introduction of governmental authorities into cultural matters.

WHAT IS A REGIME?

Still, until our time, most westerners simply could not understand what Aristotle had meant by "regime" or "constitution." How could the very same country be one thing before a political change and something totally different afterward? Also, because the individuals or projects likely to take power in Western countries were just not that different from one another, westerners could not understand what Socrates had meant when he said that every city was the "writ-large" version of the particular kind of human being dominant within it.[16]

Having lived through the twentieth century, we find Plato and Aristotle much easier to understand. The century began with boundless faith in the capacity of government to engineer health, wealth, and happiness as the agent of modern science. Yet we have lived to see governments turn Germany Russia, China, and countless other places into hells-on-earth. The list of ills inflicted on the human heart by twentieth-century regimes is very long. When we read Thucydides' account of how the revolution in Corcyra accustomed a people to ever-higher levels of mutual slaughter, it is all too easy to think of modern parallels, from the Russian Revolution to Bosnia and Rwanda and Darfur.[17]

We have also seen countries wrecked without significant violence. Thus, in 1930, Argentina might have been the world's second-richest country per capita. But by the 1960s, after a succession of populist regimes, it was experiencing food riots. By the 1990s three decades of secular socialism and corruption had driven Algeria, once an exporter of food and wine and a bastion of worldliness within Islam, to hunger and to seeking violently after Islamic purity. By the same token, we have seen Japan turn from militarism to commerce; parts of China turn from socialism to energetic enterprise; Taiwan become the first democracy in the 5,000-year history of the Chinese people; and Singapore become the first physically clean city in the long history of the vast Chinese cultural area. We know that modern Germany was built on de-Nazification and modern Japan on the radical reversal in the sociopolitical importance of soldiers and businessmen. The agents of these changes have been regimes that very consciously encouraged certain habits in their peoples while discouraging others. In sum, we have regained some of the ancient philosophers' sober appreciation of the capacity of regimes for good and for ill.

But what exactly are regimes? According to the classics, regimes are arrangements of offices and honors.[18] Each set of arrangements answers the question "Who rules?" as well as "For the good and to the taste of whom?" and "To what end?" Aristotle, remember, had divided regimes into two broad categories—those that rule in the interest of the rulers only, and those that rule in the interest of the whole polity.[19] Within each category, however, he pointed to the existence of rule by one man, rule by few, and rule by many. Each kind of regime served a different purpose and fostered a particular kind of human being. All this makes sense because there are any number of character traits within each human being. Depending on which of these traits are fostered and which suppressed, people can be tyrannical or law loving, rapacious or virtuous, dissolute or civic minded. For the classical tradition from Socrates to Cicero, the whole point of discourse on politics was to figure out how to structure regimes that would foster the appropriate character traits in a given set of circumstances. George Will claimed no originality when he wrote in 1983 that statecraft is soulcraft.[20]

The classical philosophers knew that the prominence of oligarchs who spent their time accumulating wealth would increase the polity's concern with wealth. If the rulers were engaged in trade, they would be tempted to confuse their interests with the public business.[21] They knew that where the generals' mentality dominates, the city becomes an armed camp,[22] while entrusting the city to especially virtuous men would involve the society with moral concerns.[23] They also knew that prominent men could use virtue as a cover for greed. They knew that cooperation between classes was heartily to be desired and could be encouraged by giving each class a share in the government. But they also knew that when different interests combine, they have a propensity jointly to raid the treasury. That is why each city, given the character of its citizens, needs a particular prescription to bring out the best and suppress the worst of its potentials. Arrangements of offices and honors were designed to bring to prominence certain kinds of men, whose examples would help form their fellow citizens. Laws would also legitimize some practices and delegitimize others. Finally, the laws would offer outright incentives for some activities, like showing up at assemblies, and penalize others, like sacrilege. This, in sum, is classical political science—not what is taught in Poli-Sci courses.

Regimes, however, cannot be reduced to official acts of commission or omission. They are the sum of what is prominent in society—the reigning ideas, loves and hates, fashions and phobias, hymns and epithets. They are embodied in prominent persons—the Establishment. This consists of holy men and entertainers, generals and the rich, rulers and ruffians—the makers of standards, the ones whom children imitate and adults wish they were. Sometimes—rarely—the governmental establishment imparts to society standards very different from those of the private establishment. In post–World War II Poland, for example, the Communist Party monopolized all the commanding heights of society except one—the Roman Catholic Church. Over the course of forty years, the church gradually ousted the Party from civil society, and eventually from government. But this sort of thing is rare. In most instances, official and unofficial establishments are mutually supporting and evolve together. Thus, for example, the phenomenon known as the U.S. "counterculture" of the 1960s was the very opposite of an attack on America's culture by outsiders. Rather, it was an inside job that embodied the maturation of attitudes among American elites, in and out of government, for several generations. The new rules were developed at the top of society and worked their way down. Consequently, though the nominal American Constitution remained the same during this era, the actual American regime changed profoundly because its standards, tastes, and habits did.[24]

The reason that regimes are still confused with mere arrangements of constitutions and laws is that our medieval Christian heritage leads us to think of politics as inherently separate from civil society—family, business, and professional life, the realm of knowledge, faith, and morals. But in fact, though no modern regime has the unchallenged moral authority of pre-Christian, pre-philosophical polities, all modern regimes increasingly resemble ancient rather than medieval ones. Modern governmental and non-governmental elites are integrated everywhere as they have not been since the third century A.D. Even the most liberal modern governments have material powers beyond the imagination of ancient tyrants. So, like it or not, the stakes of modern politics include the character of civil society.

In 1927, when France's government was perhaps one-third of its present size, Charles de Gaulle wrote that the regimentation it imposed "would have revolted our fathers."[25] But whether one is revolted or thrilled by modern regimes, no one can deny their enormous effect on the lives of those who live under them. Today, in much of the world, the state has taken over from churches (often by default) the role of arbiter of morality. By taxing and spending to provide for retirement and medical care, government has pre-empted the role of individuals and of their older children in providing for old age. For countless women and children, government has assumed the role of husband and father through bureaucracies that regulate their lives and provide sustenance to those who cannot or will not work. Not only in Sweden, which, as the saying goes, has laws on everything from raising children to walking dogs, parents may raise their children only so long as government does not choose to take them away. By becoming the principal financier and regulator of education, research, and professional qualifications, government has become the effective arbiter of truth. Even in the United States, religious schools must be licensed. In other countries, churches themselves must be licensed. It is difficult to find any government on earth that spends less than one-third of its people's total product. Most spend about one-half. Government is the biggest employer, awards the most contracts, and legislates so as to make all occupations expend significant amounts of effort to comply with its regulations. Government is the biggest maker of winners and losers in society. The world is abuzz with governmental schemes to remedy the ravages of governments.

HOW REGIMES LEAD

Regimes lead by example, by precept, and through the power of the purse. Adolf Hitler knew what he was doing when, campaigning against the Weimar Republic, he contrasted its archetypes—politicians whose daily business seemed to be the buying and selling of principle—with the man he presented as the model Nazi, Hermann Göring, the clean-cut hero who had routinely offered his life for his country in the skies over the western front during the Great War. Later, Göring came to personify the regime's degeneracy. Addicted to narcotics and to every imaginable perversion, the obese Reichsmarshal played while the regime was sending millions to their deaths.

Like ships, corporations, or athletic teams, regimes tend to take on the personality of their chiefs. By deploying incentives, chiefs can even manage to make subordinates put forth initiative. Napoleon thus instituted what amounted to nationwide contests for honors and rewards to be earned on the battlefield. Much as Peter the Great had done in Russia, he thereby established a new class of nobles. Most leaders ask less, and subordinates are happy enough to search out what it takes to please the boss or just to follow his lead. De Gaulle used to say that people instinctively bend themselves around power. Indeed, the effect of leaders may be likened to that of the sun, which has only to move for the sunflower to follow.

Organizations and regimes develop what the Romans called the *cursus honorum*—the path to power and profit. In the early centuries of the Roman republic, the *cursus* inevitably began with service in the army, followed by several levels of elective office and ever-higher military commands. But during the later republic, fewer patricians bothered with the military part, a trend that continued into the empire until, in the third century A.D., the Emperor Gallienus actually forbade senators and their immediate families from serving in the army. By then, of course, patricians had ceased to be powerful. They were merely rich men, groveling before every rough-hewn emperor whom the legions made and unmade.

Different paths to the top favor different kinds of people. Today's Japan is ruled by people who made their way by studying for exams and by conforming to a culture of production and service. These leaders are very different from those of the 1930s, who had become successful in peacetime by adhering to the warrior's code of *bushido.* Either kind of person would find it hard to succeed in the other's regime, just as most people who had made successful careers in the hierarchical culture of IBM would have found it difficult to succeed in the Apple corporation's freewheeling early years.

The founders of regimes quite consciously try to foster certain qualities. Thomas Jefferson thought that the self-reliance of farmers who work their own land was the indispensable foundation of American freedom. Founded on rebellion, the American regime could not remain the same if the American people lost the capacity to rebel. Jefferson did not esteem farming for its own sake, but he did not know any other nursery of independence. De Gaulle thought that his people were too prone to division. Hence, he thought that an electoral system that compelled voters to choose governments and a constitution that obliged governments to govern would help make the French people more coherent and much more serious. By contrast, President George H. W. Bush's wish for a "kinder and gentler" America was unrelated to what the voters remembered as his administration's principal initiative—raising taxes.

The personal behavior of leaders is always important, but not always in the same way. During the 1960s, for example, the Central Intelligence Agency surreptitiously filmed the goatish sexual practices of Indonesia's dictator, Sukarno, believing, mistakenly, that he would fear their revelation. These same officials shielded the equally goatish practices of their own president, John F. Kennedy, fearing, correctly, that their revelation would destroy Kennedy politically in America. They did not understand the difference between Americans and Indonesians, who expect their despots to use their positions for all sorts of gratification. Hence because of the widespread view that Americans do not tolerate scandalous sexual behavior in their leaders, when Congress made Martin Luther King Jr.'s birthday a national holiday in 1983 it sealed for seventy-five years FBI recordings of him similar to ones the CIA had made of Sukarno. By the 1990s, however, American attitudes had changed: Many people seemed to tolerate President Clinton's adultery and perjury, almost as if they had become Indonesians. Similarly, while the Roman regime of the first century B.C. demanded that Julius Caesar and his wife be above suspicion, Roman emperors only a few generations later were not politically inconvenienced by engaging in any debauchery whatever. Standards change by the acceptance of new ones.

The common practice of naming regimes, or even epochs, after the individuals who shaped them most makes some sense. True, Marxist theory and Leninist practice fully prescribed and initiated murderous totalitarianism. Nevertheless, the Soviet Union really was Stalin writ large. Its massive network of officials, who lived in constant fear of Siberia or worse, was the work of Josef Stalin. When his successors tried to run the Soviet system by different rules—without terrorizing the ranks of the Communist Party— the system began to break down. Likewise, the presidency of the United States was designed to fit George Washington, who consciously set precedents for his successors. His refusal to serve more than two terms in office, his avoidance of pomp, and his narrow interpretation of his powers indelibly distinguished the American regime from monarchy or empire. But since World War II, the U.S. government has taken on imperial trappings. Especially between 1992 and 2005 official Washington took on the aspect of a fortress. Recent presidents, like the early Roman emperors who used to play the role of mere elected officials on ceremonial occasions, have called photographers to show them eating common foods, carrying their own luggage, or making simple purchases. It remains to be seen how long the contradiction between the ways of Washington, D.C., and the presidents' pretenses of Washingtonian simplicity can endure. In the same manner, the Ayatollah Khomeini created Iran's Islamic republic in his own image. Therefore, it will endure only as long as Khomeini's successors maintain the sense of wounded, avenging righteousness that he engendered.

Regimes are also defined by the spirit of their laws. Some laws or constitutional provisions clearly aim to define the regime. The organic law that accompanied the Chilean Constitution of 1981, for example, prohibits any person from holding office simultaneously in a political party and in a business or professional association. Thus, the drafters sought the regime's primary goal: the separation of economic and political life. Sometimes regimes make laws that give them new identities. For example, after the 1948 victory of the National Party, South Africa made laws to enforce what it called "separate development" of the races within its borders. Eventually, apartheid became South Africa's consuming preoccupation. Italy's First Republic (1946–1994) was defined above all by its electoral system, which allowed parties, but not individuals, to stand for parliament. The natural result was an oligopoly in which party bosses were the only people who counted.[26]

Sometimes contending factions so strongly support or oppose a law that the outcome of their struggle is sure to alter the regime, if not to redefine it outright. This was surely the case in the United States in the late 1850s. For supporters of the Supreme Court's decision in the case of *Dred Scott v. Sandford*, the essence of American freedom came to be the capacity of owners to take their slaves wherever they wished, whereas to opponents, the long-term existence of freedom for whites became incompatible with the long-term existence of slavery for Negroes. As Lincoln said, the house could no longer stand thus divided.[27] The issue of slavery had become so important that both sides agreed that the entire regime would be defined by its resolution, one way or the other. The same is probably true of America's division over abortion and euthanasia in our time. For some Americans, the legality and propriety of these acts have become the touchstone of the good life, while for others, the definition of decency begins with the protection of life from conception to unassisted death. Regimes have been defined by less weighty controversies.

Laws that do not define regimes nevertheless help shape them as well as important aspects of people's lives. In the Roman republic, the paterfamilias had the absolute power of life and death over everyone in his household, whether slave or free, as well as the right to adopt anyone into the household. The emperors gradually took away that power, even over slaves. This was done neither out of tenderheartedness nor out of hostility to strong families. The emperors just wanted to make their courts the arbiters of as many disputes as possible, not least for the purpose of increasing their revenue. Similarly, while one may not blame the decline of the family in modern Sweden exclusively on government, it is undeniable that the Swedish government tries to reach each individual as if the family did not exist, even more than the Roman emperors did.

Laws that shape economic life affect the regime in very special ways. Most of the world, for example, does not prohibit what in the United States is known as "insider trading." Consequently, in most of the world, the trading of securities is practically confined to individuals who have or think they have privileged information. Such conditions train the average wary investor to regard investment in publicly held companies as a trap for the unwary and hence to retreat to his or her own insider realm—family-held companies.

Today, one school of economists recognizes the concept that government can shape habits through material incentives. This school's premise is the *Homo economicus* of eighteenth-century European liberalism, the individual who coolly calculates how to optimize his material position and maximize the latitude of his choices. Raise taxes so that workers get to keep less of what they earn, and *Homo economicus* will work less. Lower the difference between the rewards of positions requiring more and less effort, and *Homo economicus* will gravitate toward the ones that require less. For this school, strengthening families is merely a matter of finding the right tax advantages or crafting just the right welfare plan. To say that few actual human beings fit this model is not to argue that most people are irrational, but rather to say that the ends of eighteenth-century liberalism are not the sole or even the highest objectives of reason. This school overestimates the power of government incentives. Quite simply, not all human behavior is for sale. Still, governments have always been able to buy some people, and modern governments have an awful lot of money to spend. Hence, in practice, the straightforward statement of what one might call the "Gary Becker school"—that governments get what they pay for—is true for the most part in modern liberal societies.

Consider that before Benito Mussolini, the chief source of income and status of the southern Italian middle class was renting land. This class was already well practiced in the habits of buying and selling sinecures and lesser favors. Mussolini easily turned the members of the class into bureaucrats, their main qualification being that the Fascist system was willing to hire them as administrators for the regulatory and welfare state it was building. By the same token, the southern Italian sharecroppers who lived by their landlords' favors had never been clients of the state. But when their landlords-turned-bureaucrats offered government money in exchange for allegiance, the sharecroppers quickly transferred their old social skills to these more profitable patronage arrangements.

The very power of the state to direct floods of money into some social sectors and not others achieves what farmers do by watering and fertilizing certain fields rather than others. The very occupation of social worker, for example, never existed in all of history until our time. Western governments instituted this secular priesthood and paid uncounted thousands of people to practice it. At the turn of the twenty-first century, the environmental fad, fed largely by governments, produced another prodigious expansion of new occupations that existed by patronage alone. By the same token, decisions by vast state-funded medical plans to pay or not to pay for treating psychiatric or social dysfunctions mean that thousands of people will or will not spend their lives attempting to live by certain sets of standards and advising others to do the same. And the U.S. Community Reinvestment Act of 1977, as amended in 1992, 1994, and 1999, established a new profession, "community organizer," paid by the government and endowed with the power to coerce banks to extend mortgage loans to risky borrowers. They so filled the banks' portfolios with risk that many collapsed. But they made money and careers and built constituencies for those who administered it.

The U.S. National Defense Education Act of 1958 was based on the premise that the country needed to increase vastly the percentage of young people who graduated from college in science and engineering to meet the Soviet Union's challenge to a race in outer space. Most of the students and teachers funded under the act, however, pursued "soft" subjects rather than hard sciences. Hence the National Defense Education Act helped to quadruple the ratio of college graduates to nongraduates, vastly enlarged the professorate, virtually created a class of administrators of higher education, swelled and enriched university towns, and made politically significant the heretofore marginal tastes of half-educated intellectuals.

The tastes of any regime's ruling element are on display in society's public places. Today's rulers no less than ancient ones commission statues and murals, music and theater. The rulers' choices permit some artists to live by their art, while the artists not chosen must make it the hard way. Each set of patrons, artists, and art products embodies a viewpoint on which human possibilities are good and which bad. No European regime today would build a cathedral, any more than their thirteenth-century predecessors would have commissioned twisted hunks of metal to adorn public squares. Modern states have ministries of culture and education. There are less direct ways of gauging what the regime is about than laying side by side the proposals and job applicants to which these ministries give money and those to which they do not.

Thus in 2008 China's regime spent some $300 million on shows for the opening and closing ceremonies of that year's Olympic summer games, which involved perhaps 50,000 persons moving in impressive unison to impeccably choreographed sounds and lights. This conveyed serious, virile, even scary competence. By contrast, the show by which Britain accepted China's handover of Olympic responsibilities for 2012 consisted of an elderly man with a ponytail gyrating on top of a bus with a guitar, like a teenager, as a few extras moved around helter skelter with umbrellas.

In our times, no less than in ancient ones, political regimes correspond to ways of life. The relationship between them is like that of the chicken and the egg: It matters less where we begin to examine it than that we do so.

2

TONE AND CHARACTER

Perhaps the easiest way of making a town's acquaintance
is to ascertain how the people in it work, how they love,
and how they die.
—ALBERT CAMUS, *THE PLAGUE*

In most places, the tone of life is obvious, as if a giant tuning fork were setting the surroundings to vibrate at its frequency. No one driving into Las Vegas, Nevada, could possibly mistake the fact that the place hums to the tune of the casinos that dominate the landscape any more than visitors to the old Soviet Union could have missed the point of the giant inscriptions that proclaimed the glory of the Communist Party, the oversize statuary to its heroes, and the traffic lane reserved for Party functionaries that ran down the middle of major streets: namely, this place is ours, and if you want to get along here, it is going to be on our terms.

Businessmen who travel a lot learn quickly to discern the "business climate" wherever they land—what are the local rules for making money, and who makes them? While it is unimaginable to do business in China without paying bribes, to offer one in Japan is the greatest of faux pas—yet one must be prepared to grant Japanese business associates other forms of privileged treatment. To judge foreign climates, businessmen use skills honed, antennae developed, to discern corporate cultures. Diplomats are taught explicitly to home in on the sources of power in the vastly different places to which they are posted during their careers. Before getting down to writing official reports, they are taught to act like Alexis de Tocqueville—to take walks, to look, listen, get the feel of the place. Following these examples, a half century ago the sociologist Edward Banfield walked the streets of a small Mormon town in southern Utah and those of a comparably small one in southern Italy. In his book *The Moral Basis of a Backward Society,* he noted that while the tone of Mormon life was set by cooperation and mutual assistance, that of the southern Italian town was set by mutual jealousies.[1] Thus, he observed that while the Mormons led prosperous, gregarious, and happy lives, the southern Italians' lives fulfilled Thomas Hobbes's formula: solitary, poor, nasty, brutish, and short.

Almost always, the ruling culture and the formal government are symbiotic. Seldom does any major part of the culture exist despite the regime. When it does, it is most noteworthy. It is easy enough to make sense of a human situation, to listen to its tune, and then to begin to understand its elements. Having heard the main tone and seen the flow of the main stream, anyone may then perceive the parts of the melody, the dissonances, and the countercurrents.

TONE AND GOVERNMENT

Sending unmistakable signals about the main things of which the regime approves and disapproves is central to any regime, regardless of whether it is part of Christian, Muslim, Confucian, Hindu, or Japanese culture. Regimes survive by being proud of themselves. They rejoice in the victories over foreign or domestic enemies by which they established themselves and want to rub them in. It is a commonplace that century after century the history of Iran boils down to a struggle between the way of life depicted in the *Shahnameh,* the book of the ancient Persian kings, and the Arab-imported Muslim Koran. In 1979, the Islamic republic that the Ayatollah Khomeini installed in Iran forbade women to be seen in public without a veil or scarf over most of the face. By imposing the veil, closing businesses on Fridays, and so on, Khomeini wanted to leave no doubt as to who had won the latest round in that struggle. By contrast, the leaders of modern Turkey rightly consider the increasing voluntary use of the veil by Turkish women—including lawyers and members of Parliament—to be a threat to the regime established in 1923 by Mustafa Kemal, the central point of which was that Turkey would be a secular, Western state in which the Muslim muezzin would no longer sound the main tone of life. To that end, Kemal's regime not only banned the veil but ordained that the Turkish language—heretofore written in Arabic characters—would now be written with the Latin alphabet. Thus, he made it impossible for ordinary literate Turks to read the Koran in the original. Indeed, in much of the Islamic world, there is an important struggle between leaders for whom the Koran is either not terribly important or downright alien, and less powerful people for whom secular leaders are foreigners. Hence, anyone looking for an indicator of fundamental trends in any Islamic country might note whether more or fewer women wear veils and who those women are.[2]

Travelers to Israel, too, have noticed over the years that the proportion of men wearing yarmulkes or even black hats has risen and that the number of people who say that this makes them uncomfortable has risen as well. Until the 1980s, visitors to Israel noted the acerbity of its politics but also observed that just about all kinds of people came together in the army. That institution sounded a loud tone. Most of Israel's founders had been secular Western socialists but had been so committed to gathering the world's Jews to the Promised Land, so seared by the Holocaust, and so pressed by neighbors who forced Israel to fight for survival that they embraced military service. By the late 1980s, however, the army seemed less near to the hearts of the kind of secular Jews who founded Israel. Many, like their fellow leftists in the West, had taken to pacifist fashions. It seemed equally clear that the central preoccupation of the Israelis who count most had shifted from a united, forceful affirmation of Zionism to a divisive question: Who are the true Israelis, the observant Jews or the secular ones? Hence, because the country's defense no longer set its tone, because the regime was at odds with the Judaism of the Torah, modern Israel's dominant tone became one of discord.

Whereas a generation ago travelers to India were struck by the sad, flat note of sleepy misery under a mildly corrupt post-British bureaucracy, today they cannot help but be struck by powerful, dissonant tones that come from a revival of Hindu identity as well as from a widespread popular rejection of government-imposed misery in favor of free markets. Since the Hindu revival seems directed less at any sort of piety than at growing resentment of Muslims, identity politics sounds a loud, discordant tone in India. But at the same time, millions of enterprising, well-educated Indians of all castes and religions have taken jobs with or are contracting for foreign firms handling tasks from recycling waste to providing technical advice to Americans in computer programming. Their loud striving and achieving is awakening their sleepy neighbors. The world's second most populous nation sounds countless contradictory tones.

Travelers to China also cannot help but be struck by dissonance. On the one hand, the regime practices naked tyranny on an appalling scale. The tanks that rolled over demonstrators in Beijing's central square in June 1989, and the various officials who collect protection money and force abortion and infanticide on more than 1.3 billion people, sound a frightening tone. Just as frightening to foreigners is the 5,000-year-old habit of obedience to authority among the Chinese people, combined with evasion of rules and corruption among officials. On the other hand, the very fact that so many officials are so obviously for sale and in business for themselves sounds a tone of openness and possibility. Just as in Marco Polo's day, visitors are struck by the enormity and sometimes the splendor of buildings, artifacts, and ceremonies that result from marshaling the efforts of multitudes who live modestly. As always, these contrast with the dirt poverty of even greater multitudes. But contemporary China is more perplexing than ever because the twentieth century largely cut it off from its ancient cultural roots. The government, trying to spread literacy, simplified the Chinese language to the point that few Chinese can now read their own literature. Moreover, the Chinese language's inherent incompatibility with computers has increasingly forced society's leaders to think in English. Thus, well endowed with brains and discipline, burdened with a harsh and brittle regime, one-fifth of humanity sounds a fascinating symphony.

Visitors to the United States are usually on guard against the disorienting effects of its diversity. Nevertheless, even casual tourists get the main points—whether they like them or not. Touring the White House, they are struck that such great power should be wielded from a place exceeded in splendor by any number of palaces in their native lands. This tone of republican simplicity, reinforced by the austere neoclassical architecture of state and local governments around the country, points to the heart of the matter. Although the contemporary U.S. government resembles an empire more than it does the republic described by Tocqueville a century and a half ago, the tradition of limited government is still the most important feature of American public life—a feature that politicians ignore at their political peril. The passion of the American people for small government comes from an old refrain: Men in high places and low are liable to the same failings, and are subject to the same judgments. Most foreigners are mystified by the

American people's intolerance of politicians' public moral failings and by the fact that American politicians, especially aspirants to the presidency, overwhelmingly profess to be practicing Christians regardless of their beliefs. Well-traveled visitors know that most Americans no longer live in small towns dominated by a clapboard church or two, a little red schoolhouse, and a modest town hall. But they realize that American minds are still tuned to the emanations of those powerful symbols.

In every country, the largest buildings—the most prominently located buildings, the public buildings—are a powerful sign of who rules and why. This is as true in our day as it was in ancient times, as true in the West as in the East. The Mesopotamian, Egyptian, and Mayan temples made clear that those who lived in their shadows saw in them the meeting of heaven and earth and the unity of all authority. By contrast, in China, India, and Japan, the majesty of the rulers' palaces has always overshadowed religious shrines. In Western civilization, from the Middle Ages until very close to our own time, the biggest, best-located, and most-frequented buildings in every city and village were churches. In eighteenth-century France, government buildings began to challenge churches for size, splendor, and prominence. But until the 1960s, the Cathedral of Notre Dame continued to dominate the low-rise skyline of Paris. (The Eiffel Tower was a lonely, skinny, steel symbolic affront to that dominance, but no challenge.) In Washington, D.C., no building is higher than the Washington Monument. That is why the buildings throughout the city have seven floors at most. In the twentieth century, beginning in America, business buildings became so prominent that cathedrals are well nigh invisible in modern skylines. The Soviet Union demolished churches to make room for its signature buildings—offices for bureaucracies and apartments for bureaucrats. But the most prominent feature of the Moscow skyline today is the rebuilt cathedral of Christ the Savior. In today's America, the most luxurious buildings being built (of marble, brass, and rare woods) are federal courthouses.[3] That is where the power is.

Statues in front of buildings help set the tone. France requires all localities to clear all statues with the central government. Had it not done so, the Paris suburbs would once have been filled with statues of Stalin. In the twenty-first century these would be Islamic symbols. Other countries are not so formal. Nevertheless, in a given time and place the standards are clear. Whereas during the Renaissance Western sculptors immortalized saints and figures from classical antiquity, the most common statues from the seventeenth through much of the twentieth century were generals on horseback and political founders—signifying the primacy that peoples during this period placed on combat and nationhood. No one walking the Soviet Union's public squares could have failed to sense the regime's tones in the statuary. Even bolder than the tone sounded by the ubiquitous memorials to heroes of war and socialist labor was that sounded by statues of Pavel Morozov, the boy who informed Stalin's police of his parents' political incorrectness. Though much of the Communist legacy survived the Soviet collapse, all forms of intentional state pressures against families did not. That is why when the regime fell, Russians pulled down the statues of Morozov even faster than they did the ones of Feliks Dzerzhinsky, the founder of the secret police. Since 1992, the statues of Dzerzhinsky, Stalin, Leonid Brezhnev, and many others have lain mutilated in a weed lot behind a Moscow art school. The ones of Morozov are nowhere to be found.

In America, a sort of unofficial code has ensured that all but a handful of statues erected between about 1960 and 1985 consist of twisted shapes, the significance of which may be known only by those who manufacture them and the government officials who pay for them. Since the mid-1980s, the dominant genre of American statuary has celebrated women, people of color, and even white men—but only if they happen to be crippled. U.S. courts entertained suits in the 1990s alleging that the failure to take down statues to Confederate soldiers was an intolerable insult to the plaintiffs. The courts have not entertained the thought that doing so might insult others. In the same vein but more significant is that the U.S. Supreme Court forbade any statuary or manifestation of any kind to convey any Christian or Jewish themes on public ground. On that basis, an atheist in San Diego, California, sued to remove a cross that had stood in a city park for as long as anyone could remember. The city tried to forestall the move by giving the land it stands on to a private group. But a judge disallowed the transfer of property precisely because it would have resulted in the cross staying put. Two decades later, in 2008, the issue was working its way toward the U.S. Supreme Court. Nevertheless, without explanation, the courts allowed the city of San Jose, California, to place in its public square a statue not of the saint after which the city is named, but of the Aztecs' bloodthirsty god, Quetzalcoatl.

WHO SETS THE TONE?

Often, governments leave it to others to set society's main tone. Visitors to Saudi Arabia are impressed by the high walls that separate the royal family's sumptuous Western-style life from society's daily Koranic rigor and by how the nongovernmental religious police—for most people these cops are the regime—dictate dress, manners, and morals on the streets. In Western civilization, too, until recent decades public authorities left responsibility for marriages and morals to churches and synagogues. In America more powerfully than anywhere else, argued Alexis de Tocqueville, religion set the rules of life because, apart from the state, it ruled indirectly. Moreover, Tocqueville argued that America controlled common crime more successfully than other countries because the American people took upon themselves the responsibility of keeping public order and pursuing criminals rather than leaving it to the authorities.[4] Everywhere, the regime transcends the government.

Since few of the world's civil authorities are actually strong enough to rule the streets by their own power, they all must do so to some extent by preferring the order set by one class of private persons over that of others—in other words, by acting as if certain people have the presumption of right over others. Alan Erenhalt's moving description of the orderliness of ethnic white Chicago neighborhoods in the 1950s makes no mention of policemen—only of priests, nuns, teachers, and adults, all of whom were confident that they could inflict summary corporal punishment as well as verbal admonition on any youth they thought deserved it.[5] If asked who ruled the world, any teenager in 1950s' New York might well have answered that it was the shop owners and building superintendents who hosed off the sidewalks in summer and shoveled the snow in winter. They determined whether you could play stickball or not, along with whatever else was allowed or prohibited. The police, the judges, the mayor, and heaven itself just seemed to echo the "supers"—just as the authorities in Saudi Arabia back up the religious police and the authorities in Ireland, until recently, backed the church in family matters. *In sum, the government usually reflects the regime, not the other way around.*

In other places, however, leaving society to police itself means simply that it is left prey to its most disorderly elements. James Q. Wilson shocked many who should have known better with his observation that broken windows left unrepaired quickly change the character of a place by spreading the message that the vandals are in charge.[6] As we will see in later chapters, the presumption that those who are likely to commit violent crimes have as much right to the streets as anyone else reshaped American life. The power that violent young black men wield on America's streets has led other sectors of society to imitate their clothing—from fancy sneakers to baggy pants.

Because—by default—their hairstyles, their music, and their manners have come to symbolize virility, those who do not imitate them telegraph the kind of weakness that attracts violence. Such a mixture of incentives and disincentives has spread from the ghettos to all parts of American society. One is almost as likely to find teens with shorts down to their ankles in small-town America as in New York City—the home of the successful cable television network MTV that spreads the "gangsta" gospel. Even in the glossy pages of the *New York Times Magazine,* trendy advertisements for (very) expensive clothing feature young people properly disheveled, with just the right expression of resentment and menace. The government, it seems, let street toughs corner the market on manliness.

But there are places in the world where the tone of violence is even louder and deadlier. In Sicily, the streets are full of small knots of people speaking quietly, glancing over their shoulders, ready to tell anyone who asks that they do not know anything about anything. Neither the church nor the state has been able to disabuse many Sicilians of the assumption that the sine qua non of prosperity, peace of mind, and long life is to pay respectful attention to the Mafia's self-proclaimed "men of honor." In post-Communist Russia, the copycat "Mafiyas" wear something of a uniform—1930s' Chicago-style clothing with expensive jewelry—but they carry the same message as their Sicilian models: Officials answer to us, not we to them. In the regime of Vladimir Putin, the thugs became the officials. In Chelyabinsk as in Palermo, the mafiosi are attractive to women, the envy of men, and models for the next generation.

Government and society usually also speak the same language—using the same terms of praise and blame. Because the terms of public discourse are the lifeblood of the body politic, they sound perhaps the most telling note of all. Contrast, for example, any newspaper article or barroom conversation circa 1990 in Yugoslavia with a similar article or conversation in most of the European Union (EU) at the same time. Throughout Yugoslavia, people were eager to explain how their kind had been good but had been victimized by that other evil nationality. In fact, the visitor would soon conclude that any number of people in the bar would just as soon kill as play chess. By contrast, none of their counterparts in Western Europe expressed the kind of resentment against other groups that might justify killing them. Indeed, their talk did not contain the kind of passion about anything, whether nationhood or religion, or even soccer, that might have led anyone in any EU country to forceful offense—or, alas, to defense—of anything. Moreover, one would have gotten the impression that the very unfamiliar sight of a weapon might produce debilitating shock.

During the twenty-first century's first decade, however, the conversation in Western European bars often turned to the *extracommunitaires,* the immigrants, mostly North African Muslims, whose increasingly numerous and menacing presence was turning large parts of the cities into no-go zones for the natives. In London, Muslims marched with banners proclaiming death to infidels; in Paris they rioted and burned cars for two weeks; in Amsterdam they killed politicians and cultural icons who opposed them; and everywhere, they threatened. But the tone of conversation in the bars was a collective wringing of hands as people repeated the regime's mantra, that "they" would have to do "something about the problem." Few, however, believed that "the problem" would really get better.

The tone in Europe's bars is reflected at the highest levels of Europe's government. Reading the annual defense white papers of the major European members of the North Atlantic Treaty Organization (NATO), one is struck by the euphemisms and circumlocutions the writers use to avoid discussing the reason for this (or any) military alliance: that certain foreign peoples might do things that are so unacceptable that preparing to kill them in large numbers is both prudent and morally necessary. All such papers reiterate that the most important thing to be done is to maintain "the transatlantic link." No uninitiated person would guess that in European parlance, this disembodied term means that in certain circumstances Americans should be willing to blow up millions of human beings with nuclear weapons on Europe's behalf. Even the initiates would hardly guess what these circumstances might be, why Europe might benefit, or why any Americans in their right mind might do such a thing. Victorian discussions of sex were more graphic and enlightening than contemporary European discussions of war.

In contrast with their shyness about warfare, none of these regimes is at all shy about presenting on their government-controlled television networks graphically explicit discussions of how people contract the HIV virus. In fact, government-sponsored discussions of sex in Western Europe are almost as explicit, as lengthy, and as boring as discussions of the distribution of government benefits. Just as in most other places, the regime's sounds and silences produce a clear tone.

REGIME AND CIVILIZATION

Regimes do not spring up with particular sets of characteristics just anywhere on the planet. Civilizations set the bounds within which regimes exercise their powers over human habits. Strong as the influence of regimes on people's lives is, civilization means more. The best predictor of the quality of life in any given regime is the civilization in which it exists. The random baby born in Africa is likely to have a life very different from that of one born in North America. Indeed, a European child will have a very different life depending on whether he or she is born east or west of a line that starts at the Baltics' eastern edge and stretches southwestward along Poland's eastern border, down Slovakia's western border and along the eastern border of Hungary, then down through the middle of Bosnia to the Adriatic Sea. West of this line are relatively prosperous Catholics and Protestants; east of it, there are mostly poor Orthodox Slavs, who live in what Steven Schwartz has called "the India of the North." The world's major civilizations are more or less coterminous with its major religions and, much more roughly, with its major races.[7]

Western civilization surely covers Australia, North America, the southern cone of South America, and in some mixture most of the rest of the Americas as well, in addition to that part of Europe lying west of the line that divides Western Christian from Orthodox-Slavic civilization. South and east of both, from the Atlantic coast of Saharan Africa to Indonesia, is the world of Islam. South of that, black Africa is a mixture of the effects of other civilizations' imperfect recruiting and of tribal memories that are mostly lost while tribal identity remains. Asia, of course, contains the Hindu, Confucian, and Japanese civilizations. Each civilization is a package of habits and precepts that not only affects the way people live, but to some extent defines what it means to be happy.

Nevertheless, although every civilization determines much of this, each is open to a wide range of possibilities. Indeed, the struggles *within* civilizations are even more bitter and significant than those *between* them. In every historical circumstance, the regime—the arrangement of honors, offices, and priorities particular to the time and place—realizes some of the potentials in each civilization and pushes the others to the side. In every civilization, there are undeniable examples of poverty and wealth, family breakdown and cohesion, and civic peace with relative freedom. There have been circumstances in which Muslims, Slavs, Europeans, and Japanese have been willing and able to draw military effort from themselves, and circumstances in which they have not. Some civilizations and some cultures within them seem more malleable by circumstance and regime than others. None have given greater evidence of malleability than the Japanese, who, within a century after their leaders' decision to abandon feudalism and isolation, were led rather easily to adopt three ways of life vastly different in tone and substance: obedient pupils between 1868 and 1920, aggressive militarists until 1945, and single-minded producers thereafter. Yet, as we have seen, peoples belonging to other civilizations have changed their ways of life as well.

THE THRUST OF REGIMES

Because each of the world's main civilizations can support a variety of political cultures, our point is that within each there are regimes that foster certain kinds of behavior and personality over others.

The terms used here to describe political phenomena do not have precisely the same meaning across the world's civilizations. In textbook American discourse, "democracy" means rule by the majority of citizens, all of whom count alike and all of whom have the right to vote and to be elected to office. This understanding of democracy presupposes a willingness on the part of both rulers and ruled to abide by the same laws, to grant unto others the freedoms and powers one expects for oneself, to restrain oneself and one's friends as one would restrain one's opponents. This whole idea makes sense only insofar as one believes that every citizen, regardless of power or status, is both equal and worthy in some fundamental way. With every passing year, however, fewer and fewer within Western civilization believe this.[8] The success of John Rawls's *Theory of Justice*—in which justice is defined in terms of the power-dependent, inherently subjective concept of "fairness"—shows how far we have come in redefining the intellectual basis of democracy.[9]

Outside the West, practically no one believes that people have any right to equal treatment, or a right to offend the powerful. While polls around the world find great support for "freedom," for most respondents that word means the capacity to get what they want, and to do what they want to their enemies. What then can democracy mean for such people? The few

Chinese, Japanese, and Muslims who yearn for democracy and citizenship based on human equality (assuming they understand the meaning of such words) want things foreign to their civilization. Within Confucian civilization, the many can be fulfilled in an ethically worthy organization. Equal acceptance of social order is Confucian. But the interchangeability of roles is most un-Confucian, as is the equal worth of each member. The Islamic *umma* (the people) can be united in "the house of peace" (that is, under any truly Islamic, supranational government—something inherently problematic) or "in the path of God" (that is, fighting for one). Any Muslim's claim to leadership is theoretically as good as anyone else's. But in the Islamic world, the status of leader and led is incommensurable. The normal mode of Japanese participation is consensus, irrespective of how it is achieved. The same is true wherever Japanese cultural influence reaches—even in Korea. But this kind of consensus is consistent with winner-take-all politics. Thus, South Korea has changed governments simply because of elections. But it seems not to have shed the notion that political losers are to be jailed or disgraced.

Thus, when we think about how regimes foster or hinder civil life, and about the role of equality in civil life, we should think about what is possible in the context of any given civilization. We should also consider how the changes taking place within our civilization make problematic the continuation of our democratic institutions as we have known them.

Similarly, when we think about how regimes may foster prosperity, we should think beyond the economic institutions of economically successful countries and consider what attitudes and policies foster economic activity in a variety of contexts. For instance, consider that the culture that supports American economics could not survive were the U.S. government somehow to attempt to impose the kind of high-level favoritism—Americans call it corruption or crony capitalism—that is a major feature of life in the successful economies of East Asia. How favoritism affects East Asian economies is another question. Consider also that desire for one's own economic betterment is not the highest good in all the world's cultures. Often, the ruling passion is to be better off than one's neighbors in relative terms. This was certainly so in Edward Banfield's southern Italian village, and it is very much so in much of the Middle East and in traditional India. The point here is that we must think through to those features of any regime anywhere that foster economic activity and then try to understand what kind of economic satisfaction they foster.

The various kinds of regimes—tyrannies, revolutionary dictatorships, various kinds of military empires, theocracies and other kinds of oligarchies, and various kinds of democracies—exist within most civilizations, though seldom in pure form.[10] It makes sense, however, to begin by examining how some of the pure types affect prosperity, civility, and family; how they raise and lower the human spirit; and how they affect the capacity of a people to defend themselves among others.

TYRANNY

All civilizations are familiar with tyranny—that is, with regimes organized to satisfy the desires of the ruler. The tyrant may rule over a great European power, as did Hitler; over a medium-sized one in the Middle East, as did Syria's Hafez Assad and Iraq's Saddam Hussein; or over a small African country, as did Uganda's Idi Amin. The tyrant's passions may be petty or grand. But the results are remarkably similar: economics reduced to favor seeking; politics reduced to flattery, intrigues, betrayals, and purges; families destabilized and spirits degraded; and people killed by repression and war.

The tyrant's desire to control and to take overrides any concern he might have for the people under him.[11] That is why it makes no sense to describe such regimes as nationalistic. From Syria to Haiti, such rulers want to make sure the people closest to them get special advantages over the mass of unconnected people. This arrangement provides incentives to those closest to the tyrant to continue seeking his favor, and it makes it more difficult for people who are not connected with the tyrant to muster the economic means to oppose him. Thus, the right to import various necessities of life (as well as the privilege of importing and transshipping narcotics) in some countries—such as Syria under Hafez Assad and his son Bashar al-Assad, Cuba under the Castro brothers, and Iraq under Hussein—has been reserved exclusively for family and close friends of the tyrant. The efficient practice of tyranny, however, requires that the tyrant cause some turnover in the ranks of the privileged, both to keep the competition for favoritism lively and to prevent any of the privileged from acquiring too much wealth and too many constituents. Hence, Assad, Castro, and Hussein, like the rest of their kind, regularly disgraced some of their favorites—Assad even included his brother among those purged—for corruption.[12] Various other kinds of economic privilege—bank credit, licenses, captive customers—are the normal coin with which tyrants pay supporters. The most remunerative economic act in tyrannies is one that satisfies the person closest to the source of privilege. In most tyrannies, the laws specifically protect private property. But since the only real law is the will of the tyrant, property is held and disputes about it are resolved strictly through favor.[13]

The whole point of tyranny, of course, is that either there are no laws or, more likely, there are so many laws that willful officials can construe whomever they choose to be in violation. Hence, each official does to the powerless—and to other officials—what he thinks will advance his own personal fortunes with the one and only source of law. The only relevant political question is who depends on whose favor and why. Therefore, the politics of tyranny is, above all, self-ingratiation, and secondarily intrigue aimed at building up or tearing down others. As Hilton Root's reports to the World Bank about African governments showed, the politics and economics of tyranny are two sides of the same transaction. Privilege is the coin that pays for support, and vice versa. But since the logic of the competition leads to the search for better deals up and down the line, its logical end is the coup d'état.

The other major coin of tyrannical politics is the appearance of personal affection. Procuring women as well as providing derogatory information on real and imagined enemies are the age-old means of self-ingratiation. This is the coin that the *Book of Kings,* the manual of Persian courtiers, suggested to those who would make their fortunes at tyrants' courts centuries ago. It seems to be the currency of choice in the tyrannies of our time. Obviously, pursuit of success by such radical commitments to pleasing the boss or the boss's secretary is incompatible with respect for anyone's family, including one's own. Stalin's foreign minister, Vyacheslav Molotov, accepted cravenly his boss's offhand dismissal of his question about why his wife had been sent to the Gulag. Religious leaders, too, face the choice between public irrelevance, death, or prostitution. Whichever they choose, the tyranny makes obvious the dominance of willful self-seeking over matters of the spirit.

Tyrannies have special relationships with military force. Whether in high-tech Nazi Germany, in the Soviet Union and its satellites, or in the primitive conditions of Eduardo Macias's Equatorial Guinea, they follow Machiavelli's model of distrust for citizen militias and reliance on professional "special units." Such units live apart from regular armies and, in exchange for special privileges, do the regime's dirty work, engage in the brutal repression that others refuse to do, and, of course, purge and prod regular armies. The privileges are sometimes petty. Before the Polish government sent its ZOMO forces to crack down on the Solidarity trade union in 1981, it issued them chocolate bars—some people will do a lot for a little. But there is seldom anything petty about what such units do. Thus, in both the Gulf War and the war with Iran, Saddam Hussein's special units followed the Soviet practice of sowing land mines behind their regulars to discourage retreat. But because such armed forces are optimized for internal repression and have little stomach for real fighting, they are of little use when foreign enemies threaten. Moreover, they are unwilling and unable to call on the help of the citizenry. The more tyrannical a regime, the greater the percentage of its military forces that is devoted to containing other domestic military forces, and the weaker the ensemble. Thus, when the Kenyan army invaded Idi Amin's Uganda, it faced little organized resistance. For this reason, tyrannies typically die either because they cannot summon the strength to withstand foreign arms or as a result of coups hatched within the professional armed forces.

Modern revolutionary dictatorships have taken tyranny to new levels. Because they rule through parties, the number of tyrants, and their appetites, is multiplied manifold. Because they aim to reshape society, they infect all of it with the ethos of tyranny.

The economics of "real socialism" as practiced from Havana to East Berlin and from Moscow to Hanoi and Pyongyang had nothing whatever to do with any egalitarianism. Soviet Communist leaders lived "like gods and tsars," as Russians often say,[14] or rather, like the Communist bosses of East Germany and every other such state, secure in their own suburbs, eating special foods. Indeed, the dietary consequences of the economic stratification of "real socialism" were evident in the physical appearance of different segments of the population. The elites looked much like westerners who eat balanced diets that include meat and fresh vegetables all year round. Below the very top were thick, shiny officials who obviously had regular access to meat, but not to greens. The upper levels of the masses had the sort of pasty complexion that comes from lots of starch, while the gaunt pastiness of the rest of the people suggested they had trouble getting even enough of that. The Cuban, Chinese, and Nicaraguan Sandinista governments even empowered their grassroots officials to make sure that ordinary people did not consume more than the allotted number of calories per day. In Tanzania,

Julius Nyerere's Ujamaa villages got inmates to work by withholding food from the recalcitrant. Thus, on the lowest as well as the highest levels, economic life under "real socialism" consists of an unremitting effort to be among the rule makers and enforcers rather than among those who must live by the rules. Unlike standard tyranny, modern socialist tyranny forces everyone, low as well as high, to seek special treatment through special arrangements. No commodity has a natural price. No labor has intrinsic worth. No one has title to anything. Each and all can expect to enjoy neither more nor less than what they can get the authorities to agree to at any given time.

Stalin—with Machiavelli's *The Prince* by his bedside—set the tone for the politics of the socialist world: Purge, so that no one might ever feel secure in his position, and hence, so that everyone might be obliged to constantly seek the Party's favor at everyone else's expense. The Soviet system eventually collapsed because Leonid Brezhnev's encouragement of officials at all levels to become "rooted" in their posts turned the Soviet Union into a feudal state that was increasingly unresponsive to the center. When Yuri Andropov and Mikhail Gorbachev tried to take the Party in hand again, they did so through purges backed not by the threat and reality of bloodshed but rather by a decision to foster popular criticism of their enemies in officialdom. That violated the basic rule of tyranny that Stalin had epitomized: Only the tyrant—not any autonomous agency, and least of all public opinion—may purge officials, reward friends capriciously, and kill enemies ostentatiously. The Communists who have followed that rule have kept control. Fidel Castro managed to hang on to power by mastering his subordinates' intrigues and betrayals through bloody purges of the best of them and by practicing indiscriminate violence against opponents. Thus, he convicted and executed the popular General Osvaldo Ochoa of drug trafficking, ordered the machine-gunning of people who tried to flee the island, and made sure that the officials who were close to him at any given time had privileged access to the dollar economy with dollars from the tourist industry.

The policy of the socialist world toward families has been straightforward hostility. China went so far as to herd peasants into communes and there to physically separate the men, women, and children into barracks, monitoring menstrual cycles, granting conjugal time as a reward for work or favor, but decreeing the killing—before or after birth—of more than one child per couple. Meanwhile, of course, many officials did what they could through the exchange of favors to foster the fortunes and privileges of their children. The fabulous wealth of the families of Leonid Brezhnev and Deng Xiaoping is well documented. Nevertheless, for many more officials, the *banda,* or bureaucratic group, through which they pursued their fortunes became more important than biological families. The decline of family loyalties in socialist countries is less remarkable than their survival.

The degradation of the human spirit has been no less a policy of modern revolutionary dictatorships. Although the Nazi regime could not practically consider the physical elimination of Christians, its enmity toward the idea of Christianity was only somewhat less virulent than its attitude toward Judaism—for the same reason: they worship God. As for the Soviet Union, as late as September 1984 *Pravda* editorialized that the most mortal of the perils the system faced was the recrudescence of religion. The Chinese government closed all but 13 out of some 6,500 monasteries in Tibet. Other Communist governments closed smaller percentages—from about 90 percent of the churches in Russia to only 20 percent in Poland. But everywhere they put religion under ministries whose purpose was to banish it from public life first, then from private life as well. To all this, one must add that such regimes are always calling on the people to join in portentous programs to improve the material lot of mankind, to do wondrous things in science, and to rid society of certain perennial ills. Yet because such calls to greatness and appeals to generosity are counterfeit, they produce cynicism and meanness. These regimes produced no art, and the only worthwhile literature has been inspired by opposition. It is not surprising then that perhaps the most obvious feature of postsocialist countries is a lack of morality, sometimes described as a moral vacuum.[15]

If socialist states excelled in anything, it was in their armed forces, which absorbed upward of one-third of their economies. James L. Payne has shown that in Communist countries, the ratio of men under arms, as well as the ratio of major weapons systems to the number of citizens, was several times what it was in the rest of the world.[16] And yet, next to suppressing religion, nothing so preoccupied Communist leaders as controlling the ever-present threat of dissension within the armed forces and creating a commitment that they knew was not there to fight for the regime. In the Soviet Union, as in Poland and every other tyrannical system, the leadership relied on special units. But regimes that live by special units die by them as well.

OLIGARCHY

Most of the world's regimes, regardless of what they call themselves, are oligarchies—that is, some kind of arrangement by which relatively few people rule for the purpose of enriching themselves. Oligarchies come in numerous varieties. One kind consists of Mafias, tightly knit groups that share the loot from the meager economies of poor, small countries. Occasionally, the disorganization of large countries—such as today's Russia—lets them be governed this way. Mafia economics is short-sighted because it is purely extractive. The oligarchs' gains come from others' losses. For the few, the road to prosperity lies in fealty to a gang. For the many, selective servility and general passivity are the best way of getting by. Families thrive under Mafias because fortunes tend to rise and fall jointly, and retribution also falls jointly on families. In such systems, family members are the only people one can trust. But from Palermo to Moscow, the spirit of life is mean, and religion approaches superstition.

Another kind of oligarchy has ruled the world's free ports, from ancient Phoenicia to yesterday's Hong Kong and most of today's Asian Tigers. Since these rulers' raison d'être is to take shares of expanding trade, and since they know that trade can go elsewhere, they tend to run scrupulously fair systems of commercial law, except, of course, for occasional interventions to secure moderate privileges for themselves. Such places also usually underpin civil order and safety with draconian laws. In such places, the path to riches lies in keeping one's nose clean, keeping one's dealings simple and productive. Here, economics is least fettered by politics, and economics rewards families that pool resources to invest in business or professional education. Those close to the regime sometimes take a cut, though not often enough to raise the real cost of doing business above that of competing sovereignties. Such places are seldom known for spiritual growth, not because the governments have anything against religion, but because the inhabitants are in a hurry to make money. They had better be, because history teaches that such governments have short lives—primarily because their own citizens have neither the skill nor the inclination to form powerful armed forces. Hence, they must depend for their existence on the goodwill and protection of great powers—things that great powers seldom give for free or for long.

A third kind of oligarchy ruled ancient Carthage, the late Roman republic, Renaissance Venice, and early modern Britain. Its common feature is the tendency of its leaders to engage in great enterprises. They enforce privilege for themselves at home to foster vast commerce abroad. They build magnificent cities for themselves while fostering law, industry, the arts, and human excellence in general. And though they infrequently draw the bulk of their citizenry into the military (most such regimes have been naval powers), they organize great military enterprises.

In any given instance, however, these regimes can foster very different kinds of lives. In the eighteenth century, economic life in Great Britain was characterized by mean-spirited protectionism and exploitative mercantilism. The turn-of-the-century debates in the House of Lords over the impeachment of Warren Hastings, the chief delegate of the East India Company, laid out the conflict between economic life based, on the one hand, on restricting imports and granting special privileges to certain companies, and, on the other hand, on the economics of equal opportunity. Although Edmund Burke and Adam Smith carried the day intellectually, the great debate was not resolved until the Corn Laws were repealed in 1847, almost two generations later—after the Reform Act of 1832 had broadened participation in political life, affirmed the principle of equal treatment under law, and set Britain on the road to democracy. Venice, too, experienced a major shift in economic life in the fifteenth and sixteenth centuries. When Turkish conquests around the Black Sea gradually closed down the silk trade with China (which had been conducted by a small number of chartered importers), a host of unregulated small businesses sprang up that produced silk domestically. This, in turn, broadened the base of the oligarchy and changed the basis of Venice's prosperity. Political life in such regimes, then, depends substantially on economic arrangements. As these become less restrictive, political power tends to spread as well. Magnificence sometimes follows.

The habits of adherence to law and impartial procedure that are essential to commerce tend to spread to politics. Compare, for example, the conditions under which young Winston Churchill rose in late nineteenth-century Britain with those under which his ancestor, John Churchill, later the duke of Marlborough, had risen 200 years before. John had succeeded in currying favor in no small part because his sister was the mistress of the king's brother. Accounts of Marlborough's *cursus honorum* remind the reader of the Persian *Book of Kings*. Winston, by contrast, rose less through family connections than by the very bourgeois skill of self-advertising. Clearly, however, oligarchic regimes of this kind can as easily evolve toward the licentiousness of the very rich as toward sober bourgeois meritocracy.

The seeking after great things that suffuses such regimes extends first to the arts—in no other regimes do so many people pay so many artists for so many works of adornment and entertainment—and then to enterprises of the mind and spirit. The lasting fruits of such regimes are the works of Cicero, Virgil, William Shakespeare, Edward Gibbon, and those of the entire Venetian school that adorned the churches at which millions of tourists now gaze, as well as the civilization that they spread to the far corners of the world.

DEMOCRACY

Democracies, however, have no character except the character of the *demos* or its leaders at any given time. *Thus, in practice, democracies can resemble any other regime—even any kind of oligarchy or tyranny.* While some democracies have failed to muster the cohesion necessary to defend themselves, others have created and run military empires, sometimes moderate and other times not. Whole peoples have given themselves over to the pursuit of religious perfection, while others, just as democratically, have perfected debauchery. Tocqueville marveled that, in America, democracy had brought domestic and international peace, civility, prosperity, and morality, whereas in France, it had brought precisely the opposite. When we consider how moderate the very same generation of Athenian democrats was when it listened to Pericles, how cruel when listening to Cleon, how blindly and self-destructively ambitious when listening to Alcibiades, we are reminded of how easily and how often the German people effectively changed their character during the twentieth century as democracy spread, and we are led to ask how American democracy, the American regime, is changing.

Knowing that changes in our regime can change our capacity to be prosperous, to live as members of healthy families and communities, to raise our minds and spirits, and to protect ourselves in the world, and knowing that the social and political choices we face are sure to change our regime, we want to understand what the harbingers and the consequences of such changes might be.

We wonder what aspects of our character, of our history, which symbols, will set the tone of our lives. There are more than enough clashing alternatives. Every April 19, Americans, especially in New England, are asked to celebrate the anniversary of the day in 1775, now known as Patriot Day, when a bunch of embattled farmers near Concord, Massachusetts, "fired the shot heard round the world." By killing the soldiers of a government that had grown too demanding and inaccessible, Americans established their right to freedom. But on April 19, 1993, the U.S. government used tanks to assault a small group of cultists in Waco, Texas, resulting in the deaths of 80 people, including 25 children. Two years later, a former soldier, incensed at the Waco killings and resentful of the U.S. government's growing arrogance, exploded a truck bomb outside the federal building in Oklahoma City, killing 168 people, including 39 children. Though there was precisely no evidence that any militia was involved, the president of the United States, followed by like-minded politicians and editorialists, blamed opponents of big government for the blast, and they have since made it part of national lore that America is threatened by militia terrorism. Hence, the U.S. government closed off Pennsylvania Avenue in front of the White House and made the general public pass through metal detectors to get into federal buildings. Not least of the questions we must answer is, Which of the legacies of April 19 will set the tone among us? Or will the legacy be merely one of strife? On September 11, 2001, Arab terrorists worked within the new security systems to hijack four passenger planes and then crash two into the World Trade Center in New York City and one into the Pentagon in Washington, D.C., killing more Americans than had died at Pearl Harbor in 1941. Outraged, the American people came together, ready to do whatever it would take to undo the regimes on whose behalf the terrorists acted. But the U.S. government's primary response was to further wrap America in security measures, while its indecisive military actions abroad further contributed to dispiriting and disuniting them. Which of the legacies of 9/11 will set the tone among us?

3

THE CHARACTER OF DEMOCRACY

Free nations, remember this maxim: "Liberty
may be acquired but never recovered."
  —JEAN-JACQUES ROUSSEAU,
  THE SOCIAL CONTRACT

When Francis Fukuyama wrote in 1989 that liberal democracy's triumph over communism had ended history, he was following a long
tradition.[1] End-of-history theses have always been popular because they
promise that peoples will be spared momentous choices about how they shall
live their lives, something like "ye shall live happily ever after." In fact, however, no people is ever spared the choices by which it continues to define itself. When the Romans finally erased Carthage from the face of the earth in
146 B.C. and found themselves in a world without major enemies, they had
reason to think that their republican way of life was safe. But they could not
have been more mistaken: It was not safe from themselves. They themselves immediately set about adopting new ways, and in the process they
undid the civic, economic, familial, and religious institutions that had
made Roman republicanism so successful. The Romans did not intend to
start a century of civil wars, much less to do away with their own freedom
and decency and, eventually, their prosperity as well. Yet the Romans' new
habits inexorably brought moral decadence and the loss of self-government.
Roman society developed into one in which there were few lords and many

paupers, and the Romans' capacity for self-defense eventually deteriorated beyond repair.

Liberal democracies are more subject to changing their character radically than any other kind of regime.[2] That is because the character of liberal democracy so totally depends on the character of the people and because the people's character depends so substantially on how they freely choose to mold it. In short, today, no less than during the Cold War, we must choose what aspects of our way of life we will defend, modify, or jettison. But what do we want for ourselves? At first glance, the list seems modest.

As good liberal democrats, we want our rulers to work for us rather than the other way around. Rather than legions of bureaucrats, we want few laws that are equally applicable to all. Because we would rather be neither predators nor prey, we do not want our prosperity to depend on favors granted at the expense of others; rather, we want to be limited only by our own labor. We want to live in families, to care for our children as we choose, and to have them care for us. We want to be decent people, who treat one another as we would like to be treated—but who overawe our enemies—people whose spirits rise above the requirements for getting by in the world, which for most of us still means walking humbly with God through life's vicissitudes. Far from being modest, however, this wish list is so ambitious, so far out of the ordinary experience of mankind—including that portion of it that has lived in democracies—that few peoples have ever been granted anything like it, and then only for short periods of time and always as the result of uncommon habits bolstering rare institutions.

The questions that we Americans—and indeed all other democratic peoples—must decide about our public lives touch the very heart of the habits and institutions that make us citizens or subjects, rich or poor, that make or break families, that elevate or abase souls, and that make for military might.

SIZE, SCOPE, AND PURPOSE

The biggest set of questions regarding our civic life concerns the size of government and its competence. Size makes certain that government will weigh—or will not weigh—on a host of choices. Although size does not ensure that government will have the capacity to fulfill any particular set of responsibilities, let alone be able to carry them out well, size is a gross measure of government's incidence on civil society, on whose character everything depends. In *The Federalist* No. 46, James Madison underlined that the American regime could not be understood merely by focusing on the Constitution. The Constitution had to be seen in its proper context—as a small island of government in a big sea of civil life. Madison wrote:

> The adversaries of the Constitution seem to have lost sight of the people altogether in their reasoning on this subject; and to have viewed these different establishments not only as mutual rivals and enemies, but as uncontrolled by any common superior in their efforts to usurp the authorities of each other. They must be told that the ultimate authority, wherever the derivative may be found, resides in the people alone, and that it will not depend merely on the comparative ambition or address of the different governments whether either, or which of them, will be able to enlarge its sphere of jurisdiction at the expense of the other. Truth, no less than decency, requires that the event in every case should be supposed to depend on the sentiments and sanction of their common constituents.

The bigger government is, the less civil society can play the role of ultimate arbiter that Madison describes.

Max Weber accustomed us to dividing human relations between *gemeinschaft*, the things we do out of personal obligation to other members of civil society, and *gesellschaft*, our arm's-length economic activities. But our lives also contain a substantial measure of what we might call *machtschaft*, namely, the things that we do to others and others do to us through the power of government. This compulsive power exists alongside and intermingled with the things we do to make a living as well as with our voluntary activities as members of families, churches or synagogues, and professions. But while government is necessary to civil society, its power has always offered itself as a tool for trumping civil society. The twentieth century's typical temptation has been to try substituting government for social and economic relationships of the voluntary kind.

Thus, of the many things that we do, which should require some kind of license or permission from some government agency? What should we be able to do solely on our own account? All can agree that we want government to test the performance of drivers and perhaps airline pilots. The government qualifies lawyers, but only ratifies the medical profession's certification of doctors. To what extent do we wish to put the performance of other professions under the tutelage of government? Every government has the power of eminent domain, to take private property for public use. Should it, as the U.S. Supreme Court ruled, be able to take it for private uses that the government considers more worthy? To what extent should government be able to restrict or determine the use of private property that it does not take? How much and what kind of regulation is proper—not for economic health but for the very existence of civil society—and what kind destroys it? No one denies that government should punish murder or robbery even when committed by one member of a family against another. Certainly marriage, the contract that constitutes new families, is public business, as are its terms. But to what extent are the relations between husband and wife, between parents and children, reviewable by government? Do we want government to issue and revoke parenting licenses subject to some test? Should government have anything to say about the substance of what parents teach children? At what point are governmental attempts to preempt, supplant, or second-guess relations between individuals wrong ipso facto?

As stated earlier, the Western tradition of government is one of minimal interference in the judgments of families and other organs of civil society. Traditionally, civil and criminal law consciously reflected society's religious judgments and indeed lent secular strength to them. Since the sixteenth century, however, most Western governments (the United States being the most notable exception) have claimed the right to make laws out of the sheer sovereign power to do so. In his classic commentary on the laws of England, Sir William Blackstone wrote that the British Parliament could do anything not naturally impossible, such as turning a man into a woman. Nevertheless, until recently, only revolutionary governments (preeminently those of the French Revolution and the Soviet and Nazi regimes) have willfully departed from the rule that secular law never contradicts the fundamental tenets of religious law. Recently, however, as *machtschaft* has expanded and civil society has shrunk, governments throughout the West have tended to act as if they could make up standards as they went along and have increasingly treated religion, which they call "fundamentalism" whenever it asserts itself, as the enemy of secular order rather than as its basis.

What then is to be the role of religion among us? How should government regard the special claims of religion? How do we want to divide the power to set moral standards between civil society and government? Are religious citizens in the West to face the choice that modern regimes in the Islamic world force on their citizens, namely, that so long as secularists hold government power, their alien standards will push religion to the margins of society, make public life a mockery of everything the believer deems holy, and lead believing parents' children to mock them? But if Muslim parents want their surroundings and their children to reflect their judgments about right and wrong, they must seize government power and impose Koranic law on everyone. Thus the Islamic world has oscillated between opposing tyrannies. As Western governments squeeze civil society's traditional autonomy over morals, will Western peoples face the same bad set of choices, that if you do not want to be degraded, you must degrade others? Note that the alternative to forcing individuals to seek moral satisfaction through government would involve a renunciation of a sizable share of the claims of modern government.

Who shall run the schools—and determine what is to be taught? In 1995, 1.5 percent of American parents—all of whom paid school taxes—did not send their children to school at all. A decade later, the percentage had doubled. Another 13 percent of tax-paying parents paid to send their children to some kind of private school. Countless more wish they had the money or the courage to detach their families from the public schools. Theirs is a harsh judgment on the academic and moral competence of the schools. Comparison of test scores indicates that parents who school their children at home or in private settings are correct in their assessment.[3] But if government is rightly and fully sovereign, and if education is the foundation on which government rests,[4] then those parents who teach standards different from those taught in the government's schools are subversives by definition, while by that very definition government schools are right and proper regardless of what they teach. It follows from this that every effort should be made to stamp out private education in general and home schooling in particular.

For much of the twentieth century, certainly in Europe, government schools were the very standard of civilization. The authority of government over education was seldom questioned. In 1938, Germany outlawed home schooling, and in 2008 its government continued to subject parents and children who take part in it to forced psychiatric counseling. This has led some 800 German families to flee to Britain.[5] A state judge in California ruled in 2008 that parents who lack state teaching credentials may not educate their children at home—a ruling reversed almost as quickly as authorities learned of it, because the very demanding practice of home schooling had doubled within a decade and was continuing to increase in popularity. Today, as the competence of government to set intellectual and moral standards becomes obviously questionable, we naturally wonder what civil society loses by putting education into the realm of compulsion.

Traditionally, the inherent tension between government and civil society has been cushioned by a level of public life that partakes of civil society as well as of *machtschaft*, namely, local government. The idea that extensive government can coexist with civil society, the core of James Madison's view in *The Federalist* No. 10, an idea often attributed to Baron de Montesquieu or even to Edmund Burke,[6] rests on the capacity of large numbers of ordinary citizens to govern their own locality. It is actually far older. Large ancient cities, including Athens and Rome, were divided into tribes. Each tribe occupied a part of the city, had its own gods, settled most civil and criminal matters within its own ranks, and often voted *en bloc* within the larger polity. And of course feudal society was nothing but a welter of local privileges, obligations, and particularisms. Recently, economists have found that countries where there exist a variety of regulatory and tax jurisdictions tend to be more prosperous than countries with unitary systems. This is so because diversity spawns competition among the various local units, and competition drives each unit to be more favorable to economic activity than it would otherwise have been. In sum, there is little need in the Western tradition, and none at all in the American tradition, to make a theoretical case for the goodness of strong local institutions.

The question for us (as it has always been for those who have decided the fate of vast countries) is the extent to which we are willing to take responsibility for running the affairs of our local community, and how willing we are to tolerate communities in our country that live differently from us. Whereas the First Amendment to the U.S. Constitution prohibited the federal government from establishing any religion on the national level, religion was fully established in eleven of the thirteen states during the founding era. It remained fully established (at least by our time's standards) in countless localities, informally but very pervasively. And of course the denominations and versions thereof that they established differed across town lines. This practice endured until our time, especially in the public schools. Within living memory, public schools in America were run by units of government so small and so peculiar to the particular individuals involved that they functioned more as private than as public associations. The parents' exercise of power over them by vote over minute matters was more effective than the power that private-school parents today exercise by paying or withholding tuition. Local governments and school boards next door to one another made up rules that differed from one another but that suited themselves. They tolerated diversity next door because they could have their way at home. By contrast, now that small groups of neighbors have power over almost nothing that concerns themselves, they can only quarrel over what uniformity a faraway government should impose on everybody.

Thus, the choice with regard to schools, or social and economic matters, is clear enough: Since only a tiny percentage can take significant part in public affairs at the national level, most citizens will take part in local affairs or not at all. But they will take part only if the jurisdiction of local governments is both very small and quite powerful. Note that Tocqueville made the important distinction between government and administration. The Europeans of his time were already touting decentralized administration as the remedy for centralized government. To this Tocqueville counterposed the American example of decentralized government. He wrote:

> In America the power that conducts the administration is far less regular, less enlightened, and less skillful, but a hundred fold greater than in Europe. In no country in the world do the citizens make such exertions for the common weal. I know of no people who have established schools so numerous and efficacious, places of public worship better suited to the wants of the inhabitants, or roads kept in better repair. Uniformity or permanence of design, the minute arrangement of details, and the perfection of administrative system must not be sought for in the United States; what we find there is the presence of a power which, if it is somewhat wild, is at least robust, and an existence checkered with accidents, indeed, but full of animation and effort.[7]

However, if many different sets of people decide big questions, they will surely decide differently. Some local governments would legalize mind-bending drugs. Others would institute Singapore-style caning for their occasional use, and death for the salesmen. Rules regarding abortion would surely be different from state to state. Before the 1850s, Americans tolerated differences about slavery. But after the *Dred Scott* decision instituted one rule for all, toleration became impossible for all. How much diversity, how much freedom, can we now tolerate, and on what basis?

DEFINING ISSUES

Much depends on the issues. Abraham Lincoln taught that politics, whether at the national or local level, could not help but be nasty if its objective was to decide who was to be defined into the human race and thus protected and who was to be left defenseless. That is why he thought that *the very process of making detailed rules about slavery would corrupt the American people.* Questions about who gets what, where, and how, and at whose expense, as well as questions about which classes of people are to be somehow "protected," subsidized, or entitled—who will be "bailed out" of his financial troubles and who will not—also naturally lead to combat and corruption. The point here is that we define ourselves whenever we decide what we shall argue about and how we shall conduct the argument. Logical arguments about better and worse proceed from and produce human beings different in kind from arguments that consist of images and sound bites calculated to produce favor or disfavor. As Montesquieu wrote, the health of republics depends on public life being dominated by questions that foster rather than destroy virtue. But how do we tell the difference between issues, and how do we foster the right kind among ourselves?

Addressing the second question leads to a better understanding of the first. Even mere formalities matter. Do we—in each of our electoral districts and in our governors and presidents—want to be represented by single individuals or by parties? Since a single officeholder is responsible for everyone who voted, regardless of whether the voter voted for or against that person, and since a party is responsible only to the voters who cast their ballots for it, it is no surprise that countries where the electors must choose between party lists tend to argue over more divisive issues and do so more divisively than countries where the voters choose individuals directly. Different electoral systems also bring to the fore different kinds of politicians.

Each electoral system tends to create its own particular kind of political party. Do we want "strong" parties that can be "responsible" for turning their promises into actions by government? Or do we want parties that are only agglomerations of individuals with no power over their members and little capacity to carry out their promises?[8] Each kind has virtues and vices. "Responsible" parties tend to be filled with professional politicians, meaning professional dispensers of special privileges, lots of expertise, lots of power, and little need to care about anyone outside their own organization. Or do we want—by practice or by law—to limit the number of terms our politicians can serve, making them less expert and more responsive, if less responsible? If parties are held together by transient affiliations between blocks of voters, politicians may broker interests without care for principle. If parties are based only on ideas, they may be unable to compromise at all. Some combination of interest and principle seems to be necessary. But the twentieth century's peculiar disease combined the worst of both alternatives: parties organized to live off society, and to oppress their enemies therein in the name of lofty principles.

Expertise is one of the perennial bones of contention in republics. Do we want to be governed by people such as judges and career government employees whose claim to rule is that they know better than the rest of us? Is their detachment from politics—especially local politics—likely to make them fairer and more enlightened?[9] Is it even conceivable to detach administration from powerful interests in society, given that it is the very access to *machtschaft* that makes these interests so powerful? Are we better off with mandarins who administer specific laws according to strict rules, or with administrators who have wide discretion to achieve broad objectives, or is impersonal administration simply incompatible with government that sets out to achieve big goals with huge resources?

According to perhaps a majority of academic opinion, the wealth of nations is the result of wise management by rulers whose powers are equal to their task. According to this view, the peoples of the Pacific Rim have achieved prosperity because of what Chalmers Johnson calls "state-directed capitalism." Others call it "industrial policy," or "neomercantilism." With no little irony, the Communists in power from Beijing to Moscow who claim to be following this model call it "market economy." In a nutshell, this means that government officials, who often have interests and always have friends and enemies in business, decide which ventures to favor by direct subsidies, favored financing, protective tariffs, contracts, or tailored regulations. Peoples who export more high-tech goods than they import, so goes the argument, wind up with more money and with a better share of the world's high-paying jobs than others whose governments have not been so wisely active. That may or may not happen. But *to expect officials to treat their opponents' interests as they do those of their friends is to expect water to run uphill.*

According to another view, however, state-directed capitalism is even more dysfunctional socially than it is economically. Indeed, advantages bestowed on companies and individuals tend to pervert economic life from production to favor seeking. According to this perspective, government fosters prosperity by safeguarding property rights as well as by providing a level playing field and fair, inexpensive settlement of disputes. The first approach requires a big government that takes much and gives much with wide discretion, while the second requires a government as small and law-bound as possible. As we decide the role of government in foreign trade, in business and professional regulation, in tax policy, and in providing for old age, ill health, and misfortune, we are also deciding about what kinds of lives we will live. Deciding on the extent to which we shall be protectionists or free traders leads us to ask whether it is the objective of economic life, in addition to earning a living, to earn it in roughly the same way in the same place throughout one's lifetime, and perhaps to pass the entire situation on to one's children? Who among us will be protected while others face competition and yet others are forced to pay higher prices? Why should that be so? By what right?

To what extent shall our governments regulate? The necessary premise of the tens of thousands of pages of regulations that flow from modern governments each year is that government knows more about the right way to build widgets and run banks than their owners, or that only the hand of government prevents them from using their expertise to exploit the public. But who can guarantee the expertise of the regulators, not to mention their equanimity or honesty? Of course, since government draws its expertise by involving business in the regulatory process, government inevitably rules all banks through its favorite bankers. Moreover, it makes a big difference to what extent regulations are predictable or depend on discretionary rulings. Do officials live in fear of overstepping their bounds, or do they swagger?

By taxing any activity more, we discourage it more. By taxing it less, we decrease the discouragement. This applies to everything from the formation and size of families to charitable contributions, home ownership, savings, investment, the use of restaurants, cars, computers, and so forth. Thus, all schemes of taxation imply different levels of economic activity and ensure that some activities, some ways of life, will be surer pathways to wealth than others. By taxing the proceeds from the sale of businesses, we discourage transforming old businesses into new ones. By taxing a person's savings at death, we encourage him to waste them rather than to pass them on to his heirs.

When, at the turn of the twentieth century, Western governments embarked on becoming the major providers of assistance in old age, ill health, and personal failure, only a few imagined that government might thereby supplant rather than support the role of families in society.[10] Few foresaw that it would bring about vast changes in the composition of the labor force and even contribute to reducing the number of births to below that of deaths. Today, the economic and social consequences of pursuing social welfare through government raise questions long eclipsed by faith in government. For example, what difference does it make who is responsible for basic decisions about how much medical care each of us receives?

Not the least of the economic questions before us is the extent to which we want to pay for a class of government employees, in effect subsidizing a class of citizens with a unique relationship to power. It should surprise no one that throughout the world the most heartfelt arguments for any function of government come from the people who are paid to perform that function, and that government employees are everywhere the most determined political supporters of statist parties. Two generations ago, the U.S. government dealt with this fact in small part by passing the Hatch Act, which prohibits certain kinds of political activity by government employees. But were we to follow that act's premise, that people should be disqualified from public business in which they have a private interest, we would forbid government employees from voting. But since today in America more people are employed to govern than to make things, the size and weight of government as a political constituency has overwhelmed the Hatch Act. The public employee labor unions are great political powers, and the biggest of government's economic biases is toward itself.

Government affects economic well-being even more by influencing the "human capital" that is the principal ingredient of any economy. Do we want government leaders and policies to strengthen in people's minds the basic notion that people end up getting what they earn, or do we want them to promote the practical tenet of modern entrepreneurship that it is just as well to get ahead by orchestrating the good graces of powerful patrons? Much has been made recently of the proposition that a people's economic success is proportionate to its level of trust, that extending trust farther allows economic cooperation to spread farther. While government cannot legislate trust, governments certainly affect the level of trust in society by the degree of evenhandedness and transparency with which they enforce their own rules.

Since human capital grows in families, the character of families may well be the primary element in the creation of prosperity, not to mention its enjoyment.[11] One of the great debates concerning economic efficiency is precisely whether it is best for most women to take part in the world of work interchangeably with men, sharing both housework and child care equally with men, while leaving children in some kind of day care much of the time, or whether it is best for everyone to have women devote themselves to caring for their own children in their own homes. According to some, the Japanese people work more diligently than the citizens of other developed countries in part because Japanese families are much less affected by divorce, illegitimacy, and uncertain roles for men and women. By the same token, Mikhail Gorbachev noted that the economic contribution of women in the Soviet economy was more than canceled out by the decline in the quality of women's principal product: well-brought-up children and motivated men. On the other side, Scandinavian societies manage to do reasonably well economically with rates of illegitimacy fifty times higher than those of the Japanese. The point here is that the debate over what kind of families we should promote amongst ourselves is very much an economic debate as well.

The human content of an individual's home and family affects the quality of life far more than any material contents. Conversely, the character of families is much affected by government policy. But what is a family? Today, there is considerable objection even to defining the family in *natural* terms: as the union of a man and a woman that normally produces children. The alternative definition is *conventional:* A family is any group of individuals who live together with some degree of intimacy and commitment.[12] Although the difference between the two basic approaches to families is rooted in part in the opposition between heterosexuality and homosexuality, the difference is deeper and wider: Ought we to treat as natural the division of labor between men and women, as well as the responsibility of men for their children and for the women who bear them—and its logical concomitant, the special authority of husbands over wives and children—or ought we to treat it as just one choice among many? The traditional Christian and Jewish marriage rituals stipulate different duties for husbands and wives. Until recently, our laws roughly followed these stipulations. About a generation ago, new laws and other signals from our regime began trying to mold society according to the notion that neither man, nor woman, nor child had any particular obligation to anyone else. In our time, while many talk of the need to strengthen families, the several recipes proposed are based on radically different premises and would drive families in very different directions. Which should we choose?

Perhaps the most prominent vision of the family is that the whole nation is a kind of extended family, or "village," in which a variety of governmental institutions help raise the children, as well as provide for the sick, the old, and the indigent. According to this vision, the good society is filled with high-quality day-care centers so that women can work without guilt; with after-school programs and even midnight basketball leagues to keep children busy when they are not in school; with organized activities for senior citizens to make sure they remain independent of their adult children; and with counseling centers for all sorts of social dysfunctions, backed by teams to investigate cases of abuse and to intervene therein with education or law enforcement. One wonders how societies ever survived without Scandinavian levels of social services.

At the opposite pole is the view that further pursuit of such family policy amounts not to assistance for the family but to war upon it, and that we ought rather to reverse the incentives that government has thus far instituted to overcome gender roles. Under this category are proposals to stop taxation to get money that is now spent on hiring people to do for others' parents and children what they might be doing for their own. There are also proposals to reduce the pressure on women with young children to work by removing disincentives to marriage and to raising children from the tax code. But the main proposals under this category have to do with the legal status of marriage and birth. Thus, if the family, defined by marriage, is the only proper place for children to be conceived, rather than just another alternative, then causing a pregnancy outside marriage must be punishable; and if fathers are to be held responsible for their children, it makes no sense to give to mothers the absolute right to abort them. Different images of the family, of course, are the most prominent parts of different images of human decency.

The most fundamental struggle of all will be precisely over the meaning of decency. Every regime has its set of basic commandments, of actions that define good people and bad. The United States was founded by a group of men who held certain truths to be self-evident. The Declaration of Independence listed a small number of the truths that its signers and their neighbors accepted as divine guidance for their lives: the right to life, liberty, and the pursuit of happiness. Had any been asked for a more extensive list, they likely would have begun with the Ten Commandments. Although the American founders would not have thought of translating most of those commandments into law any more than they thought of legislating the pursuit of happiness, their list made all the difference.

Were a time machine somehow to cause any community of the founders' generation to appear among us, they would surely notice that we now enjoin actions once prohibited and prohibit actions once enjoined. Contemporary American elites, in turn, would find the founders' intolerance of pornography and their mixing of religion in public life to be violations of the First Amendment, their treatment of criminals in violation of the Eighth. They would deem pathologically anarchic their attachment to firearms, as well as their distrust of government. The founders would likely beat a hasty retreat to their time machine, pointing their muzzle loaders at the atheist, servile folks who had twisted their words and perverted their republic.

Today, those who make laws in Western society find no truths to be self-evident, and their concept of decency is a grab bag of elements for which they have developed the taste. Hence drawing up the list of the moral imperatives by which we should live has become a contest of tastes, decided by trials of political force. We thus see government telling people that happiness is doing whatever pleases them, and then putting some of them in jail for pleasuring themselves through drugs. Nevertheless, this public contest over the content of our souls determines the outcome of all the other contests we must wage.

PART II
WHAT DIFFERENCES REGIMES MAKE

4

THE SOVIET LEGACY

He that soweth discord in his own house
shall inherit the wind.
   —PROVERBS 11:29

One of the most difficult things to convey to a Western audience is how disgusting the rank and file of the old Soviet ruling class really were—how mean, treacherous, shamelessly
lying, cowardly, sycophantic, ignorant.
   —ROBERT CONQUEST, "THE IMPORTANCE
   OF HISTORICAL TRUTH"

The disaster that the Soviet regime wrought on Russia is worth pondering
because it resulted from ideas and practices that, shorn of their peculiar
Russian context, perennially tempt modern man. Because communism was
one variant of the modern way of life in which we are all immersed, because
so many of our best and brightest found its ideas so attractive that they ab-
stracted them from their monstrous reality, we would be foolish to think

that our civilization has rejected the Soviet model root and branch. Indeed, in some form, its ideas and practices are intertwined with our quotidian choices. Whether transmogrified, diluted, or disguised, they haunt us still. By no means should we think: "We could never be like that." Anyone could. So, it is incumbent on us to examine in some detail what Soviet communism's ideas and practices did to Russia—what the poisons did in their pure dose— lest we misunderstand what they are likely to do in any form to any people.

It seems paradoxical that a system that organized its people so thoroughly ended up so disarticulated economically and politically, with its people spiritually starved, snapping at each other on the streets and in their homes, unable even to make use of the armed forces into which it had poured material and human resources most unstintingly. But no paradox: The Soviet regime collapsed when its logic produced its full effects, fouling millions of human relationships among rulers and ruled alike. The more it organized, the more it ended up disarticulating. St. Augustine reminds us that even bands of thieves survive by fostering peace amongst themselves. But Karl Marx and Friedrich Engels had preached the incompatibility of human interests: All relationships, whether in government, business, family, or faith, are exploitative. Following Marx's practical guidance to socialist parties, V. I. Lenin sought a government that would rule so exclusively in the interests of its class that it would obliterate all other classes. As an instrument of this war of annihilation, he established a party of specialists in conflict—above all, internal. The Soviet Union, in short, was at war with itself economically, politically, and socially, from its first moment to its last. Naturally, having sown discord, it reaped a terrible human harvest.

Death is its proof and fruit. As the Soviet regime waned, more Russians were dying than were being born, and the living could expect to live fewer years. The neo-Soviet regime that replaced it saw deaths exceed births by about a half million per year, male life expectancy decline to fifty-nine years, and consumption of alcohol increase from about 10 to 14 liters per year per capita. Among adult men, the figure was several times higher. While record prices for oil and gas made billionaires of few of the regime's favorites, and public opinion polls registered overwhelming approval of the regime's nationalist posture, no one suggested that Russians were happy. One Russian town tried to buck this trend by giving local workers holidays for the purpose of procreation, and paying for the results. But Russian women seemed driven above all to marry foreigners—individual secessions more significant than those of political units.

THE ECONOMICS OF TAKING

The Soviet economy degraded Russia's human capital. Marx's voluminous writings nowhere contain any affirmative description of a socialist economy as an engine of production. Rather, their central theme is that *control* of the means of production is inescapably exploitative, and that the driving force in life is everyone's struggle to control them so as to exploit everyone else.[1] The natural corollary of both Marx's and Lenin's legacies is that *the primary purpose of economic activity must be to ensure the primacy of those who run it,* the Communist Party. Hence, Marxist economics is much more about taking from others than about producing.

In short, practically as well as theoretically, the Soviet economy was organized for war. The German verb that Marx used for "taking," *kriegen,* is also the word for making war. Once a class is deprived of its economic base, it has nothing to express, can neither defend nor feed itself, and ceases to exist. From the outset, for theoretical as well as practical reasons, the Soviet regime sought to deny bread to its opponents. Every Communist regime has done the same.

As regards production, the scheme by which Communist economies have been organized owes nothing to Marx. Rather, it is ideologically neutral statism, pioneered by Walter Rathenau in Germany during World War I: concentration to achieve maximum economies of scale, with each factory producing only one item at maximum capacity and the central authority allocating both capital and labor. Thus, in the Soviet Union, bureaucrats allocated resources and labor for the whole country from Party headquarters—not because Marx had so prescribed but because they followed a superficially successful example that, not incidentally, allowed the Party to crush enemies, reward friends, and secure itself.

Communist managers of farms and factories, for their part, hoarded labor and materials out of proportion to economic need—not because any Marxist text told them to but because control over people and goods meant power, status, and privileged use for themselves. "Nothing but the best for the Proletariat" was the cynical principle by which people at any given level of power took what they could for themselves. To secure themselves from above and below, Communist officials made sure that basic foods (and medical care and vacations) were subsidized and effectively rationed, and that they would do the rationing. Such a system gave workers some controlled incentives to work but prevented the kinds of sporadic riots that always made the officials on whose watch they occurred vulnerable to their rivals. Hence, the purpose of the Communist economy was not so much to produce goods and services—much less happiness for the masses—as to use economic means to maximize the Party's control over itself and over ordinary people. Thus, according to its own standard, the Soviet economy performed brilliantly to the very end.

However, a regime at war with its own people and with the world could base its economy only on compulsion: compulsion of rural populations into industrial occupations (the last of many great drives occurring in the 1960s), compulsion of women into the labor force (90 percent participation), and compulsion of the population in general to accept uneconomically low wages—effectively a kind of slave labor. Agriculture was based on compulsory collectivization and on the compulsory sale of produce at uneconomically low prices. It mattered little that the Soviets set prices this way rather than by manipulating taxes or tariffs: The power to decree prices is by no means the least of what defines tyranny.

Industrial production was organized oligopolistically, conferring on a few state enterprises the exclusive right to produce certain products, effectively compelling the public to buy whatever came out. But socialist managers used the exclusive role conferred on them to pressure state planners with demands for ever more materials and labor, plus, of course, for housing, food for special stores, access to clinics and resorts, and so forth. Like any monopolist, they charged more while producing proportionately less, so the real economic price of goods was very high. In practice, the state was caught between its natural bent to compel production and the compulsive power it had given to producers as a consequence of that bent, which reduced useful production.

Stalin resolved this dilemma by violent purges, and his successors by unbloody ones. But with every resolution, every turnover of elites, every new plan, regardless of peace or war, producers got an ever greater percentage of production, and consumers got ever less. As the productive economy produced less for more, the real economic price of goods rose. In 1928, finished consumer goods accounted for 60.5 percent of Soviet industrial production. By 1987, these goods accounted for only 24.9 percent of Soviet industrial production. The system's very logic dictated ever more work for smaller shares of the results.

That is because the logic of state direction of the economy *dictated waste.* The regime's preference for military things cannot account for the discrepancy between the high output of Soviet industry and the country's effective poverty. While official U.S. estimates for Soviet military spending of 12 to 18 percent of gross domestic product (GDP) are certainly way too low and a meaningful figure may not exist, it is difficult to imagine the military having taken up much more than about one-third of GDP or of industrial production. So what happened to the other 40-odd percent that civilians did not consume? The official Soviet answer was "investment." Official Soviet figures for investment in the economy as a whole come to an astounding 33 percent.[2] By contrast, Western economies devote some 15 percent of industrial production to capital investment. Investing more than twice as much as the West should have brought the Soviet Union wondrous growth. And indeed, when Soviet leaders threatened to bury the West economically, the westerners who believed them had in mind the high rate of Soviet investment. In reality, however, the sorts of things that the Soviets called "investment" were the opposite thereof. Mikhail Bernstam has written that Soviet industrial investment amounted to "machines that produce other machines in order to produce other machines which exact other resources in order to produce more machines."[3] In other words, waste.

But the inefficiencies went beyond that. During the 1970s, socialist countries used one and a half times as much steel and energy per $1,000 of GDP as capitalist countries. By the mid-1980s, they were using three and a half times as much. The Soviet Union produced half as much meat as the United States using roughly as much grain for animal feed as American farmers used,[4] making for half the efficiency. Moreover, the Soviet economy's use of primary commodities continued to increase even as the production of finished goods declined. Much waste, it seems, was systemic: Materials and labor were directed by powerful producers to ends unrelated to the desires of powerless consumers. Things were produced, all right. But they were akin to cathedrals in the desert—unwanted and recycled.

Inefficiency transcended theft as well. Certainly, unmeasurable parts of "lost" production resulted from individuals appropriating state property for their own use. But theft was not waste, since it satisfied human desires. Theft also made sense in terms of the system as well as in economic terms. After all, in appropriating public property, lower-ranking people were only imitating the top leadership. Hence, it was altogether reasonable that the personnel of Aeroflot reserved first-class seats for people who paid them directly, and that to get nonharmful attention from medical personnel one had to pay them personally, usually with goods or access thereto. Also, given the system, why blame the farmer who considered the state's tractor his own to plow his private plot, but not his own when it came time to fix it?

Although impossible to quantify, the human waste must have been greater than the material waste. The overstaffing of factories, offices, restaurants, garages, and so on paralleled the excess of material inputs. Arguably the worst waste of all was the employment of countless people in economically useless jobs. Legions were employed to check on others, who checked on them—from watchmen to chief assistants to the assistant chief, secretaries and drivers and janitors for functions like "political work," which no one would pay for voluntarily. Nevertheless, some of these functions, like Communist Party posts, had so much economic value within the system that people sacrificed significant portions of their lives to achieve them. But while valuable to individuals, such jobs *redistributed* wealth rather than creating it. Forcible redistribution also had a more direct cost: moral degeneracy.

Arguably the greatest source of waste was peculiar to the system. Like every other economy, the Soviet economy had managers, engineers, teachers, and plumbers. But in addition, there were lots of jobs unique to the Communist system. The *nomenklaturists* were the high-level people on whose decisions projects, fortunes, and careers hinged.[5] The countless sub-bureaucracies had to staff up to jostle with one another. Then there were the *tolkachi*—the fixers, the people worth their weight in gold who brokered favors, bargained bribes, and arbitrated claims; who found apartments, jobs, materials, and places in school; and who procured permissions and loans and all manner of documents. The state guaranteed a place in a maternity clinic and a grave site. But the *tolkach* actually made such things available— for a price. And there was the art of the *stukach,* the stool pigeon, who would make derogatory reports about someone who stood in the way at the office. Just about anyone who got anywhere did it either by using that art or by successfully guarding against it. But part of the art consisted of gauging the predisposition of the authorities to whom the report was made to take action against the accused—in other words, being sure the report went to an enemy of the accused, but only if the accused was judged friendless enough to be got. The Soviet economy, then, degraded the economic usefulness of its participants by multiplying and rewarding vile behavior and people.

There was social mobility aplenty in the old Soviet Union. After 1938, nearly all people in the ruling class were the sons of peasants. Throughout the regime's seventy-four years, countless penniless people moved up the ranks of society and acquired opulent lifestyles. Some did it on the level playing fields of sport, others on the nearly level fields of technology or the military. But the mass of those who profited from purges of others, who ingratiated their way up ladders of patronage, who made fortunes as brokers of favor, did so by excelling at the low arts of nepotism, betrayal, bribery, and flattery. Neither prosperity nor anything else worthwhile can be built on these qualities.

PLUS ÇA CHANGE . . .

Because the Soviet system was not replaced by another, the post-Soviet Russian economy is being run by nomenklaturists, to whom the Soviet economy was essentially gifted. These people usually occupy the same offices they did before 1991. Regardless of the titles on their business cards or the political labels they may sport, they brought "their habits with them."[6]

The Russian economy in our time bears no relationship to free enterprise. "The Nomenklatura," wrote former Soviet dissident Lev Timofeyev, "both acquired the freedom of private initiative and preserved their entire distributive power over state property."[7] Georgii Arbatov, once the USSR's expert on America, explained how the system worked: "An enormous and parasitic apparat gives or takes away, permits or prohibits, can fine anybody, demote anybody, often even throw him in prison or, on the contrary, raise him up."[8] It still worked this way in post-Soviet Russia, except that the regime's factions had multiplied and become independent. Then, beginning in 1999, Russia's explicitly neo-Soviet dictator, Vladimir Putin, reduced the number of factions, jailed their most prominent leaders, and brought the rest under his own control.

Who prospers in today's Russia? Millions of Russians produce goods and services, from bread to train rides, metals, and energy, that are inherently valuable. But such people do not receive rewards proportionate to their work any more than they did under communism. At the bottom of the prosperous heap are those gangsters who exact protection money.[9] These are not merely private individuals, because they work with the approval of the various police authorities—approval they must purchase. Gang wars come about when one gang pays some or all of the authorities a higher percentage of the take than other gangs are willing to pay. Thus, the Moscow police swept away the Georgian gang that had been running the used car lot by the river south of Moscow on behalf of a Chechen gang that was willing to cut them a bigger share of the business. If the Georgian gang had been on top of things, it would have matched the offer or bought the help of another of the state's security services, in which case the battle would have taken place among uniformed men, as sometimes happens on Russian streets. That is the sort of business acumen that makes *small* fortunes in Russia.

This is why people in business worry first and last about their official *protektsiya,* their "protection." This is not *part* of the business: It is the only real business. It yields the right to operate banks that recycle moneys from Western drug cartels back into Western economies, the right to buy all kinds of assets—from real estate to oil and gas to specialty metals—at prices regulated below world market levels, and the right to sell them on the world market.[10] It enables one to buy and sell currencies and securities armed with foreknowledge of events that will surely affect their value. It also enables one to receive "soft financing" from the state, just as during Communist times. And only *protektsiya,* of course, makes it possible to tap foreign money through joint ventures, as well as to administer billions of dollars and deutsche marks in foreign assistance.

But the big money in Russia comes from the oil and gas oligopoly— always under political control but largely nationalized since 2005. Prior to that, Prime Minister Viktor Chernomyrdin, a former minister of the Soviet gas ministry—and the private proprietor of 10 percent of the largest energy company, Gazprom, its privatized successor—reportedly amassed a private fortune amounting to $5 billion.[11] In 1996 the deputy chairman of the Russian State Duma, Mikhail Yuryev, claimed to me that he owned every gas station in Moscow and that he did millions of dollars of business all over the world. He had not built his business on satisfying customers, but rather on power. But in 2005 Vladimir Putin put such people out of business. He nationalized Gazprom, which made an irresistible offer to purchase Sibneft, the fifth largest company, and folded the third largest, Yukos, into the state company Rosneft, jailing its independent-minded former nomenklaturist Mikhail Khodorkovsky. But neither the Putinites nor their predecessors add value—they take it. These nomenklatura-turned-*bizhnesmeny* reap without sowing. Compared with such pure parasites, the thugs who run protection rackets work for a living and sometimes actually come close to providing a real service.

ENGINEERING DISCORD

Socialist poverty and prosperity come from exchanges between people with different degrees of access to power, and socialist politics consists of competitive oppression. This produced in the Soviet people a set of characteristics that Andrei Amalrik described in this way: "The idea of self-government, of equality before the law and of personal freedom—and the responsibility that goes with these—are almost incomprehensible to the Russian people. . . . To the majority of people the very word 'freedom' is synonymous with 'disorder' or the opportunity to indulge with impunity in some kind of anti-social or dangerous activity. As for respecting the rights of an individual as such, the idea simply arouses bewilderment."[12]

The perennial Russian practice of an autocratic, centralized empire, whose only contact with the citizens consisted of taking produce or sons, surely taught only one law: The strong do what they can, and the *muzhiks,* the common folk, suffer what they must. In other words, Russia was all too well-suited temperamentally for Communist totalitarianism. The counterargument, which also makes sense, is that the instinctive disbelief of the Russian people in government actually tempered the rigors of communism. Imagine, so goes the argument, if Communist tyranny had sprung up among Germans, a people credulous enough to give it their hearts.[13] Be that as it may, because the Soviet regime embodied the denial of all law, it wrecked human relationships by overdosing them with power.

On the surface, Soviet society was more thickly overgrown with human organization than the northern Italian cities that Robert Putnam took as his model of civic life.[14] In 1960, the Soviet trade unions had some 75 million members; the Komsomol youth organization, 32 million; the various cooperatives, 28 million; 2 million served as part-time deputies to various Soviets; and another 20 million were classified as "activists" who organized everything from chess tournaments and amateur drama to school ceremonies and sporting events.[15] People were incessantly mobilized for the widest variety of causes—from helping with the harvest to "storming" (a kind of forced volunteer overtime) at work or on civic projects. The artificial character of this human interaction exacerbated the combination of obedience and resentment for which Russians are famous. Nevertheless, some Russians remember it fondly.

Whereas according to the classical and Christian traditions, family, clan, friendship, village, and profession are natural and occur prior to politics, Lenin considered them either obstacles to be razed or "transmission belts." Stalin called them "gears and levers" by which "the realization of dictatorship is made possible."[16] Hence, the Soviet Union broke natural ties to locality, profession, and so on by adding to the injury of despotism the insulting pretense that the subjects approved of it enthusiastically. That is, the Soviet regime forced people to lie to one another's face. According to Aleksandr Solzhenitsyn, mutual lying lowered people in their own eyes and in the eyes of others, making impossible both normal society and the Communist parody of it.[17]

Solzhenitsyn ends *The Gulag Archipelago* with this comprehensive snapshot of how these effects made Soviet life lawless:

> Only in those few cases (15 percent perhaps?) in which the subject of investigation and judicial proceedings affects neither the interests of the state nor the reigning ideology nor the personal interests of comfort of some office holder—only very rarely can the officers of the court enjoy the privilege of trying a case without telephoning somebody to seek instructions; of trying it on its merits and as conscience dictates. All other cases—the overwhelming majority: criminal or civil, it makes no difference—inevitably affect in some important way the interests of the chairman of a kolkhoz or a village Soviet, a shop foreman, a factory manager, the head of a housing bureau, a block sergeant, the investigating officer or commander of a police district, the medical superintendent of a hospital, a chief planning officer, the heads of administration or ministries, special sections or personnel sections, the secretaries of district or oblast Party committees—and upward, ever upward. In all such cases, calls are made from one discreet inner office to another; leisurely lowered voices give friendly advice, steady and steer the decision to be reached in the trial of a wretched little man caught in the tangled schemes, which he would not understand even if he knew them, of those set in authority over him. The naively trusting newspaper reader goes into the courtroom conscious that he is in the right. His reasonable arguments are carefully rehearsed, and he lays them before the somnolent, masklike faces on the bench, never suspecting that sentence has been passed on him already.[18]

Solzhenitsyn's passage applies this portrait of the rule of influence exclusively to judicial proceedings. But it applied to Soviet public life in general, and the average Russian was painfully aware of how the system worked. Because they knew the rules well, Soviet subjects cowered insofar as they did not have the right connections, and they swaggered when they did. They lived in fear of trouble but rejoiced in their capacity to cause trouble for others.

Another portrait, this one of the lower ends of Soviet life, clinches the point. The journalist Hedrick Smith noted:

> I would have thought that with all the nuisances burdening ordinary Russians that they would instinctively have banded together to ease the strain of life. Within their own narrow circles they do. Yet Soviet society in general is peopled by mini-dictators inflicting inconvenience and misery on the rest of their fellow citizens, often it seems as a way of getting back at the system for the hardship and frustration they themselves have suffered. . . . I have heard Russians in more recent years describe this phenomenon as a mass settling of scores on a personal level. . . . "Put a Russian in charge of a little plot of ground or a doorway, somewhere," a bespectacled scientist ruminated sadly to me, "and he will use his meager authority over that spot to make life hard on others."[19]

To these systemic harassments, humblings, and houndings that one could avenge but not bring to justice, Smith ascribed "the quiet erosion of the spirit that takes place daily."[20] Spirits thus reduced to voluntary self-abasement, to nurturing connections by which they mean to mitigate abasement at the hands of some by inflicting it on others, are barely able to conceive of standing up for their own rights under the law, much less for the rights of others. And for right or truth in general? Nonsense. That would be neither smart nor wise, and certainly contrary to the practical training the regime imparted to its subjects.

The Communist Party was the basis of that artificial society. But despite nominally extreme bureaucratization, neither Party nor state was run by formal bureaucracy. Rather, higher officials tended to descend (physically or otherwise) onto lower ones. Then, by practicing the equivalent of the tsars' flogging of officials (or of Cesare Borgia's dismemberment of his lieutenant, Remirro d'Orco), they earned the love of vengeance-hungry subjects. Thus the Party designated from its own ranks a never-ending stream of scapegoats: traitors, wreckers, conspirators, and the criminally incompetent. Since no one could know today who or what might be thrust tomorrow into the categories of the politically incorrect, everyone learned to guard their rear, to distrust everyone else. Stalin was the teacher of this and other techniques for hoarding personal power, including fostering competing bureaucracies among whose chiefs he arbitrated. Much as during the Roman republic's decadence, Soviet public lives were built on the exchange of loyalty for the expectation of lawless favors, and lesser men were defined by the *khvost* (the tail, meaning the extended entourage of the higher-ups) to whom they belonged, while the princes were defined by the size of their "tails."

The greatest change in Soviet politics between the Russian Revolution and the rise of Mikhail Gorbachev occurred in 1968, when Leonid Brezhnev curtailed the prerogatives of the central administration to interfere in the affairs of republic and oblast divisions of the Party. After that, Soviet public life became almost feudal as the personal "tails" acquired a local character and semiformal rules came to govern the trading of patronage. The system had always allocated material goods to satisfy various ethnic groups. The constant shifting of favor had exacerbated ill feeling among them. By regularizing the system of preferences, Brezhnev's reforms tended to give this system the feel and color of law. For many, this ushered in a safe, comfortable way of life. This is the system that Gorbachev attempted to undo. But the botched undoing reminded everyone of their resentments, weakened arbitrary authority, and snowballed into the destruction of the Soviet Union. That, however, is another story.

The point here is that even under Brezhnev, but especially before that, the substitution of power for law and the personalization of power demeaned and embittered all. Since raw political power was society's currency and indeed had become the arbiter of religion, science, and human relations in general, sleazes and frauds found protectors and quashed decent folk. No surprise then that Soviet society's negative selection of human qualities raised up the incompetent, the cowards, the mean. Fortunately for the world, this habit led the Party to acquiesce not only in patent scientific frauds, such as T. D. Lysenko's genetics, but also in Mikhail Gorbachev's patently self-destructive politics. At that point, the regime's preference for worse human types over better ones finally caught up with it. As the regime was dying, a Russian cab driver told Robert Conquest: "We've been ruled by morons for forty years, and this is the first time it's paid off."[21]

Nor did Russia's post-Soviet regime make citizens out of subjects. Habits inculcated over three generations would have been hard to break—assuming anyone had intended to break them, which they did not. Visitors to post-Soviet Russia are struck by the same sense as in years past that people are terribly intent on what they are doing, that they push and shove and grasp. And conversations still offer the same explanation: that favor is a scarce commodity and that you must find the key to it. Whom do you know? What can he do for you? But because the structures of power are not so obvious as before, the guarantees are fewer, and the anxiety is greater.

FOULING THE NEST

The Soviet regime was as unfriendly to natural families as it was to other natural human institutions. But the regime's ideologically motivated campaign to wreck Russian families lasted little more than a decade. By 1936, for pragmatic reasons, Stalin introduced a set of material and psychological incentives to marriage and procreation. Nonetheless, the requirements of tyranny maintained the regime's pressure against family life. The regime's structural bias against family life was, if anything, accentuated by both the liberalization of the regime in later years and by the regime's collapse into lawlessness.

Next to religion, Lenin's Bolsheviks considered the family as the most important pillar of bourgeois society. A basic tenet of Marxism is the Darwinian position that all human characteristics result from adaptation to external conditions. Hence, the proletarian revolution that would overthrow the material bases on which all societies had ever existed would resolve what Marxists call the "contradictions" between man and woman as well as those between town and country, between intellectual and manual labor, and so on. The Marxist image of the family (like the postmodernist one) is doubly negative: It is both a den of mutual exploitation (like the rest of all societies that ever existed) and the place where the next generation is trained to perpetuate all evils. The Bolsheviks went out of their way to mock marriage almost as much as they did to mock religion. That grim lot were libertines in principle rather than for fun.

The first Soviet Constitution contained a statement on women's rights even more detailed than the Equal Rights Amendment proposed for the U.S. Constitution in the 1970s. Accordingly, the Soviet state effectively pushed women to take jobs, and it initially instituted workers' housing with the kind of communal living dormitories and refectories that exiled Bolsheviks had seen among the radical socialist workers' settlements in Western Europe. In the new industrial zones and on the first collective farms, no other kinds of living arrangements were available.

By the 1930s, the Soviets' desire to break down the family quickly gave way to more pressing ones, like industrialization. The Party went all-out (almost) to increase births. Like other Soviet producers, mothers were awarded medals designating ever-higher ranking, depending on the number of children they turned out. And parents who produced children got preferential treatment for new apartments. But the regime did not in the least relax the pressure on mothers to work, nor did it let fathers exercise any authority over their families. It was Stalin, after all, who built the cult of the boy who had reported on his parents to the secret police. The Soviet state might encourage men and women to copulate. But men and women would prosper or hang separately according to the whims of the Party. Men and women together might produce children. But children would belong to the state.

In short, the regime stripped the family of all sources of social support. The Russian veneration of virginity, abhorrence of adultery, and reverence for life, as well as the Russian belief in the responsibility of the strong for the weak, had all come from the Orthodox Church. Yet everything connected with the church now was off-limits. So was literature favorable to bourgeois ways. And so, under material and moral pressures, those ways declined. Women conscripted into labor, under double pressures of work and home, aborted most of their children (estimates of the average number of abortions by each Soviet woman hovers between five and ten) and put the survivors in day care. Life was not any more family-friendly for the new Soviet man. Knowing that he could gain nothing for his family by sweat, brains, or integrity, and that he had nothing to say about whether his children would live or die, *Homo Sovieticus* became increasingly superfluous to women and children. Increasingly, the men became the exploiters that Engels and Marx had imagined. Insofar as civil society survived, it became matriarchal.

The accounts of Western visitors, whether feminists or religious conservatives, contained the same judgments by Russian women on their men: They were boorish cads. And this did not suddenly change when the Soviet Union collapsed. Writing in 1995, a *New York Times* journalist quoted a Russian mother as saying the men "seem to have no sense of responsibility at all." Another said, "Seventy years of Soviet rule have taught men to be selfish and passive."[22] A 1989 book on Soviet women pointed out similar prob-

lems with the men. At work, they were lazy intriguers. At home, they practiced what they learned at work: The more powerful took what they could
from the less powerful. Many lived with their wives only so long as they
were served and the children were not too bothersome. Then they would
leave. They did not encounter moral censure for it, for after most of a century of relativism and fraudulent male role models, moral censure was in
short supply in Russia, whether on the upper end of society or the low. Some
men agreed to have children in order to qualify for an apartment. Then they
pushed them out. Some observers claimed that men had been conditioned
by experience to think of good grades in school, of hard work and responsibility, as female traits, which they shunned.[23]

The Soviet regime thus left permanent marks on conjugal relations as
well as on economic and civic behavior. The condition of women in Russia is
as obviously appalling to the casual visitor today as that of American Indian
women was to the pioneers. Male janitors and street cleaners are practically
unknown, as are male road construction crews. The nonmechanized aspects
of agriculture are women's work, too, as is assembly-line work. One-half of
the female workforce does heavy "drudge" work. Men, though stronger, reserve the lighter tasks for themselves. The medical profession (which is paid
very badly) and the teaching profession are also heavily female. And women
from the highest to the lowest in rank bear this burden: They do not really
expect men to do anything other than impregnate them and leave. The
defining characteristic in the lives of Soviet and post-Soviet women is that
they live as single mothers even with men in the house.[24] Thus, hard-working
Russian janitors and doctors share an experience that in the West is thought
to pertain only to unemployable, semiliterate, incontinent lower-class girls.

Among Russian women, there seems to be a desire to return to the sex
roles of old. Women eagerly practice cooking and the arts of housekeeping,
and they almost invariably dress with greater attention to style and attractiveness than American women of comparable socioeconomic status. They
want to have more children and spend more time with them. Even under the
Soviet regime, only one in five Soviet children under two was in the state
day-care system, so convinced of the evils of day care had the Russians become. To accommodate this growing antipathy, the state had gradually increased the amount of post-childbirth (half-pay) leave a woman could take
to eighteen months, which meant that the biggest state-imposed obstacle to
large families was really the size of apartments. But though Russians generally are sentimental about children, there seems to be no movement among

men to support women and children, to take responsibility for families. There is no Russian counterpart to the American Promise Keeper movement (whose members pledge fidelity to their families) and something of a consensus that childbirth and abortion are women's business. The ideal of manly life in Russia seems to have shifted from Party hack to Mafiya-connected "biznesmen." Consequently, Russian women have taken to advertising in America for real husbands who want real wives. Distaste for their men has even led Russian women to overcome racial prejudice and marry Chinese.

One man who agreed with this trend in female opinion is Mikhail Gorbachev, who wrote:

> [Because they have jobs] women no longer have enough time to perform their everyday duties at home—housework, the upbringing of children and the creation of a good family atmosphere. We have discovered that many of our problems—in children's and young people's behavior, in morals, culture and in production—are partially caused by the weakening of family ties and slack attitude to family responsibilities. . . . We are now holding heated debates . . . about the question of what we should do to make it possible for women to return to their purely womanly mission.[25]

On January 20, 1988, at what seemed the height of his power, Gorbachev told a radio audience the same thing, only more emphatically: "I think it is time to review the role of women as mothers versus as workers. Women are more important as producers of good people than as producers of fabric or whatever. I am going to propose a system of economic benefits through childhood for each child born so that it becomes economically possible for women to devote more of themselves to their families."

Unfortunately, while experience shows all too well that government can help wreck families, experience contains no guide for policies that might restore them. The main asset of Russia's families seems to be a widespread realization that socialist ways brought only misery.

DEGRADING THE SPIRIT

Fyodor Dostoevsky and Nikolai Berdayev foresaw that the socialist movement would forcibly banish God from the Russian soul and fill Russia with nihilists. The physical near-annihilation of the church did not destroy the Russian people's quest for transcendence and indeed lent urgency to their desire for "normalcy." But the regime's antireligious efforts did reduce the opportunities for the organized, mutually supportive practice of religion and for the moral discipline that is essential to religious practice.

Lenin seemed to have taken in earnest Voltaire's jocular remark that the era of human happiness would begin when the last king was strangled in the entrails of the last priest. And so Lenin and Stalin destroyed or diverted to the use of the Soviet state over 90 percent of Russia's 96,000 churches and killed over 90 percent of its 112,000 Russian Orthodox priests.[26] The rest were thoroughly infiltrated by the Cheka and its successor, the KGB, and forbidden to proselytize or even to preach. And indeed, this remnant church did its best to function as a transmission belt for the regime, persecuting priests who took their jobs seriously. The Bible and other kinds of religious literature were banned. Meetings for religious purposes or religious conversations were cause for one-way trips to Siberia. All but old people were effectively prevented from going to church. In the Catholic parts of the Baltics and in the western Ukraine, measures were even harsher. Anti-Semitism— the fight against "rootless cosmopolitans"—was also official policy. More important, everything connected with Christianity was subjected to official mockery. Taking part in that mockery was a condition for advancement, even survival.

Hence, the extent to which the regime succeeded in destroying the spiritual bases of family, faith, property, and law is less interesting than the reasons why it did not succeed even more. The short answer seems to be that the campaign quickly drove millions of Russians to nihilism and that nihilism is unendurable for very long. Visitors to the Soviet Union in the era of glasnost encountered cynicism and distrust so deep and widespread, misanthropy so bitter, that even the most ardent Communists had become frightened of it. By the late 1980s, when Communists spoke of "moral renewal," they no longer meant just the old saws about increased Party discipline and "socialist morality." But they did not know quite what they meant.

The barely surviving remnants of religion supplied an avenue of escape. Generations of Soviet rule had never quite purged the official Russian Orthodox Church of every vestige of Christianity. The church's very existence drew to the seminaries four times as many applicants as there were places. A few priests here and there actually practiced the faith. The priests who were beaten and jailed for this, and the very existence of churches that were obviously muzzled, reminded the masses that there was an alternative to the regime's morality, all the more attractive because forbidden. The regime *said* that Christianity was corrupt. But the masses *knew* that the regime was corrupt. Serious students of Marxism were equipped with a serious philosophical case against Christianity. But to the extent that they understood that case, they also understood the concept of natural law and the extent of Christianity's conformity to it. Such people also had first-hand, guilty knowledge of the Party's betrayal of its own mores. For their part, the masses, which never heard anything but unsophisticated, antireligious *agitprop,* found the glimpses of the faith's solemnities positively alluring.

Although the regime did not recognize the Christian holidays (people had to report to work), anyone walking by churches, especially on Easter, found them surrounded by crowds, pressing against the police cordons, striving for a look at the procession and trying to listen to the chants. The regime would send squads of "spontaneous" hecklers to disrupt the services. But starting in the 1970s, the crowds tended to shut them out and shout them down. Sometimes, the crowds, which were substantially made up of young people, would break through and join the congregation of old folks. When asked by strangers what they were doing, such onlookers replied that they were just curious or interested in a historical or cultural phenomenon. But it was more than that. Again, beginning in the 1970s, summertime visitors to Russia could see that many young women were wearing crosses around their necks. Visitors to the apartments of scientists or even government officials began to notice that religious icons were proudly displayed on the walls. "Oh, they are just art, part of our Russian cultural patrimony," the owners would say. And whereas in previous years westerners had been able to buy icons at good prices, by the 1970s demand had driven prices up. That interest in religious things was part of renewed attachment to timeless Russia was not a merely prophylactic explanation. By ostentatiously defining itself as the negation of the Russian past, the regime had made every scrap of the past into an instrument with which the people could deny the regime.

Personal religious practice also rose, at least superficially. Apparently, by the mid-1970s, "as many as half of the newlyweds in some areas, including Moscow, were having church weddings, and more than half of the newborns were being baptized."[27] In 1973, *Pravda Ukrainy* reported "that while one party official was lecturing on atheism, his children were being taken for baptism by his wife and mother-in-law."[28] Note well: This happened without proselytizing. The priests found themselves mobbed despite themselves. When we ask whence came this power, we are tempted to recall Machiavelli's account: While the barbarians who had defeated the Roman Empire were riding around renaming towns, they were naming their own children after Christian saints.[29] Of course, this did not transform them into instant Christians any more than the Russians who availed themselves of the church's sacraments thereby shed the spiritual habits of a lifetime under communism.

Yearning for religion is not religion. Consciousness of a vacuum does not fill it; much less do official declarations, especially when made by politicians jumping on bandwagons. Algidras Brazouskas, the reformist first secretary of the Lithuanian Communist Party who lost his country's first post-Soviet presidential elections in 1991 for being too closely tied to the past, "revealed" during the 1995 campaign that he had always been a practicing Catholic. Likewise, in March 1995, General Pavel Grachev, the Russian defense minister who started the war against Chechnya, had himself baptized in public.[30] He followed former foreign minister Eduard Shevardnadze, the butcher of Tiblisi, by one year. By 1990, Boris Yeltsin (later post-Soviet Russia's first president) had already announced in his memoirs that his mother had had him baptized as a child. Before leaving for his 1992 summit meeting with President George H. W. Bush, Yeltsin publicly received the blessing of Patriarch Alexis II. The patriarch also blessed the opening session of the Russian Parliament in 1994. None of this, however, seems to have suffused Russian public life with the substance of Christianity.

By 2008, 71 percent of Russians described themselves as "Orthodox." But since church attendance was sparse, this self-identification was more nationalism than religion. This is how the regime liked it. Hence, Yeltsin's successor, the dictator Vladimir Putin, publicly wore a cross and appeared regularly with the Orthodox patriarch Aleksei II, pointedly at Easter services. The church enjoys state patronage, and even more the state's unfriendliness to religious competitors. Thus Catholics and Protestants in post-Soviet Russia find themselves harassed in the name of Russian Orthodoxy by the very same officials who had made their lives miserable in the name of Soviet atheism.

The reasons go beyond hypocrisy. Christianity (like Judaism and Islam) is a vast complex of intellectual concepts that can be learned only through study, along with moral practices that can be adopted—if at all—only with the prompting and vigilant support of a community. The Soviet regime succeeded in reducing the circulation of religious ideas to almost nothing. Without the ideas, rituals and sacraments lose much of their power over human souls and become mere adjuncts to identity, to nationalism, or to nostalgia.

In addition, because of near-universal ignorance of what Christianity is supposed to mean for political life, discussions among Russians on how to repair the damage of communism take place on the sterile soil of economics. Everyone knows that the Soviet regime was even more about an assault on the soul and the family than it was about a certain vision of economics. But there is not enough knowledge of spiritual matters to sustain an intelligent discussion about the ethical prerequisites of classical economics or of decent politics. The contemporary Russian discussions of market economics bear no resemblance to those of Adam Smith or Wilhelm Roepke—both of whom were well-read Christians. Contemporary Russian discussions of the terrible state of family life also tend to be couched in terms of modern sociology rather than in terms of transcendental obligations. Nor is it clear that such knowledge will be forthcoming, because of the poor quality of religious instruction in the seminaries.

The cultivation of the soul is inherently a social enterprise. Ordinary people do not ordinarily soar to heights of spirituality, and all but the most extraordinary need others as examples and counselors. Outside of well-led communities, even well-motivated individuals let their mental discipline lapse. That is why there are churches and synagogues. Moreover, that is why successful churches stress personal conduct, lest men slacken their efforts to apply spiritual guidance to their own lives in the family, on the job, and in the city. The habits of the soul are formed by the habits of the whole person. It is nonsense to speak of spiritual renewal where economic practice has more to do with theft than with production, where fathers leave and mothers abort. The shortcomings of the churches might be less significant if the laws of Russia were actively promoting family, civility, and mutually beneficial economic behavior. But the regime of post-Soviet Russia is promoting quite the reverse.

Why did Soviet totalitarianism fail to eradicate religion? The reason seems to be that when any set of ideas is pressed violently upon a people, that people then associates those ideas with unpleasantness. That is why the Italian Communist Antonio Gramsci, perhaps the most perceptive theorist of totalitarianism (whose sons became Soviet citizens), advocated mostly non-violent cultural hegemony. With reasoning drawn from Machiavelli, Gramsci urged Communists to act as if alien ideas did not exist, while materially driving them from society without raising too much of a fuss. In effect, Gramsci advocated the kind of antireligious campaign later waged by the Swedish regime. Because the Soviets did not follow Gramsci's advice, they left in the Russian people the goading memory of evil so unmixed that it could serve as a reliable, if negative, guide to the renewal of the soul.

ROTTEN ARMS

Considering all of the Soviet regime's other failures, the Soviet armed forces' botched coup d'état on August 19–21, 1991, which was intended to save the tottering regime from an opposition possessed of negligible physical force, was in character. And yet the disarticulation of the Soviet armed forces is most remarkable because the regime had put all its heart, all its strength, and all its mind into building them up and keeping them loyal. The forces were big and abundantly equipped, and the apparatus by which the regime controlled them unprecedented. Nevertheless, they suffered from the brittleness common to the armies of tyrannies—once the sovereign began to totter, its corrupt members minded only their most private interests.

The Soviet armed forces were the world's largest and best equipped. Just under 4 million men managed more of just about every type of major weapon (aircraft carriers excepted) *than the rest of the world combined.* Nor did the Soviets lack quality. The list of Soviet weapons that set the world's standard begins with the AK47 rifle, moves to the BMP series of infantry fighting vehicles, to the Akuka all-titanium submarine, and on to the world's finest artillery and rocket engines by far. The SS24 mobile missile as well as the SA12B mobile antimissile system came sooner and in their time put to shame their American counterparts, the MX missile and the Patriot and THAAD antimissile systems, respectively. The Soviets had the world's only antisatellite systems, radar ocean reconnaissance satellites, naval bombers, and much more. The Skval torpedo, which literally flies beneath the seas in an air bubble of its own making, is pure genius. They compensated for areas of technical inferiority, such as the noisiness of submarines or the relative inaccuracy of missiles, by devising well-conceived tactics for employment, manufacturing greater quantities of weapons, or giving them bigger explosive yields. The privilege of rejecting the products of their industrial suppliers, plus lavish pay, made the armed forces an island of capitalism that attracted the best of the country's talents. Discipline in the ranks was exemplary, enforced by cruel hazing and backed by superior officers' authority to summarily execute recalcitrants. In operational military thought, the Soviet armed forces led the world. No American military thinker ranks with

Marshal Nikolai Ogarkhov. Had the Soviets fought a war against the West, they probably would have won.[31]

Even more awesome was the apparatus by which the regime controlled its arms. Yet since that apparatus consisted of preparations for various parts of the armed forces to fight one another for the regime's sake, it contained the seeds of its own destruction. The regime had been born in 1917, thanks to its recruitment of criminals (the men in black leather jerkins) and of small units of the Imperial Navy to act as the Party's killers. It had survived its earliest trials because a special unit of sailors and another of Latvian riflemen had been willing to shoot Russians in the regular army and to slaughter the regime's enemies as no regular forces would ever do. Also, the liveliest historical image in Bolshevik minds was that the French Revolution ended when some members of its directorate brought Napoleon into their quarrels. Against the danger of Bonapartism, the Bolsheviks deployed an unprecedented variety of special units to do three critical jobs: They were to make sure that the regular armed forces stayed loyal by authorizing the "specials" to kill anyone among the "regulars" at any time; they were to kill any dissident elements in society, no matter how large; and, finally, they were to keep one another in check.

During the Cold War, the Soviet regime had more men in some sort of special unit (some three-fourths of a million) than were in the whole U.S. Army. Lower on the food chain were the armed forces' own commando units, including the Alpha force that decapitated the Afghan government in 1979. At the bottom were the Ministry of the Interior's troops, which specialized in putting down riots. Then, interspersed within the regular armed forces was a cadre of political officers answerable to the secret police, or KGB. One part, the Third Chief Directorate, seeded all military organizations with informants and had the power to make or break careers. The other, the Border Troops, numbering some 300,000, enjoying independent supply lines, and equipped with tactical nuclear weapons, could go to war with anyone. The lines of command and control purposely crossed and overlapped. Third World regimes paid to be shown how to set up similarly ironclad guarantees for themselves.[32]

It is an understatement to say that the Soviet armed forces were a cockpit of intrigue and grudges. The regulars hated the special units, the specials hated one another, and that collective hatred, as well as individual selfishness rather than trust, ran up and down the tangled chain of command. But the mutual fears worked as intended even when (and, indeed, especially when)

Stalin purged 90 percent of the general officers and three-fourths of the field-grade officers in the 1930s, as well as in World War II, when Soviet units were taking 50 percent casualties or more. That was so because the chances of being killed for perceived disloyalty were 100 percent. When the regime stopped projecting the image of murderous resolve, the system of mutual fears and hatreds began to work against itself. Under Gorbachev the regime was willing to kill only by the tens, whereas under Brezhnev it had killed by the hundreds, under Khrushchev by the thousands, and under Stalin by the millions. The reasons why are beyond the scope of this book: The point is simply that the human qualities that had held together the military system exceedingly well under one set of circumstances destroyed that system when circumstances changed.

The Soviet Union's war in Afghanistan was never popular. But the Soviet population endured it. Then, when the authorities did not use mass executions or one-way trips to Siberia to crush servicemen's expressions of dissatisfaction, they created a little space for dissent. That space grew quickly. By the late 1980s, the regime allowed the public to disparage not just the Afghan War but many other things that Gorbachev unwisely thought he could impute to his predecessors and political enemies. The regime's subjects had a long list of complaints. The ones in and against the military were relatively minor. Thus, it apparently did not occur to the regime that voicing such complaints could set off a deadly chain reaction. In fact, that reaction moved with blinding speed.

Beginning in 1990, when the regime began to call on various military units to quell disturbances breaking out from the Baltics in the Northwest to Tadjikistan six time zones southeastward, the units and their commanders vied with one another to minimize their own exposure. The regime unwittingly fostered this disastrous competition. When one unit mangled Georgian demonstrators with shovels, the regime responded to popular outrage with punitive investigations of the unit. So subsequently, when the regime called up reservists to send large numbers of troops to do something similar in Azerbaijan, an uproar by their mothers was enough to get the order reversed.[33] The Alpha unit that killed one dozen people on "Bloody Sunday" in Vilnius thought it did not get the unanimous praise it deserved. Eighteen months later, when asked to storm the Russian Parliament in the climactic act of the regime's climactic moment, it refused. Nor did any other group of habitual murderers put itself in the slightest danger to rescue the regime.

DEATH OR RENEWAL

The Soviet monster might have lived on if it had remained true to itself. Built for war—above all at home—the regime had no choice but to wage it and keep winning. That is what Stalin did. Finished with one campaign that had destroyed one set of persons to the delight of another, Stalin would start new campaigns with new victims and beneficiaries. Within the ruling class, the countervailing levels of fear and expectation stayed high. And when one set of the reins by which he drove that class felt slack, he would pull on another. After World War II Stalin and his successors also had the good fortune of being able to feed the regime's bureaucratic constituents with the fruits of a growing empire as well as international recognition. Ordinary people were wholly preoccupied scratching out a living and staying clear of the deadly tectonic shifts going on above them.

Machiavelli writes in the first chapter of the third book of his *Discourses* that regimes die of natural decay, which they can arrest only by restoring their character. This they can do only by repeating the acts and reaffirming the ideas that had given them life in the first place. But while the Soviet regime retained its economics, its political organization, and its policies toward families, religion, and the armed forces, it emptied them of the intellectual, bureaucratic, and physical violence that had given them life in the first place. Gorbachev's regime was a "lite" version of Stalin's. War was the Soviet Union's "Spirit of the Laws." Other regimes have their own spirit. But Machiavelli's maxim applies to all regimes equally: "Lite" versions of any founding spirit are deadly. Only the real thing will do.

5

←

PROSPERITY

Commerce is the profession of equals. . . .
The most miserable [of peoples] are those
whose prince is in business.
—BARON DE MONTESQUIEU, *SPIRIT OF THE LAWS*

Things, money, and the capacity to enjoy them flow from human efforts and skills. These depend to some extent on attitudes. Every political system sets premiums on certain skills and attitudes while discouraging others. And every system fosters the economic advantage of certain kinds of human beings over that of others. How do some of the exemplar political systems of our time bring forth peculiar kinds of economic behavior, of people, as well as levels of prosperity? The modern Chinese system secures the power and wealth of officials by empowering them to permit civilians to enrich themselves even more. Permission flows down the line, loyalty and wealth flow up. The modern European welfare state has spread privilege to so many, hedged it about with so many rules, that work offers no hope more exciting than for somnolent lives. By contrast, after 1973 the government of Chile tried to separate economic life from political power, believing that the connection corrupts both.

RECIPES DU JOUR

Advice about how to make whole peoples rich is almost as common as guides to wealth for individuals. Someone is always hawking a model. During the 1960s, the Agency for International Development and the World Bank, following Walt Whitman Rostow's *The Stages of Economic Growth,* prescribed a formula to the governments of what they then called "developing countries": Use foreign aid to strengthen and centralize government, to build roads, dams, steel mills, and other infrastructure. Use land reform and taxation to break up traditional patterns of agricultural land use and traditional society. Raise tariffs and subsidies to protect industrialization and foster urbanization. Secure popular support through secularization, liberalization, and the expansion of government patronage. Fifty years later, there is no doubt that this recipe helped produce ruling parties from Chad to Chile that built political clienteles for themselves and brought disaster to their peoples. Land reform and other wrongs done to agriculture caused hunger and pushed people into increasingly dysfunctional cities. The industrial policy of "import substitution" raised prices while building up classes of workers dependent on government favor. Secularization fostered the rise of fundamentalism (especially in the Islamic world). The epitome of the "nation-building" movements was a set of ruling classes from Burma to Burundi, guarded by goons and riding through worsening poverty in their Mercedes 600s.

In the 1980s and early 1990s, the most fashionable model was Japanese. Lester Theroux, Chalmers Johnson, James Fallows, Clyde Prestowitz, Ronald Morse, and Alan Tonelson,[1] among many others, argued that the Japanese had discovered the secret of perpetual high-rate economic growth: namely, a combination of protectionism and directed investment at home and aggressive pursuit of market shares abroad. It became conventional wisdom that the Japanese economy would surpass the United States by the year 2000. Japan's economic morass after 1989 merely led devotees of the model to broaden its terms to include other countries of the Pacific Rim, including China. Like Japan, they could be expected to outperform America because they had discovered the efficiencies of solidarity between management and labor, as well as the wisdom of allowing astute public officials to manage the private economy strategically: To somehow conjoin the individual incentives of free enterprise with the superior wisdom of planners has been the Holy Grail of political economists since Mussolini's corporate state of the 1920s. Indeed, modern American discourse is full of references to the need for partnership between government and business in order to compete with the dynamic managed economies of Asia.

Today, from Moscow to Mexico City, experts from the International Monetary Fund teach the Harvard and Stanford economics departments' updated version of this catechism: Eliminate governmental budget deficits by raising taxes and privatizing state-owned firms. Make exports cheaper while discouraging imports by devaluing currencies and cutting real wages. Rely on cheap labor and high interest rates to attract foreign investment. But devaluing currencies has brought inflation, while high interest rates have discouraged internal investment and low wages have hurt both producers and consumers. And while high taxes may mean prosperity to those who reap the revenue, they are less obviously prosperity for those who pay them. Nor should privatization be confused with economic incentives, since governments often transfer state monopolies, like telephone companies, into the private hands of their friends, special powers and all. Because this recipe privatizes rather than limits government power, it tends to make the rich richer and the poor poorer.

In the wake of communism, the concoction of recipes for prosperity mushroomed into an industry. Beginning in 1990, Eastern Europe was full of emissaries touting economic models as varied as those of Sweden and Chile, but especially that of the European Union. Moscow particularly became the battleground for contrasting Western schools—Jeffrey Sachs of Harvard University and Edward Lazear of Stanford's Hoover Institution, who later served as President George W. Bush's chief economic adviser, headed two of the better-connected groups. Their proposals differed concerning the extent and timing of privatization and decontrol of prices, as well as in regard to monetary and fiscal policy. Some believed that democracy itself would produce prosperity.[2] But they shared the premise that if the right formulas were applied, Communist sows' ears could be turned into capitalist silk purses. Yet although different recipes have been tried in different countries, not even the best results—those in the Czech Republic—resemble the kind of prosperity that burst forth in West Germany after World War II or that is routine in the United States.

This leads us back to the proposition that the details of economic policy are less important than a population that is habituated to *property rights and to the rule of law.*[3] First, laws about property must be stable, transparent, and equally enforced. People will work harder and more efficiently, so goes the argument, to the extent that they are not deprived of the fruits of their labors by gangsters, arbitrary officials, or high taxes. Second, there must be a currency whose value is constant or, at any rate, predictable. Inflation is the cruelest, most destructive tax. Third, there must be equal access to the market—meaning that tariffs on imported goods must be both low and equal among products and that the government will not otherwise interfere with prices and wages. Somehow, government must avoid doing what is in its nature, playing favorites among people and businesses, determining winners and losers. Fundamentally, prosperity depends on individuals making a living by producing goods and services that others want to pay for, that others choose freely. Unfortunately, it is often easier to get rich by taking advantage of government rules, by satisfying rulers rather than customers. But getting money this way must not be confused with economic activity. Adam Smith's "invisible hand" enriches all involved in economic transactions only when all engage in them on an equal basis.

Such prerequisites cannot be established simply by some parliament passing a law. They are themselves a rare and fragile set of beliefs and habits. The question therefore comes full circle, except that we search for ways of fostering these basic beliefs and habits. That search must begin with a consideration of the factors that make it so difficult: Different regimes (and indeed different observers) have different standards for gauging what constitutes prosperity. Consequently, each and every political arrangement promotes the economic well-being of some kinds of people rather than others.

WHAT IS PROSPERITY?

We laugh too easily nowadays at the U.S. government economists who wrote in the *Statistical Abstract of the United States* in 1987 that the per capita GDP of East Germany was substantially equal to that of West Germany. They made themselves ridiculous simply by accepting the value that local authorities placed on activities in their country. All governments count their own activities as part of GDP. But counting government activities as economic assets wrongly assumes that the people on whom they are bestowed value them as if they had bought them, as if they had value. Governments have the power to endow with economic value things that no one else values and that satisfy no human need. Thus, while East Berliners placed *negative* values on East Germany's vaunted police force, trained to shoot them if they tried to escape over the Wall, our economists followed East Germany's police and counted these and other services as part of the "goods and services" enjoyed by East Germans. The same *Abstract* showed the per capita GDP of the Soviet Union as three times that of Argentina, even though poor Argentineans enjoyed beef and vegetables that all but the richest Soviets could barely imagine. But the Soviet Union was opulent in modern weaponry.

Here is the point: In any country, perusal of anything like the yellow pages reveals a variety of activities, from abortion and agriculture to X-ray supplies and zoning consultants, each of which carries with it a certain lifestyle. A city of farmers will differ from one of shopkeepers, and a city of sophisticates will differ from one of soldiers. How any city looks economically depends in no small part on how it is governed, because even the least economically intrusive governments tilt the playing field in economically vital ways. Different tilts produce different material and human results. Thus, when we speak of prosperity, it behooves us to remember that there are many ways of being rich and poor.[4]

Since time immemorial, observers have remarked on the wealth and splendor of Oriental civilizations. Economists have always known that peaks of Oriental opulence rest on broad flats of misery. But they have been tempted to suppose that only passing circumstances prevented the ordinary people who produced the Taj Mahal and the Forbidden City from turning their genius and industry to their own benefit. Hence, predictions seem to be perennial that the bright, numerous, hard-working Orientals would inherit the earth. Whereas in the past prominent observers—Montesquieu in the eighteenth century and Karl Wittfogel in the twentieth—described in some detail how the division of labor in "Oriental despotism" was part of inherently limited cultures of masters and slaves, modern writers typically discount cultural differences. Paul Kennedy, for example, discussed the prospects for China's and India's economic growth as if the Chinese or Indian masses were purely composed of *Homo economicus* and their leaders were primarily interested in maximizing economic growth for everyone's benefit.[5] Even when describing the economies of states like Saudi Arabia, where vast amounts of money, largely unearned by anyone in the society, flow to unelected rulers who spend it on themselves, economists nowadays write as if whole peoples were working for some kind of common economic well-being and would respond equally to the same incentives.

Clearly, however, prosperity is less a matter of arithmetic than of *value placed on various kinds of human activity.* It was enough for Harvard economist John Kenneth Galbraith to walk Soviet streets in 1984 to judge the Soviet Union a vibrant and prosperous society. Galbraith, remember, had long chastised American society for "public squalor amidst private wealth."[6] Even though wealth in America is obviously widespread, Galbraith called American life squalid because he did not think that the things that Americans were doing with their time and energy were particularly worthy. He had higher esteem for the things that the Soviet regime was directing its citizens to do with their time and energy and deemed their undeniable relative material privations as a kind of uncomplicated virtue.

Thus, prosperity is neither money nor things. If it were money, then the Kuwaitis, Bahrainians, and Bruneians would be among the world's richest peoples. But much of the money in these regimes pays for the extravagant lives of thousands of princelings. Other moneys go to grossly uneconomic schemes, such as producing wheat in the desert, irrigated by desalinated water. The entrepreneurs make money not from the wheat but from the subsidy. But does such money at least result in some local citizens acquiring skills? No, because the work is usually done by workers imported from Pakistan, the Philippines, or Palestine, while the locals' contempt for labor makes them ever less fit to earn a living.

Americans and Europeans were never strangers to and are ever more familiar with making money from rules, subsidies, and privileges. And in these countries as well as in the Soviet Union and post-Soviet Russia, talented persons spend time, make money, and acquire skills providing services for which governments, not customers, set the value. The American lobbyist at the service of corn growers or chemical industries, whose career path intersects with that of the sector's government regulators, means more to profits than any of the workers in those sectors do. Then there are sectors of First World economies that exist solely because they are defined and mandated by government. In these sectors, the value of activities depends on government power, not consumer choice.

Thus, under the 1997 UN-administered Kyoto agreement, European companies gained a salable credit for each ton of certain gases that they eliminated from industrial processes in designated "developing countries." The French company Rhodia SA installed equipment worth some 15 million euros in a South Korean factory and was to reap a profit from the UN program of about 1 billion euros over seven years. "I can't say the critics are groundless," said Jung Jaesoo, forty-eight years old, who ran a consulting firm advising Korean companies on how to qualify for credits. "But the Kyoto Protocol is a multilateral agreement." Jung's company, Ecoeye, shepherded a number of projects to UN approval, among them wind, tidal, solar, and hydroelectric power plants.[7] The billion in Rhodia's and Jung's bank accounts was there only because a consortium of governments placed a value on things that otherwise would have had none. The point here is that the differences between the professions of environmental profiteer, sector lobbyist, and Soviet *tolkach* (enabler) are not so great as their similarities. Above all, they are rent-collection rather than service activities, and they teach skills unrelated to anything that anyone would spend his own money on.

The point here is that all political systems affect hearts and minds in economically significant ways.[8]

WHO PROFITS?

The economic character of a people is affected by the extent to which its government lets goods and services circulate among those who produce them rather than channeling those goods to powerful nonproducers. Thus, although the habits that produce the things that make life more comfortable are important to prosperity, the *habits of equality under law that protect the wide and just spread of these things* are just as important. This means that to promote prosperity, any regime must *encourage production and discourage rent seeking.* Unfortunately, most regimes live by doing the opposite.

In the aftermath of World War II, Western economists and politicians asked how the masses of Africa, Asia, and Latin America might be brought to Euro-American standards of living. They rejected as racist all facts indicating that prosperity and poverty were due to human character. So the centerpiece of the economic recipe that the British, French, Belgian, and Dutch foisted on their colonies was to empower native elites—mostly people like themselves, alumni of the leading Western universities. But none of these elites had the slightest knowledge of or interest in production. They were masters of political patronage. Americans promoted the same people through the CIA, the World Bank, and the Agency for International Development.[9] By the 1990s, however, it was undeniable that most of the "developing countries" were not about to develop—and that the ones that had developed had done so by empowering people very different from the kinds to whom the West had given its colonies.

Remarkably in the *New Republic,* David Landes wrote that "people are different," and "this makes the story of [economic] growth very different." Landes mentioned some of the cognitive skills and personal habits that economists now recognize as the keys to economic performance and concluded that some peoples "don't like them; they don't want them, they are discouraged from learning them, if they learn them, they want out, etc."[10] This truth had always been self-evident to those willing to notice it. Alas, three generations of Western leaders chose to ignore it as they made the Third World by empowering parasites and their habits over producers and theirs.

By the time development economists touted Rostow's Third World model as the *dernier cri,* the recipe and its effects were already an old story. The following description of Mexico under Spanish rule could be applied to any current Third World regime:

> The interventionist and pervasive arbitrary nature of the institutional environment forced every enterprise, urban or rural, to operate in a highly politicized manner, using kinship networks, political influence, and family prestige to gain privileged access to subsidized credit, to aid various stratagems for recruiting labor, to collect debts or enforce contracts, to evade taxes or circumvent the courts, and to defend or assert title to lands. Success or failure in the economic arena always depended on the relationship of the producer with political authorities—local officials for arranging matters close at hand, the central government of the colony for sympathetic interpretations of the law and intervention at the local level when conditions required it. Small enterprise, excluded from the system of corporate privileged political favors, was forced to operate in a permanent state of semiclandestinity, always at the margin of the law, at the mercy of petty officials, never secure from arbitrary acts and never protected against the rights of those more powerful.[11]

In a nutshell, Western economists found a set of drunkards and proposed to sober them up by prescribing that they drink more of what had intoxicated them in the first place.

The characteristics of Third World economic life are easy enough to outline. Public employment is high, desirable, and obtainable only by favor.

When Robert Mugabe became president of Zimbabwe in 1980, the bureaucracy employed 62,036 people. By 1990, it employed 181,401. By 2008 the figure was over 250,000. Paying their salaries and operating expenses consumed over one-half the gross national income. In Ghana, 74 percent of nonagricultural employment is in the bureaucracy. In Tanzania, it is 78 percent, and in Zambia, 81 percent. Public-sector wages exceed per capita income by an average factor of 4.6.[12] But the expense of their salaries is the least of the burdens that bureaucrats place on these economies. They expropriate farms, set prices for agricultural products, and force farmers to sell their produce to the state; they control admission to universities and in general determine society's winners and losers. The loot flows upward, according to the principle "from each according to the privileges granted him." Naturally, the biggest winners are the most powerful, their families, and their friends. Almost invariably, the higher one goes in Third World governmental hierarchies, the wealthier one gets. In the Third World, the richest person or family and the most powerful such is often the same. Thus, Zaire's longtime president, Mobutu Sese Seko, who started public life as a sergeant, became one of the world's richest men. Mexico's former presidents José López Portillo and Miguel de la Madrid are generally acknowledged to have looted somewhere between $3 billion and $5 billion apiece. The family of their successor, Carlos Salinas de Gortari, may have made off with twice that. The richest man in Russia's immediate post-Soviet period may have been Prime Minister Viktor Chernomyrdin. Typically, everybody else in the Third World is a loser. Whereas life expectancy had been sixty years in white-ruled Rhodesia, it had dropped to below forty years in Mugabe's Zimbabwe.

That is because the power to loot flows downward according to a corresponding logic: "to each according to his worth as a supporter." Hence, for example, the lowest-ranking officers in Uganda were paid up to thirty times the average wage. Sometimes pay consists of the franchise to engage in a particularly lucrative business, like smuggling drugs, or the franchise to collect bribes in a certain field.[13] But ordinary commercial concessions, such as a protective tariff or the ruin of a competitor, are just as valuable. Tax rates are high, but taxes are collected only from those not well connected with the regime. Thus, an effective pyramid of taxation is established. What Edward Gargan reported about Indonesia is true of dozens of other countries: "Take a cab here or a local flight, stay in a hotel, smoke a clove cigarette, watch a private television station, make a cellular phone call, buy a Mercedes or a

Kawasaki motorcycle, put sugar in your coffee—in each case, some of the money lands in a business controlled or owned in whole or in part by a relative of President Suharto."[14]

In Aristotelian terms, this is not corruption. Rather, it is the logic by which regimes of a particular kind maintain themselves. Therefore, when we read that a Third World ruler has prosecuted one of the regime's pillars for corruption, we must think in Aristotelian terms: The prosecution is likely to be for the only act that really rots the regime, namely, disloyalty. When President Carlos Salinas of Mexico sent army troops to arrest the powerful head of the oil workers' union, Joaquin Hernandez Galicia, known as La Quina, he did so not because of Hernandez's well-known habit of translating his power into money, but because of his equally well-known ties to Salinas's opponent, from whom Salinas had stolen the election of 1988.[15] Since power is for the personal benefit of those who hold it, it is logical that those who take it away also try to strip their predecessors of their gains—to their own benefit, of course.

To survive predatory behavior at the top, those below adopt certain habits. Business skills in the Third World consist primarily of knowing the people who make the rules and doing what is necessary to get along with them—meaning knowing who is part of whose network and what payment or demonstration of loyalty will propitiate whom. Since these matters are seldom entirely explicit, wisdom in the Third World consists of trying to fathom conspiracies. Hidden combinations and occult motives are behind every rise and every fall in fortunes. Every event is somebody's thrust or parry. Explanations in terms of proper recompense for value received are reasonably considered eyewash for fools. The classroom questions that my students at the DUXX Business School in Monterrey, Mexico, asked tended to be of this sort: "We have read the published version of this event. Please tell us the real story."

The reason why inhabitants of the First World should keep the Third in mind is that habits prevalent in the countries that became known as the Third World are a set of human possibilities that any people anywhere may adopt at any time. As Argentina showed in the twentieth century, falling from the First World to the Third can be easy and quick. The Third World mentality, namely, to undercut the logic of economics by force, existed long before our time and constantly tempts us to partake of it. As Lincoln said, the notion that some men are born with saddles on their backs and others booted and spurred to ride them, the temptation to think, "You work, I'll eat," is "the old serpent" itself. That mentality attracts us as much as it has ever attracted anyone. Business, labor unions, social groups of all kinds know that by associating themselves with the state, or bringing the state to side with them, they can get more for less: set prices, captivate markets, entitle themselves, and privatize profit while socializing risk. The feeling that those who know only how to work, only to serve customers, are unfortunates or fools, that wealth comes from forcing your neighbor rather than serving him, is all too normal. What we call the Third World is more or less how most of mankind has always lived, in part because, normally, the prince is very much in business. It is we Americans, along with some Europeans, who have strayed from normalcy into prosperity and who may be returning to normalcy.

JAPAN

The contrast between good, shiny Japanese products and Third World shabbiness should not obscure the similarities that come from the similar, fateful mixture of economic and government power. That power has resulted in habitual behavior on the part of corporate and government bureaucrats that is as ruinous of prosperity as any in the world. Japan has confounded Western economists because Japanese workers are rewarded for some of the world's best labor with lifestyles all too reminiscent of the Third World. And yet they keep on working. By the turn of the twenty-first century, only a bit more than three in ten of the (cramped) Japanese houses had central heating—never mind air conditioning, in a country that makes Washington, D.C., summers feel cool by comparison. By the end of the 1980s, although Japan's per capita GDP was 12 percent above that of the United States, the purchasing power of the average Japanese was not greater than that of the average American but rather some 30 to 40 percent lower. In a sense, then, the Japanese people are getting only about one-half of the fruits of their labors. Therefore, although the Japanese people produce lots of wealth, they are not prosperous—but they are content.[16]

The cultural premises of capitalist economics—that the personal status of buyers and sellers, producers and consumers, does not affect the price of goods and services; that individuals will treat one another equally and demand equal treatment from others as they seek the best economic deal for themselves; and that economic goods are earned to be enjoyed—are even more foreign to Japan than they are to the Third World, though for different reasons. In Japan, people regard one another as the occupants of particular stations in life, each of which comports certain duties and privileges. In addition, the Japanese people believe that they are unique and compelled to cooperate in the struggle for collective survival in a hostile world. That is why there is less outrage in Japan than in the West at officials who enrich themselves, and why the officers of companies, banks, and the Ministry of Finance have exercised the kind of economic power over the kind of people that the rest of the world's planners can only dream about.

In business, the Japanese are unequal in what matters most: access to power. The great post–World War II Japanese corporations were started with privileged privatizations of government property, were immediately protected from foreign competition, and have received various forms of subsidy from time to time.[17] All sectors of business are protected by legal impediments to entry. Small shopkeepers are protected by barriers against large retail outlets. Construction of houses and businesses is regulated by the *dango* system, which fixes the level of bids. And the prices of agricultural commodities are supported by restrictions on imports. Beyond overt protectionism, the Ministry of Finance and the Ministry of Trade and Industry lend further support for high prices by encouraging companies in each sector to cooperate rather than compete—from farming to industry (the Keiretsu network of companies, affiliated through reciprocal ownership of stock and interlocking directorships) to wholesale and retail sales. Mussolini's most ambitious designs for the corporate state were a pale shadow of Japanese reality, while the results he achieved with the Italian people were far less than that.

The results should not be confused with prosperity. By the early 1990s, the Japanese people were paying $1 for a strawberry, $7 per pound for rice, $50,000 per square yard for office space, and more for Japanese goods than they are sold for abroad.[18] By the late 1980s, the value of all real estate in Japan exceeded that of all the United States by a factor of four, the average stock on the Tokyo exchange sold for ninety times yearly earnings, and companies competed with one another for extravagant expense accounts while buying famous real estate abroad at fabulous prices. Companies were bidding up prices of stock and real estate. They did it, and thought they could do so indefinitely because the ever-rising value of stock and real estate was secured with loans that the banks gave to each other, and ultimately by the Bank of Japan, with approval from the Ministry of Finance.

After 1989, however, the value of Japanese stocks dropped by more than one-half, and most Japanese investments lost money. Economists should have noted that, by seconding each other's bets, big, interconnected financiers were building a bubble economy, and that by making risk public and profit private, the ministry's wise men had proved to be the bubble's enablers. Why? Beyond comity and mutual back-scratching (stronger in Japan than elsewhere), the expansion created posts into which government officials could retire, posts so lucrative they were called *amakudari-saki*—places into which to descend from heaven. When the inflationary bubble burst in 1989, it left a highly inflexible economy in which manufacturing costs were twice as high as in America. The Bank of Japan's practice of giving away money for less than the rate of inflation did not prevent an economic "lost decade." In sum, acting as sorcerer's apprentices, Japan's big businessmen and bureaucrats wasted their people's considerable talents.

The traditional Japanese response to this, namely, squeezing each employee to produce even more, is beside the point. As Akio Morita, the man who built Sony, noted, the problem with Japan is not that its people should be working harder or better, but that the system does not allow them to enjoy the fruits of their labors. The fundamental Japanese willingness to sacrifice does not itself impose fruitless sacrifice. That is imposed by an economic system in which honest, productive labor is a ticket to places of power, but where power is oriented to the satisfaction of a network of privileges. That network produces a myriad of high-stakes bad bets as well as uneconomic preferential deals that make the difference between the high productivity of Japanese labor and its low consumption. Japan is lucky, however, that wholesale corruption at the top has not undone the retail honesty on which its wealth, if not its prosperity, rests. Other peoples' economic habits are not so sound as those of the Japanese.

CHINA

The economy of the People's Republic of China has been growing strongly since the late 1970s, averaging 9 percent per year. The World Bank once forecast that at this rate and in this way, China would become the world's biggest economy, if not the most prosperous, by the year 2002.[19] Thereafter the estimate was moved to 2020. But the forecast timing is beside the obvious point that everything about China is big, and that optimism about the

Chinese economy continues unabated.[20] This Chinese miracle is supposedly due to an artful combination of "market economics," or "capitalism,"
with political socialism. In fact, it has nothing to do with either.

Socialism is an economic concept, the heart of which is production for
consumption rather than for profit, as well as the assurance that everyone's
material needs will be met from the cradle to the grave. All of that is foreign
to China in our time. True, governments aspiring to socialism have assumed
more power over society than governments that do not aspire to socialism.
But to call a government "socialist" merely because it is big and harsh shows
how thoroughly the means rather than the ends of socialism became its
defining feature. *Statism* is supposed to be a means to socialism, not an end
in itself. The proper name for big, nasty governments that enrich their favorites and oppress opponents is "oligarchy." The Chinese regime now
claims to be socialist only in the political sense. In other words, it admits to
being such an oligarchy. Note, however, that while wealth in China comes
from labor and enterprise that bears some resemblance to capitalism, power
in China's oligarchy does not come from money. Rather, money comes by
leave of power.

At best, Chinese officials' references to socialism and capitalism are code
words denoting positions on the central question: How shall we, the bureaucratic oligarchs or oligarchic bureaucrats, get richer while maintaining
control? The theoretical answer reached by a group of well-connected Chinese economists in 1993–1994 was a "shared cooperative system."[21] According to Hilton Root, this amounts to "legitimizing for the first time
diverse forms of property rights but not identifying the socialist market
economy with any particular form of property right."[22] In other words, a lot
of people are allowed to do a lot of things, so long as they pay a cut to those
above them in the Communist Party, to the army, or to other parts of the
state. But no one can be sure precisely what the rules are today, how they will
be applied, or how they will change tomorrow. In sum, while no one could
doubt in 2008 that China's rulers were firmly in control atop a burgeoning
economy, it was by no means clear that they knew what they were doing or
that their expectation of remaining in the saddle was based on anything
other than hope.

The contemporary practice of business in China is less confusing than
the theory. *The essence of that practice is the proliferation of ways in which individuals manage to exercise some of what we call "property rights."* All these
ways, however, have one thing in common: They all involve either direct

ownership by a part of the government or Communist Party—a unit of the police or the army, or a local government (township or village enterprises accounted for 30 percent of industrial production)—or a good relationship with a branch thereof. Specifically, property rights can be exercised by officials and by those somehow connected to officials. The regime acknowledges its own great and growing pluralism, and permits its various members to enrich themselves subject only to respect for the regime itself and the hierarchy within it. This results in the exercise not of property rights as we know them but of what Root calls "loyalty rights."[23] Sheryl WuDunn has described the phenomenon as follows: "The price of capital, [indeed, she might have said 'or of anything else'] in China isn't interest. It's a bribe. Or it's the work that has gone into cultivating guanxi, or connections with the bankers and local officials."[24] As economic activity expands, however, the threads connecting any transaction with the bureaucrats who authorize it become more tenuous. But the more privileges become customs and customs rights, the greater the rulers' incentive to reassert their relevance.

The innumerable examples of this practice all point in the same direction. In a typical situation at the outer edges of entrepreneurship, an ambitious young man struck up a friendship with the manager of a large pharmaceutical factory. The manager agreed to illegally slip him part of the production in exchange for a cut of 20 percent of the sale price. Then the entrepreneur found a purchaser for a hospital who was willing to buy illegally from him, for a cut of 50 percent. The entrepreneur was delighted with the remaining 30 percent.[25] And rightly so, because if any other government official had found out, he would have exacted a cut of his share. As it was, he paid a 70 percent tax. But he invested nothing and put in little labor. Not a bad deal. Then there are the officials of ministries and counties who have gone into business for themselves, encouraging various kinds of businesses as well as making problems for them with various kinds of regulations—and then solving them for a price.

In sum, the legal system is identical to the administrative system and broadly overlaps with the economic system itself. As the modern Chinese economic system took off, Deng Zhifang, the youngest son of Deng Xiaoping, set the standard by advertising his brokerage services, sealed by a picture, for the price of 5 percent of any deal. As his father's death approached, however, the value of his services declined and the prospect of prosecution for "corruption" arose. In another way, counties and ministries became owners of factories that were established by foreign investors under specified conditions but abandoned after local officials or labor brokers changed the terms and made the deal unprofitable. This bureaucratic "death by a thousand cuts," which can involve shutdowns of electricity and water, termination of transportation routes, and labor troubles, was epitomized in a *New York Times* headline: "China, the Art of the (Raw) Deal."[26]

China's economy, however, is based on the production of real wealth. The basic and most important reason for that wealth was stated succinctly by Peter Topp, the supply manager for the largest joint venture in China in 1995, Shanghai Volkswagen: "For all practical purposes, the cost of labor in China is nothing."[27] Because Chinese workers are intelligent, disciplined, and apparently willing to work assiduously for wages that are practically nothing compared to those in the countries where their products are consumed, China has become the world's manufacturing center. Millions of workers toil in highly organized factories to turn out famous European, American, and Japanese brand names. Wage controls in the interior regions that make the "nothing" wages in the new economic regions seem generous continue to pull workers to the factories. At the same time, these workers are being pushed off the farm by unscrupulous local officials who had tyrannized farmers collectively in camplike communes through the 1960s, and thereafter squeezed them individually on their leaseholds for protection money. Thus, individual Chinese sacrifice mightily to move to the coastal regions and to acquire marketable skills. Foreign factories in China, unlike the foreign companies that did business in South Africa during apartheid, help the Chinese government keep its grip on the population—including helping it to enforce the one-child policy. Even Google cooperates in the government's policy of keeping politically sensitive subjects off the Internet.

But on top of this manufacturing base, a secondary economy has developed that has lifted hundreds of millions in the cities onto a level of prosperity unimaginable a generation ago. Personal cars and air conditioners are everywhere in urban China, as are the other products and services that characterize comfortable life. The constant improvements have excited the desires of these and other millions for even further and faster betterment. A vast class of strivers has honed sharp, hard habits. Their study habits have lifted them above westerners in science, math, and useful skills in general. They have also learned skills that allow them to evade government policy on issues from the number of children to use of the Internet.

Since 1992, when the government began sanctioning the practice of "leaping into the sea," which means leaving one's job and starting one's own business, uncountable masses of people have leapt into growing networks of families, with local officials engaging in a bewildering variety of activities based on innumerable special deals. Stories of success feed the optimism that seems inherent in so many Chinese. The result is that something that looks like economic civil society is taking hold, for which the government is eager to claim credit.[28] Still, because there is no such thing as business un-connected with some kind of official power, what is evolving in China is not an economic civil society. Moreover, one of the reasons that so many Chinese are in such a hurry is that they have reason to fear that their own special deals will not last.

The second and less important reason is the regulatory climate. The bulk of Chinese growth has taken place in the special economic zones de-creed in 1978 along the southern coast, to which Shanghai was added in 1992. Here, local enterprises doing business with foreign companies are exempted from official taxes, while the foreign companies are supposed to receive tax holidays and duty-free imports of raw material. Neither locals nor foreigners, however, are exempt from the demands of undisciplined bureaucrats intent on drawing maximum rent from the new economic activity, and who may well kill the geese that lay the golden eggs, either by squeezing them too hard or by fighting one another over the privilege of squeezing.[29] War between lords of neighboring regions for the right to each other's plunder is very much in China's tradition, as are officials who extort without caring that other sets of officials are already extorting from the same people.

THE EUROPEAN WAY

Technocratic dirigisme and paternalistic social providence came together in Europe in the twentieth century. Each of these phenomena in its own way takes power and responsibility from individuals and society. Together, these two sets of incentives have produced populations with a penchant for start-ing careers later in life and ending them earlier, working fewer hours of the day, and taking longer vacations, while looking to the state for improvement in their economic conditions. Modern Chinese are strivers. Modern Euro-peans are not.

The European welfare state has grown mutatis mutandis under every party and ideology that ruled Europe in the twentieth century—laborism, fascism, Christian democracy, radicalism, and various kinds of conservatism. Regardless of country, it has had pretty much the same components—pensions for old age and disability, unemployment compensation, health care, schooling and day care for children, and housing benefits, plus progressive taxation meant to pay for it all and to flatten disparities of income. The programs share an ideological and a practical element. Because they proceed from an integral vision of society, they are not aimed primarily at relieving the lot of the poor, but are meant rather to apply to everyone, including the very rich. But because the distribution of money stimulates group interests, each program focuses benefits on those who were able to fashion the program in the first place at the expense of the wider public. Hence, disparities in wealth and influence widen and harden.

Given the great number of state programs, everyone in society is both a winner and a loser—both at the same time and during different stages of life. In most circumstances, it is difficult to know whether one is getting more net benefit than one is paying for or vice versa. In some cases, however, it is all too clear. Since the ratio of workers to retirees in coming decades is demographically certain to be inferior to the current ratio of active workers to retirees, pay-as-you-go pension systems are obviously a bad deal for contributors that is certain to get worse.

Who gets the most out of state programs? Those who have had a hand in targeting the system to their own needs—those who have the best knowledge of how the system operates, who have the greatest affinity with the people who run the system, and who have devoted themselves to working the system. Such people fall into several categories. Everywhere, it seems that the welfare state gives members of the upper middle class some of the more expensive things they most seek to enhance their lives. In Sweden, a place in a child-care center is worth some $18,000 per year. Places in public universities are expensive everywhere. (In the United States of 2008, tuition in private universities cost some $40,000 per student per year. Real per-pupil costs in comparable public ones were not much lower.) Such services are used disproportionately by well-off professionals. As in other systems, the welfare state creates well-paid occupations peculiar to it, *occupations that would not exist had the state not created them,* such as directors of child-care centers, officials of departments of social services, benefits counselors, ombudsmen, lawyers, and so forth. These places are also filled by upper-middle-class types. Overall, it should surprise no one that the distribution of income in states that devote a higher percentage of GDP to social programs is, if anything, skewed in favor of higher-income groups than in states that devote a lower percentage of GDP to welfare.[30]

It also seems that everywhere some of the people near the lower end of the socioeconomic scale have learned to make unemployment and disability benefits, and even public subsistence, the basis of their lives. Unemployment in the European Union—rising inexorably through all phases of business cycles over more than a generation—averaged near 10 percent in the early twenty-first century (at the end of a boom in 2008 it stood at 7.7 percent and was rising), meaning that one worker in ten receives a high percentage of the salary from the previous job while supposedly looking for a job or retraining.

The rate varies by region. In eastern Germany it is one in seven; in parts of southern Italy, it is one in three. Some of those on the unemployment rolls do nothing but collect. Many more, however, especially in southern Europe, also hold jobs and simply use unemployment as an extra source of income. The same goes for disability pensions. It is no coincidence that the regions reporting the highest rate of unemployment also report the highest rate of disability. In some Italian provinces, 40 percent of the working age population is officially disabled. In one Calabrian town, the rate reached 75 percent. Of course, many of these "disabled" people work, too.[31]

Yet notwithstanding that Europeans consider unemployment to be their biggest economic problem, the European Union has a labor shortage so great that (with the exception of Germany) it semiofficially accepts illegal immigrants from the Third World, disproportionately working men. These amount to perhaps 5 percent of the European Union's population and a far greater percentage of its workforce. They are admitted simply because they are desperately needed. And they are needed because, by definition, the Europeans who are on the unemployment rolls are unwilling to work in the jobs done by non-Europeans.

Hence, the welfare state culture grows as its subcultures are fed. When generous benefits are offered to societies such as those of eastern Germany, southern Italy, Greece, or Spain, where people are already accustomed to making the most of circumstances by clientelism, such benefits are certain to swell the welfare subculture. Working the system, it seems, is a skill like any other—most easily acquired by example and in an atmosphere of approval by one's neighbors. It is as easily learned at the bottom of the socioeconomic scale as at the top and surely less consequential at the bottom than at the top.

The culture of entitlement depresses productivity in subtle ways as well. In Germany, for example, it is no secret that the 10 percent of the people who purchase health insurance outside the state system of "alliances" pay premiums that average 25 percent less than the state system's, without the latter's queues and restrictions on care. Furthermore, the administrative cost per capita is twice as high in the state system as in the private one.[32] But most Germans do not have the option of buying better service for less. They do not have that option because the very administrative personnel who make the state health-care system expensive and inconvenient also work the system to keep the "alliance" system mandatory for most people, and the rest of German society is sympathetic enough to let them succeed. After all, so many others have their own special deals. The same goes for French railroad workers who strike to demand continued subsidy of featherbedding, or to truckers who demand to retire on full pay at age fifty-five and receive support from the public.

Dirigisme might well be described as welfare for the upper classes. Its two pillars are, first, various kinds of direct subsidies to producer firms, and second, the indirect subsidy of protective tariffs and regulatory restraints. While direct public ownership of producer firms went out of fashion in Europe after the 1960s, total public support for big business has risen through "industrial policy." In France, dirigisme goes back to the privileged relationships between fifteenth-century kings, bankers, and manufacturers of cannons.[33] With some variation, similar relationships existed throughout Europe. At the end of the nineteenth century, these relationships of privilege, patronage, and military utility began to be invested with the hope that they might fulfill the socialist goal of production for social use rather than profit. In the 1920s, Mussolini married socialism with the older tradition of privilege and produced the corporate state. This hallmark of fascism consisted of setting economic policy through consultation between management, labor, and government officials—who came to the table with credits, contracts, and regulatory powers. In the aftermath of World War II, most European countries adopted in one way or another what had been the fascist system, otherwise known as "indicative" or "soft" planning. Governments and political parties came to like it because it offered power and patronage. Labor unions liked it because it guaranteed patronage and support for employment. Businessmen included in the system liked it best of all—because their inclusion guaranteed success and wealth for themselves, but they didn't have to worry too much about competition, domestic or foreign. The result has been the rise of a class of businessmen like the Agnellis of Italy's Fiat, whose profits are their own (through huge salaries and stock options), but whose losses are hidden or absorbed by the state, and the emergence of politicians who rely on them for favors, both political and personal. This is the Europe that so many American businessmen want to imitate.

The number of Europeans who make a lot of money in business is small. In Sweden in 1986, for example, only 1,100 people had an after-tax income above 200,000 kronas (nine times the average physician's salary), but 1,435 Swedes won at least that much in lotteries and other kinds of gambling.[34] The incentives to gamble are much greater than those to go into business, because the chances of going from poverty to wealth through business are much smaller than the numbers indicate. It is just not possible in Europe to rise from running a shop in one's garage to ownership of a multinational, simply because at each stage in the growth of the business the owner would not have the political pull to be included among those who are already at the next level, the ones who are invited to consult cooperatively at a level sufficiently high to get the contracts and the credit necessary to reach the level above that. To rise to the top in European business, one must either work one's way up in an organization that already has ties with the state, or become involved through politics.

Hence, it is not surprising that so much of the news in the European press is about trades of official power for money, and vice versa. This is commonly called "corruption." In Italy, some 3,000 leaders of big business and government were indicted between 1992 and 1994. In Spain, the list begins with the governor of the Bank of Spain and two cabinet ministers. In France, the season opened in 1992 with the arrest of the minister of justice, and the careers of a prime minister and a presidential candidate were ended. The particulars are always the same: money paid in exchange for lucrative government contracts or favorable regulatory treatment. The organization of the European Union may be supranational, but it is in the same business of dispensing valuable favors that the national governments are in. Since the European Commission's bureaucrats in Brussels have been setting standards for everything from bacteria in cheese to the length of condoms (precisely 15.2 centimeters), they have become the focus of Europe's most lucrative lobbying efforts. By one estimate, one-tenth of the EU's 2007 budget of €133.8 billion goes directly for fraud.[35] But far more pervasive than the trade of money for favors is the trade of favors for favors. It is also more lucrative, because regulation is where the money is made, and the jobs that have the power to designate regulators are even more valuable.

That is why it is difficult to blame the European farmers who cut one ear off their cows to turn in as proof of slaughter, so that they can collect the EU incentive payment for reducing milk production while they continue to produce milk. Like so many others in Europe, they know that their measure of prosperity depends on adjusting to government programs. The name of the game is to benefit from them, and, if one can, to influence them. For now, the game yields some returns.

In the coming decades, however, the European economic game is sure to be played for diminishing returns but increasing individual stakes, because although the welfare state's inherent dynamic is to expand and interest groups do not normally tolerate cuts in benefits, drastic cuts (either direct or through reduction in purchasing power) are inevitable. The biggest pillars of the European welfare state—old-age pensions and medical care—are collapsing under the weight of Europe's demographic inversion.[36] Fifteen years from now, four out of ten Europeans will be sixty years of age or older, and there will be scarcely more than one active worker per retiree. The huge effort that will be required to pay some percentage—but not nearly all—of the benefits under these two headings will force other claimants into unprecedented combat. In sum, the Europeans' deep injection of the state into the production and distribution of economic goods seems to have produced a set of habits peculiarly incompatible with the pursuit of prosperity in the twenty-first century.

CHILE

Chile's experience under the government of General Augusto Pinochet (1973–1990) is interesting not because the country became more prosperous (which it did, with per capita GDP rising 50 percent during the period and growing at 7 percent per year since) but because of the way in which the government sought prosperity: Countering the logic of most of the world's economic organization in the twentieth century, the Chileans sought *to separate political power from economic life.* A group of Chicago-trained economists found not just the military junta but broad sectors of Chilean society responsive to their argument that two generations of increasing state interference in the economy had inculcated habits of interest-group competition that had led to poverty and civil strife, and that reversing the country's economic fortunes would require a new set of habits. Thus, they aimed their reforms, whether obviously related to the economy or not, at shrinking the state and making it more difficult to translate political power into economic gain. It is important to underline that the reformers thought that changing habits for the long run was more important than compelling behavior in the short run.

Chileans found arguments in favor of liberal economics acceptable because between 1964 and 1973 the full logic of interest-group redistribution had been visited upon them with a vengeance—especially under the Marxist regime of Salvador Allende (1970–1973). In 1964, Chile's Christian Democratic Party, with little objection from the Conservative Party and much assistance from the United States, began what was touted as a major effort to develop the Chilean economy. To stimulate agricultural production, the government expropriated 1,408 large farms.[37] But instead of giving title to the tenants, it turned them into collectives. Almost immediately, Chile became an ever-larger importer of food.[38] The government raised tariffs to protect and stimulate domestic industries, used foreign aid to build public housing, increased social benefits, and increased public employment. But as taxes and inflation rose, economic growth fell to one-half the Latin American average and lagged behind population growth.[39] The only clear winners were those closely tied to the Christian Democratic government. As the contest for redistribution turned more bitter, so did partisan strife.

The election of the Socialist Salvador Allende in 1970 came about because he promised to do more for greater numbers of people by pursuing the same approach more energetically. With the backing of the Christian Democrats and the Socialists, he promised the country "empanadas with red wine." But only his followers got them. He officially expropriated 3,628 farms,[40] while fostering the unofficial expropriation of countless more, and raised some tariffs to 700 percent. As food and other goods disappeared from normal circulation, he tried to set up a rationing system run by local committees of his partisans. People were lining up for jobs on these committees. But these were the opposite of productive jobs. Within a year, housewives in Santiago were in the streets banging empty pots, and some people were finding jobs as *coleros,* place holders in waiting lines.

By the end of his regime, the central government had 650,000 employees (in a country of 11 million) and controlled 75 percent of GDP. It did this for the benefit of friends at the expense of enemies. The economists who wrote *El Ladrillo* (meaning "the brick," the book that roughly served as a guide to the military regime's reforms) chronicled what political patronage had come to mean to business: "Concessions on taxes or tariffs, permission or prohibition on the import of spare parts, the approval or disapproval of loans."[41] In practice, the reign of patronage meant that those who had better connections could do whatever they wanted to those whose connections were worse. And if a citizen managed to get a court ruling against the government or one of its friends, the government ignored it. It ignored some 7,000 court rulings, in fact.[42] Relief from all this is what the Christian Democrats, along with the vast majority of Chileans, sought from the military when they asked for a military coup.

They got more than they bargained for, not just because the coup set off a simmering guerrilla war with the Left, but because senior military officers intended to change long-term habits and knew that their only chance to do it was to change a deep-rooted mentality. They did not want to take power to run the system and perhaps become its dominant rent collector, or to enforce a time-out after which the system would function as before. Hence, their economic reforms would aim at more than economics. Although the desire to make such changes set the tone for the military government's reforms, these did not occur according to any plan but rather happened in short bursts (1975, 1978–1981, and 1987–1988), usually when events left no choice between disaster and leaping ahead.

Above all, and in direct contradiction to the logic of Third Worldism, the military government shrank the size of the state. By the time Pinochet left office in 1990, the Chilean people had only 150,872 central government officials to support and to obey—one-fourth of the burden they had carried sixteen years before—and the government's direct consumption of GDP was down to 8.6 percent.[43] Just as important, the government officials who remained had far fewer favors to give and far less discretionary power than their predecessors.

By diminishing tariffs and other economic favoritism, and by shrinking its own economic activities, the government made it impossible for economically nonviable or useless jobs to exist. There would be no manufacturing of cars or consumer electronics in Chile because Chileans could buy them from Japan more cheaply than they could make them. There would be no jobs for place holders in lines or for fixing public benefits because there was no rationing and few services. But there were plenty of new jobs for people involved in providing fruit and fish to the Northern Hemisphere, because that is where Chile's competitive advantage lay.

Bitter experience had taught Chileans contempt for the notion that the power to elect a government is a satisfactory substitute for the freedom to run one's daily life. Thus one of the main objectives of each of the reforms was precisely to reduce the intrusiveness and discretionary power of government. For example, the reformers decided to reduce tariffs on nearly all items to an equal, insignificant 11 percent, in large part because they wanted to do away with the power of government to make or break fortunes. If government did not have the power to grant such favors, it would not call forth from within society people who specialized in seeking them. They also transferred some inherently governmental services—roads and sanitation—from ministries to local governments, less for reasons of economic efficiency than to make it possible for citizens to approach the providers of services not as favor seekers, but as employers.

The military regime actually increased traditional welfare state benefits for the very poorest of the poor, but it virtually eliminated them for everybody else. The reason went far beyond saving money and struck directly at the view that government can be a source of economic benefit. For citizens, there would be no employment as grantors of benefits and no premium in learning the complex paths to maximizing benefits. For bureaucrats or politicians, it would be more difficult to draw rents or to build clienteles.

The substitution of private but compulsory retirement accounts for social security was excellent *economic* policy because it created a huge pool of capital for investors and yielded higher returns for contributors. But it was even more significant for people's habits because it gave the contributors themselves, rather than bureaucrats, control over their own money. Thus it turned the attention of workers from the arcana of government rules to the fortunes of the competing funds in which their contributions were invested. The institution of private medical care and a voucher system for primary and secondary education was based on the same view that consumer sovereignty is likely to produce better services and likelier to produce better people.

The reformers sought to cut the link between power and money by requiring labor and professional organizations to elect their leaders openly by secret ballot and by prohibiting people in such organizations, as well as officers of corporations, from simultaneously holding office at any level of government or in any political party. Along with the diminution in the size and scope of government, these restrictions struck at the mutual attraction that everywhere exists between politicians and businessmen as well as at the way in which political parties in most of the world have been organized in the twentieth century (more on this in Chapter 6). The result of these and other measures that reduced the capacity of political parties to reward their adherents both high and low was predictable. Whereas in 1973 one out of ten Chilean voters had been a dues-paying member of a political party, by 1990 only four out of one hundred were.[44] Since the parties could give less, fewer people were inclined to give them money.

It is important to stress that since the Chilean military's objective, especially regarding economics, was to establish equality before the law while building barriers against privilege, its success depended substantially on restraining its own members from taking advantage of their power. It did this by keeping to a bare minimum the number of officers involved in government, excluding them entirely from detailed administration, and not allowing the civilians whom they appointed to govern to build a government party per se.

There was something more than a little anomalous about a government that had taken power by the gun and that was carrying on a bloody war against armed opposition, a war that involved torture and "disappearances,"[45] trying to establish the rule of law. Nevertheless, that was the objective. The regime succeeded in separating the civil war from the economic-constitutional reforms because the war was not about policy— it was about the mutual and very personal hatred between the country's entrenched Marxist subculture and the military. Second, the economic metamorphosis succeeded despite the regime's inherent illegality because the military sincerely sought to base liberal economics on liberal legality. It could do this because the reforms removed room for arbitrariness and because the military adhered scrupulously to its own rules, including timetables for a transition to democracy.

During the subsequent two decades, the military's Socialist successors, animated by precisely the opposite political principles and habituated to governing through clientelism, vocally denigrated its military predecessors but attacked its main reforms only at the margin.

POWER, PRODUCERS, AND TAKERS

Government action cannot easily transmute the cognitive skills and work habits of any people, whether Swedes, Congolese, or Japanese. But it affects all such qualities everywhere at the margin. Government fosters hard work when it gives people reason to believe that they will not be deprived of its fruits. And it fosters the fruitfulness of human action when it channels that action toward pursuits inherently productive—both of economic goods and of respect for others' property. Perhaps the best thing that governments can do for prosperity is not to create occupations that cause humans to waste time, energy, or resources on activities that their neighbors would not pay for.

Thomas Jefferson is renowned for claiming that he did not know of an occupation other than yeoman farmer that was as reliable a nursery for the human qualities of enduring prosperity and liberty. Jefferson may or may not have been correct about the ill effects of commerce. But his general point is unexceptionable: Some occupations foster better qualities than others. Just as the U.S. government's 1876 history of the whaling industry reasonably claims that perhaps its principal product was a set of exceptionally hardy, adventuresome, and industrious people, so historian Robert Conquest cites morally degenerate men as perhaps the main product of the Soviet economy. It matters a lot that so many governments effectively steer so many talented people to master the art of the courtesan, the fixer, and the exploiter. It matters that Japanese students compete so hard for posts in the Ministry of Finance, from whose merited heights they dispense unmerited favor. It matters that public employment, based more on personal status than on productivity, sets the tone for the European workplace, and that in Chile it does not, that you are likelier to get rich in Sweden by winning the lottery than by working. Hence, we must ask the following of any government: How does it affect its people's choice of occupations among the productive, the wasteful, and the counterproductive?

Government influences economic life primarily by deciding what role coercive power will play in it. To the extent that power is a factor in any transaction, it is a part, negative or positive, of the price of the good or service traded. *To the extent that one can bring power to bear on any transaction, one need bring less of any other value to it.* That is, if one side can coerce the other into acquiescence without delivering the goods, why deliver them? The involvement of power in any transaction (unless it be for the neutral purpose of keeping all coercion away from it) will therefore lower the total economic value of the transaction. It is no accident, then, that government involvement in economic activity tends to be inversely proportional to productivity. The reason for that, however, is that government power destroys the equality of economic actors. Even power applied for the ostensible purpose of creating legal equality where social inequality prevails is problematic.

Because government is naturally the creature and ally of the strong, it is practically incapable of intervening on behalf of the weak. That, of course, is why the greater the level of government intervention in the economy, the more difficult it is for poor individuals to rise economically by economic means. That is true irrespective of the ostensible purpose for intervention.

6

CIVILITY

Men of Athens I love you, but I must
obey the god rather than you.
—SOCRATES, *THE APOLOGY*

Who can do what to whom?
—V. I. LENIN

People who enjoy the fruits of their labors are also likely to enjoy the rule of law and space for civil society, as well as family lives untroubled from the outside and such spiritual lives as they are capable of. Since such people may take part in governing, they develop a proprietary interest in their surroundings as well as habits of self-reliance, and may properly be called citizens. But citizenship is rare: Most humans have lived as members of tribes or as subjects of despots, kings, emperors, or administrators.

The habits of citizenship are formed over many years by practicing politics without mutual depredation, demonization, or millennialist goals. In turn, such politics are more likely when the reigning ideas and political

institutions repress the natural human tendency to tyrannize, while bringing out such noble and moderate inclinations as any set of people might
have. Foremost among these habits is treating one another as equals. Yet, of
course, such ideas, institutions, and habits do best where rule of law, local
autonomy, and limited government have already taken root. That is why
citizenship is so rare.

   In their 5,000 years, the Chinese people have known various combinations of administration and disorder that fall under the Western category
"Oriental Despotism." They have been obedient subjects and they have been
rebels, but they have never been citizens. In our time the People's Republic—
the latest in a long line of imperial dynasties—seems to erode the Confucian
habits on which its subjects' obedience rests, while the Taiwanese regime
seems to have built both the rule of law and a modicum of self-government,
partly by strengthening and partly by weakening Confucian habits. On the
same cultural base, the Singaporean regime has built the rule of law while
excluding citizenship. In most modern countries, however, well-established
combinations of public and private power—one form or another of the corporate state or administrative state—make citizenship as illusory as in China.
Hence we see the regimes of Italy and Mexico, which we are accustomed to
think of as differing qualitatively, as variants of run-of-the-mill political
modernity. But first, let us look more closely at the principles of law and
self-government.

LAW, LIMITS, AND DISCRETION

Oaths of office are so common in Western culture, so often mouthed cyni-
cally, so often aped in civilizations to which they are truly foreign, that we
tend to forget their momentous meaning: The official takes power by an act
of submission to a greater power. The magistrates of the Roman republic—
including the dictators—began and ended their offices by ritual submission
on the altars of the gods to the laws that had been made by the various assemblies of the Roman people. Later, even the emperors pledged (sometimes even sincerely) to follow the laws that they themselves dictated. The
kings of medieval Castile used to receive their crowns while acknowledging
a chorus of nobles saying, "Thou shalt be King if thou workest justice, and
if thou does not do so, thou shalt not be King." Like all medieval European
monarchs, they pledged allegiance to uphold and administer customs and
immunities of which they were not the authors.

When King John of England transgressed feudal law, the barons met him with swords at Runnymede in 1215 to write in the Magna Carta the law that he was supposed to have been obeying all along.[1] The difference between the king's theoretical and practical adherence to law was the subject of John Fortescue's (1385–1479) distinction between England's *dominium politicum et regale* and the increasingly lawless *dominium regale* of Spain and France. But shortly after Fortescue, Henry VIII brought England into line with modern absolutism. By contrast, in the nineteenth century, King Mongkut of Thailand startled his subjects by answering their pledges of allegiance to him with a pledge of allegiance to them.

The ruler's adherence to law, even laws of which he is the dictator, gives even to slaves some of the dignity of citizens. Aleksandr Solzhenitsyn and Andrei Sakharov knew how big (and how destructive of the Soviet system) was their seemingly modest demand that the USSR enforce its own laws. Any rule book can be a powerful bulwark. The sailor harassed to show deference can read that he is supposed to salute a superior within 30 feet and can measure a circle around his station beyond which he need not show respect. The worker whose employee manual lists the things he must do to stay out of trouble knows that "working to rule" is a fearsome weapon in his hands. Even American Negro slaves figured out that the slave codes that bound them to servitude had loopholes—including property rights that the most ambitious could use to build bank accounts to buy their freedom. By 1820, some 2,500 former slaves had bought slaves for themselves.[2] By the same token, despite apartheid's oppressive laws, South Africa enjoyed a net in-migration of blacks from nearby countries, who found unfriendly laws preferable to thoroughly lawless rulers. But laws themselves do not the rule of law make. A multiplicity of laws reduces the number of fields in which ordinary individuals, families, and churches—in short, civil society—can act at *their* discretion, while the complexity of laws empowers officials with latitude to make them mean what they wish.

The rule of law is fostered not by statutes that grant privileges, but rather, by ideas embodied in writs and made real by habits that recognize the rightful limits of government. Freedom of religion, for example, is fundamental to the rule of law because it is the threshold indicator of whether there is any human activity at all on which the rulers may not trespass. And if the rulers recognize the root—the fact that man is not government's creature—then they may also respect the trunks and branches of that fact in civil society. To the extent that they do not recognize limits in what they may do to civil society, why should they respect the rules they themselves impose? The sense of ownership that is at the heart of citizenship comes only when that ownership is not preempted from above. Only then can nonofficial persons, literally *civilians,* freely join together in civil society. Let us now look at some of the major ways in which regimes affect civic habits.

LAW AND LOCALITY

The Christian and classical traditions agree that the good man, the whole man, must fulfill responsibilities to the community—and that the highest form of relationship with the community is ruling and being ruled in turn.[3] Modern states recognize this vestigially: Although they typically confer the status of "citizen" to all nonalien natives, none allows children or the insane to vote, because they obviously cannot fulfill any responsibilities. But what responsibilities must the real citizen be able and willing to fulfill? In classical times, military service was the essence of citizenship. Service on juries and in committees to relieve disasters have been common qualifications, as has the ownership of property. Most modern states, however, have removed all these, including (for natives) the capacity to read and to understand. Whereas citizenship once required that the citizen be able to exercise independent judgment, that he not be merely the tool of others, modern states don't care about that. The bargain is straightforward: Stay out of jail, and you may vote. In some American states, even imprisoned felons may vote. But a citizenship that asks little means little, and is worth just that.

In just about all of today's nominally self-governing countries, life for all but a few so-called citizens is a series of acts of obedience to regulations affecting every aspect of life in whose making the citizen's involvement is purely theoretical, and to officials whose appointments or removals he is prohibited by law from interfering with. Although the officials are called "civil servants," civilians soon learn that the only way to avoid trouble and get what they want from them is to treat them as the masters they really are. Once every several years, nominal citizens are supposed to feel like masters because they can vote for or against a few people, none of whom have a direct bearing on their lives.[4] If they resent this, they are told to work for social mobility, so that someday they or their children might become part of the ruling class. And to top it off, the rulers chastise the people for feeling "alienated." Hence, the tendency of citizens to become cynical, wheedling subjects is unsurprising. In short, the modern administrative state is not wholly different from the ancient Chinese empire.

For all but a few, then, the only scope for citizenship, the only chance for people to take charge of their own affairs, lies in whatever latitude modern national governments give to localities. Yet rarely do the powers of local governments proceed from the presumption that citizens of a locality have the *right* to deal with any matter at all. On the contrary, in most cases modern central governments treat provinces, departments, oblasts, states, and municipalities as administrative subdivisions and delegate particular tasks to them. Sometimes they also impose on local authorities the political burden of raising whatever taxes may be necessary to carry out these tasks. But always they hand down the rules by which to proceed. Hence modern local officials are usually responsible more to the central government than to the locals who elect them. Yet whether local officials exercise powers by right or as delegates makes all the difference between citizens with habits of spontaneous cooperation and subjects with the habits of consumers of services. Nothing is so futile as giving the label "community leaders" to individuals whose standing among their neighbors depends on passing down orders and patronage from the central government. Nor is anything so self-contradictory as prohibiting localities from legislating on important matters and thereafter bemoaning the disarticulation of the community.

LAW AND RIGHT

What leads people to hold governments to law, and to exercise individual and local autonomy? History teaches us that people used to stick to customs for which they sought no explanation. Confucius's *Analects* are exegeses of customs rather than explanations of why the customs are right, and there is no non-Roman account of the liberties of the Germanic tribes, much less any Germanic argument about why liberty was good for the Germans. By contrast, among the children of Jerusalem, Athens, and Rome, social practice has been intertwined with reason for two and a half millennia, and living by law has depended on understanding the natural affinity of man for *the way things ought to be.*

Most explanations of law, however, have been of the positive kind: As Plato's Thrasymachus put it in Book 1 of *The Republic,* law or right (*nomos*) is whatever any society's most powerful members judge to be most advantageous to themselves.[5] Following this "positive law" tradition, U.S. Chief Justice William Rehnquist argued that, over time, such judgments may "assume a general social acceptance neither because of any intrinsic worth nor because of any unique origins in someone's ideas of natural justice, but instead simply because they have been incorporated in a constitution by a people."[6] Note, however, that this is contrary to the branch of the Western tradition that comes from Socrates—as well as from the Bible—and that is lodged in the American Declaration of Independence, namely that *the judgment of any sovereign can be mistaken, even about his own interest.* This branch describes law as a set of rules that are to be accepted to the extent that they are intrinsically good, and rejected to the extent that they are not.

Underlying this contrast is the fact that some kinds of behavior are naturally fit for humans while others are not. We can see this by asking whether the lifestyle promoted by the Ten Commandments that came down from Mount Sinai is inherently, naturally, a better or a worse guide to human fulfillment than a guide made up of its opposites. Imagine living by: "Thou shalt have many gods and take their names in vain; never take a day to reflect; dishonor your father and your mother; kill; steal; copulate competitively; betray; scheme to take everything your neighbor has." It would be difficult to argue that the choice between this set of laws and the Decalogue's is merely arbitrary, indifferent to human happiness, irrelevant to survival.

By the same token, each conception of law has peculiar consequences. The Declaration of Independence claims it is self-evidently true that "all men" are equally "endowed by their Creator" with natural rights to life, liberty, and the pursuit of happiness. We know from experience to what extent those beliefs are compatible with limited government and citizenship. But what if America's founders had believed that human equality was, in the words of J. C. Calhoun, a "self-evident lie"? Would America be anything like we have known it, or would it be more like the antebellum South, or like Sparta, where a minority of peers lorded it over a vast underclass? The point is that some ideas imply citizenship, while others imply the status of subjects for most men.

PROPERTY RIGHTS AND THE RULE OF LAW

Consider that self-interest can be both the foundation of the rule of law and its destruction. Self-interest was certainly in the minds of the historic defenders of law and civil society—the barons at Runnymede in 1215, the authors of the Glorious Revolution of 1688, and the authors of the Declaration of Independence in 1776. But these greats defended their own interest in law based on their recognition that it was naturally proper for them to live a certain way, and that it was right for them to have what others were trying to take away. Above all they understood the law as granting to others what they demanded for themselves. Had they understood their self-interest to lie elsewhere, the results would have been different. In short, consciousness of natural law arises from living naturally, while living unnatural ways of life makes it difficult to understand nature.

Consider property rights—the idea that individuals or families who possess things are right to have them, to defend them, and to dispose of them. Living as if one had property rights is far from a universal human experience. In ancient Egypt and other Near Eastern empires, as well as in Russia until the nineteenth century, all land belonged to the sovereign, while its occupiers were mere renters. The renters' attitude—a short-term outlook, bad stewardship, and disinterest in cooperation with others to defend it—has been the rule rather than the exception on this planet. It is all too easy to foster a renter's attitude in anyone. For example, high property taxes effectively transfer to the government the presumption of ownership and make the taxes into rent.

Yet the attitude typical of renters can also exist where taxes are low. In some cases, people who own property and make money from its use do not take full responsibility for taking care of it because that would be too much trouble, as the case of nineteenth-century Argentina shows. A poet was able to write the verse that follows because many of those who came to the Argentine pampas sought exportable profits rather than to make the land truly their own:

> *No one planted a tree*
> *And on the farms there were no sheep.*
> *Birds did not sing, the soft murmur*
> *Of bleating lambs was absent.*
> *Mothers raised sad children.*[7]

The rate of return on labor was the effective difference between many who took huge private profits from Argentina and Russian serfs. They all worked just for money, not for property. The point here is that *private profit,* which renters and investors can take as well as owners (and use-rights as well), is something very different from *private property,* which involves the duties of stewardship and defense.

By contrast, the reverential attitude toward property that Homer described in *The Odyssey* or that Fustel de Coulanges described in *The Ancient City* is a mixture of sacred right (often because ancestors were buried on the family farm) and the sacred obligation to develop and defend it, both singly and along with one's countrymen.[8] Private property is something that has to be respected and defended by the community—including, of course, by its leaders. European kings had to *ask* nobles and commoners for material sustenance because customary law and canon law recognized the rightful existence of private property, and because Europeans at the time were ready to fight for it. The development of the common law was substantially due to centuries of adjudication of disputes about property—disputes that presupposed general respect for it. The habit of exercising stewardship over property, of having one's right in property respected and of respecting others' such rights—a restrained combination of jealousy and generosity—naturally leads people to make and respect mutually satisfying rules about other aspects of public life.

However, whereas private property habituates people to the rule and defense of law, Plato taught that the mere possession of wealth does not. In Book 8 of *The Republic,* he drew an ominous portrait of society (or rather what passes for society) based not on the citizen but on the consumer. The merely wealthy man, he said, lives with all the outward trappings of social power but has none because he does not know his neighbors for any civic purpose. He is not part of any voluntary, non-profit endeavor.[9] He could not lead and would not follow in peace, but especially he could not and would not do either in war.

THE POLITICS OF REDISTRIBUTION

Because weakening the habits of citizenship is easier than strengthening them, the policy agendas that affect such habits are easier to describe negatively than positively. Surely the Roman republic up to the second century B.C. is the most prominent example of habitual civic virtues (along with strife), and Montesquieu's summation of the process by which those habits were lost is the most concise.[10] That is, until the end of the Punic Wars, foreign wars had overshadowed the violent self-seeking of patricians and plebeians, setting the tone of political life and ensuring that honor in war and public service—that is, citizenship—would be prized above private ambitions. Thereafter, as wealth became the measure of man, the Romans' habitual capacity for forceful acquisition became the means of domestic politics. Livy wrote that whenever the city took up the question of limiting landed property to the equivalent of the ancient standard of two good hectares, or the question of distributing captured lands, the city was turned inside out.[11] To sort out justice and seek advantage in the face of ambiguous law and powerful opposing interests, the relationship between patron and client became the most powerful political tie. Politics was reduced to the question of "who is to get what, when, and how." The result was ever more demanding clienteles, ever higher taxes, ever weakening civic responsibility, civil war, proscriptions unto death, and gradually, the transformation of Roman citizens into imperial subjects.

Long before Rome's political agenda of redistribution engendered partisan violence, Plato's *Republic* and Aristotle's *Politics* explained why violence is the natural end of redistributionism. Since there is no natural guide as to who should have what, and because human wants are inherently unlimited, the inescapable conflicts can be settled only by force. The only way to escape the conflicts is to hold property sacred. Two thousand years later, Abraham Lincoln was telling Stephen Douglas and his Illinois audience nothing new when he made the point that taking labor or the fruits thereof from some for the benefit of others was a game that anyone could learn to play to everyone's disadvantage. "As I would not be a slave, so would I not be a master,"[12] he declared. He also explained that race was only one of many possible bases on which the lawless invasion of property could be pursued.

The strife in seventeenth-century Britain (or for that matter in twentieth-century Northern Ireland) was between enemies who defined each other in terms of religion. But surely, strife between the English, Irish, and Scots predated the Protestant Reformation; and surely, the oppression that the English imposed on Low Church Scots was as vigorous as that imposed on Catholic Irish. Nor was it limited to the disinterested inculcation of the fine points of Anglican orthodoxy. It always involved the addictive pleasures of economic exploitation and of ethnic and social superiority. Long before communism, whenever groups came to power to improve the character of the people by imposing purer lifestyles on them, they quickly came to enjoy the power inherent in their vast task to take, reward, punish, uplift, and humiliate. And none of the rulers wound up poorer than the ruled.[13] The saying about New Deal politicians in Washington—they came to do good and they stayed to do well—is applicable generally. Our point, then, is that respect for private property is the beginning of the rule of law, and that excuses for disrespecting it are never lacking.

PARTIES AND REPRESENTATION

What is to be the relationship between modern so-called citizens and the governments that claim to represent them? This question first arose in the aftermath of England's Glorious Revolution of 1688, when the people's representatives took on the absolute powers that had been the king's. Edmund Burke was the first to warn that the new order was inherently a despotism of the constituencies, worse than royal absolutism because members of Parliament were even more likely to subordinate judgment about law and right to their constituents' dictates. Burke barely imagined party organizations that would organize the constituencies and literally reduce members of Parliament to being party employees. James Madison, who feared the prospect of such organizations, wrote in *The Federalist* No. 10 that since American legislators would come from a vast country and represent diverse and shifting interests, they could not coalesce to preempt property rights and the citizenship that flows therefrom. Madison, however, did not mention the one feature of America that eventually contributed most to the success of his design: Each individual legislator was elected singly from a district diverse enough to make it difficult for him to be captured by a single organized interest.

In the twentieth century, some parties—for instance, America's Republicans and Democrats—were more loosely organized than social clubs, with barely an agenda (this was also true of British parties up to the mid–nineteenth century). They had to be loose, ever-shifting coalitions because they were based on legislators who were elected individually and, by their own efforts or those of the people they were bound to, do the bidding of a particular locality.

But the trend of the nineteenth and twentieth centuries was toward parties organized more tightly than military units to pursue wars aimed to bring down whole cultures. The Socialist parties started the trend. Since the Socialists thought that the common good was an illusion, they sent delegates to Parliament without regard for it to press for workers' interests, and above all for the Party's interests. It is tempting to say that the Socialists were setting up alternative civil societies. But since every Socialist club ultimately depended on the Party, there was less civility in them than power. The modern, uncivil Party was the prototype of the modern uncivil state.

The rise of socialism coincided with that of the notion—best articulated by John Stuart Mill—that representative government had to represent all of society's opinions and interests and that legislatures ought to mirror interests rather than localities.[14] In other words, out of all the aspects of any person's life, legislatures ought to represent just one: the individual's interest in a party. That interest represents none of the aspects of life that bind individuals as neighbors, but rather the one aspect that tends to set the individual apart, because it depends on individual choice alone, often about abstractions. Mill's reasoning on representation meant that seats would be distributed to parties in lots equal to the percentage of the vote they received rather than to whichever individuals got the most votes in their respective districts. This system of proportional representation (PR) discourages voters from coalescing with other differently motivated voters behind an individual who will represent them all tolerably well. But it encourages them to back the party that will promote their particular interests at the expense of others'.

Legislators who arrive in office by virtue of proportional representation are *already* bound together to pursue factional interests because *they are the mere creatures of the party*. They are elected from lists compiled by the parties. The very existence of these lists presupposes and calls forth the party leaders who compile the lists. Under proportional representation, the leaders are all-powerful because they decide who is to be on the list and, above all, who will occupy the places on the list that are high enough to guarantee election, given the party's likely share of the vote. Under proportional representation, legislators work for the party leaders, who may not even be legislators themselves or who may hold no public office at all. Such leaders are elected by party officials whose careers they control. Thus insulated against pressure from the general public as well as from their subordinates, party leaders under PR are powers unto themselves. Proportional representation makes them the only truly enfranchised citizens of the state as a whole and gives them incentives to set the several parts of civil society against one another.

Some modern parties, notably the Fascists and the Communists, have provided their members with physical sustenance and moral certainty. As early as the turn of the twentieth century, socialist parties in Europe were keeping clergymen away from workers' housing, filling the resulting spiritual void with lectures on modern mores. Socialist parties possessed this century's modernist faith explicitly and organized to manufacture their members' unanimous support for it. Their programmatic focus, their practical power, and the congruence between the structure of the party and the character of modern government has strongly influenced most of the world's parties. Since then, parties of varied ideology or none at all, but organized on the Socialist model, have become laws and polities unto themselves in many countries, so that individuals' relationships with parties have counted for more than formal rights and duties of citizenship.

Although Britain never did adopt PR and France did so only for the twelve years of the Fourth Republic, from 1946 to 1958, both countries experienced a strengthening of party organizations at the expense of other political entities through the middle of the century and passed the strong-party legacy on to their colonies, usually along with PR. Italy and Germany, however, adopted PR immediately after World War I. The result was prototypical: Amid fragmented parties that had partially adopted the new Socialist-style organization (local sections controlled by regional and central committees, directorates, general secretaries and politburos, plus affiliated labor, youth, and women's organizations), the more compact, more fully disciplined Socialist parties were able to maneuver more adroitly to capture targeted sectors of the electorate and make and unmake coalitions. But the newest, most radical Socialist parties—the Fascists and the Communists—enjoyed the greatest advantages because they had carried organization, discipline, and antagonistic ideology to their logical conclusion: the establishment of gangs that brought "extra-parliamentary" pressure to bear on the political process. The black- and brown-shirted thugs who beat rank-and-file political opponents in the streets, intimidating their leaders, became the only real citizens of the Communist-Fascist regimes.[15]

It is important to note that the full logic of modern political parties, and its effect on the habits of citizens living under them, could manifest themselves only *after* these parties had taken hold of state power and used it to feed and discipline their own organizations. Prior to that, they lacked the power to shut down opposition. When Benito Mussolini himself, for example, ran afoul of the Socialist Party in 1915, he was cut off from his Party job (as editor of the Party newspaper) but remained free to get another job and to organize his friends into a rival party. Once Mussolini's Fascist Party took state power however, no other job would be available to apostates from the Party, much less the freedom to organize opposition.

Once upon a time the Party's affiliated labor unions had worked with the Party in the expectation that it would advance the unions' own goals. But when the Party gained power to prohibit alternative unions as well as to reward and punish the unions' officials more than the members could, the unions became (in the terminology of the Communists) "transmission belts" for orders from Party chiefs to union officials bound to obey them. The rank and file became ciphers. The same goes for all other "sectoral" or "mass" organizations affiliated with the Party.

Far from being confined to the Nazi and Communist parties, colonization of the economy and the use of social organizations as political transmission-belts—the choking of civil society—are the rule in modern big-government states. Only the tightness of the grip and the degree of colonization are different. Since giving jobs and favors is a powerful tool of party-building—and government power in the modern world is nothing if not power over jobs—modern parties have aggressively sought involvement in the economy precisely to "colonize" both government and private employment, to reward the friends and punish the enemies of the party. From Israel to Italy and Japan, regimes that employ PR tend to have parties that are more disciplined, whose control of the social organizations associated with them is greater, and whose colonization of the economy has gone farther than parties that do not live under PR. In such regimes, elections do not determine who governs. Interparty deals do. Consequently, in such regimes, voters are less able than elsewhere to "throw the rascals out." How can they, when the "rascals" in the several parties fight as they might over the division of society's spoils rather than cooperating on the essentials—shutting out competition from upstarts? Throughout the Western world, for example, budgets are passed through comprehensive deals between the leaders of all major parties. Increasingly, this is so in America as well. Mutatis mutandis, modern parties support and defend the administrative bureaucracies and associated interest groups that really govern modern states.

But by what right do modern parties and states rule?

SCIENCE VS. CITIZENSHIP

Modern states negate citizenship in a way and on a basis not wholly different from that of the millennial Chinese imperial bureaucracy: efficient administration. No sooner had France's revolutionaries revived the concept of citizenship in Europe than Napoleonic practice and Hegelian theory sucked political equality and self-rule out of it and defined the modern state in terms of scientific administration. In nineteenth-century France, Prussia, and their imitators, the state set standards for schools, professions, and localities. While elected assemblies in the new regimes might debate abstractions, theory and practice barred them from dealing with the rules by which people lived. The fundamental reason for this was the unremarkable belief that because human beings are *un*equal in so many obvious ways, everyone is better off when the masses are kept out of business best handled by professionals. Of course, the masses must consent—but really, they must consent only to the proposition that they must consent. Only in Switzerland and America did the theory and practice of popular government take deep root. In sum, citizenship and the rule of law are problematic throughout the modern world, and most problematic in the regimes that most partake of modernity.

Science, or the pretense thereof, is the source of the modern administrative state's intellectual and moral authority. When a polity decides that its business, its controversies, are beyond the capacity of citizens to understand, and its business too complex for them to administer, and hence that only certified experts may deal with them, power logically passes to "the experts," and, above all, to those who certify the experts as experts. Thus the polity's ordinary members cease to be citizens. Aristotle teaches that political relationships—that is, relationships among equals—depend on persuasion. Conversely, persuasion is the currency of politics only insofar as persons are equal. Whereas equals must persuade their fellows about the substance of the business at hand, despots, kings, or aristocrats exercise power over lesser beings by pointing to their status. The argument, "Do what we say because we are certified to know better," is a slight variant of "Do what we say because we are us." But do those who rule on behalf of superior knowledge really know things the knowledge of which makes them so unequal as to endow them with the right to rule? What might such things be?

The problem is patent: To the extent that the matters to be decided rest on expertise, any nonexperts who claim a civil or natural right to refuse to follow the experts in fact abuse those rights. At most, nonexperts may choose among competing teams of experts. But on what basis may they choose? If the questions that the experts debate among themselves are fundamentally comprehensible by attentive laymen, "science" would be about mere detail and citizens would be able to decide the big questions on the basis of equality. But if the "science" by which the polity is ruled disposes of essential questions, then citizenship in the sense of Aristotle and of the American founders is impossible and the masses should be mere faithful subjects. And if some voters dig in their heels or place their faith in scientists who are out of step with "what science says"—quacks, by definition—then they undermine the very basis of government that rests on expertise.

Note, however, that removing the polity's business from the arena of politics to the cloisters of science does not reduce the contrasting interests that the polity's parties have in that business. It just restricts the competition and changes its rules. Whereas previously the parties had to address the citizenry with substantive cases for their positions and interests, now translating those positions into scientific terms expressed by certified persons means that the parties must fight one another by marshaling contrasting scientific retinues, by validating their own and discrediting their opponents' experts. It follows, then, that the modern struggle is over control of the process of accreditation, and that the arguments the masses hear must be mostly ad hominem, seldom ad valorem—not least because the experts deem the masses incapable and unworthy of hearing anything else.

Because Americans believe that "all men are created equal," they tend to identify the concept of citizenship with that of self-government: Equality under the law means equality in the making of laws. But while that is analogous to the thinking of Athenian democrats, it is strange to modern European theory, never mind to modern practice in America. That is because it is as plain in our America as in all places and at all times that some men *do* know the public business far better than others. From this follows the universal presumption that the people in charge should be the ones who best know what they are doing. Hence, inequality of capacity argues for political inequality. *Such inequality is compatible with some conceptions of citizenship, but not with the American or democratic versions thereof.*

The French revolutionary intellectuals and merchants who reintroduced the term "citizen" to Europe applied it to the peasants as well. But that was talk. They knew that if the masses governed, they might well have them guillotined rather than the nobles and priests. And so they set up, and Napoleon perfected, a system of government that consisted of bureaucracies. The difference between these and the royal bureaucracies they replaced was that the republican ones were supposed to be aristocracies of merit. This is the continental model of the state, best explained by G. W. F. Hegel in *The Philosophy of History* and by Max Weber in his description of the *Rechtstaat,* the "rational-legal state." Access to this ruling class is theoretically equal, typically through competitive exams, and its rules should apply equally. Just as in the ancient Chinese imperial bureaucracy, the substantive decisions should be made by those who know and care best: the examination-qualified bureaucrats who embody the state. In modern governance, in addition to embodying the state, the bureaucrats are supposed to be the carriers of the developing human spirit, of progress.

The modern state, then, is quintessentially government of the many *by the few*. Ancient political theory was familiar with this category, distinguishing within it the rule of the moneymakers for the purpose of wealth, of the soldiers for glory, or of the virtuous for goodness. But modern thought has reduced government by the few to the rule of the experts. Expert in what? In bringing all good things, it seems. *In our time, such knowledge is called science, and is important enough practically to negate human equality and hence citizenship.*

By the 1950s this had become a problem in the Anglo-Saxon world as well as on the European continent. In 1954, the U.S. Supreme Court decided the case of *Brown v. Board of Education*—whether schools segregated by race fulfilled the Fourteenth Amendment's requirement for "equal protection of the laws" to all citizens—not by reference to any legal or political principle on which the general population might pronounce themselves (one such principle was available in Justice John Marshall Harlan's dissent in *Plessy v. Ferguson,* the case that *Brown* overturned), but rather by reference to a "study" by sociologist Kenneth Clark concluding that "separate is inherently unequal." This was a finding supposedly of fact, not of law. Debates within the Court and in society at large subsequently have been focused not so much on what is lawful as on contending studies about the effects of competing policies. A large chunk of education policy shifted from citizen control to judicial-scientific control. The scientization of American political life was just beginning. In *Massachusetts v. EPA* (2007), the court agreed with what it called "predominant scientific opinion" that carbon dioxide emissions cause "global warming," and hence ordered the EPA to regulate those emissions—essentially America's economy. The American people's elected representatives had not passed any law concerning "global warming." No matter.

In his 1960 Godkin lectures at Harvard, C. P. Snow, who had been Britain's civil service commissioner for fifteen years, addressed the Americans' worries by telling them that "In any advanced industrial society . . . the cardinal choices have to be made by a handful of men: in secret and, at least in legal form, by men who cannot have first hand knowledge of what these choices depend upon or what their results may be."[16] In short, public figures must be figureheads for scientists who are formally responsible to them but whose minds are beyond common understanding and scrutiny. Snow concluded that society's greatest need was for change, and that scientists were the proper originators of it because among them were "socially imaginative minds."[17] While scientists should not administer, he said, they should be part of the Establishment along with administrators.

He illustrated his point by contrasting the clash in Britain between two scientists, Sir Henry Tizard, innovative, progressive, and very much a member of the administrative-scientific Establishment, not incidentally Snow's personal favorite, and F. A. Lindeman, a scientist close to Winston Churchill and even farther from the Establishment than Churchill. According to Snow, Lindeman polluted science and administration with politics, while Tizard's contrary scientific and administrative opinions were supra-political because Tizard was a member of the Establishment.

As Snow was writing his lectures, President Dwight Eisenhower was dealing with the same subject as he prepared his farewell to the American people after eight years in the White House and a lifetime in the U.S. Army. His oft-cited warning about the dangers of a "military industrial complex" was part of the address's larger point: the danger that big government poses to citizenship. For Eisenhower, the alliance between scientists and administrators so dear to C. P. Snow was taking politics captive and polluting science itself. Whereas Snow had taken pains to identify science with public policy and to call true scientists only those who got along with colleagues, and especially with administrators, Eisenhower pointed to these things as subversive:

> A government contract becomes virtually a substitute for intellectual curiosity. For every old blackboard there are now hundreds of new electronic computers. The prospect of domination of the nation's scholars by Federal employment, project allocations, and the power of money is ever present and is gravely to be regarded. Yet, in holding scientific research and discovery in respect, as we should, we must also be alert to the equal and opposite danger that *public policy* could itself become the captive of a scientific technological elite.[18]

The importance of the contrast between Eisenhower and Snow becomes obvious when we question underlying premises: What subjects, what judgments, qualify as "science," meaning matters so far beyond the horizon of ordinary human beings as to disqualify commonsense judgment about them? What can any humans know, the knowledge of which rightly places them in the saddle and others under it? What are the matters on which the public may have legitimate opinions, and on what matters is it illegitimate to speak except by leave of certified experts? Moreover, how does one accede to the rank of expert? Must one possess a degree? But neither Galileo nor Isaac Newton had any, never mind Thomas Edison. Must one be accepted by other experts? But scientists are not immune to groupthink, to interest, to dishonesty, to mutual deference or antagonism, never mind to error.

By the time Eisenhower spoke, the criterion he had warned about had become dominant: In our time, one accedes to the rank of expert by achieving success in getting grants, primarily from the government. Anyone who has worked in a university knows that getting government grants is the surefire way to prestige and power. And on what basis do the government's grantors make the grants that constitute the scientific credentials? Science itself? But the grantors are not scientists, and they would not be immune to human temptations even if they were. Personal friendship, which C. P. Snow touted, is not nearly as problematic as intellectual kinship, professional and political partisanship. In sum, as Eisenhower warned, politicians are tempted to cast issues of public policy in terms of science in order to foreclose debate, to bring to the side of their interests expert witnesses whose expertise they manufactured and placed beyond challenge.

Testifying to a joint congressional committee on March 21, 2007, former Vice President Al Gore argued for taxing the use of energy based on the combustion of carbon, and for otherwise forcing Americans to emit much less carbon dioxide. Gore wanted to spend a substantial amount of the money thus raised to fund certain business ventures. (Incidentally or not, he himself had a large stake in those ventures.) But, he argued, his proposal was not political, and debating it was somehow illegitimate, because he was just following "science," according to which, if these things were not done, Planet Earth would overheat and suffocate. He said: "The Planet has a fever. If your baby has a fever, you go to the doctor. If the doctor says you need to intervene here, you don't say 'well I read a science fiction novel that tells me it's not a problem.'" But Gore's advocacy of "solutions" for "global warming" was anything but politically neutral acceptance of expertise. As vice president until 2001, as well as afterward, he had done much to build a veritable industry of scientists and publicists who had spent some $50 billion, mostly in government money, during the previous decade to turn out and publicize "studies" bolstering his party's efforts to regulate and tax in specific ways. Moreover, he claimed enough scientific knowledge to belittle his opposition as following "science fiction." Gore received a 2007 Nobel Peace Prize for his work. But that work was political, not scientific. Not surprisingly, some of his opponents in Congress and some scientists thought that Gore and his favorite scientists were doing well-paid science fiction.

Who was right? Gore's opponents, led by Oklahoma senator James Imhofe, argued that the substance of the two main questions, whether the Earth was being warmed by human activities, and what if anything, could and should be done about it, should be debated before the grand jury of American citizens. Gore et al. countered that "the debate is over!" and indeed that nonscientific citizens had no legitimate place in the debate. Yet he and like-minded citizens claimed to know enough to declare that it had ended. They also claimed that scientists who disagreed with them, or who just questioned the validity of the conclusions produced by countless government science commissions to which Gore and his followers had funneled government money, and which they called "mainstream science," were "deniers"—illegitimate. Equally out of place, they argued, were calls that they submit to tests of their scientific IQ. *Whatever else one may call this line of argument, one may not call it scientific. It belongs to the genus "politics."* But, peculiarly, it is politics that aims to take matters out of the realm of politics, where citizens may decide by persuading one another, and places them in a realm where power is exercised by capturing the commanding heights of the Establishment.

Thus on July 28, 2008, Speaker of the House Nancy Pelosi explained to journalist David Rogers why she was right in forbidding the Congress from voting on proposals by Republicans to open U.S. coastlines to oil drilling. Using fossil fuels, she explained, causes global warming. Forbidding votes that could result in more oil being used was her duty because, she said, "I'm trying to save the planet. I'm trying to save the planet." No one would vouch for her scientific expertise. But she was surely saving an item in the agenda of her party's constituencies, which rightly feared defeat in open debates and votes.

In the same way, in September 2008 Secretary of the Treasury Henry Paulson and Chairman of the Federal Reserve Board Ben Bernanke told the Congress and the country, backed by many in the banking business, that unless the Congress authorized spending $700 billion to purchase the financial assets that the banks and investment houses considered least valuable, the entire financial system would collapse and the American people would lose their savings, jobs, homes, and so on, and that authorizing that money would avert the crisis. But none of those who proposed the expenditure explained why the failure of some large private enterprises and their subsequent sale at public auction would cause any of the above-mentioned catastrophes. There was no explanation of how the money would be spent, how the assets to be bought would be valued, or why. The arguments were simply statements by experts in government as well as finance—whose repeated mistakes had brought about the failures that were at the center of contention, and whose personal interests were involved in the plan they proposed. The strength of their arguments lay solely in the position of those making them. They were the ones who were supposed to know. And when, a month later, the same Paulson, backed by the same unanimous experts, told the country that the $700 billion would be spent otherwise, and as they committed some $8 trillion to somehow shore up the rest of the economy, the arguments continued to lie in the position of those making them, combined with the clamor of those who would benefit directly from the government's outlays. These managers of trillions proved competent by definition—but only by that.

The confluence of political agendas with the attempt to describe political choices as scientific rather than political, and the attempt to delegitimize opponents as out of step with science, is clear in the 2005 book by journalist Chris Mooney, *The Republican War on Science.* Typically, Mooney disclaims substantive scientific judgment and claims *only* the capacity and right to discern the *"credibility"* of rival scientists and their claims. Note well, however, that propositions or persons are credible—that is, worth believing—only to the extent that they are correct substantively. Arguments such as Mooney's, Paulson's, Pelosi's, and Gore's most certainly aim to convince citizens about certain substantive propositions, but—and this is key—*they do so indirectly, by pretending that they find certain propositions credible and others not.* Credible are the ones of which they approve in the places of which they approve: the government bureaucracies or universities. Because of their authoritative provenance, they argue, their judgments need not refute the opposition's arguments, or even refer to their substance. Since science—meaning the Establishment—is supposed to have settled the arguments intellectually, its public partisans need only heap social contempt on the outsiders.

Mooney writes that because "American democracy . . . relies heavily on scientific technical expertise to function [public officials] need to rely on the best scientific knowledge available and proceed on the basis of that knowledge to find solutions,"[19] but that modern Republicans have put themselves "in stark contrast with both scientific information and dispassionate, expert analysis in general." The Republicans, he writes, are caught in the confluence of corporate interests and conservative ideology, primarily religion. Hence, Republicans have "skewed science" on every important question of the day, from stem-cell research to "global warming, mercury pollution, condom effectiveness, the alleged health risks of abortion, and much else."[20] They have "cherry picked" facts and, most ominously, even cited scientists to back them up. Mooney worries: "If the American people come to believe they can find a scientist willing to say anything, they will grow increasingly disillusioned with science itself."[21]

That worry is serious. Let us be clear about it. Convincing people that public affairs—from what you may teach your children, to what taxes you should pay, to whether all should use condoms—must be decided by the "scientific" pronouncements of members of a certain class challenges the Aristotelian-American concept of popular government all too directly. To succeed, any attempt to impose things so contrary to American life must confront two political hurdles as well as a fundamental feature of human nature itself.

First, since the partisans of rule by scientific management eschew arguments on the substance of the things they want and rely instead on the cachet of the scientists whose mere servants they pretend to be, their success depends on maintaining a pretense of substantive neutrality on the issues—the pretense that if "science" were to pronounce itself in the other direction, they would follow with the same alacrity. But this position is impossible to maintain against the massive evidence that those who hawk certain kinds of social or environmental policies in the name of science are partisans of those policies, and that these policies are the preference of a particular sociopolitical class.

Second, it is inherently difficult for anyone who fancies himself a citizen to hear from another that he is not qualified to disagree with a judgment said to be scientific. Naturally, he will ask: If I as a layman don't know enough to disagree, what does that other layman know that qualifies him to agree? Could it be that his appeal to science is just another way of telling me to shut up because he knows better, and that he is justifying his view by pointing to his friends in high places?

Perhaps most incident to citizenship is the substance of the most important claims made on behalf of science. The central one, of course, is about the nature of humanity. On December 20, 2005, deciding the case of *Kitzmiller v. Dover School District,* Federal District Court Judge James Jones prohibited the Dover, Pennsylvania, schools from teaching the *possibility* that human beings are the result not of chance but of "intelligent design." To partisan applause, he ruled that science had shown, proved, that all life, including human life, is the result of chance, that it is meaningless, that entertaining the possibility of the opposite is religion, and that doing so in a public school amounts to the "establishment of religion," and hence is prohibited by the First Amendment. Leave aside the absurdity of maintaining that the authors of the U.S. Constitution entertained any part of this reasoning. Consider first: Nobody really *knows* how life, particularly human life, came about (cf. the legal meaning of the word "knowledge"). Moreover, anyone who intimates that Charles Darwin's *The Origin of the Species* is science knows neither that book nor science. But second and more to the point, any polity in which some impose upon others as *official truth* the proposition that human life is meaningless—a nihilism that is unprovable and counterintuitive—is as hostile to science as it is to citizenship.

Now, neither Judge Jones nor Chris Mooney, any more than Nancy Pelosi or Al Gore, or Henry Paulson, never mind C. P. Snow, would see their assertion of science against their political opponents as any restriction of citizenship. Nor would it be such, were citizenship to consist of obeying impartial administrators. But insofar as citizenship implies equal right to weigh upon public policy, privileging any class or party means disenfranchising another. Mooney is almost as candid as C. P. Snow is (and more so than Gore and Pelosi) that science serves the predilections of the academic and governmental class with which he identifies. Judge Jones adamantly professed his nonpartisan disinterestedness—as well he might have, since disobeying his ruling carried civil and criminal penalties. But the denial of partisan interest is absurd. The partisans of scientific administration merely confuse their preferences with science. The preferences on which the administrative state runs flows from founts—universities and government— that have been dominated by self-described progressives for most of a century. It would be strange were this pretend science not partisan. Nor is it strange that those who share preferences should privilege themselves and their preferences in public life. Perhaps if what Mooney calls "conservatives" were to dominate these commanding heights of society someday, they might do the same. But the point here is that regardless of which party plays this game, it is a game that all can play—to the detriment of citizenship.

CIVILITY REAL AND FAUX

We know that only in a minority of regimes can large numbers of people take part in public affairs on the basis of equality, and that in most regimes, order and the defense thereof result mainly from compulsion. Nevertheless, travelers and readers of history are struck by the near universal existence of at least some patriotism along with some order just about everywhere. Thus, while keeping in mind the distinction between citizens and subjects, it is important to draw still another distinction—between the patriotism and order that arise from the citizens' common ownership of the regime, and that which comes from the subjects' adherence to some of the regime's goals— which usually include its survival against enemies, foreign and domestic.

In modern times, nationalism has most often masked the absence of citizenship. Recall that while the French Revolution failed to recreate the pre-Christian communities of ancient Greece and Rome,[22] it did succeed in raising consciousness of national differences to levels unprecedented since the Dark Ages. And no doubt the lively sense of patriotism they worked so hard to build helped the regime to draft and discipline its armies as well as to compel its brand of civil order. But that is just the point. Despite their talk of the natural rights of man and of society's corporations, the French revolutionaries sought to bend towns, churches, professional associations, and the schools they built to the service of the state—or to kill them. Alexis de Tocqueville's practical point in *Democracy in America* was to disabuse his French countrymen of any illusions that the revolution had turned them into citizens. By describing the genuine American article, he showed Frenchmen that their patriotic enthusiasm did not in the least affect their status as subjects of an administrative state.

Between the French Revolution and World War I, the European regimes that more or less aped France succeeded brilliantly in identifying themselves with the nation. By the end of the nineteenth century, the peoples of Europe had bound themselves emotionally and unconditionally to their regimes. The ties were so strong that even the Socialist parties of Germany and Austria, for all their antimonarchist talk, never dared to try to break their members' solid habits of civil obedience. When the war came, predictions of resistance to the draft proved unfounded. In August 1914, resistance averaged 1.5 percent throughout Europe.[23] Like everybody else, the Socialists marched into the meat grinder with merry patriotic hearts—just because the order to do so had come down from the top. The spirit of self-sacrifice was over-abundant. By and large, the European regimes of the nineteenth century were beloved. For the most part, they were the most law-abiding regimes of all time—the "state of law" having become something of an object of worship in Germany, more or less imitated elsewhere. And yet the fact that these Europeans loved the machines in which they were cogs did not make them any less cogs. It masked the fact that they had long since lost the habits of self-starting citizens. When the Great War's stupidity discredited nationalism, the European regimes were left to rule masses of mere claimants.

The postwar Fascist movement was an attempt to resurrect the prewar regimes by multiplying the dose of nationalism. Mussolini was the last Jacobin. By militarizing society's rituals (there were "wars" on crime and on low productivity as well as on mosquitoes), by focusing the people's attention on enemies foreign and domestic, by radically expanding the welfare system to secure the "home front"—and not incidentally, by increasing the size and brutality of the state's administrative apparatus—the Fascists managed to put some order into political processes that had been degenerating into chaos. Thus, Mussolini's Italy—and even Hitler's Germany until the outbreak of war—gave the impression of order, purposeful energy, and widespread patriotism. But these regimes had no citizens. Mussolini's Fascists abandoned him as soon as it became profitable to do so, while the German people, having been seduced by the Nazis until 1939, thereafter submitted to ever-more-violent rape. Civic enthusiasm was absent.

After World War II, too many Europeans failed to see that the nationalist pageantry with which Third World leaders were surrounding themselves was a bad copy of fascism. Some Europeans, aghast at the increasing lack of civic commitment in their own sleepy welfare states, were tempted to envy what seemed to be the civic vitality of the Third World. The most renowned European political scientist of the twentieth century's second half, Sir Ralf Dahrendorf, even envied the patently fraudulent civic vitality that East Germany had forced upon a population held captive behind the Berlin Wall.[24] True, Third World regimes have little trouble whipping up crowds and raising armies. But, whereas citizenship is full partnership in a regime, the masses of the Third World are partners only in being exploited and manipulated into ethnic hate. At least in the Communist world ordinary people learned to hate communism.

THE CHINAS

Despite the vast differences between Chinese and Russian cultures, the Communist regime in the People's Republic of China fostered human habits somewhat similar to those produced by Communist rule in Russia, before returning to the old path of oriental despotism. By contrast, the two non-Communist Chinese states, Taiwan and Singapore, have regimes very different from Communist China's, and promoted different human qualities.

The People's Republic

Even more than the Soviets, the Chinese Communists tried to destroy the moral as well as the material basis of society. After killing landowners and forcing peasants out of their family hovels into the sex-segregated barracks of agricultural communes, they lectured the inmates about the evils of Confucian ethics while trying to inculcate a new morality based on devotion to the state. During Mao Tse-tung's time, the public—especially the young—was exhorted to emulate Liu Weuxue, a young man who reported a landlord who had stolen from his former field what were now the people's peppers. In the 1990s equivalent, schoolchildren were forced to buy books about Lai Ming, a boy who reported on two of his classmates who had struck up a romance before the age permitted by the state.[25]

Like the Russians, the Chinese had been the subjects of empires that had toyed with lives and property. But in China, unlike in Russia, emperors had not claimed to own all the land, and the Chinese Confucian tradition had been an even stronger support than Eastern Orthodox Christianity for the idea that righteousness and political power are not identical. True, the Confucian tradition has little to say to individuals except that they should conform perfectly to a virtuous social order. But Confucian demands on the virtue of rulers are so exacting that those who claimed that any given emperor had lost the "mandate of heaven" found it little more difficult to make their case than those who claimed the mandate. Moreover, the counsels of perfection that Confucius extended to individuals tend to make them almost as morally self-possessed, almost as likely to stand aside from government and criticize it, as Christians or Platonists. And although China had been ruled by a centralized empire, its very vastness also gave it some experience of local autonomy. In short, then, although China was not accustomed to living under the rule of law and did not have social institutions (other than the family) independent of rulers, it was not wholly bereft of bases on which law and civil society might have arisen. Communist rule, then, was even more disruptive of Chinese ways than it had been of Russian ways.

The effect of absolute power on those Chinese who exercised it was roughly the same as the effect on their Russian counterparts. Mao Tse-tung's physician revealed that Mao's taste for young girls was as insatiable as his thirst for power and typical of that of Chinese emperors.[26] Biographies of other top Communists stress the groveling and betrayals that they had to practice on one another to survive. Change the proper names, and Chinese Communist stories would be interchangeable with Soviet ones. The story of Kang Sheng, for example, could easily be a composite of the biographies of the most murderous chiefs of the Soviet KGB.[27] The method of governing in Communist China was—and remains—what Kenneth Lieberthal has called "fragmented authoritarianism,"[28] the familiar Soviet pattern in Brezhnev's time where bureaucrats are responsible both to the chain of command leading to central Party headquarters and to the local network of interests. In twenty-first-century China, the bureaucrats form informal networks through which they seek their personal interests and those of their localities while building their case for advancement in the central bureaucracy. Impress your superiors from Wuwei or Tongliao, and your next assignment may be in Lahzhou, and then someday maybe in Beijing. But in China, as in the Soviet Union, that means spending money and producing things primarily for show. Bureaucratic efficiency is the enemy of all efficiencies. Moreover, insofar as an official really does make his garden flourish, he becomes rooted in it, and dangerously independent of his superiors. This problem is as pervasive in China's latest dynasty as it was in previous ones.

The effects on those who must put up with a government just as lawless as the Soviet Union's but occasionally more intrusive—the enforcement of the government's one-child policy, as we will see (in Chapter 7), marks a new low in the history of tyranny—may have been best described by Chinese visitors to the mainland from Taiwan. They noted that mainlanders work only when the boss is looking, that officials live well and demand bribes from the poor, that anything, including admission to schools, may be had for a bribe, and that "lack of sincerity," cheating, and extortion are prevalent. They noted that there has been a general decline in traditional Chinese virtues.[29] It takes no special sophistication for a traveler to see that everything is for sale, from immunity for oneself to the ruin of one's enemies.

And yet the very first thing that struck me when I visited China in 2007 was that the imperial bureaucracy, currently called the Communist Party, was obeyed habitually regardless of the content of its orders. No contrast could be greater than the *generic* respect, empty of substance, paid to Mao Tse-tung's memory. Though his successors changed nearly all his policies, they remain his heirs and govern through the Party bureaucracy that he established. For rulers and ruled alike, the substance of policies seems to be much less important than the fact that the dynasty and its organ continue to function. Again, this seems to be the continuation of millennial Chinese history.

But modern China's economic vitality is new, and its effect on civil and political life is unknowable. Though corruption is rife, much advancement in the society and economy, if not in government, now depends on exams and performance. This has fostered a set of expectations about the rule of law that the authorities defy at their peril. Moreover, the very scale of more or less free economic activity requires habitual adherence to rules. And as the Soviet Union found out, officials who sink roots in local communities may value their comfort and those roots above loyalty to the center. Becoming the world's center of manufacturing has meant that hundreds of millions of Chinese have left their villages for cities and factories. To what extent and on what basis the regime will secure their obedience is open to question. No doubt, the People's Republic of China can make soldiers out of such human material—indeed, such deracinated people may be recruited by any number of military factions within the Chinese regime. And since the regime itself has no purpose other than the competitive enrichment of its members, there is every reason to believe that persons so habituated will hasten the recurrence of the Chinese cycle of civil war. The very concept of citizenship, however, clashes with Chinese reality.

Taiwan

The Nationalist regime on Taiwan differs from the mainland Communist regime not so much in the degree of brutality involved in its founding[30] as in its purpose and organization and therefore the habits it fostered. Chiang Kai-shek shaped the Nationalist regime according to the ideas of Sun Yat-sen, who founded the Nationalist Party, and according to the bitter experiences of the 1936–1949 civil war, which Chiang had lost. Sun had tried to blend the Confucian tradition, Western political philosophy, and Christianity.[31] That syncretic blend's intellectual incoherence is less important than the fact that Sun's successors wanted to preserve the Confucian way of life and to somehow graft Western, liberal politics onto it. Also, Chiang knew he had lost the civil war in large part because his regime had been captured, paralyzed, and betrayed by interest groups in the cities and countryside that sold out the regime. So, reason and necessity pushed him to found his regime on Taiwan in a way that would crush independent centers of power, fuse Confucianism with Western ways, discourage the rise of corruption, and lay the bases for broad support, freely given.

Chiang's first constitutional act, like Mao's, was the expropriation of large estates. But Chiang performed this revolutionary act for a conservative purpose. That unlawful act could become the foundation of law because, like Machiavelli's model prince, Chiang's most injurious act was his first, his biggest, and nearly his last. He divided lands among peasant farmers, to whom he gave *full title,* while to the former owners he gave bond payments that made them stakeholders in Taiwan's budding industrial economy. Only time, however, could redeem Chiang's promise to respect property rights scrupulously and to depoliticize the economy. But that respect eventually became the foundation of the rule of law on Taiwan. The free, honest market in agriculture immediately provided a measure of prosperity for the native Taiwanese, and that, in turn, foreclosed serious opposition. Since the regime was not at war with the population or with its customs, it raised no barriers to upward mobility—including involvement in the ruling party and, eventually, in the free opposition that the party promised from the beginning. The government decided to own and operate primary industries so that it could ensure that the economy met its military needs without having to develop corrupting links to private wealth. The private industry it encouraged would be small: "In essence the decision to 'go small' was the industrial equivalent of land reform. Both policies preempted the rise of powerful interest groups."[32]

The effective constitution of Taiwan, then, presupposes the Confucian ideal of the autonomous and virtuous individual in harmony with the community; the Chinese tradition of large, hardworking, patriarchal families that seek (and in Taiwan have found) a minimum of interference with their affairs; and the consciousness that the country has to "make it" if it is to withstand the threat from its huge neighbor. These are not the Western foundations of the rule of law. The Taiwanese regime owes nothing to any idea of human equality, because Confucianism both ancient and modern is a culture of different duties for different stations in life rather than an exegesis of a nature common to all humans. Still, the rulers of Taiwan chose from the beginning to institute equal treatment by law regarding economic matters. When habits of economic equality had taken root, they chose to follow their logic to equal treatment regarding political matters as well. Yet the notion that fathers and sons should have equal standing before the law in social matters would be regarded as totally subversive, if anyone thought of it.

Although Taiwan calls itself the Republic of China, Chinese culture does not contain the idea of a republic, much less Montesquieu's notion that the chief political requirement of republics is a virtuous population. Nevertheless, the Confucian tradition knows even better than the Western that virtue is essential to all political life. Hence, it fears freedom, above all because of its often corrosive effects on virtue. Since Taiwan has been completely free for only some two decades, it is difficult to tell whether or to what extent freedom is undermining the good habits that undergird its constitution. The divorce rate, though not high by Western standards, has doubled since 1980 (thus becoming the highest in Asia) and alarms the Taiwanese.[33] Also, since both politics and economics on Taiwan are free, they have begun to mix all too freely. The newspapers are full of stories about the purchase of votes, and the rising price of influence indicates that its value must be rising, too. Finally, no Confucian composure could fail to be shaken by the indecorous sight of legislators fistfighting on the floor of Taiwan's National Assembly. Taiwan is the first Chinese republic. But the diseases of violent faction and redistributive economics can kill Taiwan's adherence to the rule of law just as surely as in any other republic anywhere.

Singapore

Singapore's rulers argue precisely that their suppression of political freedom is the precondition for the maintenance of the rule of law and, therefore, of all other good things. The People's Action Party, founded by then Chief Minister Lee Kwan Yew, and led by his son Lee Hsien Loong, uses the powers of the state, including such machinations as lawsuits against political opponents tried before biased judges, and the government's official influence over business, to effectively shut out the opposition. Anyone else is treated with scrupulous fairness under laws that make perfect sense in terms of both Confucianism and capitalism. Civil society exists by sufferance. Lee Kwan Yew, now Minister Mentor, his family, and the ruling party's main functionaries are paid very well, but they are not the richest men in the country, and no one has charged them with using their power to skim the profits of business. Machiavelli would have been surprised at the regime's success in this very difficult feat, but not at the results of its having done so. The residents of Singapore consent to be governed because they are doing fine and have few complaints besides the high cost of the good life.[34]

But although they are satisfied as consumers of government, they have no experience of citizenship. Lee may be right that Taiwan's freedom is destroying the virtues needed to maintain the rule of law and the good life.[35] It is quite another thing for him to argue that those virtues are now safe in Singapore. Since he, their guardian, is someone Confucius might well have approved of, they are safe enough with him. When he dies, they will be in the hands either of his heirs, whose virtue is anyone's guess, or of the Singaporeans, whose expertise as consumers of mostly lawful government should not be confused with any capacity to produce it.

Does citizenship mean reliable reception of government services, or does it mean self-government? Throughout the twentieth century, governments have justified their power by claiming to deliver more and better services. Some deliver better than others. But it seems that governments run as providers of services train those who live under them to be subjects rather than citizens.

MEXICO

When we draw sharp lines between modern Western democracies and less democratic modern regimes, we are too kind to ourselves. To a greater or lesser extent, all modern regimes promote themselves as nonpolitical administrators of the only reasonable agenda: the assurance of ever-improving economic circumstances in a socially liberal, scientifically driven, secular society.[36] Some regimes take more than others, and some preside over more orderly material well-being than others. Regardless of performance, however, modern regimes foster among those who live under them similar habits of social and political atrophy.

The Mexican people's habitual acquiescence to authority is rooted in the ways of the pre-Columbian Aztec and Mayan subjects, who became the servants of Spanish conquerors. One can notice the difference in the *degree* of social deference between most of Mexico, where this legacy is strong, and the northern deserts, where Spanish settlers found no one to enslave and had to work for themselves. Mexico does not lack laws. But enforcement is a commodity to be bought and sold.[37] Bureaucrats get along fine with the businesses they regulate because they get paid off, as do their superiors. The judges decide on the basis of payment and pressures on either side of the case, and the police are in business for themselves like everybody else. Just like in Europe, one must get at the enforcers of regulations through the "right," meaning extralegal, channels, or through status, which implies access to such channels. However, in Mexico the regime's currency, the *mordida* (literally, "the bite"), is monetary rather than social.[38] In Mexico, the cash bribe enables an unconnected man to purchase influence as well as a well-connected one. Cash is easier to get than status. If anything, in Mexico the possibility of citizenship is less remote than in Europe, because the Mexican people only act as if they believed in the system. In fact almost no Mexicans believe in technocracy, whereas many Europeans do, even a few Italians.

The dictator José de la Cruz Porfirio Díaz (1877–1911) began the practice of bolstering his government's prestige by claiming that he had put it in the hands of *los científicos,* the scientists (that is, the economists), who were disinterested and knew best how to lift the country out of poverty. Though this was thin cover for kleptocracy, it was very much in line with the European Progressive movement of which he fancied himself a member. The several factions that overthrew him fought the revolution that ended in the presidency of Lázaro Cárdenas in 1934 and coalesced into the Institutional Revolutionary Party (PRI). Just as kleptocratic as its forebears, the PRI claimed to have a sure-fire recipe for prosperity that was just as *scientific:* the nationalization of petroleum and other basic industries and the distribution of land to peasants (without title). The government would administer the oil and the land. The Party and thus the regime formed an alliance between those who controlled the labor movement, based mainly in the nationalized sector; those who ran the government agency that controlled the peasants; and the major industrialists. Opposition parties were either bought off or cheated in the vote counts.[39] Meanwhile, the PRI politicians began to pass themselves off as more scientific than *los científicos.* After all, they were the ones who decided who was scientific and who was not. Just like elsewhere.

In both Mexico and modern Europe, the only theoretical question in public life is who has the formula for general prosperity, while the only practical question for individuals is how to make the connections needed to ensure the maximum flow of favor. Until 2000, elections mattered not at all in Mexico because the one and only ruling party had co-opted society's lead-ing interests (including the opposition parties, to a considerable extent) and endowed the regime as a whole with monopoly power. When Vicente Fox won the presidency for the National Action Party (PAN) in 2000 and was followed by Felipe Calderon, another *PANista,* the monopoly became an oligopoly, just like in Europe. But Mexico's parties differ from one another more than Europe's parties do: Whereas PAN, based in the north, calls for U.S. style governance, and the Mexico City–based PRI harkens back to the old days, the Democratic Revolutionary Party (PRD), based in the south, talks of just that: revolution in the Third World sense. Hence the weight of the voters' choice in presidential elections is substantially greater in Mex-ico than in Europe.[40]

Mexico is squeezed between its people's bitter experiences and their im-ages of America. Especially in the north, the label "U.S." is the cachet of quality, of things that are as they should be. This is evident in tastes for food as well as sports—American football rivals soccer—and above all in groom-ing and behavior. Posters on the northbound lanes of the highways, placed by the governments of northern states, show happy young people who look like Americans, implying that the closer you get to the United States, the more you become just like them. Because this feeling is characteristic of northerners in general and of the middle class in particular, because it is very different from the attitudes that animate the parties based in Mexico's cen-ter (the PRI) and south (the PRD), it is very much a bone of contention. Mexico then is a case in which ordinary voters, though bereft of citizenship, do determine their country's general orientation simply by voting once every six years.

ITALY

The Italian people have no such power. Italy's regime is a variant of a type found from Crete to the shores of the Arctic. But while the differences be-tween Italians and Swedes are as great as those between Europeans and Mex-icans, and each regime came to be via peculiar historical paths, all share common features: The relationship between parties and interest groups is more important than that between voters and parliaments; local government is nearly powerless; the state has colonized society; and the only power—and money can't usually buy it—is connection with those who decide.

Although the parties that run twenty-first-century Italy bear names different from those of the post–World War II period, they run a system whose foundations were laid in the 1920s and 1930s under fascism and nourished in the postwar period when the victorious Allies distributed the Fascists' organs of control for the economy and society among a bevy of parties. Though the Communists and their Socialist allies lost the 1948 elections decisively to Christian Democrats, Liberals, Social Democrats, and Republicans, the winners subsequently reorganized themselves along Fascist-Communist lines—instituting general secretaries, central committees, and so on, and basing their power on patronage. Since then, Italian politics has consisted of competition to colonize the public and private sector with patronage posts.

The case of the Christian Democrats stands out because they chose specifically to rely ever less on independent organizations of Catholic laymen, as little as possible on the variable opinion of voters, and ever more on networks of recipients of patronage they could control. They did this because they believed—like the Communists and Fascists—that politics is about taking away from enemies to give to friends, and that only support that is bought and paid for can be relied upon. To disenfranchise voters even further, they developed the habit of cooperating with the opposition, both in or out of government, in a practice called *consociativismo,* loosely translated as "bipartisanship." As a result, voters got the same result no matter how they voted. Citizens who wanted favors could work through any party—Catholic or Communist. But anyone who wanted impartial treatment had nowhere to go. The result has been six decades of economic, political, and moral corruption.

But Italy is not unique. In Sweden, which never experienced fascism, the Social Democratic Party and its popular organizations loom even larger over economy, society, and Parliament than all the Italian parties combined do in Italy. The tradition of nonconfrontation, of effacing differences among leaders, is much stronger in Sweden than in Italy. And the basis of the Italian regime's legitimacy, no less than the basis of legitimacy of the Swedish, German, or French regimes, is the assumption that government knows what produces security, prosperity, and fairness, and that it can deliver them. Italians, however, have fewer illusions than the Swedish, Germans, or French.

The modern Italian political agenda has consisted of redistribution—wholesale among the parties, retail among their adherents. On the wholesale level, formal and informal additions to the governing coalition are "paid for" by grants of exclusive rights to patronage. Thus, the Socialists' payment for supporting the government in 1963 began with the right to staff the electric power industry. However, it certainly did not end there. The first installment of the payment for Communist support in 1974 was the addition of a third channel to the state TV network, both for the Communists' use as a propaganda tool and as a fount of patronage. Below the highest level, each party's "mass organization" lobbies for places and for control of the countless contracts that the state issues for everything from moviemaking to welfare.

Between 1990 and 1993, a loophole in the constitution allowed Antonio Cossiga, president of the republic, and Mario Segni, son of a former president, to place before the Italian electorate a referendum on a portion of the Proportional Representation electoral law that secured the parties' oligopoly. The voters' near unanimous expression of disgust changed the formalities of the system. All the major parties either died (Christian Democrats and Socialists) or morphed by splitting and changing their names (the Communists). A new electoral law at least formally linked governance to elections. And in fact, elections since then have been between broad coalitions of the Left and the Right. But that is largely illusion. On any given day in 2010, as in 1950, the headlines in the press will be about interparty and intraparty bargaining over who is to be appointed to what post in what regulatory agency or "parastate" body. Italy, like Sweden, is thus not run by laws interpreted by courts, but rather by administrative acts of officials who work in agencies that owe nothing to Parliament and who are selected by the parties in the ruling coalition. This is the law, from Crete to North Cape.

In the modern administrative state, then, impartial law is a bother. Whereas law presumes the impartial settlement of contrasting interests through adversarial proceedings and reference to objective truth, European regimes offer cooperative striving for consensus and comfortable adjustment. Chronicling even a fraction of the jobs, contracts, sinecures, licenses, school admissions, exemptions, and exactions retailed through political patronage in Italy alone, let alone all of Europe, would be an immense task, and the results would fill a library. Losing a job, contract, or benefit because of shifting powers above carries no onus—but the inability to land on one's feet denotes shameful impotence. The only fatherland to which one can repair is one's own faction, and the only right in property or in law is the mutual obligation of favors and loyalties.

Suffused as it is by the Italians' penchant for pleasant living and soft cynicism, Italy's way of life is arguably more tolerable than that of other Europeans. But the mildly competitive hedonism of contemporary Europe never generated its own military defense. It is difficult to imagine Europeans nowadays offering their lives for their country. Contemporary Europe's way of life has been possible only because it was protected by the United States.

THE UNMAKING OF CITIZENSHIP

Socrates obeyed the laws of Athens unto death because he believed that the duty of citizenship was worth dying for, even though he sought virtue higher than the kind that came from citizenship. This chapter has set forth ideas about what it takes to be a citizen in several different regimes, and what civic qualities several kinds of regimes engender. In the end, the possibility of citizenship depends on the presence of the habits of virtue and freedom that produce the rule of law. However, citizenship also requires the possibility of ruling and being ruled in turn, of sharing decisions big and small. At best, modern regimes engender few of the habits of citizenship.

Law is restraint, and the rule of law is the acceptance of restraint by those who could most easily not accept it. But law requires that this self-restraint be regular and predictable. Most regimes are clusters of discretionary powers and are not suffused with ideas that logically lead people to limit their own discretion. Why should there be limits on the power to do good? Nothing would prevent the Swiss, for example, from using their powers of referendum to sweep away their local prerogatives as mere obstacles to progress. They do not do this, though, because they have grown accustomed to acting as if they did not have the right to do it even if they wanted to. One virtuous habit protects another. Similarly, the authors of the U.S. Constitution were keenly aware that they had erected mere "parchment barriers" against bad popular government. George Washington dedicated his First Inaugural Address to the "truth more thoroughly established than [any] that there exists in the economy and course of nature an indissoluble union between virtue and happiness."[41] Jefferson, in his First Inaugural Address, invoked the principles of natural law that had justified America's struggle for independence to establish "this sacred principle, that though the will of the majority is in all cases to prevail, that will to be rightful must be reasonable, that the minority possess their equal rights which equal law must protect, and to violate must be oppression."[42] Abraham Lincoln repeated that anyone who had the power to make a free man out of a slave would also have the power to make a slave out of a free man. Indeed, his argument against

Stephen Douglas's popular notion that "popular sovereignty" should decide whether there should be slavery in the territories or not was that the power to decide such things implies that some men are to others as gods, while others are as animals. Therefore, for the rule of law to exist, not even *vox populi* may be confused with *vox Dei*. Alas, in many modern regimes, the most authoritative voice is that of an official, or of a potentate of an organization "close" to a ruling party who does whatever he can get away with.

In most of the world, Plato's Thrasymachus rules, and such citizenship and civil society as exist do so by sufferance.

7

FAMILY

The disciples said to him, "If this is the law of
a man with his wife, it is not expedient to marry."
—MATTHEW 19:10

Each culture is largely defined by the ways in which men and women within it come together to raise children, and each regime defines itself substantially by how it affects those ways. That is not to say that every regime has a "family policy"—the very term is a latter-day Western presumption of government power. Seldom do laws place intolerable burdens on families, and never can laws make families. But every regime affects families by making the conditions in which they live. In our time, the passions that surround the relationship between government and families has so obscured the relationship that our discussion must begin by considering what a family is and what it is not.

FAMILY AND NATURE

Not all arrangements for procreation, never mind for intimacy, can properly be called families. Aristotle noted that the barbarians of his time treated women as slaves,[1] using them for the heaviest, meanest tasks as well as for sexual satisfaction. Children were simply another product that the strong got from the weak. But husbands and wives, Aristotle wrote, are natural partners in the household—equally rational beings who adjust their particular contributions to the common good through mutual persuasion.[2] Their relationship is political. Early Americans also noted that the American Indians used their women like "mules." Why? Thomas Jefferson argued that the Indians did not know the natural law. He wrote: "Were we in equal barbarism . . . our females would be equal drudges."[3] When Western travelers applied the term "wives" to the multiple women taken by African or Asian potentates, they did so for lack of a handier term to describe arrangements that were based on force, that were revocable at will, and that involved obligation on one side only—or that, at most, were deals between families that exchanged women for goods.

Such arrangements do not involve husbands, wives, and families, properly speaking. They are closer to the practices of four-footed herbivores, among which the strongest males gather the biggest herds of females. The Muslim polygamous unions, however (like polygamy under the law of Moses), have an element of family about them because these unions are indeed marriages—though not in the Aristotelian sense—that produce families. They are entered into, conducted, and broken by law, however imperfect. Some laws, though, such as the customary requirement in Hinduism that widows be burned alive on their husband's funeral pyre, cannot naturally coexist with the notion of family. The natural notion of family, of course, is the basis on which the U.S. Supreme Court declared that the practice of polygamy by Mormons in the state of Utah mocked the very basis of family, namely, the full reciprocal commitment on the part of one husband and one wife.[4]

In the particular case of Mormon polygamy, the Court's conclusion went beyond its logic, because the Mormon polygamist husband's allegiance is supposed to be to all wives equally, and Mormon law binds all through eternal duties. The Court, however, was responding to the demand by the vast majority of America's husbands and wives to define family strictly by the fullest realization of the natural relationship between men and women, which can only be based on "one to a customer." In the nineteenth century, governments did not imagine the currently fashionable redefinition of family to include any consensual living arrangements, much less were they tempted to entertain any notion that the family might be the root of all social evils.

The very notion of defining or redefining families is a thinly disguised argument for the proposition that the natural family is no better than any other human arrangement, and may be the worst of the lot. Thus, practitioners of what were once called "deviant" lifestyles want to pin the family label on relations between homosexuals less because they think there is little difference between homosexual and heterosexual relationships than because they want for homosexual couples whatever deference natural families normally receive. Yet this desire cannot be fulfilled for logical as well as practical reasons. If families are not natural and permanent unions of one man, one woman, and their children, in addition to others related by blood and marriage, they are the products of infinitely variable choices. And if that were the case, no one could deny the label "family" to sometime unions of one man with many women, of one woman with many men, of many men with many men, and so on. Why deny it to any combination of bisexuals, pedophiles, and necrophiliacs or to practitioners of sex with other species or with one's own offspring? If it were so, what deference would it deserve?

Yes, in practice, marriage is a creature of positive law: It is as the relevant local statute defines it. Yet to the extent that the label "family" is restricted to some living arrangements and not others, the criterion for the restriction must be defensible on the basis of nature rather than of what anyone may happen to want. The acceptance of nature as the criterion, however, drives the argument back to one man and one woman, united to reproduce and raise children.

Fashion in the most influential Western intellectual circles has long dictated that mankind is composed of discrete individuals whose relations are purely consensual, and that these relationships are called "families" when they involve housing and sex. Note, however, that under this view, while each individual is independent of every other, all individuals must rely on the state alone to resolve disputes among themselves or even to know what is disputable. To the extent that individuals' relations with their cohabitants— their "families"—are conventional, contingent rather than natural, each individual's relations with the state must be noncontingent. That is because since within contingent relationships there are always disputes about who is to do what, the state from time to time must delegate authority to some over others and call it family policy. This line of reasoning follows inexorably from the twin pillars of modern social thought: autonomous individuals and omnicompetent governments. However, this way of thinking about families hardly resonates beyond contemporary intellectual circles.

Ancient barbarians and American Indians gone the way of the buffalo would shake their heads at it for their own reasons, as surely as would Aristotle, Jefferson, or a typical housewife in Omaha.

Modern social thought, however, does not view all freely chosen living arrangements with equanimity. Its third pillar is fierce hostility to natural families. This was never more succinctly stated than in the pages of *Time* magazine by Barbara Ehrenreich, who wrote that the family—and she hastened to specify *"even the ostensibly 'functional,'* non-violent family"—"can be a nest of pathology and a cradle of gruesome violence." For women and children, claims Ehrenreich, "home is statistically speaking, the most dangerous place to be." A husband is a woman's worst enemy, and "for every child . . . who is killed by a deranged criminal on parole, dozens are abused and murdered by their own relatives."

This is highly misleading. It is a truism that victims and criminals are likely to be close to one another, since all crimes of violence occur not at random but proceed primarily from acquaintance. But the batterers of women are typically not husbands. Rather, they are "boyfriends" or other kinds of live-in and transient intimates in relationships that were themselves considered crimes until recent decades when views like Ehrenreich's became dominant in Western regimes. Calling such living arrangements "families" and then imputing violence to families is an example of the chutzpah that passes for intellectual integrity nowadays.

Ehrenreich makes clear the reason why she and the Establishment whose views she represents so hate families: "The family, with its deep, impacted tensions and longings[,] can hardly be the foundation of everything else. In fact, many families could use a lot more outside interference in the form of counseling and policing."[5] In other words, the very idea of relationships presumed to be natural is very bad, both because it restricts individual choice and *perhaps, above all, because it presumes itself to be privileged against the state.* Any claim of independence from the state is deeply subversive of modern regimes. The state should foster just about any other kind of living arrangement. The state, the power she supposes supreme, is the focus of her affections.

Hence, states should start improving upon the natural family by freeing people from it. In 1970, Gloria Steinem laid out the basis of a feminism that became a goal for many influential Americans: the overcoming of specifically male and female functions through the power of government. She looked forward to the day when courts would assign to wives (not divorcées) a percentage of their husbands' income, and when government would mandate that housing complexes be designed to force people out of traditional patterns. This line of argument is a crude reprise of Friedrich Engels's *The Origins of the Family, Private Property and the State,* which starts from the premise that each and every individual's interest is naturally opposed to every other's, and proceeds to overturn the primordial law of economics, namely that the division of labor of which marriage is the prototype is the foundation of human prosperity. Contemporary sophisticates dumbly echo the old Marxist saw: Come the revolution, all peculiar relationships to production will fade away—the family first.

However, families are defined neither by governmental nor by private choice, but rather by the biological relations between parents and children, who are produced by natural intercourse between men and women who have undergone a process of "naturalization" into one another called marriage. Marriage is indeed a matter of choice. But it is a choice that precludes all such subsequent choices. Indeed, the process by which women leave their parents' homes for new ones has always had the solemn quality of an adoption or a change of allegiance. In ancient Greece and Rome, it involved the renunciation of one set of gods and ancestors to accept another.[6] Being a son or daughter or a father or mother is a fact of nature, not a matter of choice. Marriage is the supposition that husband and wife become related as if by nature. The proper behavior of sons to fathers, of husbands to wives, and so on has been the stuff of the world's philosophy and literature.[7] But until our own time, few who have written on these matters imagined they were doing other than explaining what already exists in nature.

The whole premise of the modern state, of course, is sovereignty—namely, that nothing is beyond its reach. While some modern regimes have sought to reshape or "redefine" families, others have affected families in the wholehearted pursuit of economic progress without really meaning to. Let us look at how each element of family life can be influenced by regimes and then examine how some exemplar regimes of our time have affected family life.

LAW AND MARRIAGE

Marriage is the mingling of separate bodies and interests. Although either partner may manage the material goods, these are possessed in common. Even to raise the question of each partner's separate material interests is to envisage the dissolution of the marriage. How much more important and less soluble than common property is the sharing of lives, of the only years when we can lay claim to good looks, vigor, hope; the joint bearing of fortune and misfortune; of children who irrevocably belong to both and who concern us from before their birth until our deaths—if not longer. Add to this that being married means living in constant adjustment to another, and it is obvious that to marry is to trade in a life that is one's own for one that is not. *No wonder that people who marry want some assurance beyond the other spouse's private promises that they are not spoiling their lives.* These promises must be public, because both spouses want family, friends, authorities secular and religious, to somehow protect against bigamy, adultery, nonperformance, abandonment. Of course, no third party can guarantee against an unhappy marriage. But the secular difference between marriage and cohabitation is precisely the expectation that to some extent the public will weigh in against whichever partner might be inclined to violate the terms of the deal.

Marriage, therefore, is everywhere a creature of law. But governments just as often affect marriages by not enforcing laws as by enforcing them. The Hindu women who are killed—sometimes by burning—because their families have failed to deliver the proper installment payments on their dowries to their husbands' families are wronged by the government of India, as well as by their assailants, because the government fails to enforce the law banning dowries as legal conditions of marriage that it made, ostensibly to end this practice. In the cities of West Africa, despite widespread protests by women, governments have stopped trying to enforce marriage laws, which has led to an informal system of female-headed households in which men are visitors. By contrast, Saudi authorities have enforced the Islamic law by which a man may take a second (or third and fourth) wife only if he can afford to support all as well as one. Hence, any Saudi woman who marries and finds that her husband downgrades her materially and morally by taking another wife has every reason to blame the king. In practice, even tentative enforcement of this law has pushed Saudi society a bit toward monogamy. By the same token, the institution of no-fault divorce in Western countries has changed the rules to the disadvantage of those who counted on public support to maintain their marriages so long as they abided by its rules. Thus, Western governments have pushed their societies toward West African lifestyles.

Marriage is as important to society at large as it is to married people. The notion that young men are turned from savages into useful citizens by the women they mate goes back to the earliest Sumerian epics and is a constant theme of literature and sociology. Civilization happens when individuals produce more than it takes to sustain them. Persuading anyone to work for anyone but himself is hard. That is why marriage makes civilization by tying a man's sexual satisfaction to his producing for others far more than he needs for himself. Monogamous marriage—the agreement that a man, no matter how powerful, will take no more than one woman—brings social peace and makes political equality possible by ensuring that all will have a chance to mate. Because laws against adultery help to ensure that one's mate will not be taken away, they are the most basic affirmations of social security—a security worth far more than promises today to tax workers tomorrow. By contrast, where law allows multiple wives for those who can afford them, it guarantees that there will be masses of men frustrated physically and marginalized socially—in other words, that there will be trouble. But marriage underpins society most of all by turning young men and women into fathers and mothers—people who practice self-sacrifice every day—who have a stake in social order, who are the likeliest to protect it against enemies foreign and domestic, and who alone can ensure that the next generation will not wreck it.[8]

This is why every regime, sooner or later, tries to bolster marriage, each in its own telling way. Even the Soviet regime that openly mocked it in the 1920s, and largely destroyed the institution of Russian Orthodox marriage, reversed course in the 1930s and tried to give some substance to its own institution of marriage. It did this not because of any homeyness on Stalin's part, but rather because the country's birth rate was collapsing and communally raised children were proving to be unmanageable. The laws of Middle Eastern and Latin countries treat marriage as a financial deal between two families, making sure that the property that each family puts in through gifts or inheritance flows only to the natural heirs of both. Anglo-Saxon laws deal principally with making sure that common property stays that way.

Marriage laws everywhere deal less with marriage itself than with the disposition of children and property in case of separation or divorce. Islamic law shows two contrary faces. By granting wives divorce in cases of their husbands' egregious misconduct, the law acts as protector of the weak, of the innocent, and arguably of marriage itself. By granting divorce at will to men, however, the law acts as an adjunct to the power of the male, whom nature and society have already endowed with greater power, and provides men with an escape hatch from marriage itself. Similarly, before the Irish people voted narrowly in a 1995 referendum to allow divorce, the advocates of a yes vote argued that divorce was an escape hatch for the oppressed of either sex and that it would increase the chances that surviving marriages would be happy, whereas the opponents' poster read, "Hello divorce, good-bye Daddy"—the contention being that men would use the law to escape their obligations to women and children.[9] In other words, laws on divorce depend on the lawmakers' perception of the problem to be ameliorated, as well as on the interest of those who draw advantage from them. In Western countries, the constituency for no-fault divorce consists disproportionately of people possessing what economists call "marketable sexual characteristics"— women in their physical prime and successful middle-aged men.[10] By contrast, older women and ordinary men tend to oppose it. Children, of course, hate divorce viscerally.

The rights and duties of husbands and wives differ from regime to regime. Islamic law is unequivocal about the husband's duty to provide material sustenance and is backed by custom, which requires a man to show a certain level of material security before he will be allowed to marry. This requirement, especially given the declining economies of the Middle East and the difficulties of sexual relations outside of marriage in the Islamic world, has made married status the envy of legions of poor young men, many of whom emigrate to the West. In the West, marriage laws that compelled husbands to support families have been replaced by divorce laws that compel ex-husbands to pay to liquidate their obligations to them. This has rendered divorce attractive to men who can afford to pay, as well as to women who expect the settlement to grant them the material bonuses of marriage while shedding the onus of the man. More important for the long run, men have noticed that while the courts will make them pay for children sired within marriage, they do not hold them responsible for ones they sired informally. So modern divorce laws discourage men from undertaking the responsibilities of marriage at all and undercut the imperative to fulfill any of the responsibilities that flow from it.

The Old Testament law is that sexual intercourse between an unattached man and woman constitutes indissoluble marriage.[11] And indeed, the very definition of society is that, somehow, a man who lies with a woman assumes for her and for any child who might be conceived a responsibility far beyond money. This proceeds from the natural fact that the offspring of *Homo sapiens,* unlike that of any other creature, develops his potential only as the result of many years of care by both parents.

The human experience seems to be that where husbands exercise much authority, they bear correspondingly great responsibility, and vice versa.

Christianity is as clear as Judaism and Islam: The man is the head of the household. The English common-law principle that "a man's home is his castle" once applied just as much to his authority over wife and children as it did to his property. As a consequence, Anglo-Saxon courts traditionally refused to entertain suits by wives who challenged the husband's authority over domestic matters. For example, the decision about whether the household should move was deemed the husband's prerogative; the wife must follow. The maximum link between lost authority and shed responsibility is found in the case of slave husbands, who could hardly be authoritative with their families while their masters showed them no respect, and whose orders regarding their own family they could not gainsay. Likewise, the decrease in the status of husbands in China, which resulted from two decades of life under the Communist agricultural commune system and from the state's one-child policy, also shows the corrosive effects of powerlessness.

Early in the twentieth century, Western states began to superintend the family lives of industrial workers on the assumption that minimal standards had to be imposed for the sake of the children. Today, from Helsinki to Perth, women and children have only to wave a hand, and the state, in effect, will take over the husband's role as provider and as source of authority. It is therefore not surprising that throughout the Western world, especially in those sectors of the population that are the biggest consumers of state services, married men are working less and are abandoning their families at unprecedented rates.[12]

While men can slough many of the burdens of husbanding onto women or the state, women are pretty well stuck with the burdens of their sex. Unless they always use contraceptives themselves and live essentially male sexual lives, they can count on pregnancy, and then on children claiming their strength. The race of men who will help with housework more than occasionally is a figment of modern mythology.[13] Inescapably, then, women must care for children and home. Must they, in addition, work outside the home? And if women can happily provide as well as dispose of material goods, if they can direct as well as nurture—in short, if they can happily perform all the functions of the household—what need have they of husbands? The truth is, few women who have fulfilled all the functions of the household have chosen to do it. Nearly all have been pushed to do so by the death of husbands, by their irresponsibility, or by their inability to make ends meet. And in some cases, they have been pulled by the idea that it would be wrong for them not to try—an idea fostered by women who are in careers that are exciting and fulfilling. But of course, most jobs for women as well as for men are drudgery. Could it be that feminism's main result has been to impose more work and loneliness on women?

Marriage is the quintessential division of labor. And in fact, Nobel Prize–winning economist Gary Becker has shown that in the case of marriage, as in others, divided labor is efficient labor:[14] Married men are more productive workers than unmarried men because they bring to work (along with added incentive) the energy they would otherwise have had to expend on matters that their wives are taking care of at home. By the same token, women do a much better job raising children when they are not bothered by the demands of a career. And yet the modern state has promoted the entry into the workforce of women with young children, while teaching that women should rebel against men who do not do housework. As has often been pointed out, much of the paid work done by women outside the home involves caring for others' children and parents. Thus, many women carry out impersonally the same tasks they once performed for their own families, while they themselves are clients for the services they provide. The difference is that they pay in taxes for the services they receive and are paid by taxes for the services they provide. In sum, the employment of women in public social services is based on the assumption that functions once performed within families can be performed more efficiently and impersonally through state institutions.

Governments create incentives for this way of life by eliminating laws that give married men advantages in competing for jobs. Furthermore, modern tax systems take no account of the worth of the social services that wives at home provide for their own families. To pay for professional, impersonal social services, taxes must be high. This in itself diminishes family income and pushes women to work outside the home. Tax systems do not take into account the cost of raising children, and in some advanced countries actually penalize marriage and children. In Canada, for example, a married couple with three children earning $60,000 per year in 1992 was liable for $17,824 in income taxes if the income came from one worker. But if the husband got a less demanding job and sent the wife to work, the same income was taxed at only $10,725. If they then got divorced and cohabited, the tax dropped to $7,580.[15] Why marry? And if a man gets married, why should he support his family?

Surely the greatest incentive for women to work outside the home is the growing expectation by husbands that they do so. The state's official position is that women are quite equal to men and that their worth is to be measured on the same scale as men's. This notion is inherently attractive to men because it allows them to place little value on what women do at home, but above all because it absolves them of the duty to regard women as people to whom they have special duty. The state's official position is that men have every right to demand that the woman with whom they live pay her way. That being so, why should you strain? Send her to work.

And so, the outstanding fact of the second half of the twentieth century may be less the collapse of communism than the increasing burdens placed on women. "The reality," says a study by the New York–based Population Council, "is that trends like unwed motherhood, rising divorce rates, smaller households and the feminization of poverty are not unique to America but are occurring worldwide."[16] All these trends have one thing in common: They happen in households that husbands have either left or where they never lived to begin with. In northern Europe, these account for over one-third of households, and in the United States, for just under one-third. These households are relatively poor, despite the fact that "women tend to work longer hours than men, at home and on the job."[17] No one should be surprised that hours worked by someone under great stress are less productive than hours worked by someone who is well rested and cared for. Thus, with the exception of Japan and parts of the Islamic world, mankind, including the Chinese of Singapore, Hong Kong, and Taiwan as well as the Koreans, seems to be following the West, albeit at a slower pace.[18]

Western regimes have further embittered relations between the sexes by sanctioning the intrusion of police into domestic quarrels and by doing away with ancient customs that prohibited husbands and wives from testifying against one another. But nothing shows the attitude of modern law toward marriage better than the self-contradictory principle established in one way or another in codes and judicial practices that marriage does not entail the presumption of sexual consent. In other words, governments are emphasizing the legal rights of wives vis-à-vis the rest of their families, decreasing their time with their families, and shifting their financial dependence from husbands to bureaucrats.

PARENTS, CHILDREN, AND THE STATE

During the twentieth century, almost every government on the planet tried to substitute itself for parents in some way. The practice of uniformed children exercising in unison while mouthing state slogans, and bearing such names as Young Pioneers (Soviet Union), Vanguard (Syria), Balilla (Italy), and Hitler Youth (Germany), hollowed out the authority of countless parents in the twentieth century. Today, the government of Japan may interfere less with parents' upbringing of children than any other. But before World War II, its effort to make the younger generation into tools of the state was the equal of the Soviet Union's and was even more successful. The schools taught a version of Shinto made to order by the Ministry of the Interior to draw lines of authority directly from the emperor (in practice, the government) to each child, with parents playing supporting roles. The military-style educational scheme was bolstered by uniforms and by after-school time filled with military exercises and songs of allegiance to the state.

People who think they know how to raise the next generation better than parents have persuaded Western governments to interpose between parents and children.[19] In T. S. Eliot's words, they have tried to establish systems of child rearing "so perfect that no one will need to be good."[20] The policy of Western governments has been to proclaim children's rights, then to endow officials with the power to exercise those rights on their behalf against parents. Indeed, one influential author urged that "the legal status of infancy . . . be abolished" and that the state no longer take one person's childhood into account when considering that person's relationship with another.[21]

The first of these children's alleged "rights"—not only for a few poor abandoned children but for everyone—is to day care. Every Western government has established or has tried to establish such an entitlement and to expand it. The push comes not from the recipients of such services but from their providers, from the class of government employees and social service professionals who run such things, as well as from the imperative of collectivist ideology. The second is the right to be free from "child abuse." Most modern states, either by law or regulation, can punish or severely inconvenience parents for inflicting any kind of corporal punishment on their children. Whereas once the policeman would take errant youths home for punishment, now parents are supposed to take errant children to the state for analysis, therapy, and correction. The state, not the parent, has become the ultimate authority.

Then there is the right to be free from sexual abuse. In the name of it, modern states have built inquisitorial apparatuses that assume that fathers routinely sexually assault children and that justify their own existence by finding "telltale signs" of abuse in children, taking these children from their parents, extracting or manufacturing testimony, and prosecuting the parents. Accordingly, throughout the Western world, state schools routinely sow distrust of physical contact with parents. The state also gives children the means to take vengeance for wrongs real or imagined by asking them for confidential reports on their parents' drunkenness and drug use—shades of young Pavel Morozov. Some parents have taken the logic of these laws to its conclusion: They have taken teenagers they no longer want to manage to hospitals or police stations, to rid themselves of them.[22]

There is no conclusive proof that the state's growing role and parents' diminishing role in the lives of children are the cause of the upsurge in the variety of pathologies affecting children in the modern world. But the correlation between an individual's committing a crime and being raised without a father is high and largely consistent throughout the world. It is even higher for people who have grown up under the direct supervision of the social service authorities.[23] And yet, with the exception of the countries in the former Soviet empire, governments are responding to the obvious decline in the condition of children by increasing their involvement in their upbringing.

The modern state has also weakened ties between adults and their aged parents. Social security systems have advanced their stated purpose of making retirees independent of their families. Since, however, the payment of social security pensions depends on collecting taxes from those very children, the dependency on the younger generation is there, in spades. But whereas once the dependency was within individual families, now it is collective dependency through the collection by the state of high taxes on the younger generation. Once the sanction was moral. Now it is political. Moreover, while earlier generations handed down their accumulated wealth to their children and received care in turn, the generation that has dominated modern countries during the last quarter of the twentieth century and the early years of the twenty-first has paid to the state in "social contributions" large amounts of money that previous generations had laid up for the children's inheritance.

Modern states also levy steep taxes on inheritances. Their premise is simply that the community does not mind if an individual dissipates his wealth by gambling, by dissolution, or by taking cruises. He may burn his cash. But if he attempts to pass it on to the family, the state will take most of it away. In sum, because of the state, older people have less to give to their families and can expect less from them in their last years. Thus, while modern retirees look to the state for help, their children bear the state's taxation for social security—without the combination of gratitude and obligation that earlier generations held for their aging parents, and with the realization instead that the state will not be able to deliver to them what it is delivering to their parents. Both generations seem increasingly united in one sentiment, however: resentment of the state.

No claim of politicians is more fatuous than that the state is a big family or even a "village." Villages, of course, are composed of real families, of churches, schools, and other associations that take neither orders nor money from the state. Above all, families are bound by blood and serve the natural purpose of raising children. Aristotle described the rule of parents over children as "royal"—absolute power exercised for the benefit of the ruled.[24] And indeed, during the age of absolutism, kings were wont to describe themselves as fathers and their peoples as their children. But, unlike fathers, kings granted privileges to some subjects over others, not disinterestedly for their children's benefit but rather to shore up support for themselves. Modern governments, lacking the legitimacy of kings, live by trading privilege for support. To be precise, they purchase the support of whole classes of people by granting privileges, and sometimes jobs, to the entire class. One of the biggest of the constituent classes of modern government is that of the employees of social service agencies—the masses of social workers, psychologists, teachers, consultants, administrators, and hangers-on whose business is to interfere with families. If the people at large are the children of the state, then these social service employers are the big brothers and sisters, who get the authority and are paid to exercise it—not exactly what happens in natural families and villages. More important, the institutions of pseudo-families and pseudovillages crowd out those of the real ones.

There are no examples of states that make families. We have seen how the totalitarian Soviet Union well-nigh wrecked Russia's families. Let us now examine how Social Democratic Sweden did it even more thoroughly and how Japanese governments are balancing the contrary pressures of modernity and of their own culture.

SWEDEN

The fate of the family in Sweden and other modern social democracies since the 1950s shows that government can achieve a relationship between the sexes resembling that of the Soviet Union without Soviet-style brutality—

if it is willing to use all the powers of the modern state, and if the people are more docile and more trusting of government than Russians. Indeed, although in recent years even Swedes have come to believe that the welfare state must be cut back, there is no sentiment in Sweden or in the rest of Europe for the restoration of the family comparable to the nostalgia for family in Russia.

Swedish family policy began in 1934, ostensibly as an effort (common throughout Europe during the interwar years) to stimulate the birth rate through financial incentives to married couples to have children. The original package of aid to families included assistance for mothers who were looking for work. But this was only a minor part of the Social Democratic Party's agenda, which was fully laid out in Gunnar and Alva Myrdal's book *Crisis in the Population Question* (1934). The purpose of the Myrdals' book and the Party's agenda was the same: to create "the economic independence of married partners." Among other things, that would require a certain kind of sex education as well as the spread of contraception and abortion. Because Swedish society at the time was as familial as any in the West (and more prudish than most), public opinion caused parliamentary rejection of these proposals. The public would have been even more outraged if the Myrdals' ultimate objectives—the promotion of all kinds of "common living arrangements," the abolition of sex roles, and "living alone"—had been put before Parliament. The Myrdals' agenda lay dormant until the 1960s, when the government set out to pursue it piece by piece, at first under the cover of some traditionalist rhetoric and only gradually avowing its revolutionary implications.

The centerpiece of the government's effort was to push and pull women out of the home into the labor market. The push came from Sweden's steeply progressive income tax. By first permitting married couples to figure their tax bills separately and then mandating them to do it, the government made clear to every Swedish husband that by far the most efficient way to raise his standard of living was not to work harder himself, but to send his wife to work. The government also offered women jobs in large numbers in the growing public sectors of education, welfare, health, and bureaucracy. Seventy-five percent of public-sector employees are now female, making Swedish bureaucracy—the day-to-day control of society—women's work. The government also subsidized jobs for women in the private sector, and in 1992 established quotas for female hiring in private companies. Companies that fail to meet the quotas are fined by special labor courts. So, recruitment of women is heavy. Moreover, the state's schools and public services depict the few women who shun work as "parasites." Thus, 91 percent of Swedish women between the ages of twenty-five and fifty-four spend most of their days in cubicles, although over one-third do so less than thirty-five hours per week.[25]

Second, the state taught Swedes that marriage is just another lifestyle. Swedish sex education, compulsory since 1956, teaches that the sexual urge is to be satisfied like any other, and that to limit its satisfaction to marriage is wrong, period. The state teaches sexual technique, encourages sex at will, and provides free contraceptives and abortion. State schools exalt sexual un-inhibitedness as the vital proof of personal independence (about the only kind of independence celebrated in the land of social constraint) and equality between men and women. This is very popular, especially with men. Far from countenancing social disapproval for out-of-wedlock pregnancy, the state offers more support to unmarried mothers than to married ones. Like everyone else, they receive greater allowances for each successive child. But unlike married mothers, they also get preferential housing allowances, welfare allowances, and fully subsidized child care. Not surprisingly, Sweden has the world's lowest marriage rates; one-half of births are now out of wedlock, and one-half of marriages end in divorce. Marriage has become a minority lifestyle. Since the Swedish state also keeps statistics on the behavior of cohabiting couples, it takes note of the fact that they split three times as often as divorce-prone Swedish married couples do. In other words, even cohabitation is losing ground to the dominant lifestyle—casual contact. Perhaps the most significant demographic fact in Sweden is that, as of 1980, one-third of all Swedish households were composed of just one person, and in progressive Stockholm, 63 percent of inhabitants lived alone—that is, in one-person households.[26] What family?

The government has altered the quality of human contact, too. State schools teach "gender equality" for the purpose of transcending the differences between men and women. This is not feminism or any other kind of exaltation of female peculiarities. It is a tendency, already well known to Alexis de Tocqueville, "to make of man and woman creatures who are, not equal only, but actually similar. They would attribute the same functions to both, impose the same duties, grant the same rights; they would have them share everything—work, pleasure, public affairs."[27] It is a political project the end of which is to transcend the human condition. That, of course, was Friedrich Engels' point, the point that all thoroughgoing revolutionaries share: to re-create man in their own image.

To whittle down the differences between the roles of the sexes, the state has also spent advertising money and has paid fathers to take time off from work so that they might do more child care and housework. But studies have shown that although husbands or live-in men accept the benefits, they do only 7 percent of the housework and 18 percent of the child care.[28] Swedish men, then, have it easy. The state, however, has made their status in Swedish homes more precarious by requiring the police to arrest men for domestic violence without evidence or even without complaint, based on mere suspicion. Without formal convictions, men so charged can be compelled to undergo counseling and can be deprived of benefits at work. So the only way to have relations with a woman without being liable to such treatment is to maintain a separate household—one more reason for the growing popularity of living alone and making sure that sexual contact is casual.

The regime adds physical incentives to the financial and legal ones. Following guidelines of government planners, Swedish architects are designing smaller individual living units, which must share communal facilities such as laundries and play areas. This wealthy imitation of Soviet-style communal poverty discourages mothers, fathers, and children from getting into the habit of behaving as a unit and makes three-generation homes quite impossible.

Swedish family policy is also based on high-quality day-care centers. The cost per child is about $15,000 per year, mostly subsidized by the government. The centers boast ratios of up to one caregiver for four children. If one adds the people who work on buildings and grounds, cooks, cleaners, and administrators, these centers employ up to one person for every two children—roughly the ratio a child might find in a traditional home.[29] In the end, then, the industrial method of child rearing does not employ fewer people than the natural family. Swedish arrangements for raising children are not more efficient, even in terms of inputs, not to mention the quality of the product, than the natural family. However, Swedish family policy aims less at socioeconomic efficiency than at a certain kind of social engineering— to train children to focus on sources of authority other than their parents. In this it succeeds. The state caps off this policy by offering allowances to adolescents to help them move out of their parents' apartments and begin *independent—nay, state-dependent—living* as soon as possible. The child's connection with his parents, or indeed with any person he chooses voluntarily, will surely be less substantial than his connection with the state. About *that* relationship he will have no choice at all.

And just to make sure that no one—either father or mother—wears the pants in a Swedish family, in 1979 the state outlawed spanking of children—only the state may punish. Moreover, the state can decide without formal judicial proceedings to take the children wholly to itself. Even before the child-protection wave of the mid-1980s got underway, it did so frequently—to the tune of some 22,000 times every year.[30] At that rate, in the United States over three-quarters of a million children would be removed from their parents every year. If one accepts Swedish claims to have mitigated most social pathologies, the only explanation for such high rates of intervention is that it is an assertion of control. Control so thorough needs no assertion.

The consequences of the Swedish state's victory over the family in a generally prosperous and physically healthy setting belie the argument that the way of life in America's black ghettos is due to poverty (much less to race). Swedish illegitimate births (the term is not allowed in Sweden) and abortions at close to the rate present in American black ghettos are just the beginning.[31] Free-floating men and women who do without each other except for biological purposes are another consequence. Workers whose declining commitment to work results in absentee ratios of 20 percent on Mondays and Fridays are yet another.[32] Teenagers who have the world's highest suicide rate, who drink and take drugs,[33] and who must be disciplined by the police at rates far above those of other native Europeans fill out the picture—except for the fact that the generation to which this applies is the first to have been raised under full-fledged family policy. The full effects of that policy will be felt in subsequent generations.

JAPAN

The family habits of contemporary Japan result from a combination of the Yamato people's ancient ways and policies adopted by post–World War II governments to imitate to some extent the ways of their American conquerors. In old Japan, women were beasts of burden and objects of pleasure. Visitors to prewar Japan noted that the workforce was heavily female, that the meanest jobs seemed to be reserved for women, and that whether it was a matter of girls rather than boys sweeping schoolyards, of women giving up train seats to men, or of wives serving husbands in addition to everything else they were doing, the society seemed to run on women's backs.[34] In especially lean years or poor families, girl babies were often killed at birth. The only partial exception seemed to be in upper-class families, where women were fully occupied in caring for their families. The Japanese people, however, deviated partially from what one might call standard barbarian practice because regardless of how heavily they used women, they made sure that marriages were universal and honored. In Japan, everyone has a place, no matter how lowly. After World War II, the government reformed Japanese family ways by partially spreading the customs of the upper class to the rest of the country and by elevating marriage still higher in social esteem. As usual, the Japanese reformed themselves in part to become more efficient international competitors, and as usual, they succeeded.

Laws and customs encouraged one-earner households primarily by reserving career-track jobs for men; by giving married men preference in hiring, pay, and promotion; and, secondarily, by taxing married couples at much lower rates than single people. Japanese women went to work in their teens as before, and for relatively low pay. But when they got married, which practically all did by their mid-twenties, they retreated to their families, returning to outside employment, if at all, only after their children were grown. The expectation that every young woman was a lady-of-the-house-to-be and that men were to bear the main burdens—which quickly caught on in public opinion—shifted the nature of women's work away from mean labor further toward services. In the Japanese armed forces, for example, women soldiers are taught to arrange flowers, one of the skills required of the traditional upper-class wife. There are career women in Japan. But the norm is that a woman's principal career is the nurture of her family.

Japanese women prepare for marriage systematically with classes in various household skills, including arranging flowers. When they marry (unmarried people in their thirties are looked down on), women become *oku san*, "Mrs. Inside." They run family finances, doling out allowances to their husbands, and do just about everything else necessary in the domestic realm. This domestic support system has made it possible for postwar Japanese men to work exceptionally long hours. Women still serve men in ways that make westerners wince. But one gets the impression that, like Japanese workers on the job, they are doing their work to perfection, doing the equivalent of oiling and shining their machines to make them run better.

The new way of marriage is built on the Japanese devotion to duty. Mothers shine their children inside and out to help them compete in the very high-stakes contest to enter higher-ranking schools. They also care for aged parents on either side of the family. It is considered disgraceful for adult children not to care for their parents. The Japanese extend some duty even to the children whom they kill by abortion: They make little clay shrines to them to propitiate their spirits. Everyone has a place in Japan.

The laws—strongly backed by public opinion—discourage single motherhood by not allowing tax deductions for children (except by death of the spouse or divorce). Out-of-wedlock children and their mothers also face officially sanctioned discrimination in schools, jobs, and housing. There is enormous social pressure for young unmarried pregnant women to either get married or abort the baby and for adolescents to keep faith with their parents. The government, in short, is very proud of Japan's low rate of single motherhood and believes that the country's success, its very identity, is due to its people coming from two-parent, patriarchal families that take care of both children and grandparents. Because it wants to maintain the status quo, "the Japanese political establishment find the concept of sexual equality about as welcome as smallpox."[35]

Yet the new model Japanese family is eroding. Whether because both mothers and fathers are under too much pressure to perform their roles perfectly or because people are following latter-day Western ways, the fact is that Japan is suffering the same demographic implosion as Western European countries. Couples are marrying later, and the birth rate has fallen to 1.4 per woman, meaning that the county's population will fall by about 60 percent over the next century. As Japanese people grow older, they are less likely to be cared for by their children. The government is offering large financial bonuses to couples that have more than two children.[36] But the bonuses hardly satisfy the financial burden of raising children in Japan, let alone the human cost. The prime minister once even suggested that saving Japan might require discouraging women from seeking higher education. But he quickly retreated.

In fact, the establishment—"out of concern for Japan's cherished international image"—has paid lip service precisely to the need for women to fill traditional male roles. As noted Japanologist Robert Christopher has written, "In Japan, where bureaucratic pronouncements are taken considerably more earnestly than in the United States, this sort of thing has impact." "As recently as the early 1970s," Christopher observed, "polls showed that 80 percent of Japanese women believed that a husband should work and a wife should take care of the house." But "by 1976 . . . only 49 percent still held to that belief, and by 1978 the figure had dropped to only 46 percent."[37] Polls notwithstanding, the actual behavior of the Japanese people has been much more oriented toward distinct roles for men and women. Sooner or later, however, actions catch up with words. Moreover, the Japanese government has given substance to its rhetoric by visibly recruiting women for some of its more glamorous bureaucratic posts. The point here is that while a government may earnestly want a particular kind of family behavior, it may get quite another kind by virtue of its own words and deeds. Mixed signals are always difficult to decipher.

POWER AND EXPERIENCE

Anyone who might want to restore family life to Sweden would have to contend less with the laws of that country than with the attitudes that have come to dominate the thinking of Swedish people over the past forty years. They would have to begin by recalling how shocked the Swedish people of the 1930s were when the Myrdals' agenda was partially unveiled, and how a determined elite changed public opinion gradually over a generation through exhortations and concrete incentives. But any non-Swede who thought of imitating such radical surgery on his country's character would have to keep in mind that most peoples are not as docile as the Swedes. In the Japanese case, any regime that wanted to preserve the Japanese family could count on docility even greater than that of the Swedes as well as on basic Japanese attitudes that are very approving of families. But the regime would also have to understand which habits made Western society so powerfully imitable in the first place and how these have changed. Then the Japanese would have to do something they have not done since 1868—something original.

Perhaps the most powerful factor in disposing people to accept or reject leadership is massively bitter experience. The Russian people rejected communism's teaching about families—in word if not in deed—because it was part and parcel of an ordeal that the Communist regime imposed on Russia. This does not mean that Russia is about to regrow prerevolutionary families. But it does mean that works and policies aimed at fostering habits of family responsibility are likely to find more favorable responses in Russia than in, say, Sweden, where the attempt to feminize men and androgynize women does not yet have a bad name. In Japan and elsewhere, demographics and other developments are convincing people that, somehow, men should become more manly and women more womanly. But habits seldom reverse course without some impulsive experience, and even then, they do so slowly. In Russia, the argument for male responsibility is convincing mostly women. But it is among women, after all, that civilizations take root or wither.

8

THE SOUL

The mores of our fathers produced excellent men, and these excellent men preserved our ancient mores and the institutions of our ancestors.

—CICERO, *DE REPUBLICA*

Since parents and children, workers and consumers, rulers and ruled possess the inalienable human tendency to think about better and worse, to consider whence they came and whither they are going, to like and to dislike, it is not surprising that human habits depend heavily on what happens in our minds and on how that shapes our souls. Consequently, no issues are more contentious or more defining of regimes than those that deal with right and wrong, as well as with everything else that touches man's relationship to God.

Most who marry, raise children, and care for parents do so under some kind of religious injunction. Any secular laws in this field are bound to satisfy those who adhere to religions that those laws support, and to alienate others from the regime. Religion also defines the boundaries of economic behavior. No regime in the Islamic or Chinese cultural area has the option of running an economy based on the assumption that people will work, save, and follow rules like those of the Protestant capitalists described by Max

Weber. Running the American economy as if its leading lights were still parsimonious Protestants is also increasingly chancy. And since public life is substantially about who or what is to be honored when and how, people are sure to ask whether those whom the regime chooses really reflect the right order of things—an order instilled in most people's minds primarily by what they believe about God.

Most regimes act in the interstices of the predominant religion. In a few extreme cases, regimes become partisans in religious struggles, either waging a kind of war on religion in general or trying to institute a new set of beliefs and standards about the most important things. When they do this, they bet their lives. Culture wars, of which religious ones are the most violent, tend not to be good for habits, religions, or regimes.

THE WHOLESALE STRUGGLE

In the ancient world and in much of today's Asia, struggles over the right way of life have not necessarily referred to the supernatural. Custom and (later) philosophy were guides at least as important as the gods. By contrast, in the Abrahamic traditions all controversy about conduct is fundamentally theological. Though it is possible in Judeo-Christian civilization to discuss matters of the heart and soul in other terms, nevertheless with all due deference to Aristotle, our ethics derive from commandments, and natural law draws its authority from nature's God. So inevitably, all sides in the wars over human conduct in our time have focused on religion.

The very essence of modern Western government has been the attempt to tame and even to eliminate religion. In the sixteenth century, Protestant as well as Catholic princes quickly realized that mere civil life, not to mention the good life, was hardly possible when two or more sects were fighting to the death to impose every item of their confession and ritual on the others.[1] But recall that mere religion was only one among the many causes that drove Europe's wars of religion. Well before the Reformation, Europe's kings had been gathering powers—including, preeminently, power over religious matters—and were bidding for sovereignty. Religious quarrels afforded sovereigns the chance to take sides, and then to seize for themselves the strongest and wealthiest organizations in their realms in the name of Catholicism or Protestantism. Whether in France or Scandinavia, the state made itself the *tertius gaudens,* the ultimate winner, of religious strife.

The concept of "established religion" is an early modern *political* concept, not a medieval religious one. Europe's medieval kings did not try to run the church, while the absolute monarchs who followed were not terribly interested in the details of the faiths they managed. They wanted the church's approval of their sexual exploits, of their suppression of rivals, of their taxes, and of their wars. They therefore vested themselves with baroque rituals almost as elaborate as those of the Caesaropapist Eastern churches. Not medieval clerics, but the official churchmen of the absolute monarchs of the sixteenth and seventeenth centuries, both Catholic and Protestant, claimed thaumaturgic powers for their masters, elaborated the doctrine of the divine right of kings, and lived on tax monies. The attitude that these modern regimes fostered toward religion may have been best summarized by Edward Gibbon in his description of early Roman imperial attitudes toward various modes of worship: "[The religions] were all considered by the people as equally true; by the philosopher as equally false, and by the magistrate, as equally useful."[2]

Most observers of society have agreed with Gibbon's emperors about the usefulness of religion. Survey evidence from the United States—roughly replicated in just about every other time and place—shows that religious observance correlates positively with all sorts of desirable human characteristics. According to the 1993 National Longitudinal Survey of Youth, an intact family that attended church weekly averaged an income of $50,000 per year, versus $39,000 for intact families that did not attend church at all.[3] Moreover, it seems that churchgoers make more money because they have the kinds of personal habits that naturally lead to income,[4] since even broken families that attended church weekly made $2,000 more than irreligious intact families.[5] Copious research also shows an unbroken link between religious practice and family stability. And people who go to church commit crimes at a much lower rate than those who do not.[6] In short, there is not now and never has been a better predictor of prosperity, family, and civility than the faithful practice of Christianity or Judaism.[7]

Appreciating religion for its tendency to produce faithful and fruitful subjects is not religion. Even Stalin found it useful during World War II to style himself a Defender of the Faith. Thus, not just Louis XIV but also Montesquieu, and not just King William but also John Locke sincerely touted the indispensability of faiths they did not necessarily share. Few governments in the world have been *overtly* hostile to religion, and when they were it was only until horrid consequences forced them to try something else.[8]

Ideas and practices have their own logic, however, and by the end of the eighteenth century, the consensus of European regimes had come to be that though religion might serve society's lower tier, it would be best for the educated classes to foster useful intellectual and moral habits outside the churches—indeed, that religion itself was dangerous, an obstacle to all good things.

In the West then, the public struggle for the soul is carried on largely between the state and organized religion. Relationships between church and state fall roughly into the category of embrace, enmity, and neutrality. In the discussion that follows, keep in mind that religiosity and clericalism are very different things, and that some regimes have been friendly to clerics but hostile to religion, while others (though fewer) have taken the opposite approach.

THE RED AND THE BLACK

Western history, and here the history of Islam must be included, shows that the state's embrace of religion tends to corrupt both the state and religion. Few literary passages are more poignant than the ones in canto 32 of Dante's *Il Purgatorio* that symbolically reenact the Emperor Constantine's conferral of the status of state religion on Christianity. As an imperial eagle's feather falls on the cart that symbolizes the church, the voice of God himself comments: "Oh, my poor vessel, how badly you've been loaded!"[9] This is followed by the image of the church's cart, driven by a whore—the pope—who is engaged in intimacy with a giant (the king of France, who had just taken the papacy to himself at Avignon); the giant then beats her whenever she tries to turn her eyes away from him.[10] Dante's poetic argument is drawn from standard Christian theology: The functions of church and state are so inherently different that when either party tries to wield the powers of the other it makes a mess of both.[11] The church is corrupted both when it exercises secular power, as the popes did in Dante's time, and when it accepts a privileged status in exchange for giving temporal rulers influence in its affairs, as happened in the Greek and Russian Orthodox churches.

In Europe's absolute monarchies, Protestant and Catholic churches paid for their official status through compromises that dimmed their spiritual attractiveness. As a result, the former papal states of central Italy have the lowest rate of church attendance in the country. They bred Benito Mussolini as well as the Italian Communist movement. In Protestant Europe, the areas where the church was most closely associated with the state—Sweden and the Netherlands—have the lowest rates of religious observance.[12] The pattern occurs again and again. In Germany, the Adenauer government's attempt to fuel the country's post-Nazi religious revival by financing churches and synagogues with a church tax on registered members seems to have discouraged membership.[13]

The case that shows most fully what happens when religious and secular authority mingle is that of Islam and, specifically, the Islamic Republic of Iran, established by the Ayatollah Khomeini in 1979. Well before he entered politics, Khomeini had earned respect for piety and expertise in Islamic law. Like Islam itself, he embodied leadership in secular as well as spiritual affairs. That he brought bloody war and economic decline is incidental; secular leaders in the Middle East have brought their peoples the same. More to the point, Khomeini saddled Iran with a class of rulers who made all kinds of secular decisions (many of them naturally in their own interest) and who tried to justify them on the basis of Islam while using secular force to purge the people of impious habits. This simply rang false, and would have even if the decisions had been good and the regime had not been pretending to be holier than its subjects. Moreover, few, if any, of the governing mullahs who followed Khomeini had ever made reputations as men holy or wise. Thus, as an astute observer said of Khomeini's successors, "No mullah or religious student . . . nor any Iranian in need of religious counsel would seek a judgment [a *fatwa*] from Khamenei [the ayatollah who succeeded Khomeini]."[14] As a result, the people of Iran have been left poorer spiritually, as well as in every other way.

Direct persecution of religion is seldom as disastrous as outright embrace—as long as the persecution does not amount to the physical extermination of believers, as it did in seventeenth-century Japan's extermination of Christians, as almost happened in Hitler's Holocaust of European Jews and to the Tibetans under Chinese rule after 1959. Certainly, the Islamic practice of levying a special tax on Christians and Jews—the infidel tax—never stifled the Christian or Jewish faiths in the Ottoman Empire. Nor was it intended to. Often, indeed usually, religious persecution has nothing to do with the soul. Government persecution of non-Muslims in today's Middle East is far more political than it is religious, as evidenced by the fact that Arab governments persecute various Muslim associations even more vigorously than they do non-Muslims. In such cases, persecution's effects are physical, and hence spiritually neutral.

When religious persecution clearly aims to destroy a people's identity, however, and the persecution consists of half measures, it often strengthens the faith. This is certainly what happened in Poland under the Communist regime between 1945 and 1989 and in Nicaragua between 1979 and 1990. These regimes taught atheism in the schools, ridiculing and restricting the Catholic Church in innumerable ways. They even established alternative Catholic churches that they controlled. They hoped that the church would wither as society's most ambitious elements moved away from it. But the church fought back by increasing its spiritual demands on believers and offering the people a choice between lives lived in the integrity of the faith and those lived by the standards of a corrupt regime. It gave examples of prelates who put their bodies between the regime and ordinary believers. As a result, the churches, the confessionals, and the seminaries were filled to overflowing.

Neutrality toward religion seldom means that a regime does not care about it, although that seems to have been the case in postwar Japan. The rate at which the Japanese profess affiliation to some religion (19 percent) is comparable to that of modern Europe.[15] But there seems to be no ongoing struggle for the soul of Japan, at least not in the sense of any controversy over transcendent truth or the individual's relationship with the universe's creator. Shinto, the ancient religion of Japan, lacks any concept of an afterlife and any ethical system related thereto. Buddhism is the basis of many Japanese customs and, together with Shinto, encourages a cult of ancestors, prevalent festivals (Japan may have more of these than any other place on earth), and mystical feelings for natural phenomena, such as flowers or the moon. In the first part of the twentieth century, the Japanese government effectively fabricated a version of Shinto to reinforce even further the Japanese tendency to obey superiors. The ploy worked well enough to stifle dissent to a mindless war. In the aftermath of defeat, however, the Japanese people were left spiritually empty. This does not mean that the Japanese lack conscience or character, but rather that these as well as habits come almost exclusively from adherence to the expectations of the group to which an individual belongs. Society is Japan's soul, and this is where the struggle is.

In sum, religion's substance and the regime's attitude toward it have enabled peoples to live certain kinds of lives and disabled them from living others. Let us see how they have done so in several societies: in ancient Rome, where changing pieties over a thousand years went along with radically different ways of life; in twentieth-century Europe, where the ideas and policies of elites have banished religion perhaps more effectively than the Soviet policy of persecution did; and in Israel, where the split between observant and nonobservant Jews seems to be creating two peoples out of one. All these experiences shed light on our own.

MANY ROMES

When the Roman Senate disposed of Romulus, the city's bellicose founding king, at the end of the eighth century B.C., it sought out as his successor Numa Pompilius, who had a well-established reputation for piety and peace. During the next forty years, according to Plutarch, the city gained such "discipline and schooling in religion" that its character was thereafter marked by love of law and reverence for oaths.[16] Numa trained the Romans by establishing countless rites and priestly orders. He even made sure that the private rites of Roman families were consistent with the public rites. In short, he wrapped every facet of life in divine red tape. Numa himself seems to have been the sort who revered nature and who thought, as Greek philosophers were later to write, that decent human behavior is right by nature. He forbade making images of gods, discouraged blood sacrifices, and tried to infuse rituals with ethical content. But his rude countrymen simply got into the habit of religiously following the procedures he prescribed. They associated doing so with what at the time was the greatest good—winning wars—and feared that failure to observe rites and oaths would bring the greatest evil, which was losing wars. Early Roman religion was an innocent compact between the gods and men: *do ut des*—"I give so that you may give." Abounding tales of ancient Roman justice—of Regulus, who delivered himself to death rather than breaking an oath; of Scaevola, who burned his hand for having failed to keep one despite his best efforts; and of countless other instances where advantages were forgone or sacrifices endured for the sake of solemn promises—tell the story of a people so mentally tough that they became irresistible.

Livy's account of the later Roman republic shows us that religion had become more sophisticated and more manageable. Greek influence had brought to Rome a trove of interesting stories about individual gods and goddesses. The Romans superstitiously sought the gods' personal intercession on a wide variety of affairs. But the divine personages of Virgil's *Aeneid,* the epic of the Augustan age, had specific personalities, likes, dislikes, and conflicts. Relationships with them had no ethical content. They were useful, but like Juno, who fought Aeneas, they could be defeated. Still, overall, the gods favored Rome; and Rome's advantage was the highest good. This was useful to magistrates. Livy wrote approvingly about a Roman consul who pressured the augurs to give favorable omens for battle. When the consul did not get them, he argued publicly that the augurs had botched their job, killed them, and gained a victory. However, Livy decried another consul in a similar situation who overtly disparaged augury and caused the armies to mutiny. Those were the days, wrote Livy, perhaps without irony, "when disinterest in the gods, common in our century, had not yet become prevalent, nor did everyone interpret laws and oaths to their own advantage."[17] The Romans quickly learned what to do with a religion of success: Use it, but do not believe it.

Livy and Virgil wrote after the Roman republic had died of an overdose of self-seeking, culminating in civil war. The gods had not brought peace. Augustus had. Thus, the epics and histories of the early empire celebrate the Caesars, not the gods. The law itself had become imperial Rome's effective religion. The many new religions current among the empire's diverse populations usually did not challenge the law (when they did, they were crushed), but neither did they lend any support to the laws. The old official religion was celebrated with more pomp than ever, but it was believed no more than any other, probably less. Christian hagiography aside, the policy of the empire, broken only occasionally, was religious tolerance. Nevertheless, the official religion drew more negative attention from the tastemakers of Rome's high culture. That is why by the time of the empire Rome's cultural leaders had nothing in common with plodding old Numa Pompilius. The theaters were full of plays for every imaginable festival, and the plays were such, as Augustine said, that the actors could not rehearse in front of their mothers. The gods were almost always shown in the throes of debauched sex or engaged in farcical plots. The laws, therefore, were without religious support. Anyone who felt the urge to keep a commitment at his own expense and considered the gods found ambiguous counsel at best. Except under the philosopher-emperor Marcus Aurelius, the laws themselves had only the sanction of force, and force was mitigated only by evasion or corruption. Hence, generous souls increasingly were drawn to unofficial or foreign cults. So it happened that the followers of a crucified Jew taught habits more consonant with the old Roman virtues than Rome's official religion did.

When the barbarians were overrunning the empire, Christians had reason to mock the impotence of the debauched gods and their debauched followers. Rome's victories had been the old religion's glory. The Romans had even invented a goddess, Victoria, and built altars to her. But, wrote Augustine, Victoria had not made the legions victorious. The legions had made Victoria. And the legions had been made by steady habits forged in the piety of Numa's simple obedience by the great and the humble alike. Those habits had been discredited gradually by people at the top of the regime. They had become more sophisticated and less credulous, though also more self-indulgent and better at sloughing their burdens onto others. By the fifth century A.D., Gibbon tells us, the barbarians who came and went through Rome found interesting human qualities only in the empire's Christians and in its whores.

EUROPE

The French and Italian branches of the liberal tradition that stems from the French Revolution treated religion as an enemy. The German, British, and Scandinavian branches treated it as a competitor. Later, liberals in most places gave up liberal ideas for some amalgam of Marxism and Freudianism, firmly embedded in statism. The pure versions of these doctrines, in addition to the late nineteenth-century vitalism that merged with other elements to form fascism, have taken most European souls from Christianity and Judaism. Indeed, all these doctrines have won converts within the churches themselves. This unequal struggle for the souls and habits of Europeans has taken place over education, abortion, euthanasia, and the treatment of political enemies, as well as over the very place of religion, and of right and wrong, in public life.

Education used to be the business of clerics, and its ultimate purpose was to enable people to understand God's word. Christian (and Jewish) teachers used to start with Plato's blueprint: The study of practical things would lead to the study of mathematics—the preeminent theoretical discipline—and to astronomy, then to philosophy. On top of this pyramid was theology. This scheme applied from the lowest level of instruction to Europe's great universities.

The French Revolution's promise of "free and compulsory" secular schools was not redeemed until Jules Ferry's long tenure as minister of education in France's Third Republic after 1875. The schoolmaster, inculcating the curriculum devised by the Ministry of Education, was to free the younger generation from superstition and to fill its minds with practical knowledge and zeal for the fatherland. Copied mutatis mutandis throughout Europe, this institution was everywhere acknowledged to be an offensive weapon against religion. In Germany, the public schools became part of Otto von Bismarck's *kultur kampf* against Catholics. In Italy, the pope urged Catholics to boycott the schools. The public schools divided society sharply between the nonreligious who attended them and the religious who fled them.

Nineteenth-century secular education, however, was not so different from religious education. Not until well into the twentieth century, when the schools adopted the gospels of Charles Darwin, Sigmund Freud, and Karl Marx, did they teach aggressively different views of man's origin, man's character, and man's relationship to man. Even so, through most of the twentieth century, European secular education taught confinement of sex to marriage, hard work, and fulfillment of civic duty even unto death. Only during the last one-third of the century did secular education fulfill its antinomian potential. In Sweden, the high schools teach a compulsory two-year course that presents the world's religions equally as figments of fetishist imagination. They stress the Hegelian-Feurbachian thesis that humans attribute their best qualities to God (that is the meaning of the Marxist concept of alienation), along with the psychoanalytic view of religion as a compulsive neurosis with infantile characteristics. In the second year, they present the practical or ethical side, touting the morality that has been developed in Sweden, which is essentially the platform of the Swedish Social Democratic Party. Everyone is obligated to pay taxes, to show social solidarity by not striving too much or being judgmental, and to avoid being prudish about sex.

This kind of attack has been far more effective than those launched against religion by the century's harsh totalitarians. As we have seen, the Soviet Communists' frontal assault, including explicit indoctrination into atheism, did not succeed fully because it caused people to associate opposition to biblical religion with all sorts of unpleasant things. More seductively, the Fascists had asked people to worship human vitality in general and in themselves—especially in the nation-state.[18] They offered the churches (and in Italy the synagogues, too) a part in this pageantry of ersatz spirituality. Had they held power longer, they might well have succeeded in displacing religion. Still, the French Revolution's altars to *la patrie,* fascism's sound-and-light shows, and communism's exorcisms and excommunications (recall East Germany's adulthood ceremonies, which some Germans are now reviving and which were meant to supplant confirmations and bar mitzvahs)[19] took their toll and prepared the way for the success of a way of life very close to nihilism.

In every European country, religious practice has waned. Whereas 41 percent of Americans attend church or synagogue weekly, and over 80 percent report praying regularly,[20] in Sweden only 4 percent attend church weekly, while in the European Union generally, weekly attendance averages 18 percent. Without Ireland, where about 60 percent go to church every week, the EU average would be about 12 percent. European tourists gaze at cathedrals as uncomprehendingly as they do at the pyramids, for they are equally products of alien civilization.

A book by a respected French diplomat notes Europe's moral disorientation and proposes as a remedy nothing less than a "religion without God."[21] But this is already Europe's officious religion, and persons like the diplomat-intellectual are its priests. In the universities, in government service, and in the prestige press, biblical religion is either nonexistent or treated as a problematic vestige. In its place, European governments promote self-worship (the very word "soul" has been replaced by the word "self") thinly disguised as earth worship.

The new religion's commandments range from the purely fashionable ("Thou shalt not eat fat, which is bad for you and the environment, nor smoke tobacco—but marijuana is okay") to the serious. The primordial one is: "Thou shalt have no truck with the God of the Bible, lest he outshine thee." Its twin corollaries are that the state outshines each of us—hence "Thou shalt obey the state, the source of all truth, prosperity, and status"— and "If ever thou dost doubt the authority for these commandments or of the state, remember thou that it flows somehow from our Mother Earth, our fragile planet, through Science, which is beyond thine understanding."

The source of authority having been established, the practical commandments follow: "Pay thine taxes and struggle with all thy might to get more from and through the government than thou hast paid"; "Whatever you say or think, if it's true, useful, or pleasant to you, it's true and good"; "Thou shalt abort, or at least speak of abortions as the ultimate act of liberation, and regard denigration of abortion as heinous"; "Thy children belong in day care, thy parents in nursing homes"; "Thou shalt copulate at will, counting this as thy great freedom"; "Thou shalt keep guard over thy neighbor for any sign of evasion of regulations and promptly report the same."

More than most, this religion gives its adherents a dose of the ultimate human thrill: feeling superior to the irreligious, and the sense of entitlement to wield power over them. Its god, "the Planet," speaking to humankind through its priests, indicts humanity's original sin: polluting the planet with excess population, poisoning it with chemicals, scarring it with mines, and causing global warming. In its dogma, the source of that sin is the biblical lie that man is somehow superior to the rest of nature. But the dogma says that human life is no more worthy than that of animals or even of plants. Hence this religion's Great Commandment: "Save the Planet!" bids believers to live lives that are obviously "green," thus to purify themselves from the ideas and people who are "enemies of the Planet." Then it endows believers with the right and duty to minimize the enemies' "footprints" while feeling better about themselves.

Judaism and Christianity teach that all men are subject to one God and hence to a single standard, the various iterations of which stem from the Ten Commandments. But modern Western governments, by rejecting biblical religion, entitle themselves to make up standards as they go along. Proclaiming that "values"—the moral bases for preferences—are inherently arbitrary (in Max Weber's words, "demonic"), they feel entitled to impose their own values in the name of tolerance. To the powerful, the great attraction of this moral relativism is precisely that it lets regimes stigmatize and disadvantage people who assert values different from theirs, or to deny the existence of standards to which the powerful also are subject. Arthur Koestler and George Orwell identified the moral relativists' ultimate enemy: the soul that is stiffly independent because its anchor is beyond the reach of the regime.

Moral relativism's logic—justifying whatever the powerful may want—has led modern regimes to invert the ethics of Judeo-Christian civilization. As these regimes were being established in the 1930s, they called "economic justice" what had previously been called taking others' property—robbery. In France, the ruling Popular Front's explanation for taking over the country's wealth was the same as Willie Sutton's wry reason for robbing banks: "That's where the money is." As the welfare states matured, their ruling coalitions—retirees or the soon-to-be-retired, in addition to various kinds of "disabled" and welfare clients, the subsidized industries, the government contractors, and government employees—loaded taxes on young workers and called it "social justice." Elsewhere, it has been noted that interest-group politics has a logic that drives it toward what Lincoln called the counsel of the "old serpent": You work, I'll eat.

The secular religion's logic has led Western governments to aggravate the other diseases of the soul that follow from self-indulgence. Having promoted promiscuity, they have dealt with its consequences by distributing condoms. The government of France even sponsored a tongue-in-cheek TV commercial urging young men to use them "to please Mom." And of course, Western governments provide free abortions. For drug addiction, they provide clean needles and an income. For those who do not wish to work, subsistence. For crime, jails. In short, modern European government is paying to subsidize the way of life that is the consequence of its secular religion, and it is paying even more heavily to alleviate the discomforts of practicing it. Note, however, that one subsidy comes from abroad. In a nutshell, Europe's official religion has not produced men who even think about defending themselves militarily. For more than half a century, the United States of America has provided Europe with military defense. Had it not done so, European regimes would have been swept away.

In sum, although the European regimes' new religion manufactured non-Christians, it did not fill the souls that it emptied. Its chief legacy seems to be to further sharpen the choice between biblical religion and nihilism.

ISRAEL

In December 1996, a poll revealed that 42 percent of Israelis thought that a civil war between religious and secular Jews was likely.[22] And in fact, since the 1960s, both religious and secular Israelis seem to have exacerbated the conflict of visions that existed at the Jewish state's conception circa 1900. During the generation leading up to the birth of Israel in 1948, both sides made compromises, on which both sides reneged late in the century under the pressures of military events and social developments in Western society. As the years passed, the religious became more antisecular, and the secular became more antireligious. No one can say when or whether the harshness of politics across Israel's religious divide passed the point of no return. But no one can deny that religious politics after the mid-1980s seemed to be producing two nations.

The Zionist movement that created Israel was largely the creature of secular Jews like Theodor Herzl and Chaim Weizmann, *fin de siècle* Socialists who, like the formerly Christian Socialists of their kind, believed in human perfectibility rather than in God. They also believed that Jews and Arabs could live together in peace in the Promised Land. Non-Socialist Zionists, including Ze'ev Jabotinsky, a classical liberal, did not share the socialists' expectation that the Jewish state could come into being without conflict with the Arabs. Nor did they embrace the vision of a society embodying the European Enlightenment's utopian dreams. The early Zionists were Europeans who happened to be Jews, who had had enough of attempts at assimilation, and who wanted their own country for their own nationality. In this they were no different from other Europeans of their time. Each major nationality had a state. Why not the Jews? They looked on the religion of the Torah as an embarrassment, quite as much as their post-Christian fellow Socialists looked down upon Christianity.

That is why religious Jews, especially the few already in Palestine, viewed the Zionists as triple abominations—they were nonobservant nonbelievers who presumed to hurry the time of the Messiah. They aimed to set up a society just as foreign to Jewish law as any in Europe, and they would make a lot of trouble to boot. Nevertheless, the prospect of resettling the Land of the Promise convinced a few Orthodox rabbis, such as Samuel Mohlever that the Lord might possibly be using profane vessels for holy purposes. In the interwar period, as Europe became more menacing, even the anti-Zionists of Agudat Yisrael joined in the settlement, if only to minimize the damage that the Zionists might do to Palestine and to Judaism. But although all these factions worked out compromises, they kept the separate organizations and divergent outlooks that define Israel's four basic political groups today—two of them secular, Labor and Likud; and two religious, those in the National Religious Party and those Hasidim even further alienated from secularism. (The Kadima Party, founded in 2005, seems to be a hothouse hybrid of short duration.) Of course, in Israel the religious groups mix promiscuously with the secular ones for political purposes.

It is inherently difficult to sort out the many different relationships that various Israeli Jews have with the laws of the Torah and that each group has with the state of Israel. Perhaps one-fourth of the Jews in Israel try to live by the whole *Halacha,* the law of Moses, and send their children either to the state's religious schools or to religious schools of their own supported by the state. Of the remaining three-fourths of the population, consisting of Jews broadly termed "nonobservant," most follow varying percentages of the law. Perhaps four-fifths keep some kind of fast on Yom Kippur, even in secular Tel Aviv, and nearly all accept with some gladness the quiet that descends on the country during the Sabbath, the preholiday preparations, the religious marriages, and other Jewish symbols that pervade society. Aggressive secularists who despise such things may number no more than one in eight Israelis.

The state of Israel is based on a set of postwar compromises between the secular David Ben-Gurion and Orthodox rabbis, an arrangement since that time called the "status quo." According to this agreement, religious identity, marriage, and divorce would be under religious law administered by Orthodox rabbis. Public transportation would not run in the country as a whole on the Sabbath but would run in non-Orthodox neighborhoods. Most businesses would close. All state eating establishments would follow Jewish dietary laws. Religious schools would be funded by the state, which would also run a more or less secular system. (In the contemporary United States, the Israeli secular system would be insufferably religious.) But Israel as a whole would be a secular state where people could follow their own ways. The state of Israel would emphatically *not* be a creature of Abraham's covenant, but rather of the United Nations. It would never consider razing the Muslims' Dome of the Rock from the Temple Mount, and rebuilding the Temple. Secularists saw the state of Israel as the affirmation of a Jewish identity whose meaning owed more to lively memories of persecution than to the law and the prophets. *Indeed, the only decoration outside the prime minister's office is a painting of the Holocaust, not a menorah.* The religious, for their part, were happy enough that the people of the Covenant could worship God in the land of the Covenant. Present dangers helped forge solidarity over the underlying sentiment that others were not true Israelis, or perhaps even true Jews.

In 1967, when war delivered the Wailing Wall, East Jerusalem, Judea and Samaria, the Sinai, the Golan Heights, and the Gaza Strip to Israel, the status quo began to unravel. Many observant Jews were energized to think that the Lord had given them the whole Promised Land, which they could not now give up. A large number of secular Jews joined them in this belief and formed the Gush Emunim and Tehiya parties, which united the secular and religious Jews in what might be called a new nationalism and pushed politics to even sharper confrontation with the Arabs (assuming that were possible). This further discomfited some Socialist Jews who felt that their lives and comforts were being endangered more than necessary in the pursuit of ideals they did not share. The rise of Arab terrorism within Israel pushed both hawkish nationalists and dovish Socialists to see each other as a major obstacle to the different kinds of peace each wanted. During the 1970s and 1980s, secular leftist Israelis underwent the same kind of cultural changes as similar people in Western countries, tending toward growing antimilitarism, diffidence of religion, and sexual liberation. Finally, the immigration of large numbers of Sephardic Jews, who tended to be more observant than Israel's original mix, and the observant Jews' higher birth rates, combined to shift the character of the country in an ever more religious direction. More men were wearing yarmulkes and black hats, more were wearing earrings, and fewer were in between. By the 1990s, Israelis were growling at one another across a religious divide.

Even the army, the institution within which all but a faction of the Orthodox had joined for the common good, began losing the trust of both sides. The Right and the religious opposed the army for carrying out the policy of removing some settlers from the Sinai to implement the peace treaty with Egypt (and later for removing settlers from Gaza). Some rightists felt that the army might not be counted on to protect settlers in Hebron (some rabbis have called for soldiers to disobey such orders). The secularist Left objected because trust in force was the reason the intransigent part of the population was not eager enough for peace.

Across society, both sides accused the other of encroachment on the status quo. Ugly words were spoken and ugly incidents began to take place. Secular Jews began to drive honking caravans into Orthodox neighborhoods on the Sabbath. Teddy Kollek, Jerusalem's longtime secularist mayor, asked rhetorically what might be done about the Orthodox element's reproductive prowess. And in fact, the city's demographic shift cost him his job. Orthodox rabbis effectively denied Jewish status to the foreign non-Orthodox, implying that their secular brethren could not be classified as Jews either. And then both factions, supported by friends abroad, began to engage in name-calling, blaming each other for the acts of Arab terrorists. In 1995, when Prime Minister Yitzhak Rabin was shot by a deranged Jewish settler who claimed that he had done the will of God, the secularists blamed the opposition in general and observant Jews in particular. And after another psychologically unstable Jew committed an act of terrorism against the Arabs and claimed religious authority for it, the Left retaliated by saying that religious Jews were nothing more than interlopers in the Zionist dream.

The constant complaint of the biblical prophets was that the people lived the law with their bodies but not with their souls. Today, many Israeli secularists go so far as to speak ill of the way of life of those who live under the law. Since the Torah is the only possible source of spiritual substance for those who call themselves Jews, the reduction of the Torah to a bone of partisan contention weighs heavily on Israel's spirit. Division into two sets of people habituated to contempt for each other's spiritual substance poses a mortal danger for any country, but most of all for one that rests on a religious foundation. No more than any other can Israel's house stand divided.

RELIGION AND REGIMES

What can any regime do with the spiritual habits of the people it governs? Regimes cannot make Christians out of Muslims, or Jews into Zoroastrians. Few try such nonsense. They can only abet processes by which people become better or worse Christians, Jews, and so on. Nor can regimes create new religions. Those that have tried have ended up with peoples alienated from their old faith and cynical about the new. All religions have civil relevance, but there is no such thing as civil religion. Regimes can work only within the parameters set by the religion. Some, like Shinto, lend themselves to being bent to a regime's purposes more than others: The Bible and the rest of Christianity's intellectual corpus made the Nazis' attempt to bend Christianity to its purposes ridiculous. In general, a regime only has the choice of supporting the religion under its domain or trying to weaken it. As we have seen, weakening religion is feasible in several ways. Strengthening religion is probably beyond the reach of any regime, except in the sense that a regime may simply leave some social functions to be carried out by religious authorities. Yet even here, it is important to distinguish between the Saudi practice of leaving matters of morals to the religious police, and the seventeenth-century Swedish practice of deputizing the church to carry out state policy.

Regimes can have the most devastating effects on the spirit of those who live under them, as well as on the body politic, by taking sides in spiritual struggles. Civil wars tend to be the most devastating of wars, and religious civil wars are the worst of civil wars. And yet regimes define themselves precisely by taking sides on the questions most important to those who live under them. Statecraft is also the art of the soul, because it involves choosing which spiritual matters to treat as fundamental. But to choose principles that are right by nature, that intrude minimally on the prevalent religion, and that habituate people to religious peace is statecraft's most difficult part.

9

THE ULTIMATE TEST

It is truer than any other truth that if where there are
men there are not soldiers it is the fault of the prince,
and nothing else.
> —NICCOLÒ MACHIAVELLI, *DISCOURSES*

To the extent that a people's habits do not produce military forces that win wars, these habits are a mortal disease. The preparation and employment of force is the most indispensable of any regime's functions. The task that the regime's leading personages must perform is always the same: to competently direct those responsible for military operations, to inspire devotion and instill quality performance among them, and to make sure the forces match the regime's military and civil needs. Some civilian leaders direct military force more than others. But all are inalienably responsible for victory or defeat.

POWER AND HABITS

People, not things, generate military power. Regimes that nurture the proper habits find they have military power when they call on it, while those that trust in economics or technology or diplomacy or sociology to provide it are disappointed.

No view is more prevalent or more mistaken than that money is the sinew of war. But history abounds with instances of wealthy peoples defeated by lean and hungry ones. Alexander's poor Macedonians cut through Darius III's wealthy Persian Empire like a knife through butter. Genghis Khan's tent-dwelling, dung-burning Mongols did the same to the Chinese and Persian plutocrats. George Washington's rag-clothed Continentals defeated the wealthiest power of the age. Wealthy Americans were defeated by poor Vietnamese. And, of course, the wealth of the impotent Romans only excited various barbarians to take it. For this reason, when King Croesus of Lydia threatened Solon of Athens by showing him his gold, Solon told him that war was made with iron. Guns compel butter. Even more to the point, iron is wielded by men, whose ultimate efforts cannot be bought, but rather result from certain habits. Nor can money, unlike character, make the difference between prudence and foolishness, or energy and lassitude, in war.

Thucydides' liveliest set of images show Athens, which had all the ingredients of great power, coming to ruin because it had lost the key habits of public-spirited moderation. At the outset of the Peloponnesian War, Pericles told the Athenians that they should be confident of victory because of their capacity to draw wealth from their overseas empire. He also told them that their strength lay in their character, which combined lust for magnificence with patriotism and love of right measure. In that regard, he warned them not to try to add to their empire during the war.[1] But because, after Pericles' death, the intemperate Cleon and the disproportionately ambitious Alcibiades made their respective vices prominent among the Athenian people, Athens' character changed. Quite literally what had been foul became fair, and vice versa. Diodotus found that to get the Athenian Assembly to listen to arguments for decent acts, he had to couch them in indecent terms. When Nicias countered Alcibiades' immoderate suggestion that Athens attack Sicily by showing how inherently senseless, dangerous, and militarily difficult that operation was, as well as how much it would cost, the Athenian people heard only about the cost. They threw stunning amounts of money at the enterprise, but little judgment. The force they sent was magnificent. But its splendor did not make up for its lack of cavalry, the military mission's lack of clarity, or the rifts between its chiefs and the city.[2]

Nor does power come from technology. Probably since before biblical times, when the chariot ruled the battlefields (Egyptians sometimes even attached scythes to the axles), people have been tempted to think that victory belongs to those possessed of the latest wonder weapon. Certain tactics, such as the Greek phalanx and the Roman triple-rank line, have led to similar suppositions of invincibility. In the late twentieth century, it was fashionable to think that nuclear weapons, and then precision-guided munitions, made the human ingredients of military power irrelevant. The fashion in the twenty-first was that constabulary forces were the key to victory. But this is as much a fancy as previous notions that crossbows, artillery, or machine guns turned offense or defense into mere technicalities.

Machiavelli uses the example of fortresses—by also referring to artillery and cavalry, he makes clear that he means technical factors per se—to show that one can make few mistakes worse than to regard *any* technical factor as operating independently of human factors.[3] In and of themselves, fortresses can either be useful or not. But the fortress mentality (or the artillery mentality, or any other principled reliance on things or techniques) is invariably fatal to military habits. We should recall that the Maginot line of fortresses on the northeastern border of France's Third Republic was inherently quite useful for channeling enemy attacks and economizing French forces. But the French used the Maginot line not as an adjunct to strategy but as a substitute for it. The Maginot mentality led the French people to think that France's military problems had been solved on the cheap, which fed ruinous habits that spread throughout French society. The same goes for the mentality induced by any other instance of military technolatry.[4]

Even the number and dedication of soldiers is not to be confused with military power. Thus, when Mao Tse-tung asserted that China did not fear nuclear weapons because there were more Chinese than any set of weapons could kill, he was missing an important fact. Even if all Chinese had been organized militarily instead of only a minuscule percentage of them (and these, badly), the Chinese had neither the means nor the schemes to prevent any of the world's major powers from doing whatever they might wish to any part of China. By the same token, the Zulu troops that Britain defeated in 1879 were dedicated and trained to a perfection that the Romans might have envied, and they were led well. But run-of-the-mill machine gunners trumped world-class spearmen. The point is that numbers and dedication of troops are merely parts of the military equation.

Where there are proper military habits, able leaders can combine them with money and high-tech weapons to produce military power that stands a chance of winning. Crafting such combinations takes statesmen. Where these are lacking, money and materiel are wasted. In 1940, France had more tanks than Germany. But French generals had resisted calls to organize their tanks into armored divisions. The regime could not bring itself to correct the military's smug inertia because it did not want to challenge the country's pacifist habits. Pacifists argued that armored divisions were offensive weapons unworthy of a peace-loving country. Because this sentiment lent support to its narrow self-interest, the military failed to tell the public the truth: that armored divisions—indeed, just about any weapon—may be used for defense as well as offense. Because one set of bad habits at the top of French society abetted another set of bad habits at the bottom, all the money the country spent on tanks could not prevent the Panzer divisions from parading the Nazi eagles on the Champs-Élysées.

THE ULTIMATE RESPONSIBILITY

Since the regime sets the tone for military institutions as well as for the rest of society, the character of the military depends substantially on that of the regime's leading personages. If they do not lead armies themselves, they must somehow lead both the leaders and the led. The difficulty of this task is vastly underrated in modern Western countries and nowhere else. But that is not all: Military institutions also contribute to the tone of society at large.

On a wall in Istanbul's Topkapi Museum are the vestments and swords of the Ottoman sultans. The plain tunic of Mohamed II, conqueror of Constantinople, once fit a fit man. His unadorned sword was obviously dented by steel and bone. As one moves along the exhibit, the vestments get wider and fancier, the swords more ceremonial, until those of nineteenth-century sultans indicate that their owners were fitter for sedan chairs than saddles and that they could no more dent shields than they could lead armies. During these 300 years, the nature of the Ottoman regime did not change. It was still an Oriental monarchy with an army composed of large numbers of people who were essentially slaves kept in line by dread, and of smaller numbers of special units, especially the Janissaries, who had been raised from childhood to be loyal shock troops and henchmen. When the Janissaries respected the sultan physically, they focused on winning his battles; when he controlled them by playing some against others, the best they could manage was to oversee the empire's shrinkage. Finally, when the sultans had nothing more in common with military leaders, the "Young Turk" military officers ceased to respect them and their bureaucrats. Thus, these officers first became an interest group within the regime, then they set up their own—modern Turkey.

Even though the Prussian regime was very different from the Ottoman Empire's, Prussia underwent an evolution analogous to Turkey's. Quite simply, whereas until the mid–nineteenth century the senior officer corps had been broadly representative of the aristocracy, its social base thereafter narrowed to a sector of East Prussian landholders who came to think of the army's interests as more important than those of the regime. Conversely, the rest of the regime, from the Kaiser down, progressively lost confidence in its own military judgments. As it decreased its involvement in military affairs, it received less and less respect from generals, and gradually lost control over them even as these gained greater weight within the regime. That is why during World War I, General Erich Ludendorff was able to take over the Reich effectively without either the army or the regime realizing that anything radical had happened. But that army, although efficient enough in military operations, wrecked the country by pursuing a two-front war that violated statecraft's most elementary tenets. The generals' ignorance of statecraft combined with the rulers' military impotence to produce a ruinous military supremacy.

Nazi Germany shows the obverse of the same predicament: A group of chaotically undisciplined civilians whose führer was the epitome of personal indiscipline imposed their ways on the armed forces. Special units proliferated, not only to perform the standard tyrannical functions of slaughter and counterchecking, but also because any number of military leaders were corrupted into seeking special channels of influence and privilege. After July 1940, Hitler's management of World War II became militarily indefensible and was harming the professional military as much as the country in general. Yet the military never seriously resisted because the regime had so impressed its own chaos, mistrust, and lack of honor on it. In this case, the civilians' assertive ignorance of military matters combined with the military's political corruption to produce a civilian supremacy that proved even more ruinous than Ludendorff's military supremacy had.

Sometimes armies influence the character of regimes more than regimes influence that of armies, and sometimes armies pass their peculiar disease— or health—on to society at large. Ever since Juan Perón reshaped Argentina in 1943, every part of the regime—government agencies, parties, and allied organizations—has exercised some exclusive economic privileges. The armed forces, too, have run dozens of companies and profited from it. By contrast, the armed forces of neighboring Chile accepted the earmarked taxes on the copper industry but managed nothing, holding themselves aloof from the country's politics and preserving old-fashioned, modest probity. In 1973, when Chile's congress asked the armed forces to overthrow Salvador Allende's rapacious regime, Chilean tanks literally stopped at traffic lights, and the subsequent military regime remade the country in its image. In 1982, when Chile's military ruler Augusto Pinochet built a luxurious presidential palace, the frugal habits of the public and of the military made it impossible for him to move in. Nor did his successors.

In the ancient republics, military service was synonymous with citizenship, and rightly so, because the ultimate practical question in public life anywhere is, Who will uphold the laws, arms in hand, at the risk of his life? Even in the ancient world, especially in Carthage, the argument was made that other kinds of contributions—especially money—could be just as valuable to the community; therefore, so goes the argument, such contributions entitle those who make them to as full a voice in civic life as those with military service. But this is most convincing to those who have not given or are not about to give up the best years of their lives to the discomfort and danger of military service.

A set of difficulties arises when regimes purchase the military service of citizens or foreigners. As we shall see, various schemes have been tried with varying degrees of success to alleviate some of the consequences of straightforward purchases. The best-known instances of straightforward purchases— by city-states in Renaissance Italy—were the object of Machiavelli's historic critique of mercenary forces: When citizens do not fight for themselves, they neither learn military skills nor form patriotic habits of the heart. And governments that hire mercenaries do not form links of habitual command and obedience with citizens. Worse, bought armies seldom fight as well as armies composed of citizens, and when they win (rarely), they often replace the government.[5]

Common sense has always prescribed a cure for such ills, namely, citizen-officers as well as citizen-soldiers. But these words are difficult to translate into reality, regardless of whether the regime is an oligarchy or a democracy, because citizens who have gained the power to rule others seldom allot to themselves any of society's unpleasant functions, let alone the dangerous ones. And no function is less pleasant or more dangerous than soldiering. Where low-ranking soldiers are concerned, it is possible for regimes to have the advantages of citizen-soldiers without inconveniencing the powerful of the land by taking the young and the poor. More rarely, leading citizens have been able to convince the population at large to pressure its children to give their lives as soldiers. But, as World War I and its aftermath in Europe showed, even the perception that the blood tax is being assessed unfairly or for insufficiently worthy reasons is the stuff of revolution or of outright social dissolution. In sum, officers are either the same kind of people who run the country or they are not. And that makes for big differences in society.

The Israeli experience is a reminder that what the classics taught about the role of military forces within civil societies is still valid. Although Israel today extends to the Arabs within its borders all civil privileges of citizenship, it denies them military service. Because the rest of the Israelis cannot rely on them when the chips are down, the Arabs are not really citizens. Because it is difficult for a man to rise in Israeli society without fulfilling thirty-three days of military service every year, military experience is a closely examined part of resumes, and marks of military distinction are marks of social distinction. Thus, at the top of Israeli society are men habituated to physical courage and responsibility for life and death. At a minimum, foreign affairs is not a spectator sport for any Israeli. Also, perhaps the concept of the common good is not as abstract for them as it otherwise might be. Since the most prestigious military units—the special forces who scale rocks and rescue hostages—require special physical performance, teenagers from the best Israeli families pay for and sweat through courses to prepare to compete for the privilege of serving in them. Hence, there flows toward the top a stream of young men habituated to exposing themselves to risk.

Finally, societies where almost every man is a soldier are always pervaded by a radical sense of equality, because nothing so entitles a man to look upon his fellows as no more than equals than the common hardship and danger incurred in military service. The resulting informality is often mistaken for a lack of respect. But it really signifies that respect is spread rather evenly. One of the peculiarities of Israel is that this spirit of equality exists in a people whose economy runs on patronage and who therefore have to make their way by wheedling favors. Anybody can "get to" just about anybody else through some mutual acquaintance made in the army. Also, while Israel's Socialist economics tend to push women out of the home, and women serve in the army, Israeli families receive a patriarchal push from the fact that men are the society's obviously indispensable protectors.

Soldiers and veterans are not always pillars of the rule of law. In the Roman Empire, after military service had ceased to be an act of citizenship and became a profession, the military and ex-military simply composed the dominant interest group. But when citizens are soldiers, they are in the best moral position to assert the basic demands of citizenship: to be treated as fairly as anybody and to be left to run their own lives. They are in a good practical position to press their claims, because through their years of service, they have acquired the capacity to lead and to follow according to rules. They have also learned how to accomplish the most unpleasant civic duty of all: rebellion. Even Stalin had to be a little careful of World War II's veterans. The defense of the Russian Parliament that sealed the Soviet Union's fate in 1991 was possible only because a large number of Red Army veterans, and some active units as well, defected to the Russian rebels. The defense of the Lithuanian Parliament in 1990 against KGB forces was organized by a Lithuanian-American who had served in the U.S. Special Forces.

Machiavelli explained that a regime that hires its soldiers devalues and diminishes patriotism. It soon loses perspective about peace and war and forfeits respect at home and abroad. A few have recognized the importance of universal military service to the formation of citizens but dispensed with it nevertheless. In the post–World War II period, the countries of Western Europe maintained conscription formally while allowing about one-half of the eligible young men (almost all from the upper classes) to simply not show up when called. By the 1990s, such blatant discrimination against the poor was dividing European societies much as it had done in the United States during the Vietnam War. And so, in May 1996, the government of France gave up two centuries of conscription, which it had valued for habituating different classes to equal and joint endeavor. For this, it substituted a one-week class on civic obligation, compulsory for all young men and women. The class teaches that that obligation exists. Its existence teaches that it does not.

ARMS AND THE REGIME

Just as any regime's reach must not exceed its grasp, its military forces must fit its character and its objectives. Before the Punic Wars, republican Rome seldom sent armies of more than 50,000 men beyond the Apennines. Because these armies were relatively small, hordes of barbarians would occasionally defeat them. But as the barbarians drew closer to Rome, the city and its peninsular hinterland turned populations into masses of soldiers. In 347 B.C., near today's city of Pisa, one band of Gauls was annihilated by

1.5 million Romans. And one century later, whenever Hannibal wiped out a Roman army, the extended city would bring forth another as if nothing had happened. Early republican Rome could not send big armies far because the legions were made up of ordinary citizens whose family fields and shops could not spare them for long. But since every man was a soldier, emergencies could bring out masses for short periods. Rome did not have to send big armies far away because the only faraway wars it undertook were those its consuls planned on winning with relatively small forces. The armies did not have to stay long after the victory, either, because the Romans quickly inserted colonists into newly conquered lands who could defend them to some extent. The colonists did not have to fight often because Rome let potential attackers know that the penalty for attacking Roman colonies would be sure, swift, and terrible. In short, ancient Rome drew a very sharp line between peace and war, and none at all between citizen and soldier.

By contrast, as soldiering was becoming common only among the dispossessed who were willing to exchange ten years in the legions for the promise of land in the provinces, late republican Rome began the practice of stationing large armies far away. Large standing armies abroad allowed Roman generals the luxury of long campaigns. This made it possible for Roman consuls to deal with peoples such as the northeastern Germans, the Scythians, and the Goths by making a little peace and a little war. The provincial legions remained strong well into the imperial era. But their vigor, the growing practice of hiring barbarians into the ranks, combined with the loss of military habits in Italy, caused the Roman Empire to implode many times before the center rotted completely and the barbarians put it out of its misery.

The point here is to recognize the necessary proportion between any regime's military organization and the regime's objectives. Consider that nineteenth-century Britain was able to control a vast empire, including such warlike people as the Afghans, with fewer than 20,000 men abroad at any given time. For this, the organization described below sufficed. By contrast, note that the Soviet Union occupied its East European empire with almost 1 million soldiers, and that a superbly equipped and ruthless Soviet force of 250,000 was unable to hold Afghanistan. Maintaining the Soviet empire required near-universal conscription and the economic militarization of society. The reason these two empires required such different levels of effort and such different kinds of relationships between society and the military lies in the very different purposes of the two empires. Whereas the British worked through the local power structure wherever possible, did not dream of threatening what the locals held dearest, and offered them a way of life that many found attractive, the Soviets backed locals who sought to force their countrymen into uncomfortable molds. The Afghan mujahideens' war made sense only as a defense of threatened Islam. And the Russian people's rejection of their regime's war shows a disconnect between the mentality of the conscript army that had to be used in a conflict of that size, on the one hand, and the partisan purposes for which the regime fought the war, on the other.

EUROPE'S ANCIEN RÉGIME

Prior to the French Revolution, Europe's regimes fostered a set of habits at both the top and the bottom of society that fit the regimes' domestic order and served the pursuit of their moderate international objectives.

In Britain, where the military habits of the seventeenth and eighteenth centuries lasted through the nineteenth, Rudyard Kipling wrote that "Sergeant Whatshisname" could "make soldiers out of mud."[6] The duke of Wellington had described that mud as "the scum of the earth" and had been happy to say that the British system had turned into useful fellows men who otherwise would have been useless or worse. A generation earlier, Frederick the Great had described his recruits as "the dregs of society." But he, too, was confident that training would turn them into useful soldiers. And so were his French counterparts. The soldiers of Europe's *ancien régimes*—up to one-third of whom were foreign adventurers—were enticed or forcibly impressed into regiments, where sergeants drilled them in loading and firing muzzle loaders regardless of the carnage around them. They were also taught to march and to make bayonet charges. Discipline was everywhere enforced by horrible physical punishment. Yet by the turn of the eighteenth century, Britain's duke of Marlborough and Louis XIV's minister Francois Michel Le Tellier, Marquis de Louvois, had discovered that soldiers who believed that their officers cared about them fought better than those who did not. Thus, both Britain and France sought to make enlisted military service something that would enmesh the soldier or sailor in habits of obedience. The regiment or the ship would become the enlistee's only real family and country. Punishment would then become less important as a motivator. The liberal British preferred enlistments for twenty-one years but often abandoned old soldiers to pitiful conditions. The paternalistic French went further and established a chain of old soldiers' homes, of which the magnificent Invalides in Paris is the centerpiece.

The middle classes and ordinary farmers would not have stood for attempts to recruit them into such lives—which is why the free English of America were so horrified when the British navy kidnapped some of *them* for service. Nor would ordinary British or French subjects have stood for impressment. Ordinary people served in the very part-time militias that were relics of the old feudal retainers. But the *ancien régimes* relied ever less on armed representatives of a free society, whom they feared as breeding possible resistance and as militarily unreliable. Even Adam Smith, applying the Hobbesian ideology typical of the period, believed that men motivated by dread would face danger more surely than men accustomed to freedom. Hence, the old regimes relied ever more on men who could be counted on to behave as if they had been bred to obedience. Ironically, the exploits of royal armies, composed of society's dregs and led by its cream, inspired middle-class spectators to think nationalistic thoughts, thus paving the way for the nationalist regimes and mass armies of the nineteenth and early twentieth centuries.

The most significant aspect of the old regimes' military arrangements, however, is how they trained officers, almost all of whom were noblemen, to be loyal to the king. Military leadership had been the old nobility's raison d'être. Many, if not most, nobles were all too eager to lead troops. Their families cultivated habits of courage and honor aplenty. And recall that the sixteenth and seventeenth centuries had been full of wars between nobles and kings. By the eighteenth century, however, European kings were selling to their nobles the right to pay to equip the regiments they would lead, under the superintendence of royal bureaucrats. Still, the great nobles were not easy to train. The Prince de Condé and the Vicomte de Turenne were loyal enough to Louis XIV. But the first was a prince and the other a count. Although Louvois was Louis's minister, he could no more order such blue bloods around than William III could push Marlborough after the victory of Blenheim. Leadership had to be subtle. The domestication of the military nobility was accomplished not just through repeated acquiescence to royal wish but also through the introduction into the officer ranks of commoners who had shown merit. The Prussians led the way here, followed by the French. But when the British took up the practice, they went the others one better and granted knighthoods to able commoners. The old regimes thereby trained a class of military leaders that was identical with themselves.

The military tools at the disposal of the old regimes fit their objectives of survival and limited aggrandizement. They wanted to avoid radical changes abroad quite as much as at home. Soldiers were relatively difficult to rake up and were expensive to maintain for life. In campaigns, the ranks of armies were cut between one-third and one-half by disease, desertion, and casualties. There was thus every reason to use armies sparingly. Still, they would go anywhere and do anything asked of them. The officers, too, were even more willing to go for glory. But the idea was not to let them get too much of it, nor too much rapport with their troops. Such armies and navies were just right for genteel, limited warfare. The grand prizes were the succession to the thrones of Spain or Austria, the allegiance of the Netherlands or some princeling in Germany or Italy, or the possession of some colony. Thus, though there was bloodshed and bravery and honor aplenty, commanders also recognized when someone else's timely march or placement of artillery had so prejudiced the survival of a fortress or the outcome of a battle that surrender was an honorable option—and a safe one. In the Franco-British war over the Netherlands, for example, captured officers would go home after promising in writing to abstain from further action during the current conflict. Instances of cruel imprisonment, such as that which the British inflicted on Americans aboard ships in Charleston harbor in 1778, were most rare. In this way, the old regimes' military practices fostered habits consistent with themselves.

NAPOLEONIC FRANCE

Appetite comes from eating. So goes an old French proverb. Just so, Napoleon's appetite for conquest grew with each victory—and so did his military needs. In the end, those needs outstripped the capacity of the regime to supply them, even though the regime had been organized primarily for that.

The Napoleonic regime really was organized like an army. The old regime had slowly substituted feudal functions and powers that had been vested in countless guilds, towns, and nobles by royal officials. These assumed responsibility for roads, bridges, public health, basic industries, and even the breeding of quality draft horses. Not least of the kings' motives for this had been to increase their capacity to draw military power from society. The revolution swept away the remainder of society's spontaneous hierarchies—what Tocqueville called "intermediary bodies" and Burke, the "little platoons." It pasted the label *commissaires* onto royal officials, while multiplying their functions and powers. Since their regime was fighting for its life from beginning to end, the revolutionaries were even more militarily motivated. For this reason as well as to imitate the ancient republics, the revolution introduced universal conscription.

Napoleon, first consul and then emperor, who claimed to be in the line of the Caesars, took these trends to their logical conclusion and created the first modern regime conceived for people-to-people war. No Caesar had ever established a network of schools to qualify the best of society's young for administration, health, and all the useful trades. The Napoleonic regime marshaled society's many occupations and functions into "corps." Every part of society was encouraged to think of itself as an organ in a body marching forward. Napoleon had organized a Ministry of the Interior to make sure that the various social functions were coordinated and delivered materiel. Conscription delivered the personnel. The country was cut into departments, within which towns were marked out, roads named, and houses numbered, so that orders from the very top could move the very bottom. The Parliament itself was the "legislative corps," with its assigned function, just like every other part of society, in a scheme intended to produce military power.

War is supposed to be one of the means of statecraft. But the Napoleonic regime—thereafter widely copied throughout the Western world—had no end other than war. A regime's purpose is supposed to transcend that of the army, but in this case, the purposes were identical. Therefore, while the army triumphed and society was well trained to supply its needs, triumph fed habits of spiraling ambitions that could never be satisfied.

Napoleon asked a lot of the regime. In 1804, he drafted 60,000 men. The following year, he took not only 80,000 from the newly eligible but 100,000 from among young men who had become eligible in earlier years but not been taken. Six months later, he asked for another 80,000. In 1811, as he prepared for the Russian campaign, he took 120,000 from the current crop of eligibles and 100,000 from all the preceding ones. In 1812, he took 120,000 and incorporated another 100,000 from the old territorial militias. As he began to suffer more defeats than victories, the demands grew even larger. But even the victories were costly: The campaigns of 1806 and 1807 killed 200,000, and the Russian campaign alone wiped out 300,000.

Making such sacrifices required a particular set of habits. Napoleon instilled them in officers and men alike quite simply by running the army, according to de Gaulle, as "a perpetual contest, of which the emperor was the organizer and judge, the reward of which was glory."[7] And, he might have added, profit as well. Just as men advanced in the various civilian corps by demonstrating competence in competitive exams, they advanced in the armed corps by demonstrating superior performance in combat. Napoleon's descent upon the most heavily bloodied regiment after the battle of Abensberg was typical: He asked for the bravest officer and made him a baron with a lifetime pension. Then he asked for the bravest soldier and made him a knight of the Legion of Honor, also with a lifetime pension. The emperor, in short, built a brand new, endowed nobility. He made some of his marshals into kings (Sweden and Naples), others into dukes. He made counts out of colonels and barons out of captains. And formerly humble farmers who had earned their way into the Imperial Guard or who had been decorated with the Croix de Guerre could count on prestige that would compel the respect of officials throughout the regime. Napoleonic France was truly the land of opportunity, where nobodies could become princes by their own valor. To entice the many to risk their lives for rewards that could only go to the few, the emperor freely handed out symbols of recognition, such as special hats or rations of wine or decorations for the musket. He taught his senior officers to spread downward the impression that the leader sees all, appreciates all, and gives a just reward. And so, because restless daring flowed downward, Napoleon's armies moved faster and fought harder than others.

The regime's denial of just measure, however, destroyed the habits on which its success rested. The source of the trouble was that Napoleon only pretended to aim at peace. His army and his country gradually found out that he was lying to them. His first campaigns had been continuations of the wars of the revolution, caused as much by France's neighbors as by the French. Between 1800 and 1806, Napoleon aggrandized France beyond the hopes of its kings, though not wholly without reason. Before every battle, he would tell his troops that after this one, they could go home. But after every battle, there was a bigger one to face. As Napoleon threw more men and more guns into battle, he ceased to care about the quality of his instruments or about what would happen to them.

His expressions of concern for his men had begun to ring hollow. In the end, the regime and the army crashed at the same time because recruits did not know how to fire muskets that in any case were defective, because cannons fell off carriages built out of green wood, because society began tolerating draft evasion, and because some officers quite naturally began to enjoy some of the rewards of their efforts. Still, at Waterloo, the outcome was a near thing.

SWITZERLAND

Life in Switzerland is much less exciting than it was in Napoleonic France, and the Swiss Army is no more fit to hurl masses of conscripts against great powers than it is to send small numbers to hold down foreign posts. It is fit for only one mission: to defeat invaders. For this, a country of 6.7 million can generate an army of twelve divisions (the U.S. Army has ten) and twenty-six brigades, armed with some of the world's best equipment. Of course, Swiss forces completely lack, among many other things, the mobility and capacity to sustain the long supply lines that the armies of great powers possess. But the Swiss Army's civil function and military mission require no mobility but rather steadiness, teeth rather than tail.

The Swiss regime consists of provincial burghers who have no desire to be anything else. Even bankers in Zurich and Basel, as well as people in the universities and the media, share that mentality. Long ago, they realized that they would have to pay for their peace and quiet by getting rich and poor to cooperate in an army capable of mighty defense, but nothing else. Until the seventeenth century, poor Swiss boys had hired out all over Europe as state-of-the-art pikemen. During Europe's wars of religion, the fact that different bands of Swiss served with Catholic and Protestant princes fostered strife among the cantons. The Swiss therefore came to realize that given their own religious and ethnic diversity (they speak German, French, Italian, and Romansch and practice both branches of Protestantism as well as Catholicism), to have peace among themselves they would have to take no part in foreign quarrels. Hence, the Swiss regime became characterized by its pursuit of internal social peace and international peace, traits that have become habits. The superabundance of guns in Swiss hands contributes to both.

The Swiss Army is a militia that requires every fit man to perform twenty-eight years of service—forty years in cases of emergency. No one is allowed to refuse promotion to higher rank (and responsibility). Men who are exempted for good reason pay extra taxes, and refusal to serve may be punished by expulsion from the country. This means that for twenty-eight days for twenty-eight years of their lives, men of every socioeconomic category have to practice entrusting their lives to one another. Since military units are small and each draws mainly from its own locality, the men get to know one another very well, and there naturally arises among them the same kind of bond that old regime armies tried to manufacture among their low-class recruits. But Swiss soldiers come from all classes, meaning that the bonds are formed on a higher human level and that the society as a whole, and not just the regiment, benefits from widespread mutual confidence. Beyond the army the regime also produces habits of mutual trust because people in each locality administer their own affairs, and national as well as cantonal issues are often settled by referendum. Switzerland certainly does not have the kind of divergence in tastes and manners among men in the upper reaches of society, especially the media and the universities, that one finds in other advanced societies.

By design, these common tastes and manners include violence. In Zurich, for example, a holiday is set aside to introduce young boys to shooting at human silhouettes. And can one even imagine a college professor or a TV news anchor in America who is also a colonel of artillery? In Switzerland, such people are common. Thus, while no one would describe the Swiss as particularly jolly or loose, relations among them are remarkably smooth; and though the Swiss are anything but egalitarians, their habit of treating one another with respect and by the rules is well established. In sum, the habits generated by the recruitment and training of the armed forces concur with those generated by the rest of the regime.

The Swiss military has not been fully tested in war since the time of Napoleon, when it gave a good account of itself. But its skills and dedication have been sufficient to deter attack ever since. During both world wars, the German military simply figured that taking Switzerland would cost more than the country—never mind mere passage through it—was worth. In 1940, the German plan for conquering Switzerland, dubbed "Tannenbaum," called for using twenty-one divisions against the Swiss. Had the Swiss Army been deployed on the borders, the Germans' superior mobility and firepower would have punched holes in it, surrounding and destroying it in short order. But had the Swiss Army retreated as planned to its alpine redoubts, twenty-one divisions might not have been enough, and the fight's duration would have been anybody's guess. In the only trial between Swiss and German forces, the Swiss came out ahead: On their way to France, German aircraft violated Swiss air space. In the ensuing fight, the Luftwaffe lost seven planes to one for the Swiss.

Note also that the Swiss enjoy in unusual measure the usual advantage that accrues to military forces that are operating on known terrain. Not only are passes, roads, and bridges mined, but any enemy would be operating in effect on the Swiss Army's training ground, where every artilleryman knows by heart the settings for hitting precisely every point in his field of fire, where the field of fire emanating from every bunker has been studied for generations, every line of communication covered optimally by generations of reservists, and every tactic rehearsed on the very battlefield where it must be employed. Some of the Swiss preparations—such as airplanes stored in mountain tunnels—are so expensive that they can be paid for only over many years. But because the Swiss regime's commitment to military matters does not depend on shifting perceptions of external threats and opportunities, but on constant attention to one mission, that commitment can be steady.

Because Switzerland is the land of steady habits, where nothing exciting ever happens, many regard it as dull—even as many thought Sparta dull. But in Switzerland as in Sparta, dullness and longevity go hand in hand by design—and the army serves to keep it that way.

PART III

OUR CHARACTER

10

TOCQUEVILLE'S AMERICA

The foundations of our national policy will be laid in
the pure and immutable principles of private morality.
—GEORGE WASHINGTON, FIRST INAUGURAL ADDRESS

Amerca's image, albeit hazily perceived, has drawn millions of immigrants, and has prompted much of the world to transform itself. But
it is less an image of America as it actually is than a portrait drawn from a
reality best described by Alexis de Tocqueville over a century and a half ago,
much of which is forever past.

Tocqueville described a way of life that combined characteristics that
Europeans had thought incompatible: unprecedented freedom along with
morality, as well as popular participation in government, along with unprecedented respect for law. The American phenomenon, he explained, is
due to the prevalence of habits of equality, of religious devotion, and of
practical responsibility in the exercise of local government. He showed that
the founders' thoughts reflected the American people's ways, and vice versa.
The original American regime's prosperity is to be understood in terms of
its civility and its religion, while its religious habits are to be understood on

their own terms as well in terms of civil equality. Finally, Americans became "most free" because, like the Swiss, they were "most armed."

AMERICAN PROSPERITY

Every Thanksgiving, the *Wall Street Journal* runs as its editorial two descriptions of Massachusetts. The first, written upon the Pilgrims' arrival in 1620 and entitled "The Desolate Wilderness," describes a place that promised hunger and cold, as well as danger from "wilde beasts and wilde men." The second, written years later and entitled "The Fair Land," describes solid prosperity and boundless confidence. What turned one into the other? Certainly not any economic "plan," or any economic policy whatever. The very words would have been incomprehensible to early Americans. The poor colonists did not become prosperous through any transfers of wealth. If anything, the mother country's stewardship was exploitative. Nor did prosperity come from the availability of extraordinary natural resources. Massachusetts is not Argentina. Its soil is poor, its weather worse, and making farm land out of virgin forest with hand tools is enormously laborious. The colonists surely worked hard, but probably no harder than the Russian peasants who carved out of the Siberian forests nothing that attracted the world. So, neither superior connections, nor resources, nor circumstances, nor even mere effort—much less wise economic policy—turned America's sub-poverty into super-prosperity. Rather, self-interest pursued in freedom and driven by Christian morality built habits of disciplined and thoughtful labor. Material plenty came from a wealth of human qualities unleashed.

The American founders wrote often of what had to be done to foster prosperity. But few of their utterances on the subject strike modern readers as economics. Rather, they look like political moralizing. And indeed they are. From countless pulpits, Americans heard the king of England's claims on them denied in words similar to those of John Allen: "As a fly or a worm, by the law of nature has as great a right to liberty and freedom (according to their little sphere in life) as the most potent monarch upon the earth: And as there can be no other difference between your lordship and myself, but what is political, I . . . take leave to ask . . . whether anyone who fears God will oppress his fellow creatures?"[1]

Such expressions restated John Locke's premise that whosoever mixes his labor with anything thereby acquires a natural right to it. Thus countless orators rhetorically asked whether the king had plowed their fields, and if not, what right he had to any of their produce. Thus also Francisco de Miranda told the story of an ordinary Virginia farmer who demanded of General Rochambeau payment for fields trampled by his troops and, when rebuffed, returned with a humble sheriff to vindicate his property rights against the great man's army. A people so imbued with the combination of equality, righteousness, and industriousness, remarked Miranda—like Tocqueville after him—could not but prosper.

The effect of the so-called Protestant ethic on America is often remarked upon, usually with some reference to grim determination. But there was nothing grim about early American economics. First, it is impossible to read early Americans' accounts of their economic exploits without being struck by the joy they took in their accomplishments. From the days of John Winthrop until the 1920s, America grew on the exuberant sense that human accomplishment serves the will of God. Second, early Americans acted on the belief that economic activity—so long as it was conducted on the basis of equality and without the admixture of compulsion—is the path to domestic and international peace. Eschewing power politics, Thomas Paine, whom the Continental Congress chose to be responsible for foreign affairs, wrote: "Our plan is commerce."[2] In his pamphlet *Common Sense,* economic freedom at home and free trade abroad were more than paths to wealth and peace: They were the paths of righteousness, along which the Good Shepherd of the twenty-third psalm leads mankind for his name's sake.

Just like property rights and free trade, sound money and frugal budgeting were not matters of economic policy but of morality. Thus in 1780, the Reverend Samuel Cooper, in a sermon largely about sound money and the maintenance of national credit through minimal expenditure, used the expression about America having "a national character to establish," a phrase George Washington used in his campaign for payment of debts owed to the Continental army. Cooper also reminded his economically eager parishioners that there is a big moral difference between making money through honest labor and doing so through the acquisition of privilege. The latter, he said, breeds habits of servility: "Servility is not only dishonorable to human nature, but commonly accompanied with the meanest vices, such as adulation, deceit, falsehood, treachery, cruelty, and the basest methods of supporting and procuring the favor of the power upon which it depends."[3] Cooper would not have been surprised at the economic results of communism and Third Worldism. *His fellow Americans would have diagnosed the poverty of these systems as a moral rather than as an economic dysfunction.*

The founders were not unanimous on economics. Alexander Hamilton was a mercantilist who thought that trade was about getting special deals. He also wanted to make the U.S. government into the country's most potent investment banker. But he was overruled on these matters by most of the rest of his fellows, with whom he generally agreed on the moral bases of economic action. Jefferson was deeply suspicious of the habits that nonfarming occupations would bring to America. Nonetheless, at the end of his life, fifty years after having written the Declaration of Independence, he rejoiced that his country was becoming a hive of industry and commerce because it was happening on moral bases of which he approved.

AMERICA'S CIVILITY

America had been made town by town. Physical isolation made it likely that local government would be the only real government, that disagreeable royal governors would be circumvented or ignored, that factions too out of tune in any given town would simply set up their own town, and hence that higher levels of government would be built on cooperation within and among localities. American public life, in short, was not made by conquerors or delegates but by free citizens. By the mid–seventeenth century, no one had to try to build citizenship in the colonies—only not to erode it.

The authors of the U.S. Constitution expressed the strongest fears about the effects of popular government on the national level. That is why they enumerated the specific tasks of the federal government and why the Constitution does not even contain the most important word in the language of modern politics, *sovereignty*. Nor does it refer to *sovereignty's substance, the capacity to define one's own power*. They were happy enough to leave sovereignty where it already existed—with the inhabitants of localities and states.

Tocqueville was thus moved to explain why the colonists thought popular sovereignty on the national level was inconsistent with good citizenship: "The general business of a country keeps only the leading citizens occupied. . . . It is difficult to force a man out of himself and get him to take an interest in the affairs of the whole state, for he has little understanding of the way in which the fate of the state can influence his own lot."[4]

The American founders knew that since most people had neither the knowledge nor the personal affection needed to deal responsibly with national affairs, they would do so as party and prey to some faction. But they also knew that in regard to matters close to them, people have "an infinite number of occasions . . . to act together; and [to] feel that they depend on one another. That is, the same people are always meeting and . . . they are forced in a manner to adapt themselves to one another. . . . Some brilliant achievement may win a people's favor at one stroke. But to gain the affection and respect of your immediate neighbors, a long succession of little services rendered and of obscure good deeds, a constant habit of kindness and an established reputation for disinterestedness are required."[5]

Tocqueville aimed his explanation at European statesmen, some of whom were already bemoaning ordinary citizens' sullen indifference and exhorting them to revive local civic life. But Tocqueville noted that such statesmen, "in making municipalities strong and independent . . . fear sharing their social power and exposing the state to anarchy." "However," he added, "if you take power and independence from a municipality, you may have docile subjects but you will not have citizens."[6]

European politicians, in short, would tell people to be vigorous and to participate. But since they reserved all important matters to their bureaucrats, they were effectively telling people to get excited about trivia or about the things that the leaders wanted them to be excited about. Meanwhile, they were imposing on localities school curricula, urban planning, and the agendas of interest groups as well as of social reformers, just as during the French Revolution, European states had hired prefects to oversee mayors in their administration of central directives.

Tocqueville, however, reported that New England towns (whose population of working-age men was typically in the low hundreds) had nineteen elected officials and yearly elections. Most men would have several turns in some office. In Tocqueville's America, as in Aristotle's *Politeia,* the distinction between "the people" and "the officials" was primarily chronological. Thus, New Englanders fulfilled Aristotle's definition of citizens—equals who rule and are ruled in turn and who are fully responsible for the city. When the public safety was threatened by crime, they did not merely call the police. As Tocqueville noted: "In America the means available to the authorities for the discovery of crimes and arrest of criminals are few—Nevertheless, I doubt whether in any other country crime so seldom escapes punishment. The reason is that everyone thinks he has an interest in furnishing proofs of an offense and in arresting the guilty man. . . . In Europe the criminal is a luckless man fighting to save his head from the authorities; in a sense the population are mere spectators of the struggle. In America he is an enemy of the human race and every human being is against him."[7]

It made sense: The same people who made the laws enforced them. The legislative, executive, and judicial powers were separate in theory. But the same people who voted for ordinances acted as officials and served on juries. For the same reason, when it was time to fight the Indians or the British, they formed their militias, much as Roman citizens had, elected their officers, and went out to fight. They were no more paid to fight than they were paid to vote or to serve as jurors.[8]

The various localities not only erected peculiar rules about the Sabbath. They established religion, regulated speech, tarred and feathered the obnoxious, and, yes, tolerated slavery or not. Tocqueville was by no means enthusiastic about the "wisdom and quality" of American local legislation. But he recognized that "there is prodigious force in the wills of a whole people"[9] and that officials backed by popular laws "dare to do things which astonish a European, astonished though he be to the spectacle of arbitrary power." He therefore warned, "Habits formed in freedom may one day become fatal to that freedom."[10]

All of this is to say that citizenship is a good, relative to the objectives of the city at any given time. Tocqueville, like many Americans, saw different kinds of polity arising in the South and the North. The Civil War that eventually engulfed both regions was all the fiercer because it was fought by young men brought up to treat the *res publica* as their own. But Tocqueville used the American example to teach that local independence, however dangerous, is the irreplaceable ingredient of citizenship. At the turn of the twentieth century, when urbanization and the ideology of efficiency through scale had diminished many Americans' participation in meaningful local affairs, the direct democracy movement (initiative, referendum, recall) tried with modest success to resuscitate civic involvement in an America where the distinctions between ruler and ruled had become clearer and more solid. But neither these reforms nor subsequent ones ever restored Tocquevillean vigor and civic life in America.

Tocqueville had also noted that vigorous political life at the local level was a useful guardian against the excesses of representative government at the national level. He had observed various interested parties trying to influence government in America. But because they could not capture—no one could—a government so diffuse, they were reduced to trying to gain the attention of a variety of legislators, officials, and their successors. This, too, was very difficult. In short, because they had to deal with public opinions, American interest groups had to talk a lot and to moderate their demands. By contrast, as Tocqueville said, interest groups and political parties in Europe were organized "to act and not to talk, to fight and not to convince." "There is nothing civilian about their organization and indeed military ways and maxims are introduced therein," he wrote. "One also finds them centralizing control of their forces as much as they can and placing the whole authority in very few hands."[11]

In America, however, or in any country where local politics is meaningful and where representatives are elected one by one, each representative must pay more attention to the needs of constituents than to the demands of any party.[12] To get a grip on many representatives, the party would first have to gain control over many constituencies—and this is what James Madison bet would be hard to do. But Madison's confidence in the people's disinterest in nationwide factions was based on his assumption that they would severally be absorbed by the politics of their districts. By contrast, when people become accustomed to focusing on political matters that do not involve local cooperation and to obeying rules made by people they do not know and cannot control, said Tocqueville, "their habits too are trained; they are isolated [from one another] and then dropped one by one into the common mass."[13]

Among such peoples the capacity for citizenship will gradually atrophy. It does not matter that the agenda imposed on them is more enlightened than the one they would have imposed on themselves, or that the professional officials to whom they turn are more competent than the amateurs or part-timers they replaced. Tocqueville did not report that America in the early nineteenth century was administered well, or enumerate the social services that local governments delivered. But he did tell his European readers that the American system produced free men, citizens such as Europe could barely imagine.

The French Revolution had just swept Europe with the claim that its version of equality and liberty would produce a brotherhood of citizens such as the world had not seen since the Roman republic. Hence, throughout Europe, officials took on Roman names: prefects, consuls, procurators, tribunes, censors, and so on. Yet the Europe of Tocqueville's time had nothing in common with the Rome of Cincinnatus and Cato. With the exception of Switzerland and parts of Germany, Europeans had long since forgotten how to look to one another. So when they overthrew one set of masters, they simply accepted another.[14] Throughout Europe, administrative organization quickly came to resemble that of the early Roman Empire—orderly, capable of marshaling human energies, and passionate about foreign wars, but devoid of citizenship and always liable to disruptive popular movements. Napoleon, in short, had been the revolution's legitimate heir.

The Americans were not Romans because Christianity did not allow Roman-style single-mindedness about aggrandizing the city, and because individual freedom enabled self-interest. Nonetheless, the Americans cultivated the Romans' civic virtues—the self-sufficiency of families made for real equality and liberty—while constant cooperation in local affairs built habits of fraternity.

THE AMERICAN FAMILY

In America as elsewhere, habits of fraternity begin at home. America's economy and its civic life were as they were because America's families taught piety, the sanctity of commitment, the performance of duty, the pursuit of righteousness, and the value of work. Since the founders had no doubt that popular government was possible only among virtuous people, they treated marriage as a preeminent part of the divine order of nature and as the foundation of private morality.

Members of the founders' generation got married in church, where they heard the familiar injunctions from the King James Bible: "Wives, submit yourselves unto your own husbands. . . . Husbands, love your wives even as Christ also loved the Church."[15] They also heard: "The wife hath not power of her own body, but the husband; and likewise also the husband hath not power of his own body, but the wife,"[16] and "What therefore God hath joined together, let not man put asunder."[17] The educated ones kept Aristotle in mind, who wrote that marriage was a friendship both useful and pleasant and also "a friendship of virtue if [husband and wife] are good."[18] Thomas Jefferson wrote of marriage in these very terms: "While one considers them [women] as useful and rational companions, one cannot forget that they are also the objects of our pleasures."[19] In short, the founders' generation believed that men's and women's interests were complementary, and they saw marriage as the divinely ordained, naturally good way to organize life. George Washington had started his presidency by pointing out that public life must be grounded on private morality. His successor, John

Adams, devoted husband of Abigail, was even more specific: The "foundation of national morality must be laid in private families."[20] He went on to say that children learned the meaning of morality, religion, and respect for law from the habitual fidelity of their parents to one another.

The founders had no doubt that marriage meant a monopoly of lawful sex. Every colony and town had laws against sex outside of marriage and, of course, against sodomy in all its forms. Fornication was often punished by exhibition in stocks. Adultery was dealt with through heavy corporal punishment and heavier fines. Marriage laws obliged husbands to support their wives and to pay the debts they incurred. When Jefferson supported a local ordinance for punishing deficient husbands by confinement at hard labor, he did nothing remarkable.[21] Since divorce could be granted only in outrageous cases—mainly adultery, in which case the adulterer was not allowed to remarry—ordinary women could be confident that their men would not go when the wrinkles came. The law built a community of interest on the expectation of mutual performance and permanence.

That interest, according to Tocqueville, was pursued according to "the great principle of political economy." He wrote, "They have separated the functions of man and woman so that the great work of society may be better performed. . . . You will never find American women in charge of the external relations of the family, managing a business or interfering in politics; but they are also never obliged to undertake rough laborers' work or any task requiring hard physical exertion. No family is so poor that it makes an exception to this rule."[22]

This is why Jefferson, James Wilson, and their contemporaries were so shocked at the sight of Indian women bearing the brunt of labor; they would have been even more shocked at Soviet labor practices than latter-day Americans were—not because they thought using women for labor was inefficient, but because it violated the order of nature. Tocqueville made clear that Americans of both sexes concurred wholeheartedly in this assessment of the natural role of each. Americans thought that human associations large and small must have a head, that the natural head of the household was the husband, and that the purpose of democratic equality was to regulate necessary powers, not to destroy them. American men, he noted, "constantly display complete confidence in their spouses' judgment and deep respect for their freedom because they relied on their wives for management of the household. Wives in turn took pride in their husbands' authority and hold him accountable for it."[23] Just as each level of government—federal, state, and local—was supreme in its own jurisdiction, American women ruled the "domestic sphere" autonomously as nowhere else.

Tocqueville also noted that Americans applied to relations between the sexes the same kind of spirit that they applied to legal matters in general, namely, equal treatment. Adultery was punished equally, and American husbands no more than wives boasted of amorous exploits. But the Americans tempered equal treatment with recognition of the sexes' physical inequality. Whereas in Europe rapists were treated leniently and juries often refused to convict, Americans hanged them routinely. Tocqueville found this remarkable because in general America's criminal laws were milder than Europe's. Americans were so adamant about rape not because of any unusual possessiveness about women—Europeans were more so—but rather because, "as the Americans think nothing more precious than a woman's honor and nothing deserving more respect than her freedom, they think no punishment could be too severe for those who take both from her against her will."[24]

Tocqueville did not imagine that the laws did anything more than defend the American family. The laws had not built it. Rather, he argued that the American family was bound by natural ties and that the contribution of the law was to let nature take its course. Had Americans tried by law to make the family what it was, they probably would have failed, because "trying to add something, [the law] almost always takes something away."[25]

Far from suggesting that American-style families would spring up among any and all peoples if they were left in some kind of lawless state of nature, Tocqueville was careful to point out that marriage in America was this way also because Americans, as Puritans and traders, were accustomed to "a continual sacrifice of pleasure for the sake of business."[26] Americans valued high standards of human performance and were accustomed to holding themselves and others responsible for meeting them with "great strictness." Freedom left no excuse for bad performance. The American way of consensual marriage left no room for extramarital love. As Tocqueville noted, "there is hardly a way of persuading a girl that you love her when you are perfectly free to marry her but will not do so."[27]

Early America, then, was a network of families. American cities, like all cities, had prostitutes and some amorphous people on the margins. But to grow up into a normal adult, a boy had to become a husband, and to become a woman, a girl had to become a wife. Few men or women stayed out of marriage—because to do so was to stay out of society. The occasional out-of-wedlock birth produced "bastards," most of whom were quickly adopted. Not until the late nineteenth century did the need arise for social institutions to deal with "foundlings." No doubt some parents were abusive toward their children as well as toward one another. But the Americans of Tocqueville's day did not understand, much less believe, his warning that government might someday try to superintend their domestic lives. Nor would they have taken seriously anyone who told them that their way of life itself was abusive. The American men and women of that age would not have understood (as many Europeans already did understand) the notion that people should make up their own definition of a good man or a good woman, or that these definitions might change with government policy, or that anyone might command them to become gender-neutral. They knew they were free, and they believed what the Declaration of Independence said about their freedom being derived from "the Laws of Nature and of Nature's God."

THE AMERICAN RELIGION

"The religious atmosphere of the country was the first thing that struck me on arrival in the United States,"[28] wrote Tocqueville, and throughout his account, he reiterated that to make sense of America, his readers had to realize that religion really did pervade every aspect of life, that religion was "the first [of America's] political institutions." That was true precisely because clerics had no official power. Even more remarkably, the pastors and priests liked it that way.

Tocqueville's European experience had taught him the difference between religion and religiosity. In America, he looked for hypocrisy and found little. He wrote that "in the United States the sovereign authority is religious, and consequently hypocrisy should be common. Nonetheless, America is still the place where the Christian religion has kept the greatest real power over men's souls; and nothing better demonstrates how useful and natural to man it is, since the country where it now has widest sway is both the most enlightened and the freest."[29]

He found religious fervor in the depth of the forest, where pioneers would travel for days to encamp around the tent of a circuit-riding preacher, and in the homes of rich New Englanders, who would give up comfort to preach the gospel in the wilderness. He found it in the schools—

almost universally run by clerics. He found it in private as well as in public—in short, everywhere, and everywhere without compulsion.

To be sure, the very earliest settlers in Massachusetts had come from Christian sects on the edge of heresy, which had made little distinction between secular and divine law. But neither Plymouth's William Bradford nor Boston's John Winthrop had been theocrats in the mold of Muhammad or even of John Calvin. None ignored, much less repudiated, Christ's distinction between duties to God and to Caesar. The confusion of ecclesiastical and secular authority in the earliest settlements—people were in fact whipped and fined for sin—was naturally due to the fact that each settler band was simultaneously a practically sovereign civil polity and a self-governing religious congregation. It would have been a lot to expect of any given bunch of dog-tired people living on the edge of survival and meeting to transact their common business that they would draw fine lines between the civil and religious items on their agenda.

The settlers were motivated both to freedom and to a greater degree of civil and ecclesiastical perfection. John Donne's sermon to the Virginia Company in 1622 was a typical mixture of exhortation to add to "this kingdom," meaning England, and "to the kingdom of heaven." The Mayflower Compact of 1620 also dedicated the signers to "the glory of God and advancement of our Christian faith, and honor of our king and country." As the colonies grew, the two sets of ends were reconciled rather quickly in terms of practical tolerance, because dissidents could always move out—as Roger Williams did when he moved from Massachusetts and founded Rhode Island. Practical necessity required each congregation to support itself and govern itself. In practice, Catholic and Jewish congregations were organized like Protestant ones. As Americans of different religious persuasions spread out, they lived profitably side by side. Consequently, as historian Paul Johnson has argued, "America was born Protestant"[30]—Protestants, Catholics, and Jews developed Protestant habits—and each congregation vied with the others for civic success and godly lives. Thus, George Washington could write to the Jewish congregation in Newport, wishing it success in its own house and supposing that it wished Christians success in theirs.

This pluralism was not, as some claim, a "collapse of the idea of total Christian society."[31] The very notion that society, much less the polity, should be Christian had been relegated to heresy ever since St. Augustine had published *The City of God* in the fifth century. In America, each congregation was free to be as Christian as it wished, in the way that it wished, and so was every other. Nor should anyone read as religious indifference Washington's assurance to the Jews of Newport that in America they observed their religion not by tolerance but by right. On the contrary, American Christians welcomed Jews because they were the senior branch of America's religious family. Washington did not write and would not have written a similar letter to Muslims, much less to organizations of Thuggees, peyote smokers, or militant atheists.

So, while the laws of the several colonies did not force anyone to belong to any congregation or to perform any religious rite, it was impossible to take part in public life except as a member of some congregation—just as it was difficult to do so unless one was married. Since the country was built by, of, and for the faithful, anyone who was faithless was very much a stranger. Moreover, every town and every colony had some ordinances that put certain forms of ungodly behavior beyond the pale. Maryland's 1649 act concerning religion, later known as the Toleration Act, for example, set fines for denying the existence of God and for various acts of blasphemy.[32] Such laws, however, were nonsectarian and were indeed less religious than civic, since they defined the common denominator on which the polity stood. They did not force anyone to revere Jesus. But *they kept irreverence private and out of public squares dominated by reverence.* Hence, Tocqueville wrote that "Christianity itself is an established and irresistible fact which no one seeks to attack or to defend."[33] Merely to stand away from God, however, was to cease being part of the body politic, because all ranks of society identified with Christianity and liberty, and judged them essential to their institution. He added an example: "While I was in America, a witness called at assizes of the county of Chester (state of New York) declared that he did not believe in the existence of God and the immortality of the soul. The judge refused to allow him to be sworn in, on the grounds that the witness had destroyed beforehand all possible confidence in his testimony."[34]

Tocqueville wrote that he had "met no one, lay or cleric," who did not agree that "the main reason for the quiet sway of religion over their country was the complete separation of church and state." Clerics and laymen alike quickly came to realize that involvement with politics burdens the faith with "the ill feelings that must necessarily attach to political enterprises from time to time."[35] Moreover, when a church is in any way subject to political authority, it loses the one claim by which it can trump politics—namely, that it speaks for the transcendent authority of God. State churches, he wrote, tend to serve the interests of the state and are always sooner or later fatal for the faith. Hence, the state constitutions of New York, Virginia, North and South Carolina, Tennessee, and Louisiana explicitly excluded clergymen from public office. All the others did so by custom. This was so even in the states (nine of them in 1775) that extended special favors of "establishment" to one or more sects. Thus, while the political sermon was a major fixture of American life, the cleric who delivered it could not himself touch public business.

Even before the First Great Awakening of the 1730s, clergymen were the best known—indeed, the only widely known—people in the colonies, and the advancement of piety was a prime goal of public policy. James Madison's 1789 speech on behalf of the First Amendment to the Constitution made clear that the amendment was being introduced at the behest of several states to protect their peculiar religious arrangements—all meant to foster the practice of religion. Paul Johnson summed it up as follows: "Hence, though the Constitution and the Bill of Rights made no provision for a state church—quite the contrary—there was an implied and unchallenged understanding that the republic was religious, not necessarily in its form, but in its bones, that it was inconceivable that it could have come into being or continue to flourish, without an overriding religious sentiment pervading every nook and cranny of its society."[36]

From the beginning, religion in America had been less ritualistic and more literal, and hence more intellectual, than elsewhere. Protestant services were substantially lessons. American Catholics and Jews imitated them. Tocqueville noted that on the Sabbath, America came to a halt, and that after church the typical American read the Bible. Nowhere else in Christendom was the Old Testament read so much and the notion of God as lawgiver so widespread. The tendency of Americans to equate themselves with the children of Israel was so great (note the predominance of Old Testament names) that it spread to Negro slaves as well. By the time of the Great Awakening, preachers, notably Jonathan Edwards, were already linking this re-Judaized Christianity to natural law. This kind of preaching substantially stiffened morals—something immediately obvious to visitors.

In the public realm, this religion of law fostered the notion that all power under God must be accountable to Him. Hence, anyone who could understand the laws that God had written in nature and in the hearts of men could and should judge the actions of the powerful. The American Revolution and the tradition of limited government that flows from it can only be understood in this light. Anyone suggesting that the American Revolution was about claiming the "rights of Englishmen" either is unacquainted with the fact that English law had been neither more nor less than the will of the Crown ever since Henry VIII, and that it had passed to Parliament whole after 1688, or else is referring to the preexisting but longeclipsed medieval conception of right, which proceeded from natural law. Rather, the American Revolution was driven by the sense that the sovereign power was wrong, unnatural, and ungodly. It was also inconvenient. Tocqueville did not think the U.S. Constitution was as powerful a guarantee of limited government as religion, which, he said, "prevents [Americans] from imagining" and forbids them to dare "all sorts of usurpations." "And if anyone," he wrote, "managed to conquer his own scruples, he could not likely conquer those of their partisans."[37]

The litany of invocations to God by American statesmen, of their reminders to their fellow citizens to stick close to the divine laws because they were the only bases for good republican laws, is long, repetitive, and beside the point here—that point being that early American statesmen did "everything and nothing" to foster the religion on which their regime depended. Tocqueville, after lengthy treatment of the importance of religion to the American regime, has only the following to say about its preservation:

> What I am going to say will certainly do me harm in the eyes of politicians. I think the only effective means which governments can use to make the doctrine of the immortality of the soul respected is daily to act as if they believed it themselves.
>
> I think that it is only by conforming scrupulously to religious morality in great affairs that they can flatter themselves that they are teaching the citizens to understand it and love it in little matters.[38]

Not by accident did American politicians, especially presidents, come to speak of their offices as "pulpits." Nor is it an accident that long after the founding generation had passed away, American political discourse was suffused not just with Christian symbols—America (with Canada tagging along, as usual) is the only country that observes a national day of Thanksgiving—but also with the framing of issues in terms of natural law. Perhaps the best illustration of this is the coincidence that the House of Representatives passed the resolution asking President Washington to proclaim a National Day of Prayer and Thanksgiving[39] on the very day, September 24, 1789, after it had passed the First Amendment to the Constitution, by which it had shielded America's massive, public, and fervent practice of religion against the interference of the federal government. It is worth noting the lack of ambiguity in Washington's response: "The providence of Almighty God, to obey His will, to be grateful for his benefits, and humbly to implore His protection and favor . . . that great and glorious being who is the beneficent author of all the good that was, that is, or that ever will be, that we may then unite in rendering unto Him our sincere and humble thanks for his kind care and protection of the people."[40]

Shakespeare and the newspaper—the two pieces of writing that Tocqueville found everywhere in the forests, towns, and cities—filled the space in the souls of early Americans that was not filled by religion. In sum, the early American soul was not terribly complex. Its pleasures were "simple and natural," seeming to consist of success, both material and spiritual.

THE HUMAN PRODUCT

The founders made the laws and the laws made the founders. And they were the wonder of Europe. George Washington was probably the first international celebrity, receiving awed letters and visitors from throughout the Old World. Europeans marveled at the Americans' bearing. Their walk and their manners bespoke freedom, dignity, and confidence. Europeans knew that although the Americans did not live in splendor, they were somehow richer, happier, and freer than they. Alexis de Tocqueville was only one of an endless series of foreigners who traveled to America to find out its "secret" recipe. The most perceptive of them, however, focused on human qualities, as Tocqueville did. From the very first, Americans themselves have considered how to spread their way of life to the rest of mankind. But the sober judgment of America's founding generation was that the American way of life was made possible by a set of qualities that other peoples did not possess. Might they ever? More important, would these qualities survive in America itself?

The deepest reflection on this subject was John Adams's in his *A Defense of the Constitutions of Government of the United States of America,* as well as his *Discourse on Avila,* veritable surveys of mores and laws around the world.[41] Adams saw mankind's prosperity everywhere eroded by greed, laziness, and rapacity. He saw freedom rendered impossible by lack of self-restraint on the part of great and humble men alike. He saw debauchery and luxury ruining domestic life; and ignorance, superstition, and hardheartedness barring man's way to God. In short, all mankind was drowning in sin, and the American people were blessed to have their nostrils just a bit above the muck. If the Americans were diligent, if their laws continued to encourage hard work, self-control, fidelity, and piety, they might retain their present happiness and be the city set on a hill, the city that might enlighten the world.

As for the rest of the world, Adams's analysis added only Christian morality to the advice of Greek and Roman manuals for liberal education, that is, for training man in the habits necessary to get and maintain freedom.[42] These maxims, along with the Christian faith, were known in Europe long before the founding of the American republic. The Europeans never put them into practice, but perhaps the sight of America's happiness might inspire them to do it.

11

←

WHAT ARE WE DOING TO OURSELVES?

We have now a national character to establish.
—GEORGE WASHINGTON

No one would argue that the U.S. government set out to engineer the vast differences in civic and economic life, family customs, and souls that separate contemporary America from the nation of the founders. Nevertheless, whether deliberately or through unintended consequences, government has been an important—arguably the primary—engine of innovation. Certainly it is difficult to think of any contemporary ideas or practices that have become part of American life despite the government's strenuous fight against them. In America as elsewhere, government, the Establishment, sets the tone.

Outside of the nineteenth-century struggle over slavery, few Americans before our time have felt that one part of society was deliberately enlisting government in an effort to shove an alien way of life down their throats—much less that it had succeeded in doing so. But no one could have conceived of Supreme Court decisions since the 1950s that would take schools out of the hands of local citizens, drive religion out of public life, privilege obscenity in public discourse, create "protected classes," and establish abortion, or of laws that would empower and finance parts of the private sector to influence the public, all of which would ordain a way of life tasteful to about half of the American people and disgusting to the other half. The changes that have taken place in American life since the 1950s have long intellectual and social pedigrees. But they did not grow from the grass roots. Rather, they were wrought upon America from the top, preeminently by a regime that used government—and preeminently its least representative branches, the judiciary and the bureaucracy—to carve the larger society into its own image. Social engineering, however, begets counter-engineering. Social engineering also naturally leads its intended human raw materials to go limp on the engineers, or to go off on their own.

THE AMERICAN REGIME

Unlike previous American regimes, the current one is backed by modern government's vast reach. A century ago, the J. P. Morgans and Jay Goulds may have been economically more important than Archer Daniel Midlands's Duane Andreas or General Motors' Rick Waggoner. But today's tycoons have more power over ordinary people than the trusts of a century ago, because while the old robber barons had to do the robbing themselves, today's CEOs can count on the government to do it for them by manufacturing markets for them, by tailoring rules that stifle competition, and by bailing out their blunders. U.S. car companies stood a better chance of taking the public's money by working their contacts in Washington than by selling cars. Until the mid–nineteenth century, anyone who wished to set America's tone had to appeal to countless more or less autonomous individuals, families, and localities. Circa 1900, Horace Mann and John Dewey set the tone for American education through persuasion alone. Government did not funnel one-tenth of America's GDP to them, as it does to those who set today's tone in education: the teachers' unions—a major constituent of the Democratic Party. A century ago, when government accreditation was in its infancy and taxes were low, all you had to do to start a new school or college was to start it. In our time, government accredits the accrediters, and the taxes it imposes to support the established schools preempt the private money that might go to new ones.

The modern American regime—the Establishment—contains most of the officials of the U.S. government as well as the majority of state and local employees. Also included is the leadership of countless business and non-profit groups who profit from—indeed who live by—their connection with the government officials whose proclivities they share. As the regime changes, it pushes some persons and groups out and pulls others in. Excluded are those of whatever rank or station out of sympathy with the ruling regime, who do not accept its fashions, customs, and preferences or who otherwise do not acknowledge the Establishment's right to deference and privileges.

The regime rules more by fashion—strict, pervasive, unforgiving of nuance—than by statute. It defines itself by its icons and taboos. By violating them, even the president of the United States may place himself beyond the Establishment's pale. Between 1981 and 1984, when President Ronald Reagan spoke of the Soviet Union as an "evil empire" on its way to the scrap heap, even his nominal subordinates—never mind America's tastemakers—disregarded him, because Reagan was entirely contradicting the conventional wisdom. Because Reagan's view of the Soviet Union was "irresponsible," "over the top," it disqualified him for membership in the regime in the 1980s as thoroughly as disputing "global warming" disqualifies anyone, regardless of scientific station or argument, from membership in the regime of our time.

The regime also defines itself by the juncture of its members' interests and identities. Thus senators, congressmen, and other officials who do not cooperate in funding the Establishment's "private sector" exclude themselves from the deference normally accorded persons of their rank. Hence, as the financial panic of 2008 was unfolding and the Treasury Department sought Congress's unprecedented appropriation of $700 billion to relieve the banking sector of responsibility for its assets, its officials assumed that they needed to consult only the legislators of both parties who did not question their wisdom. Those outside the presumed consensus just didn't count. In the face of hostile public opinion, and as if that opinion and the congressmen responsive to it were unworthy of refutation, the plan's advocates, Democrats and Republicans together, argued simply that to oppose their plan was to stand in the way of collective wisdom. There was nothing substantive in this argument: You had to support it if you wanted to be among those who get invited to serious places and are taken seriously. The regime resorts to such bipartisanship, amounting to uni-partisanship, whenever important matters are at stake.

This herd behavior is so attractive in part because it absolves the members from having to explain why what they are doing is right or to acknowledge error. It is enough for each to state that he is part of bipartisan consensus. Self-esteem as a substitute for substance is even more important in the regime than in ghetto schools. Hence, after the above-mentioned appropriation failed to stop the panic, none of those who had assured the public that it would do so felt the need to explain why they had been mistaken. Because there is really only one party at the top, the regime may not always be right, but it can never be wrong.

The regime's private sector includes all those organizations and individuals who have their position in society because officials favor them. Companies like Archer Daniel Midlands, the nation's biggest grain broker, prosper as they do because of the U.S. government's subsidies, tariffs, and mandates for using grain alcohol as a motor fuel. The major automakers, which have "helped" to set tariffs and environmental regulations and have joined with the Department of Transportation to produce the "car of the future," the multibillion-dollar "alternative energy" industry, the multitrillion-dollar Federal National Mortgage Association (Fannie Mae), the major investment banks, and innumerable other similarly connected businesses, also contribute money to politicians and support officials by testifying before Congress and helping to form public opinion.

But it is not just corporations that can find themselves in—or out—of the Establishment's favor. The regime also brings key actors from the medical profession and nonprofit sector into its orbit. The abortion industry is as large as it is primarily because many state governments pay abortion providers to perform abortions and because the federal government pressures the insurance industry to fund abortions that are not paid for publicly. Planned Parenthood receives some $300 million per year in federal funds to promote them. In the nonprofit sector, hundreds of "public interest groups" or "nongovernmental organizations" are wholly or largely financed by government. The environmental lobby is paid for almost entirely by government. Labor unions for teachers and government employees exist largely because government makes membership in them a condition of employment and allows compulsory collection of dues. Without exception, the nonprofit groups on the receiving end of government largesse happen to be politically liberal. They objected to a law requiring them to disclose their financial relationship with the U.S. government whenever they testified before Congress on the all-too-factual grounds that they were in the same business as the government, sought the same ends, and were effectively extensions of it. By the regime's logic, they are entitled to the money.

We can see that logic most clearly when the character of the regime changes: Some groups that had been in are pushed out, while others that had been outside become pillars of the regime. Until the 1960s, the National Rifle Association (NRA) was part of the regime. It received surplus U.S. government guns and ammunition, and its members were allowed to use government ranges and were encouraged to run shooting clubs in schools. The association was close to officials at all levels of government because the officials generally took it for granted that teaching kids to shoot was a good thing, that American military power was a good thing internationally, and that it was good domestically for the American people to be armed. During the same period, the Boy Scouts of America were similarly intertwined with government, especially with schools, because the people who were running Congress, state governments, and school boards believed that the way of life associated with self-reliance, with reverence for God and country, and with individual and collective defense was good. The Eagle Scout (it took twenty-one merit badges to earn the title) was the epitome of American youth.

During the 1970s, when the Boy Scouts' promotion of morality and religion went out of fashion in the regime, the courts began to take seriously arguments that the Boy Scouts were a nursery of inappropriate attitudes toward women, homosexuals, and the environment. At the same time, the regime began to think of American military power as problematic for the world, and of the American people as prone to violence. At the same time, the NRA became a pariah. By the same token, during the years when the NRA and the Boy Scouts were in, groups such as Planned Parenthood and the Sex Information and Education Council of the United States (SIECUS) were out. Since the 1970s, these groups have been part of America's schools more than the Scouts and the NRA ever were.

Just like advocacy groups, some media organizations are in, and others out, of the Establishment. The *Washington Post,* the *New York Times,* and the major broadcast networks are in. Officials fall over themselves to talk to them. The Central Intelligence Agency, a byword for secrecy, has always given secret briefings to its favorite reporters, who become its conduits to public opinion. For CIA and other U.S. government officials, talking to a reporter from the liberal *Washington Post* is a sign of distinction. Talking to one from the conservative *Washington Times* is punishable disloyalty. Conversely, nothing frightens the media establishment more than the prospect that it might not get privileged treatment as officious conduits of official opinion. Thus, in 1980, the media greats gave a collective sigh of relief when the newly elected Ronald Reagan, having lambasted the establishment media during his campaign for president, sought an invitation to dine with the owner of the *Washington Post* as soon as he got to the Oval Office. The order of the regime would not be upset after all.

After the election of Ronald Reagan, the *Washington Post*'s "Style" section, true mirror of the regime's ruling tastes, published a front-page article, only half tongue-in-cheek, about how the new administration's feared appointment of thousands of role models very different from their predecessors would make passé a long list of people, institutions, customs, magazines, and culinary and personal habits while making others the new standard. It speculated that cohabitation, for example, was to be replaced by marriage and children. Early rising would crimp the Georgetown salons' soirees. Aristotle would have nodded: New regimes mean new people and mores. But as it happened, neither the *Post*'s favorite people nor its favorite habits went out of style, because the new president appointed mostly Establishmentarians. Nevertheless, the *Post*'s publication of the contrasting lists of customs and tastes accurately reflected the Establishment's proclivities and its phobias.[1]

BEING IN

Because the regime is the jealous arbiter of its own membership, trying to exercise any of the functions that it reserves for itself makes any outsider liable to ridicule, to slander without recourse, or worse. Contrast, for example, the reception that regime insiders gave in 2008 to the candidacies for president and vice president, respectively, of Senator Barack Obama of Illinois and Governor Sarah Palin of Alaska, who were roughly the same age and had spent roughly the same amount of time in public life. No one argued that the senator had accomplished more than the governor or tried to show that he knew more things than she. Nevertheless, he was accepted while she was not. Authoritative figures of both parties, conservatives as well as liberals, asked aggressively how Palin could dare to stand for such high office and belittled her for doing so in the most demeaning of terms, while celebrating Obama's quest, in his own words, as "the audacity of hope." Why? Because Obama was part of the regime's ideological, financial, and, above all, social network, while Palin looked and acted like an ordinary American. He had the proper regime identity. She did not. The fact that Palin did not try to speak like a member of the ruling class, that she appealed to ordinary folk in their own idiom, underlined that she lacked the primary qualification for admission: being part of the Establishment, having been invited in after giving proof of fealty. In their insistence on this, our nobles are no different from those of the Roman Empire, whose motto was *Quod licet jovi non licet bovi*—"What is proper to gods is improper to cattle."

That is why lawfully appointing non-Establishmentarians to positions of responsibility puts them in danger of personal destruction. Three years of criminal prosecution made it impossible for Ronald Reagan's secretary of labor, Ray Donovan (1981–1983), to function. Though he was fully exonerated, his ordeal ruined his otherwise productive, prosperous life. When Clarence Thomas was nominated to the Supreme Court in 1991, the regime used a former employee's wholly uncorroborated accusation that he used inappropriate language toward her constituting sexual harassment to etch in the public's mind an indelible image of Thomas as lewd and stupid. Neither truth nor law can defend you. The regime can always impanel an officious-sounding group to declare that although an upstart has not broken any law, his or her actions "may have been illegal or improper"—as happened to Attorney General Alberto Gonzales for firing U.S. attorneys whom he had a legally uncontestable right to fire, and to Governor Palin for firing a state trooper who had used a Taser on an eleven-year-old boy. Accusations are ubiquitous commodities. Calls for "investigations" by persons with access to the media are sure to produce recurring headlines that "raise questions." The target may as well contract leprosy. Hence, appointees or even candidates disagreeable to the regime must choose between spending their time in office profitably for themselves by not interfering with the exercise of its privileges, or by resisting those privileges at great personal cost. By contrast, being "in" means that unless you are caught with both hands stuck in the cookie jar, you have a presumptive right to respect as well as to power.

Being part of the regime means seldom having to be sorry. For example, on April 28, 1997, U.S. Attorney Eric Holder filed a motion before Judge Royce Lambeth asking him not to consider a suit arising from a government wiretap, in which Secretary of Commerce Ron Brown was heard selecting private participants in a U.S. trade mission according to their record of contributions to the Democratic Party—the prima facie evidence of conflict of interest or bribery was obvious. Ten days before, Holder had said of Secretary Brown: "He played a substantial role in my becoming U.S. Attorney. He's the guy who made the calls . . . when the names were being sent up."[2] Holder dealt with Brown's conflict of interest by compounding it with his own. But the judge granted the motion, President Clinton appointed Holder to be deputy attorney general, and a decade later President-elect Obama appointed Holder as attorney general. That is how things work.

The limit case was that of President Bill Clinton who, after lying under oath in a 1998 judicial proceeding broadcast worldwide—the textbook definition of perjury—found the mainstream media and a nearly united Establishment turning their ire against those who wanted to prosecute him. And when Fannie Mae, the U.S. government's semiprivate guarantor of half the nation's mortgages, defaulted to set off the financial panic of 2008, the U.S. Treasury treated Congressman Barney Frank, chairman of the committee that oversees the corporation, who received money from it, whose homosexual lover was one of its executives, and who had shielded its practices from reform, as part of the solution, not part of the problem.

Hence, being part of the regime means having it made. When government officials need members of advisory panels or expert witnesses to justify saying yes or no to whatever projects they want or don't want, they find authoritative voices among the people to whom and in the places to which they send the grant money—the Massachusetts Institute of Technology, the Council on Foreign Relations, and so forth. These are the very same places where the officials themselves are employed between stints in office and where ambitious young people know that they can find ladders to climb. Being part of the regime, whether as a legislator, a bureaucrat, an academic, a journalist, a businessman, an entertainer, or someone engaged in a sociopolitical cause, is all about being connected with the connected, and sharing with them distaste for the unconnected. It means being able to draw support from and to move between its parts. Thus, journalists can become officials and then businessmen, as Richard Burt of the *New York Times* did between 1981 and 1989. Because each of the regime's hands washes the other, its members can count, if not on support for all that they do and are, at worst on criticism muted by basic acceptance.

Never has it been so necessary as today for an American to be part of the Establishment to exercise his full human powers. As the late social critic Christopher Lasch pointed out, whereas once upon a time the "American dream" consisted of making one's way without being burdened by people with more privileges than oneself, now it consists of the prospect of climbing out of the ranks of the ruled into those of the rulers, from the ranks of those who count only theoretically to the ranks of people who count for real because they're connected.

GETTING IN

Like all regimes, ours puts a premium on selecting its own members. How does one get into the American regime, and how have the paths to entry changed? Once upon a time, not so long ago, America's very variety and freedom meant that persons unconnected with the regime could rise to greatness through genius in business or science. Microsoft's Bill Gates, the last person to have trod the lonely path of the Rockefellers and Morgans, was able to do so only because he invented a wholly new field that required neither permits nor qualifications—Gates had dropped out of Stanford. But in any existing field, whether in medicine or energy, the American entrepreneur must obtain credit and permits in ways more reminiscent of Europe or even of the Third World than of America. Hence, getting in means more and more having the right introductions and the right pedigree, and that means making yourself acceptable to those who are already in—on being co-opted. Increasingly narrow of access, self-referential, and self-interested, our Establishment seems content with its own decline—moral as well as intellectual.

The general rule for entering the ranks of the blessed, whether in business or government, the media or academe, is that one must succeed in matching the blesseds' preferred resumes, as well as their tastes, but especially *by deferring to their prerogative to co-opt or not.* One must also make it easier for them to insulate themselves from competition while appearing to serve some lofty purpose. The reward for pleasing those above you is that thereafter you need not strive to do anything else.

Though there is nothing remarkable about the fact that, in America as elsewhere, some of life's most valuable things—jobs, contracts, or privileges—are reserved for "authorized persons," it is remarkable that the American people have gradually come to accept as rightful the power of those who dispense them. That is all the more remarkable because the contemporary American way of privilege, which combines co-option with semi-naked quotas and set-asides, negates so directly America's traditional (one may say former) maxim that people should earn what they get. Other peoples also reserve their most prestigious and powerful positions for special persons. Other regimes are even more self-referential. But few processes of selection have trashed merit quite so explicitly as that of today's America. Contrast

France, where competitive exams, blindly graded, secure admission to and advancement in academe and government. There and wherever admission to special status depends on exams, it is possible to claim that those who enjoy such status have a right to it. Not so in America.

In our governments, rules governing civil service exams notwithstanding, co-option has always been the rule. Lately, even the exceptions have been curtailed. Once upon a time, not so long ago, any American could assert the right to employment in what is arguably the nation's most elite bureaucracy, the State Department's Foreign Service, just by scoring higher on the written and substantive oral exam than anyone else—just as any Frenchman could assert the right to employment in the Conseil d'Etat on the same basis. But after 1979, the oral exam ceased to be substantive and objective, and the Foreign Service examiners were empowered to make subjective judgments about the candidate's suitability. Just like at the CIA and elsewhere, the exam became a thin cover for co-option. Then, in 2006, the Foreign Service dropped the exam completely for young black people who had come up through the patronage of Congressman Charles Rangel. Secretary of State Condoleezza Rice celebrated the event. She had not taken the test either.

Being counted among America's "best and brightest" usually begins with admission to the "best" colleges and universities. Leave aside the question "best for what?" (A lifetime in academe taught me that the student, not the institution, is far and away the primary factor influencing what he will learn, that the most highly rated institutions tend to demand the least from their students, that for most students learning is well down in the practical list of priorities, and hence that for all but a few there is little difference between Princeton and Podunk.) In practice, "the best" means "the hardest to get into," as well as the most prestigious. This definition is as circular as it seems.

Once upon a time, as recently as the 1960s, the offices of admission of American colleges were small because their job was simple: Choose the applicants who scored highest in the Scholastic Aptitude Test (SAT), who had the best high school grades. Occasionally, look at letters of recommendation for something special. As colleges expanded later in that decade, admissions officers became recruiters who peddled prestige, and students became customers who bid for it. The colleges competed by advertising the average SAT scores of the students they admitted. Thus in the 1970s and 1980s, the schools that were already prestigious became even more so. Harvard or Stanford might not teach Johnny much. But the fact that Johnny could get into such places certified that he was a pretty sharp guy.

In those very years, however, these same colleges began to move away from meritocracy. In 1987, Stanford announced proudly that half of the applicants it had *rejected* had SAT scores above 1400 (before the test's standards were lowered). Not looking closely, one might have supposed that Stanford had rejected them in favor of folks who scored, say, above 1500. But no. In fact, by this time Stanford and every other major college and university had begun admitting *smaller* percentages of high scorers in order to accommodate growing percentages of lower scorers who fit the admissions officers' views of who ought to be admitted to the Establishment—and not just blacks. A generation later, it had begun to dawn on the American public that Johnny's feat of getting into the likes of Harvard was evidence only of the fact that Johnny fit Harvard's prejudices. That's all. At least for undergraduates, the prestige colleges were selling only prestige—a currency backed only by itself, whose value can only decline.

The controversy over "affirmative action," or preferential treatment, for blacks, important as it is in itself, obscures an even more important issue, namely, to what extent affiliation with those universities and other institutions that are the analogues of well-connected businesses should depend on the subjective preferences of incumbents, and to what extent such institutions should be open to all, depending on transparent, objective criteria that apply equally to all.

While the effects of co-option on blacks and whites are disputable, the practice of admitting persons to the ladders of the regime by nebulous criteria surely has endowed the incumbents in America's top places (overwhelmingly white) with the power to choose whom they will allow to compete for their posts. Restriction of competition has made for insulated living at the top. As shared tastes, educational background, life experiences, attitudes, deportment, and interest substitute for brilliance or achievement as criteria for admission to the regime, the members of our ruling class think increasingly as a group, disagree with each other less and less, and are ever readier to think well of themselves and to be surprised at their failures or just to deny them. As each succeeding generation of our regime proves less competent than the preceding one, the American people have every reason to shudder upon reading that the nation's highest posts are occupied by those whom our top institutions have certified as the best and brightest.

It is important to reemphasize that the following account of how our regime is affecting the habits that affect our prosperity and so on is emphatically *not* a complete picture of America in our time—principally because it is not, except tangentially, an account of the many forces working in the opposite direction. At the very least, the regime has covered with hypocrisy its tendency to greater power and exclusiveness. But virtue may well demand payment from the debts that vice thus incurs.

What follows is an account of our regime's effects.

POWER AND PROSPERITY

The U.S. economy today is being shaped not so much by economic policies as by a degradation of economically useful habits and the proliferation of economically useless jobs, caused by the ever-increasing injection of government power into the world of work. Liberal and conservative economists pay little attention to this.

Liberal economists have argued that America's prosperity is being undermined by excessive private consumption and insufficient public investments. They argue that private profligacy, coupled with free trade, is deindustrializing America while raping the environment. They urge higher taxes and tariffs, along with more nontariff barriers to trade, and recommend an "industrial policy" that will rein in consumption, get America out of international debt, and guarantee good "green" jobs for our children. We should be producing the good things in life, they say, without upsetting the environment.

The premises of the liberal economists are false. America is not an international debtor, but very much a creditor, because total income to Americans from overseas investments is greater than total payments to foreign investors.[3] Large corporations have indeed shed middle managers and moved manufacturing to low-wage countries. But this is a result of inescapable principles of economics favoring comparative advantage. No one has ever shown how one people may violate such principles without paying the price. But the premise that really underlies liberal economics is one that is seldom, if ever, avowed: namely, that Americans value the wrong things, that the view the American people have of the good life is wrong, and that Americans must give up the low-density living arrangements they have preferred since colonial days and live like Europeans, closely packed and using primarily public transportation. The problem, as liberal economists see it, is how to *change* the American public's view of the good life. Hence the liberal critique is not about how to increase or even maintain America's prosperity, but about redefining it while making the laws of economics yield results different from the results they have always had. The objective of the liberal economists, then, is to obtain economic power with which to refashion the way Americans live.

That is their objective when they write of the need to repair America's crumbling infrastructure. The proposition that the American economy is hampered by crumbling roads and bridges, and that it is more difficult to move people, goods, and data around the United States than elsewhere, is ludicrous to anyone who has traveled the world. Liberal proposals for "investments" of the bricks and mortar kind make sense, however, as patronage to favored contractors and unions—as instruments of power. Sometimes, such projects are touted as general economic stimuli, Keynesian means for injecting money into the economy. Whether such roads and bridges benefit the general public is less certain than that they benefit the persons who are paid to work on them. Conversely, it is just as certain that the money paid to these recipients becomes unavailable to anyone else. Even more certain it is that such infrastructure money will go directly to the persons best connected with the grantors, enriching them, and above all that it must empower the grantors. Thus, in America as in the old Soviet Union or in the Third World or anywhere else, "investment" in any item of public work that is undertaken except pursuant to specific demand for it will yield political patronage at a high economic price.

"Investment in human infrastructure" is direct patronage to social service providers and their clients. President Clinton claimed that each dollar spent on education, early childhood vaccination, and job training would pay off up to tenfold in increased production and reduced government costs.[4] This is part of the argument that President Lyndon Johnson made in the 1960s to justify expanding welfare and job training as part of the "war on poverty." But the populations targeted by these huge investments became more economically dependent on the government and produced greater burdens for the criminal justice system than before. Realistically, such investments pay off only in the coin of political support. In sum, liberal economics may be bad economics. But it is sound clientelistic politics of the kind practiced from Chicago to the Congo.

Nevertheless, liberal talk of social investments at least points in the general direction of the key relationship between prosperity and human capital. Most conservative economists nowadays—the neoclassical public choice theorists—ignore the warnings of their intellectual ancestor Wilhelm

Roepke about the indispensability of good character for the proper functioning of markets. Instead, they assume the constancy of character and diligence and posit that all people rationally seek to maximize their material well-being. Unlike their forebears, the neoclassicists cannot account for the farsighted self-restraint and self-discipline that lead some utility-maximizers to make economic contributions to themselves and others, or for the shortsightedness that turns other utility-maximizers into consumers of social services, or worse, into people who make money by gaming government programs. This has led some of them to set aside their objections to socializing risk and hence to fostering "moral hazard" in the business world, and to join liberals in keeping failed banks and businesses out of bankruptcy.

Public choice economists usually do not understand that the meaning of free enterprise differs radically for people of different moral dispositions. Therefore, although the conservatives' policy recipes—they prefer private to public investment, free trade to managed trade, and low taxes to high ones— tend to be better for economic growth than those of the liberals, conservative economists are apt to ignore what is gnawing at the habits of the heart of a people that once turned a "desolate wilderness" into a "fair land." Thus, Gary Becker has recalled something of the moral emphasis of an earlier generation of economists: "The effects of a free market system on self-reliance, initiative, and other virtues," he wrote, may be more important to prosperity than technical market arrangements. Becker has pointed to welfare as a destroyer of economically essential virtues, and to affirmative action initiatives as programs that help people get ahead not through their own accomplishments but through their membership in favored groups. Aid to small and large businesses that subsidizes their profits and insures them against losses, and regulations that protect companies against competition, are other examples he cites of economic policies that can impact a people's economically useful habits.[5]

The best economists, then, look to noneconomic causes and effects.

THE REAL ISSUE

Even the middle class, little less than the rich and the poor, is losing personal discipline, substituting self-indulgence for the practical moral code that used to be the basis of the American economy—namely, living within your capacity to earn and realizing that laying claim to things you cannot pay for is a recipe for ruin. At stake is whether modern America, like the America of the founders, will value the habits that make for productive lives, or, like so many other regimes, it will teach people that having is better than producing, thereby fostering mutual depredation.

Financial imprudence has become as much a hallmark of modern American life as financial prudence was of yesteryear. According to a May 2008 report by the Institute for American Values, credit-card debt in America rose from $238 billion in 1989 to $937 billion in 2007, and the number of payday loans—in which a person signs over his forthcoming paycheck for a portion of it today—has doubled each year. Companies run ads on television cheerfully informing people that they do not have to pay the full amount of their credit-card bills or taxes: Spend now, repudiate later. Meanwhile, the states encourage the gullible to buy lottery tickets—with odds of winning the big one like those of being hit by lightning. And these attitudes toward spending and gambling are by no means limited to the bottom of society: In our time, millions of middle-class people have bought homes caring less about the price they committed to pay than about the prospect that they could flip the property at a higher price or simply walk away from unrealized gain without suffering loss. Then they clamored for the government to save them from the consequences of their choices. They had every reason to believe that the government would try to do this because the American economy's top personages long ago persuaded the U.S. government to shield them from bankruptcy and keep them in their places at taxpayer expense. The financial panic of 2008 consisted of nothing but a chain of debt repudiation, the final link of which was the taxpayer—a transfer of wealth away from responsible people for the sake of the irresponsible. In sum, "moral hazard" flows downhill in America just as it does anywhere else.

In America as elsewhere, once people become comfortable with the notion that they are entitled to what they want and that the government is somehow responsible for securing their desires, redistribution replaces production as the focus of economic activity. At stake in the struggle between different sets of economically relevant habits is not just the amount of material possessions that the American people will enjoy but also the extent to which the American people will have at their disposal the material means of personal independence and habits of self-control.

CORRUPTION AT THE TOP

Using the government to leverage your business, or making money by satisfying it rather than customers, is a corruption far deeper and more contagious than merely taking bribes, because it abets the temptation inherent in all government to foster redistribution rather than production and service.

Those in power need not seek opportunities for self-enrichment. Such opportunities knock at their doors and well-nigh knock them in. In most cases, transactions of influence and money go well beyond specific governmental quids for explicit, specific private quos. The 1990s' big corruption story involved the relationship that Tyson Foods, Arkansas' largest poultry processor, and several of that state's banks and savings and loans may have had with the state's first family. Tyson's chief counsel was instrumental in multiplying the First Lady's investments in cattle futures a hundredfold, from $1,000 to $100,000. The Madison Savings and Loan president paid the governor's personal gubernatorial-campaign debts, and he had no problems with the state's banking examiner, who was appointed by the governor. What the great do in a grand way, lesser folks do as they may. Thus, President Clinton's secretary of labor, Alexis Herman, made between $500,000 and $1 million, according to her federal disclosure form, on a silent partnership with a man whose interests she recommended to her mentor, Secretary of Commerce Ron Brown. The same man had made a $50,000 campaign contribution to President Clinton, and Brown used the power of the United States to obtain special treatment for him in Japan.[6] There is no way of knowing how much money he made there. More recently, the Chicago hospital that employed Michelle Obama raised her salary from $121,910 to $316,962 after her husband's 2006 election to the U.S. Senate. When the hospital's spokesman said that she was "worth her weight in gold," he probably understated her value.

Yet all such things are important only paradigmatically in relation to what is becoming the new American economic regime at the top: sometimes called "access capitalism," the way of much of the rest of the world.

Since the New Deal, America has come to know what other countries know even better: the political entrepreneur. The first of this kind in America, Henry J. Kaiser got close to Roosevelt administration lobbyist Tommy Corcoran and garnered through him almost one-third of America's war production—all on government credit—"cheap at twice the loan," he would say. And he worked on cost-plus contracts. Of course Kaiser produced airplanes and lots of other useful things. But when he was allowed to buy his facilities at a few cents on the dollar at war's end, he resembled a modern Russian privatizing nomenklaturist more than a character from a Horatio Alger story who made money by adding value.

Corporate favoritism for the rich and the upper middle classes, not welfare for the poor, has driven the process first sketched by Mancur Olson, and later described by Jonathan Rauch,[7] by which interest groups have hardened the arteries of the American economy and are turning it, notch by notch, from a machine for production into one for redistribution. Here, as elsewhere, "as a society becomes more and more dense with networks of interest groups, as the benefits secured by groups accumulate, the economy rigidifies."[8] Not so differently than in the Soviet Union or Argentina, entrenched interests use the government in order to collect more while working less, and individuals learn that productive activity is less rewarding than government-related activity. How this logic unfolds is an old story: Because the benefits' recipients can never be satisfied, the government must respond to growing demands by becoming more "taxy," thus pushing society's producers into passivity or worse.[9]

Because the new path to riches is knowing what the government wants, ever greater attention and effort must be shifted away from production and toward fitting into government schemes. Thus businesses have found that they can make more money by cutting down on the number of production workers and experts in the business while hiring more government affairs consultants. Though lawyers produce nothing, they are paid more than engineers because government makes their services really more valuable. A biotechnologist who has worked for the Food and Drug Administration (FDA) can name his price with a drug company. And what utility would not pay top dollar to someone who has worked for the Environmental Protection Agency (EPA) on approving smokestack scrubbers? Lest anyone doubt that such high salaries (passed on to the public through higher prices) are fair recompense for substantive expertise, consider why the Lockheed Corporation hired one John McMahon, deputy director of Central Intelligence, to be president of its Missiles and Space Company. The company builds high-tech products, and McMahon, whose career had been in personnel security, never knew the difference between a pixel and a pixie. But his knowledge of the people who gave out contracts justified every penny of his astronomic salary.

For that reason, as we issue more regulations, *more of us will have to go to law school than to schools of science and engineering.* Moreover, the decisions we make about the relationship between government and the economy will have more to do with our material well-being than any economic decisions. Consider, for example, the price of things. During the 1980s, the press was indignant that aerospace contractors had charged $500 for a hammer, $600 for a toilet seat, and $7,000 for a coffee pot. But it wrongly assumed that someone had pocketed the difference between these sums and the $15 or so that these items should have cost, or that they were made of gold or "unobtainium" by herds of Ph.D.'s. None of that. These plain Jane items were produced as part of larger projects that involved several subcontractors as well as reviews by different government committees at different stages of the job. This forced entire factories to march in place as workers waited for others to meet contrasting specifications and as engineers were shuttling to Washington. By the same token, the high cost of drugs reflects the years and somersaults required to gain approval by the FDA for a new product. As for nuclear power plants, which could easily provide the cheapest form of electricity known to man, the process we have set up for building them requires as much lawyering as engineering over decades to get one up and running. One can only sympathize with the aerospace company vice president who told me: "If the government wants paper instead of metal, we'll take the money to the bank just the same."

Rauch estimates that what he calls "the parasite economy" costs the country some 5–12 percent of GDP.[10] In comparison with most of the world, that is not bad. By previous American standards, it is awful. Even worse is that the U.S. economy is moving ever farther into the orbit of government. That is because, as James L. Payne has shown, the legislative process is close to monopolized by witnesses who are petitioning for more rules and expenditures. Only 1 witness out of 145 wants fewer of them.[11] Congress calls such witnesses precisely because they are claimants.

The financial crisis of 2008 was made inevitable by the government's decision to force banks to extend mortgages to persons they judged not creditworthy, as well as by the decision of banks and investment houses to pyramid onto one another ever more highly leveraged financial instruments. The existence of these instruments, combined with the government-mandated collapse of lending standards for subprime borrowers, encouraged otherwise qualified borrowers to overextend themselves. None did so more than those best connected with banks—such as the managers of hedge funds, endowment funds of Ivy League universities, and state pension funds. But when the financial bubble created by preferential financing burst, the very people who had created it sought to be rescued by government commitments of preferential financing. That necessarily aggravated the shortage of private capital and sent large businesses scrambling for some share of government-guaranteed capital.

By the end of 2008, as the value of stocks rose and fell almost exclusively on news of how much the government would give to whom in exchange for what, a radically new (for America) economy loomed. Its shape was clearest in the car business. Forced by government into debilitating cohabitation with the United Auto Workers union, obliged to produce unprofitable small cars, the major U.S. automakers were bankrupt. The Republican president, his elected Democratic successor, and Democratic leaders in Congress agreed that the government should keep the companies in business with public money on condition that they produce the kinds of "green" cars that the regime thinks the American people should drive. But few bet that the American people would buy such cars. In short, it seemed that the auto industry, like other large components of the U.S. economy, would purchase the government's preferential financing by committing to produce things that satisfy the government rather than customers. Unless the government somehow did away with customer choice, this sort of thing would be mere waste. Were government to try giving monopoly powers to its effectively nationalized industries, it would be worse than waste—a path for the American economy straight to the Third World.

CORRUPTING THE BOTTOM

Lower-class corruption is straightforward. In 2008 some 13 million American children were on welfare, and 28 million—9.4 percent of all Americans—received food stamps.[12] Other welfare programs—housing assistance that pays the rent, energy assistance that pays the utility bills, and Medicaid that pays the doctor bills—have grown even faster. In twelve states, the combined worth of just these five programs (there are seventy others to choose from) to a welfare mother of two amounts to over 90 percent of the mean wage in the area. In Hawaii, Alaska, Massachusetts, Rhode Island, and the District of Columbia, these combined benefits actually exceed the after-tax income of the average worker. And in each of the fifty states, the combined benefits exceed the take-home pay from a minimum-wage job (in some by a factor of three). To this must be added the fastest-growing welfare program of all, Social Security Disability Insurance (SSDI) and Supplemental Security Income (SSI). In 1994, the number of people supported by these programs, which affect the middle class as well as the poor, actually exceeded those supported by what was once the biggest program of all, Aid to

Families with Dependent Children (AFDC),[13] which was transmogrified after 1996 with its expenses much reduced.

The welfare relationship is not merely a quantitative economic transaction. Its importance is in the habits it fosters. Note that in southern Europe welfare is often just a fraudulent way to add to income from honest work. That is not so corrupt, especially given the local cultures. The different quality of the welfare transaction in America, however, may be glimpsed in the fact that roughly 40 percent of those eligible for benefits do not take advantage of them because they are too proud to become part of a culture of dependency so at odds with normal American ways. The government tells them they are entitled to be relieved of worries and toil. But, like the bedraggled wolf in Aesop's fable who chose not to share the well-fed dog's dish—and collar—they prefer to eat whatever meager portion they can earn. Once upon a time, private and local charities honorably supported the lame, the blind, the injured. To the able-bodied of questionable character they offered minimal sustenance in exchange for hard labor, thereby fostering personal honor and the habits that flow therefrom. When the U.S. government made welfare an entitlement, however, it collapsed the distinction between bad fortune and bad character. It validated the habits of the takers and effectively labeled honorable scruples as stupid.

Now consider the economic consequences of the moral content of the welfare culture. Quite contrary to the intent of the statute that created it, AFDC became the main support for the sexually irresponsible. Its requirement that the "family" have no one producing income meant that the presence of fathers would be uneconomical. More children meant more money. But social workers and police knew very well that many welfare mothers were not really "single," that is, bereft of men, and that the money that the government paid for the children's support supported them less than it did the men who impregnated the mothers. Typically, these itinerant "boyfriends" made sure that they were with their women on the day the check arrived, popularly called "mothers' day." The U.S. government in fact made it possible for such males to hang out, fight, and deal drugs. While the church on the corner may have told them to be productive, the U.S. government gave them the material and moral means to disdain the jobs for which they qualified as unworthy sources of "chump change."

To remedy these frightful habits even more than to save money, Congress passed and President Clinton signed the 1996 Welfare Reform Act that made welfare the responsibility of states and set some conditions on the states' receipt of block grants to fund it. Foremost among these was the requirement that adults (women) receiving the money either work or do some kind of community service, and a (flexible) prohibition against remaining in the program for more than five years. States were allowed to make cooperation in determining children's paternity a condition for benefits. This caused a precipitous drop in the welfare rolls and a shift to other programs.

The welfare attitude is not a racial problem. Most of the Americans who take advantage of government assistance are white, and the *percentage* of lower-class whites who live this way is climbing rapidly toward black levels. Indeed, as welfare critic Charles Murray pointed out, the biggest difference between the black underclass and the growing white underclass is the geographic concentration of the former and the geographic dispersion of the latter.[14] Most important, the welfare culture is multiplying among all races, because bit by bit, social workers are breaking down the moral stigmas that Americans used to attach to the culture of the underclass. The welfare population is also growing biologically through growing rates of illegitimate births. The main economic consequence is that if the trends identified by Murray continue, one in seven Americans, soon more—will be noncontributors to society, or worse.

Social Security's welfare programs (especially SSI) may be the most harmful of all. Whereas in other countries disability programs mainly support the otherwise decent grassroots clients of politicians—mere partners in theft—in America they have grown into support mechanisms for social pathologies. That is because the government has classified alcoholism, drug addiction, and various kinds of personality disorders (aggressiveness, boorishness, tendency to steal) as federally subsidizable disabilities. Children, too, are eligible to be classified as "disabled" if they exhibit "mental impairment." In 1990, the Supreme Court redefined this category to include children who do not act in an "age-appropriate" manner. Thus, whereas once parents had only incentives to make their children act their age or better, the U.S. government now gives them $600 per month or more for every child who can demonstrate immaturity or below-grade performance.[15]

Because of subsidies for bad habits and the official erasure of stigmas on behavior that civil society once discouraged, we are raising up more and more people who are more likely to turn the fair land into a desolate wilderness than the other way around.

CORRUPTING THE MIDDLE

The U.S. government's corruption of the economic habits of the great American middle class—the geese that have laid history's greatest trove of golden eggs—has been more subtle. As elsewhere, the promise of security has been the effective bait. Middle-class entitlement programs, especially Social Security and Medicare, have led people to believe that in exchange for substantial contributions, they will receive, absolutely guaranteed, services that are worth more than what they pay. This might be called the "insurance-plus" mentality. Reality, however, amounts to "insurance minus." And the minus consists of lost habits and families as well as lost money.

For its first three decades, Social Security's Old Age and Survivor's Insurance, established in 1937, was a pay-as-you-go chain-letter scheme end-loaded against collecting. Workers and employees paid in tiny amounts (0.5 percent of wages), and some people (only a handful compared to the number of recipients today) received benefits that, though modest, were much greater than what they had put in. Since average life expectancy in the United States in 1935 was only 61.7 years, few would ever collect, and not for long. *Then, as now, Social Security was primarily a tax, veiled by thin pretense.* Like Otto von Bismarck, who invented social security, twentieth-century American politicians bought the votes of *prospective* retirees by using the contributions of young workers, to whom they promised that their time would come. Meanwhile, they pocketed the money and spent it. Hence, promises that benefits will be paid are backed by precisely nothing. Zero. The contributor has no property right whatever in any of the money he pays in. Besides, for many years after 1935 very little money was being paid out.

The government's implicit promise that everyone would get much more than they put in trained people not to ask who the money belongs to, what happens to it when it's paid in, and by what magic it should come out bountifully on the other end. Beginning in the 1960s, however, as more people lived long enough to collect and fewer were being born, paying retirees became possible only by increasing the Social Security payroll tax again and again. By 1980, the payroll tax exceeded the average worker's income tax. But the new constituency of recipients was convinced easily enough that they had a right to the benefits, which Congress had increased, because they had "earned it." They had learned to treat as sacrilege questions about how the increase had come about. The increased taxes, however, led workers to ask for some assurance that the money taken from them would be returned to them in the form of Social Security payments. The government answered with the Reform Act of 1983, fathered by a bipartisan commission (when everybody is responsible, nobody is responsible), which consisted of a whopping increase in the payroll tax to 12.4 percent dressed in mumbo jumbo about putting the "trust fund" on a sound basis forever.

As a consequence of the 1983 act, the Social Security system began to take in lots more money than it paid out. All the excess went nominally into the "Social Security Trust Fund." Yet talk of "trust funds" thinly veils the fact that when the Internal Revenue Service (IRS) turns the Social Security contributions over to the U.S. Treasury, the Treasury spends them *the instant* it receives them, as it does all other moneys. In return, the Treasury gives the Social Security Administration a set of IOUs that can only be redeemed through the willingness of future politicians to tax future workers to pay them. In 2008, the U.S. treasury "borrowed" $674 billion from the Social Security Trust Fund.[16]

Like any Ponzi scheme, Social Security yielded enormous increases to those who were the first to collect. A typical worker retiring in the early 1970s before the big jumps in Social Security taxes took place and surviving into the 1990s may have received a hundred times more than what he or she contributed. Between the early 1970s and the early 1990s, however, the odds reversed rapidly. A nominal worker retiring in the mid-1990s and surviving for twenty years will be lucky to get an increase of 2 percent on the money contributed. A typical baby boomer retiring in 2010 and surviving for twenty-five years may get 40 cents on the dollar. From there, the curve will drop steeply. This is not a very good return, especially compared to most long-term investments in the stock market. In short, the U.S. government has led millions of Americans to lend it trillions of dollars under false pretenses. Consider what a middle-class Social Security contribution of $3,000 would yield if it were invested and compounded each year for forty years at the stock market's historical 9 percent rate of return (which would be similar to what is done in Chile).[17] The resulting $1,880,000 would provide some $126,000 per year for a fifteen-year life expectancy after age sixty-five, whereas the Social Security Administration will have a difficult time keeping its promise of a maximum of some $24,000 per year.

Since it is known with near certainty how many retirees there will be circa 2020, and with absolute certainty how many workers will be there to support them (since those workers have already been born), and that the ratio between retirees and workers will be about 1 to 2, as opposed to the current ratio of 1 to 3.3, we know that keeping up with payouts would require nearly doubling Social Security taxes. Alternatively, the U.S. government must repudiate the promises of Social Security by some mechanism, probably by inflation.

Social Security has been a smashing success, however, in changing the economic habits of Americans. Prior to Social Security, Americans secured their old age through savings and through their children. Families planned to pass on such nest eggs as they had to their children. Social Security, however, promised people independence from their children. And the estate tax, or death tax, ensures that their children cannot depend on whatever inheritance the parents might have saved up for them. True, until the late 1960s, the benefits that Social Security paid were insufficient for any but the most penurious independent living. Nor, until the 1970s, did Social Security taxes take enough from personal income to hamper the accrual of private nest eggs. Only in the 1980s did Social Security make private nest eggs well-nigh impossible for average workers to build.

Nevertheless, Social Security pointed the way to a new model of family economics. The government encouraged adults to dream of retirement not among the children and grandchildren who would be their heirs, but in Winnebagos heading into the sunset bearing the standard bumper sticker: "We are spending our children's inheritance." Ironically, of course, although the folks in the Winnebagos may be independent of their children as individuals, they are very much dependent on the younger generation collectively, because Social Security payments are a growing negative inheritance pressed upon the children and grandchildren of retirees by the U.S. government. But that negative inheritance is passed on in the name of an anonymous generation rather than for beloved parents. Hence, rather than encouraging generosity, the government is encouraging people's natural tendency to be even less generous collectively than individually.

The other major middle-class entitlement, Medicare, is to be understood as the prototype of social services—and as the future toward which our Establishment is driving America. Its operative feature—individuals pay some third party that then guarantees the delivery of services—has long since conquered the habits of middle-class Americans. Before the Medicare law was passed in 1965, there was only one major health maintenance organization (HMO) in America. Fee for service was the rule, and health insurance was the exception. By the turn of the twenty-first century, health insurance was the rule, HMOs the model, and some states had made it unlawful for fee-for-service medicine to compete with insurance-based medicine. The habits associated with the new way of medicine are very different from those fostered by the old. Under the new system, even people who have a wide choice of doctors, as under the best insurance policies or Medicare, are *supplicants*.

In the old days, people went to the doctor and contracted fees for each service. They might or might not consider price, but in any case, they hired the doctor. If he did not satisfy them, they could hire another. Under the new systems of "managed care," middle-class Americans and their employees pay month after month to insurance companies or HMOs, which then hire and pay the doctors. The contributor (who, ironically, is no longer considered a payer) then goes to see "gatekeeper" physicians who decide what, if any, treatment the patient should receive. The real payer, the patient, has no power vis-à-vis the doctor.

Middle-class Americans have been attracted to managed care for some of the reasons they were attracted to Social Security, among them *the promise of unlimited benefits in exchange for limited payments*. Earlier forms of health insurance paid only a percentage of costs, and then only after the patient had paid substantial amounts out of pocket. The HMOs promised to pay for everything. Pay a small premium, and get unlimited use of the miracles of modern medicine! But the premiums turned out to be not so small, and the gatekeeper physicians, whose future careers now depend on satisfying their employers rather than their patients, were encouraged to make cutting costs their first priority. Effectively they administer a system of rationing.

For those upper-middle-class people who either have personal relationships with the doctors or with the "payers," or can expect to have their arguments taken seriously because of their status, the new system does not require behavior much different from the old. But lesser beings now have to cajole and often to plead, first with doctors and then with insurance companies.[18] To make their case, they have to research their health problems themselves, and they may be forced to hire a lawyer, because the cards are stacked against them. Meanwhile, the supplicant's condition worsens. In sum, in the illusory pursuit of a bit more than their money's worth, middle-class Americans now need bureaucratic skills that their parents did reasonably well without.

The party that won the 2008 elections is committed to "universal health insurance." It made no secret of its intention to present the insurance

companies that are the current system's formal "payers" with the choice between a future in which they carry out government policy secured by government financing and mandates—like the car companies—on the one
hand, and, on the other, government regulations that squeeze them into
bankruptcy. Enactment of "universal health insurance," while not increasing the number of doctors or CAT scan machines, would entitle all to use
them freely—but, as in any and all nationalized systems, only theoretically.
Those who run the system would have to ration access as never before, perhaps by lengthening waiting lines. American patients would be forced to
learn the skills all too familiar to other peoples—how to work the system as
if life depended on it. Because it does.

In sum, then, the U.S. government is habituating Americans to pursue
national well-being in ways that would have seemed strange to the country's
founders and, indeed, to most Americans before the 1960s. The economic
habits being fostered in the upper, lower, and middle classes, though different, share two features: the search for security and advantage, and the rejection of personal responsibility. These features are destructive not only of
prosperity but also of civic, family, and spiritual life.

CITIZENSHIP

If Alexis de Tocqueville were to return to America at the turn of the twentieth century, he would find the Constitution he had described dead in all
but formal and vestigial aspects. So would Madison, Hamilton, and John
Marshall. Instead of few laws to which citizens adhered with pride of au-
thorship, they would find an incomprehensible infinity of regulations, and
hordes of haughty officials propitiated by a nation of increasingly resentful
subjects. He would find that a government with so many favors to give and
to withhold was producing a nation of favor seekers, that the government that
had taken upon itself the job of righting social wrongs had so stimulated
the articulation of grievances that it was producing a nation of enemies. Tocqueville would see the inhabitants of American towns taking their concerns
to the state or national capitals just like the Europeans of his day had to do.
He would meet legislators elected from districts designed to be "safe" for
blacks, whites, or Hispanics, for Republicans or for Democrats, and he
would conclude that the American people were being divided to be ruled.
Tocqueville would notice the scarcity of prominent citizens in public places.

He would find they had retreated into buildings, suburbs, and gated communities governed for practical purposes as if the public laws did not exist. He would be struck by how much citizens concerned about crime talked about the police and the courts, and how little they considered their own responsibility for public safety—and he would conclude that Americans were becoming Europeans.

FROM THE RULE OF LAW TO THE WHIM OF MAN

The rule of law in America is eroding in theory and in practice. It long ago ceased to be a secret confined to the law schools or to readers of Texas law professor Lino Graglia that the rulings of the Supreme Court have nothing to do with the text of the Constitution or with the intentions of the founders and everything to do with the political preferences of the judges and their political associates off the bench. In 2008, four out of nine justices wrote that the Constitution's recognition of the right "of the people" to "keep and bear arms" in the Second Amendment means that individuals have no such right, while in 1973 six justices found a right to abortion in "an emanation of the penumbra" of the Fourth Amendment. In short, there is little support in the legal establishment for the proposition that judges should be restrained by the text of law.

As for the spirit of laws, the attack on the 1991 nomination of Clarence Thomas to the Supreme Court showed that liberals deem as dangerous nonsense the notion that natural law can restrain or inform government power.[19] Conservatives, for their part, tend to oppose the expansion of government power. But they do so merely because that is their preference—as a mere assertion of will. Former chief justice William Rehnquist, for example, wrote that the "Constitution's safeguards for individual liberty . . . assume a general social acceptance neither because of any intrinsic worth nor because of any unique origins in someone's ideas of natural justice, but instead simply because they have been incorporated in a constitution by a people."[20] In saying this, he essentially granted that all constitutional judgments are of inherently equal worth. In sum, for the Right as for the Left, the will of the founders is no better than ours. This leaves each of us to ask why we should not push our own will *à outrance*.

Congress, too, has abandoned constitutional restraint. It no longer bothers to cite authorization from Article 1, Section 8, of the Constitution when it legislates a national drinking age, makes nationwide rules for the health-care industry, mandates hospital stays for specific conditions, sets rules regarding the environment or disabled people, or nationalizes banks or industries. But Congress's propensity thus to legislate is a small part of the problem.

In practice, since 1935 most "laws" in America have not been of the sort taught in civics class—passed by the Congress or state legislatures elected by the people, and enforced in detail by courts that hand down the judgment of juries composed of one's peers. Instead of being governed by laws, in fact, for the most part citizens are governed by regulations. Bureaucracies make the actual rules and then administer and enforce them. Most often, ordinary people are treated in accordance with "agency policy"—or rather some bureaucrat's interpretation thereof—instead of in accordance with laws or even published rules. That is because when the Supreme Court let its ruling in *Schechter Poultry Corp. v. United States* (1935)—which said that Congress could not delegate legislative and judicial powers to its creature, the National Recovery Agency—pass into oblivion, it effectively amended the Constitution to allow Congress to delegate its powers to bureaucracies both unelected and unlimited by the Constitution.

This was the beginning of the "alphabet soup" agencies that exercise quasi-legislative and quasi-judicial powers—as well as executive power. From the citizen's standpoint, there is nothing "quasi" about these powers. They are more absolute than ordinary criminal and civil law, and far less accountable. They do not accord their subjects trials by jury. Often, officials choose to impose rules via regulatory agencies that they have failed to impose through legislation. Thus, Massachusetts Attorney General Scott Harshbarger, having failed to convince the legislature to ban the manufacture and sale of handguns with certain characteristics, simply prevailed on the state's Consumer Protection Agency to do it. In our time, as the proponents of carbon taxes pondered the fact that voting for them would mean suicide for most congressmen, they laid plans to impose those taxes by simply having the Environmental Protection Agency issue the rules and set the fees. In this way, the price of carbon-generated energy could be raised to the desired level without anybody having to cast a vote or sign a bill. All would be done anonymously in the name of science. People in the know in today's America no longer bother with legislatures. They go where results are easy and for which they need bear no responsibility—the bureaucracies or the courts.

The rules for dealing with bureaucrats are not written in any civics book. These fall under two headings: first, "rules are for outsiders," and second, "[expletive deleted] flows downhill." The first means that if you have managed to rise to the level of those who sit on agencies' advisory boards, you need fear neither rules nor those who make them—because these know you can always have a chat with their boss and make rule number 2 work against them, very personally. Most people, however, are not in the same league as the bureaucrats' bosses. So they must wheedle at the system's edges.

The rule of law means that the government is bound by rules known to all and administered equally "by the book." But modern American bureaucracy has so many rules that not even the officials who administer them can know them all or apply them consistently, while those who live under them cannot possibly take refuge behind compliance. The Federal Register issues 200 pages of densely written regulations every day. The Internal Revenue Service manual consists of 260 incomprehensible volumes. The Occupational Safety and Health Administration rule book has some 4,000 chapters. Any willful official, or simply one under pressure to get ahead, can find a taxpayer, a homeowner, or a business in violation of some regulation because of how he filed his tax return, how he modified his house, or how he runs his business. This is easy enough, especially since some agencies hand out a majority of their citations not for substantive violations of regulations but for faulty recordkeeping or inadequate filing of forms. In today's America, any business can be shut down, every individual can be mightily inconvenienced, if not ruined, for administrative violations unrelated to substantive ones at the mere discretion of a couple of officials. And if one inspector or auditor thinks something is okay, that is no guarantee that another inspector will not wreck you. That is because different officials know and care about different rules, or they understand them differently on any given day—or simply because some like the looks of you and some don't.

Making matters worse, no taxpayer, even if armed with the Internal Revenue Code, or landowner, likewise prepared with EPA regulations, could cite any of these regulations in his own defense with hope of success, because the courts have consistently held that agency regulations and a fortiori policies are merely guides to administrative action. And since administrative judges are hired, fired, transferred, and promoted by the same agencies whose cases they are supposed to review, the agencies have a sure advantage in conflicts with members of the general public. Modern American bureaucrats increasingly look at citizens as if to say: "I can do anything I want to you, and there's not a damn thing you can do to me, so when I say, 'Jump,' you had better ask, 'How high?'" Prudent individuals quickly realize that the best chance they have for safety before a force they cannot control is to humor it.

The irony is that those who originally advocated the explosion of rule-making in the 1960s, including Federal Circuit Judge J. Skelly Wright and others, thought they would thereby be protecting the citizen against bureaucratic discretion.[21] But the opposite happened. Between 1978 and 1992, the number of penalties assessed by the IRS jumped tenfold, and the number of liens it placed against property jumped by a factor of three, as has its preemptive (that is, prior to any court judgment) seizure of assets.[22]

Seizure has also become the standard modus operandi of other regulatory agencies, thanks to the recent and very radical revival of the old but long dormant legal principle known as civil forfeiture, whereby a criminal forfeits the property used in the commission of a crime. In today's America, a bureaucrat armed with that principle can seize property, even without ever bringing formal charges, simply on the allegation that it might be used in the commission of a crime.

Civil forfeiture was revived as a measure against drug dealers. But according to researcher James Bovard, 80 percent of the people whose property is seized under the drug laws are never formally charged with any crime. The percentage of those whose property is seized by the Environmental Protection Agency and the U.S. Fish and Wildlife Service and who are never even charged, much less convicted, is even higher. The Supreme Court has ruled that even a person's total innocence does not protect that person's property from civil forfeiture.[23] What a weapon against a citizen! For whatever motive, an official accuses a citizen of a vague or unsubstantiated offense, then inflicts punishment on the spot by seizing the person's land, machinery, or transportation. A livelihood—and perhaps a family—is ruined. The citizen can go to an ordinary court to try to prove his innocence, but that costs money he may not have, and that perhaps was just taken from him. And the prospect of attempting to fight bureaucrats who stand to lose nothing—and are backed by in-house lawyers—is not very encouraging. The citizen who is unlucky enough to draw the attention of a willful bureaucrat is typically reduced to doing at least part of what the bureaucrat wanted, plus signing a waiver of his right to sue.

Since 1965, American legal procedure has increasingly turned citizens into resentful subjects and wheelers. Nowhere is this clearer than in regard to economic regulation. Take agriculture. Since the 1930s, American agri-culture on all but artisan scale has been effectively run by government-mandated marketing boards. These boards are composed of leading growers in each crop who advise the Department of Agriculture about such vital matters as how to set arbitrary standards of quality (products that do not meet the standards may not be sold at any price). This system has turned into a machine for driving small farmers out of business. It is supposedly le-gitimized by periodic referenda of the growers, run by the department. But the department itself collects and counts the ballots and permits no oppo-nent to verify the integrity of the process. So, as in the rest of modern Amer-ican administration, there is a lot less money to be had in fighting the system than in going along with it, and if possible, joining it.

Receiving the Food and Drug Administration's seal of approval is fraught with even more arbitrary rewards and punishments. Evaluations of both "safety" and "effectiveness" depend on subjective criteria. What percentage of laboratory animals must be free of what symptoms after what dose was taken, and for how long, in order for the drug to be considered safe? How much improvement must human testers show with what dose before it can be considered effective? Depending on the subjective answers, people in busi-ness can become wealthy or poor. People who are familiar with the process and on good terms with those who run it are the only ones who can suc-cessfully argue for test criteria. Any drug company would be foolish if it did not hire—for a lot of money—the most prestigious, well-connected con-sultants it could. Former employees of the FDA are best, in no small mea-sure because their prosperous presence tells current employees that if they act right, then they, too, can get high-paying jobs with drug companies.

When a company tries to stand on its rights, however, terrible things can happen. Thus, in 1990, Sporidicin, a well-established producer of disin-fectants approved by the EPA, was notified that its product now had to be certified by the FDA as well. The company was not pliant enough, arguing that its product had been sufficiently tested. On December 13, 1991, the FDA and the EPA together raided its headquarters and seized all its prod-ucts. The pretext? The product had passed 239 tests, but the FDA said it had failed number 240. The government had no case, but it had the power to keep the company shut down. In the final settlement, the company only had to agree not to violate federal advertising rules in the future—and, of course, not to sue. But the damage had been done.[24] How does one avoid trouble with the regime when one is not a member? In America, as elsewhere, one hires members—legislative lobbyists, bureaucratic lobbyists, lawyers, and the like. At the bottom of the food chain, the prudent builder will hire from a list of expediters and contractors who have good personal (that is, financial) relationships with the inspectors.[25] In the Soviet Union, they called such people *tolkachi.*

The U.S. bureaucracy's new discretionary powers are all the more galling because the government is so loath to punish its employees for harming citizens. Even when, in a highly publicized incident, an FBI sniper murdered the wife of a fugitive who was standing in a doorway holding her baby, the government issued only mild reprimands to its own. It did not even apologize to Richard Jewell, the security guard whom the FBI ruined by publicly accusing him on the basis of precisely no evidence (unfortunately for him, he fit a profile) of setting off a bomb in Atlanta during the 1996 Olympics. Federal prosecutors now obtain indictments in 99 percent of the cases they bring to grand juries. Prosecutors routinely use unethical methods to get indictments. The case of *Moore v. Valder,* in which the judge punished the unethical methods of the prosecutor, was a rare exception to the rule.[26] That is why, when the IRS agent who is auditing you laughs in your face, it makes little sense for you to think of the *Federalist Papers.* In such instances, it is easier to understand why so many Russians still have an affection for Stalin, who regularly threw to his subjects the bones of those who oppressed them directly.[27] Alas, it is easiest of all to think the servile thought: "To get along, go along, minimize the damage, and look for a way to get yours." That is how subjects nurse their grudges.

THE RULE OF SPITE

As the rule of law recedes, it becomes easier to get satisfaction at the expense of one's fellow citizens. Thus, Lance Morrow summed up the new pseudo-legal litigiousness in *Time* magazine:

> The busybody and the crybaby are getting to be the most conspicuous children on the American playground. The busybody is the bully with the Ayatollah shine in his eyes, gauleiter of correctness, who barges around telling the other kids that they cannot smoke, be fat, drink booze, wear furs, eat meat or otherwise non-conform to the new tribal rules taking shape. The crybaby, on the other hand, is the abject, manipulative little devil with the lawyer and so

to speak the actionable diaper rash. . . . Both these types are fashioning some odd new malformations of American character. It all adds up to what the *Economist* perceptively calls a "decadent Puritanism within America: an odd combination of ducking responsibility and telling everyone else what to do.[28]

These latter-day American epigones would just be sad fun if they were not a growing part of the regime. In fact, their actions are significant primarily because certain classes of Americans now enjoy legally "protected status" over others. It all began with the civil rights movement of the 1960s, when some Americans found moral satisfaction, personal power, and careers in branding others of their fellow citizens as racist. Racially motivated injustices have always been part of American society—though less than of any other multiethnic society in history. (Compare, for example, India, Rwanda, or even Belgium.) Reducing them is a noble objective. Surely for a substantial part of the civil rights movement, that objective was uncontaminated by ignoble motives.

However, no movement could be an exception to the rule that power corrupts. As Congress was passing the Civil Rights Act of 1964, its sincere, ingenuous sponsor, Hubert Humphrey, already felt compelled to deny in the strongest possible terms that the bill might be used to advantage some at the expense of others in jobs and education. But Howard Smith, the bitter segregationist Virginia congressman, had a firmer grip on reality. He knew that Humphrey's followers would quickly turn power gained in the name of antidiscrimination into power to discriminate, and that this would cause massive troubles in American society. Therefore, to cause trouble among those who had caused him trouble, to foster litigiousness among the liberals themselves, he added the word "sex" to the list of bases on which discrimination would be prohibited. He need not have bothered, because the movement was heading on its own toward expanding the bases on which the judiciary and the bureaucracy—meaning themselves—could interfere in interpersonal affairs. In 1967, Congress added the stipulation that workers over forty years of age also had the right to sue for discrimination in employment—and, in practice, for everything else. Since then, the list of protected classes has lengthened, and more Americans have learned the joy of gnawing on one another.

What this meant became unmistakable in 1976 when the Supreme Court, in *Meritor Bank v. Vinson,* established a woman employee's right to sue for sexual discrimination not on the basis of a tort (as specific, intentional damage recognized in common law) but rather on the basis of subjective feelings of discomfort. Protected status means that some people have the right to get mad at others and hurt them, while the others don't have the same right against them. In 1990, Congress followed that logic to its *pons asinorum,* its point of absurdity, by adding people with various handicaps to the list of the protected.

It is hardly surprising that many people, offered the advantages of protected status, quickly learned to flaunt it. Thus, in the womb of the federal bureaucracy, the judiciary, and its allied groups in society, the germ of the Civil Rights Act begat affirmative action, and affirmative action begat race norming, sexual quotas, suits for racial and sexual harassment, and sensitivity programs, as well as the legions of officials who make their living in them (Alexis Herman began her rise to fortune as one of them). As a result, one nice grievance, and one can be rid of an enemy, lock in a career, or just make enough money to retire. And to think that once upon a time to do these things you had to make a better mousetrap!

As Harvard professor Mary Ann Glendon has pointed out, defining any contest in terms of rights "impedes compromise, mutual understanding, and the discovery of common ground."[29] Such contests make for haughty winners and sore losers.[30] Perhaps, above all, it makes government power the arbiter. Robert Reich and many other liberals knew that the expansion of special rights would increase the level of contention in society and make lawyers as a class the managers of the new conflicts. They got more or less the results they wanted.

UNEQUAL EQUALITY

"Affirmative action," once unleashed, immediately became a part of American life, particularly in universities. It was quickly taken up by government itself as well as by large corporations. The pretense was soon dropped that it involved only aggressive searches for qualified, now-protected-but-heretofore-victimized students or employees. Quickly, it became a system of outright preferences. But precisely why should person A be advantaged at the expense of person B? Almost anyone can recite an accurate schedule of racial-sexual handicaps for jobs, promotions, and schools in his or her field. Yet rare in the literature is a straightforward defense of preferences. Within our Establishment, straight talk about preferences simply does not happen.

And so, to the corrosive effects of the policy must be added the corrosive effects of dissimulation, of living by lies.

Almost simultaneously with the practice of preference, there arose the practice of penalizing dissent with it. Labeled "racism," "sexism," "ageism," and so forth, the New Age crime of discomforting a protected person through speech can now be prosecuted formally by lawsuits (which have increased manyfold since 1969) for compensatory (and, since 1992, for punitive) damages. But the number of suits is dwarfed by informal actions brought before kangaroo courts within the workplace. No impartial juries, no rules of evidence apply to these proceedings. The offenses are defined only by the feelings and the status of the parties involved. Opposition to preferences for protected classes is prima facie proof of guilt (a position supported by the Supreme Court's decision in *Romer v. Evans* [1996]), as is humor about the whole matter.[31] At stake are promotions and demotions, who is up and who is down, who gets what—but, above all, who "gets" whom.

A reporter for the *New York Times,* obviously not realizing the self-indicting nature of the claim that there is a class of human controversy in which one side is right 95 percent of the time, breathlessly reported the following as typical: "A. T. & T., which has won considerable respect for its policies, says that 19 out of every 20 complaints received [for sexual harassment and discrimination] are valid." Almost by definition, the only accusations for New Age crimes that get to first base are those levied against people who lack the proper support within the workplace to turn them against the accuser. Such accusations are another unaccountable, pseudo-legal weapon of the preferred against the unpreferred, of the politically powerful against the politically weak, of the regime against gate crashers. By the turn of the twenty-first century, however, our regime's enthusiasm for discrimination suits had cooled. The liberal community's near unanimous support of President Bill Clinton in the face of evidence that he had preyed on women subordinates underlined the political nature of judgments on such matters. More important, during the previous quarter century every corporation and institution had been roiled by accusations of harassment and discrimination. No one could be sure of safety. Old Howard Smith had gotten his revenge after all.

But academic, governmental, and corporate America's passion for affirmative action continued because it continued to give officials (overwhelmingly white men) the capacity to dispense with objective criteria in hiring and promoting in general, not simply with regard to particular classes of employees, but with regard to individual employees. Affirmative action makes it possible to reward friends, to punish enemies, and to safeguard one's own position. Some years ago, following an impassioned plea by Judge Stephen Reinhardt, of the Ninth Circuit Court, to a Stanford Law School audience for acceptance of affirmative action because there are too many white men in high positions in the legal profession, I asked Judge Reinhardt whether he would agree to resign his post if the president would assure him that it would be filled by a qualified nonwhite female. As the audience laughed at his embarrassment, Reinhardt stumbled that the interaction between the concepts of professional qualifications and affirmative action is more complex than it seems. It is also very simple.

In practice, the distinction is not between formally protected classes and formally unprotected ones. In practice, not just any black gets preference over just any white, and not just any woman is preferred over any man. Under the system, lots of whites of both sexes get preference over other whites of the same or of the opposite sex as well as over people of other races. Affirmative action is about neither race nor sex. It is about politics—not the grand kind, but the seamy variety. It is about patrons and clients. People like Judge Reinhardt would prefer to work with another white man who belonged to his personal or political *khvost* than to have a black woman who was not pliant enough personally or politically. Still others use the freedom from standards that affirmative action provides to hire people who will not threaten to outshine them. In sum, then, affirmative action is about adding to the power of those who already have power and obliging those under them to build the personal political relationships that override objective criteria and immunize against New Age accusations. If liberal education is the formation of minds and hearts fit for freedom, affirmative action teaches some very illiberal habits.

The fading of the American tradition of the rule of law has produced new "rights." The beneficiaries of such rights are resentful,[32] and the new victims are bitter at having been deprived of theirs. We are becoming habituated to using power to obtain advantages at the expense of others. Thus, the civil rights industry has produced "unprotected classes" that publicly nod and privately simmer at charges against them that they know are not true. Moreover, as court decision after court decision emboldens homosexuals and feminists to condemn the lifestyle of average Americans, these feel increasingly as if they live in hostile territory.

LOCAL PREROGATIVES

A local tradition as strong as America's is not erased easily. But the U.S. government has gone a long way toward doing it. Demography helped. As cities grew, each to the size of an empire, classic American civic life became impossible in them. Thus, by the middle of the nineteenth century, New York City's school board was dominated by aristocrats, and by the turn of the twentieth, the class of bureaucrats whom the aristocrats had hired had become the new rulers. But in most of America, local government remained largely Tocquevillean through the 1950s. In fact, as city dwellers moved to the suburbs after World War II, they reestablished—at least for a few years—something resembling the kind of civic life they had lost in cities. A commuter to a job with a large corporation could still be a volunteer fireman and a power on the school board or town council in his suburb. By the late 1950s, however, as the suburbs expanded into one another, the idea gained ground that services such as zoning, police and fire protection, sanitation, and schools had to be handled professionally and on a larger scale. Elected mayors gave way to city managers, all but the most important of whom became liaisons with county departments that were really extensions of state bureaucracies responding to federal priorities. By 1990, in one of the most extreme of these steps, the state of Washington, through its Growth Management Act, required county governments to adopt countywide policies binding on the cities within them. In effect, the state abolished local government.[33]

The biggest abolition of citizenship came in the administration of schools. Whereas at the turn of the twentieth century in an America of 80 million people there had been some 105,000 school districts, by 2002 an America of 280 million had fewer than 15,000 school districts. When the roughly 9,000 districts that serve tiny populations are subtracted from this number, it becomes clear that most Americans live in public school districts with populations as large as those of states in James Madison's era. Moreover, the bureaucrats who run those districts regard as illegitimate the citizens' attempts to influence them. Thus, New York schools chancellor Joseph Fernandez declared in 1995 that individual parents could not be allowed to stand in the way of the distribution of condoms, even to their own children. If parents could thwart the professionals on that, said the chancellor, they might do anything. He had a point.

Federal courts accelerated the breakdown of American federalism and literally turned the Constitution on its head by pushing local government out of the regulation of behavior. By declaring unconstitutional those laws that prohibited loitering, disorderly conduct, and the sale of pornographic material, and by restricting authority over zoning, the courts made it impossible for those local voters who wanted to maintain control of their community to do so. The federal courts laid down detailed rules on everything from the extent to which a citizen may defend himself to what indignities he must suffer from those who flaunt loud music or obscenities "in his face." As these rulings took effect, American towns and cities began to segregate themselves as never before, using real estate as the sorting mechanism. The reason is straightforward: The capacity to move to a more expensive neighborhood, to live among similarly expensive neighbors, had become the last way in which an American could affect the quality of his surroundings.

For many people, however, the courts curtailed even that freedom. The main device was court-ordered busing of schoolchildren from one part of a district—or in some cases of a county or even of a metropolitan area—to another for the purpose of achieving racial balance or simply to overcome economic geography. Consequently, city public school districts thus lost all but the poorest of their white students. In Boston, the National Guard had to be called out to restrain parents who realized that because of federal judge Arthur Garrity, they would henceforth have to choose between moving away, paying private school tuition, or letting their children be used as guinea pigs. "White flight," the regime called it, indicting as racists those who would not submit to its policies. Hartford, Connecticut, was typical. White residents fled the city limits, and by 1993 90 percent of the public school students were black or Hispanic. In response, the federal courts crafted a plan to forcibly bus suburban children into the central city. By 1996, the bargaining and the appeals had ended; the luckless districts were identified; the usual, futile mantras about stable neighborhoods were intoned; and another sad round in the game of musical neighborhoods began.

Those who cannot afford to move are condemned as antisocial. This is what happened to people in the lower-middle-class community of Yonkers, New York, during the 1980s, when the federal government and the courts brought their full pressure to bear to force them to accept a federal low-income housing project in the community. The courts declared the Yonkers City Council vacant, deposing its elected members. But new elections brought in even fiercer opponents. Finally, the federal government simply dispensed with the fiction that the people of Yonkers had anything to say about the quality of their lives or the value of their homes. Of course, the judges did not choose to put the project in nearby wealthy Scarsdale, where their own kind live, where the regime lives. Nor do courts and bureaucracies release convicted felons to the neighborhoods where judges and court officials live.

The ultimate form of flight is the gated community—groups of houses surrounded by walls with guarded entrances. There are some 150,000 of them in America today, along with countless apartment buildings with equivalent security arrangements, and the number is rising. Inside, the pathways, even the landscaping, are the private property of the corporation to which the residents belong. Everything is ruled by the corporation's bylaws, enforced by private guards. These guards know what public officials used to know but were persuaded to forget: the difference between citizens—those who pay them—and everybody else. In places like this, and indeed within the private shopping malls that have replaced public shopping districts, some of the judicial revolution that occurred between the 1960s and 1990s might as well not have happened. In such private places, parks do not have to be designed to eliminate the nooks where people can find privacy but where criminals can hide. Packs of youths cannot loiter and intimidate, and parents can let children play without guard. Some of these "communities" have their own private schools. Such places, however, should not be confused with the American local governments of Tocqueville's time. They are not places where mutual obligations are exercised, where people rule and are ruled in turn, where they can enforce their views of the good life. Rather, they are fortresses, and their residents are refugees who purchase and consume minimal order. And the courts may not long permit the arrangement.

Nothing shows the growing lawlessness of the American regime more than its reaction to Proposition 209, passed by the voters of California in 1996 to prohibit racial preferences. The words of 209 are precisely those of the Civil Rights Act of 1964, whose authors also indisputably intended to banish racial preferences. Yet the very courts and executive branch that enforce the 1964 act regard that act as if it had said precisely the opposite of what it says. Not surprisingly, within days of 209's passage a federal judge ruled that 209 was unconstitutional for attempting to apply the very words of the 1964 act in their plain meaning. The Clinton administration joined the American Civil Liberties Union, the National Education Association—indeed, practically the entire regime—in asking that the appellate courts overturn Proposition 209. The fundamental, practical reason why the regime did so is that, as I have mentioned, group preferences are a legal shield behind which the regime runs a patronage system. The underlying theoretical reason is that 209 seeks to reinstate the older American legal principle that rights and duties pertain to individuals alone, whereas the federal courts have increasingly placed group rights over individual rights.[34]

In 2008 the people of California adopted, by referendum, Proposition 8 to amend the state constitution by defining marriage exclusively as between one man and one woman. Voter petitions had put Prop. 8 on the ballot after the state supreme court had ruled—without textual basis—that the state constitution mandated recognition of same-sex marriages. The regime simply refused to accept the election results. The very court whose legal basis for action the voters had undone scurried to find another, while the governor, Republican Arnold Schwarzenegger, backed by the media, encouraged people so inclined to intimidate the Catholic and Mormon communities whose votes had prevailed.

Clearly, the modern American regime lives by a constitution that increasingly consists only of its own will.

CRIME AND CRIMINALS

Nothing wipes away civics textbook illusions about the relationship between citizens and public servants so thoroughly as a typical encounter with the police. Here is an account of one by a writer for the *New York Times Magazine* who was strolling down a street in Los Angeles: "An immaculately groomed patrolman came up and, as his glance took me in, planted a meaty paw on my chest. 'Get off the street,' he said, and shoved me back. . . . The casual nature of both words and gesture, the arrogance of it, I suppose as well as the hostility . . . took the breath away."[35]

Except in small towns, this herding attitude is typical of modern American bureaucracy, extending from federal agencies down to lowly airport security, and unless such bureaucrats get unlucky and bully someone from the regime, they can take pleasure in throwing their weight around. Most Americans over the age of fifty can remember when police were blue-clad, lightly armed, nonthreatening figures who seemed to know the difference between their masters and the bad guys. They were eager to solve crimes and seemed upset if a single burglar in their area went uncaught. The paradigm shifted in the 1970s. In part because of the war on drugs, police became heavily armed. Because of the civil rights movement, on the one hand, and the Supreme Court's expansion of the rights of criminals, on the other, they began to apply harsh procedures to all. Unionization helped to insulate them from complaints, and bureaucratization and the expansion of their jurisdictions insulated them from their fellow citizens. Perhaps the practice of riding around in patrol cars—or the tendency to watch too many movies about paramilitary operations—further skewed how they viewed their role. Whatever the reason, they now run around wearing windbreakers and baseball caps with their agency's name printed on them, or sport paramilitary gear, and they do not give out names or badge numbers. If they were as effective at maintaining the public safety as the police in Singapore are, the average American might not mind so much.

But their performance seldom rises to Singaporean levels. Los Angeles is the paradigm for perhaps the most typical police behavior of our time: During the riots that blackened a square mile of that city in 1992, the police absented themselves for about twenty-four hours and left store owners to defend lives and property as best they could with their own weapons. When the police returned as the rioters retreated, they did not try to arrest every rioter. But they did handcuff and take away such store owners as they found standing armed guard over their life's work. Thus the cops earned again the label that the area's Spanish-speaking residents pinned on them long ago: *los cobardes,* "the cowards." In 2006, in the wake of Hurricane Katrina, police brought to New Orleans from several states fanned out across the city's unflooded parts and confiscated the weapons of the residents who had stayed through the storm and were guarding their homes. The paradigm is this: American police in general seem to have designated as their main enemy—as the criminal they cannot tolerate—the citizens who protect themselves. In fact, the police have effectively lobbied for the disarmament of law-abiding citizens and for punishment of those who "take the law into their own hands."

Consequently, whereas Tocqueville had found America the safest and most law-abiding of places because citizens defended their own lives, property, and honor with their own arms, in our time American cities may be among the world's most unsafe places. In these cities, courts have consistently held individuals acting in undeniable self-defense liable for injuries to the assailant. Courts will protect a loud-mouthed youth who shouts obscenities at a woman, but punish the woman's husband or the youth's father who punches that mouth. The regime has brought this about—not the people. Carlos Bea, the San Francisco judge who vacated a judgment against a cab driver who had pinned an armed robber to a wall with his cab, became a popular hero in 1992.

The law enforcement establishment's constant refrain is that the country is violent because ordinary citizens are violent and that controlling citizen violence through gun control is the key to safety. But this is nearly the reverse of reality. Thus, a perceptive observer has written: "Crime is rampant because the law-abiding, each of us, condone it, excuse it, permit it, submit to it. We permit and encourage it because we do not fight back, immediately, then and there, where it happens. Crime is not rampant because we do not have enough prisons, because judges and prosecutors are too soft, because the police are hamstrung with absurd technicalities. The defect is there in our character. We are a nation of cowards and shirkers."[36]

Though overdrawn, the point touches the essence of the matter: the general population's increasing passivity—a passivity encouraged and even demanded by our regime. How important this is may be seen by what happens when the mere possibility arises that the general public might not be so permissive of crime. While the so-called underlying causes of crime have continued to rise, homicide rates in Florida and Oregon dropped by one-third within a year of the passage of laws permitting ordinary citizens to carry concealed firearms.[37] This effect occurred even though only a tiny percentage of the population has availed itself of the privilege. It occurred because the mere prospect that victims might be "hard targets" has given potential criminals an immediate incentive to restrain their appetites.

Controversies over crime are part of a cultural struggle. When Mario Cuomo was governor of New York, he felt strongly enough to denounce his state's numerous gun owners—who, after all, had committed no crime—as "hunters who drink beer, don't vote, and lie to their wives about where they were all weekend."[38] By this measure of civilization, such people are worse than criminals because they exhibit insufficient faith in the regime and adhere to ways now alien to it.

In sum, the replacement of the rule of law by the rule of rights as defined by the regime has given new meaning to citizenship in America. Liberals and conservatives now battle essentially within a society framed by, in the words of a wise contemporary, a "confiscatory nanny state run by people who 'know what is best' for everyone; a state that promotes class envy, which in turn causes social unrest, and which in turn 'requires' government 'solutions' concocted by the same social engineers that created the problem; a state that bestows 'rights' on favored groups and individuals and confiscates those of others less favored, with all the pomp, ceremony, and arbitrariness of a feudal lord blessing or punishing a serf."[39]

12

THE CULTURE WARS

[One man's] vulgarity is another's lyric.
—U.S. SUPREME COURT, *COHEN V. CALIFORNIA*

In most places and times, the differences in manners and morals—what we call lifestyle—between the members of the regime and the rest of the people have been quantitative. The richer and more influential have done the same things that those on the lower rungs have, only with greater abundance and ease. When such differences become qualitative, however, they call forth mutual contempt. In rare historical cases—the Jacqueries of the late Middle Ages or the French Revolution—they break up societies. But even small differences in manners and morals can cause big troubles when they are rooted in religious differences. In the rare cases when regimes differ substantially from their population and try to press the manners and morals of their religion on society, that population is likely to see the process as a corruption of its ways and view the regime as an enemy. Thus, the Shah of Iran made his regime liable to revolution when he flaunted the elite's non-Islamic ways and tried to press them onto the general population. In short, cultural splits between the regime and large numbers of the people are always troublesome, and culture wars are doubly so.

Cultural conflict in today's America is not a figment of the imagination. Whereas in 1948 three-fourths of the American people said they trusted the U.S. government to do the right thing by them, by 1994 three-fourths answered that they did not trust the government.[1] By 2008, only one-fifth trusted the government. Much of the shift would surely have occurred regardless of the cultural context and policies of the regime, simply because the government takes and gives much more than it did fifty years ago and because the distance between ruler and ruled has grown. But the gap would not have grown so large had there not been a growing recognition by rulers and ruled of differences in manners and morals—and a growing mutual dislike. In the world's most diverse society, parts of which retain some of the ways of its founders, the distinction between ordinary people and the regime is anything but neat. Still, there is no mistaking the messages about family and religious matters that the regime has injected into American society: Marriage, for example, is a temporary contract of convenience, in no way preferable to "alternative" lifestyles. All human relationships are contingent on consent except those with the state. The public schools and social service agencies know better than parents what is good for children. Religion may be all right for commoners, so long as they do not take it seriously and keep it out of public places. But in public, all must practice the regime's secular religion. The purpose here is not to keep score in this conflict, but rather to note how cultural differences have engendered public policies that divide Americans.

THE VILLAGE VS. THE FAMILY

Although families and the idea of family still set the tone for most Americans, the modern American family wields less authority over its members and is less important in their lives than ever before. It is smaller because fewer children are born into it, because adolescents move out of it sooner, and because aged parents seldom move in. And because of divorce, it has a shorter life expectancy than just a generation ago. Most important, fewer Americans over eighteen (51 percent) are married than ever before—a drop of 21 percent in over a generation. And for a substantial sector of the population—the blacks—marriage has become a minority lifestyle. By 2000, fewer than a third of black households had a married couple.[2] Some 45 percent of blacks have never married, as opposed to about one-fifth of whites. And whereas in 1950 fewer than 5 percent of American children (all races combined) were born outside of marriage, in our time 22 percent of white children and 69 percent of black children are.

Although American families are still unusually strong in some respects—fewer than 2 percent of married people report having had extramarital affairs during the previous year—divorce is so prevalent that, by some estimates, a white child has only a 30 percent chance of reaching the age of eighteen with both natural parents living together in the home, and a black child has less than a 5 percent chance of this happening. Because mothers now work, children get some 40 percent less time with their parents than they did a generation ago.

Far from decrying the weakening of the American family, the modern American regime seeks to hasten it by word and deed. Elite spokesmen have treated the traditional American family as a bad myth, an anomaly that is not passing quickly enough into the dustbin of history. Congresswoman Patricia Schroeder (D-CO) made notorious the proposition that only 7 percent of American families now fit the "Ozzie and Harriet" model, which in her circles is a model of hell. But Schroeder meant that in only 7 percent of households are *two* children present—not one or three—along with a mother who has never earned a penny. In fact, however, most households with children have a working father and a predominantly homemaker mother.

Equally misleading is the claim that only 27 percent of American households with children under the age of eighteen are headed by a married couple. According to the 1990 U.S. census, however, 27 percent was the figure for U.S. households that have two parents and children. Another 9 percent of households had children with only one parent or with guardians. But the 2000 census showed that 81 percent of white families (defined as two or more people related by birth, marriage, or adoption) were headed by a married couple (down from 89 percent in 1970), and that 72.5 percent of households where children are present were headed by a married couple. A large and growing percentage of households, however, are not families at all but rather singles, empty nesters, and so on. That is because, from the ghettos to the campuses of elite universities, the kinds of relationships between men and women that used to produce families are less and less evident. And that, in turn, is because the modern American regime gives examples, makes laws, and runs programs hostile to all that marriage implies.

MARRIAGE

The academic literature explains the tone that the American regime has set regarding how men, women, and children ought to relate to one another. Open marriages, same-sex marriages, and cohabitation are often portrayed as involving more opportunities for individual development and for sharing—especially for women—than male-headed heterosexual households. To become less oppressive, traditional male-female arrangements must take on some of the characteristics of these others. That is why the regime's "secular arm"—the U.S. government agencies and courts—usually speak of fostering not "the family," but the plural "families." As for children, the regime view is that neither children nor parents have special rights or claims on the other. In this same vein, Barbara Bennett Woodhouse, professor of law at the University of Pennsylvania, wrote that the law should regard children as "having a direct relationship with government," that the relationship between children, parents, and the state should be regulated by the state, and that "children's welfare bureaus, juvenile courts, and of course the expansion of public schools [should push] at the borders of the domestic realm."[3] In short, children belong first and foremost to a community defined by something other than marriage. That is also the point that Hillary Rodham made in 1974 in the *Harvard Law Review* and that she made again later, as Hillary Rodham Clinton, in her book *It Takes a Village,* albeit with an anesthetic coating. That is the wisdom that our regime is pressing on the American people, and it is the source of the ongoing culture war over the American family.

There is no dispute over findings that marriage is the healthiest lifestyle. A 1995 survey of obituary pages showed that the median age of death was seventy-nine for married women but only seventy-one for unmarried ones. For men, marriage made an even bigger difference: The married ones died at an average age of seventy-five, whereas the single men died at an average age of fifty-seven. (The latter discrepancy may be due in part to the early mortality of homosexual men.) A check of the *Washington Blade* (a paper for male homosexuals) obituaries showed that the median age of death was forty-three for those without AIDS and thirty-nine for those with it— evidence that AIDS is not much more lethal than the gay lifestyle itself. In its study of "Marital Status and Health, 1999–2002," the U.S. Centers for

Disease Control and Prevention found that, regardless of race or economic status, marriage correlated positively and substantially with every measure of health other than proper weight.[4]

There is no doubt about the very positive effect of marriage on the prosperity of men, but even more on the prosperity of women and children. The "feminization of poverty" and the dramatic rise in the proportion of children living in poverty, about which so much has been written, result quite simply and entirely from the growing separation of women and children from men. Indeed, the great divide in the economy, politics, and society of this country is between those who are part of families (including, interestingly, widows) and those who are divorced or have never married. The socio-economic gap between blacks and whites, like the gap in health, nearly disappears when marriage is taken into account: Black married couples earned 87 percent as much as white married couples in 1995.[5] In sum, the presence or absence of marriage literally creates two different nations.[6]

In the minds of those who set our tone and make our laws, however, the undisputed benefits of marriage weigh less than its congenital sins: Marriage is based on unequal gender roles, limits the professional development of women, inhibits the sexual freedom of all, and shuts people off from the wider community. That is why the regime sometimes "supports" families as a rope supports a hanged man.

In *Griswold v. Connecticut* (1961), the Supreme Court began to use the notion of the marriage-based *family's* sacred privacy to read into the Constitution a right of *individual* sexual privacy that it later applied to all people, whether married or not, and that subsequently led it to diminish the status of natural families in American law.[7] In *Roe v. Wade* (1973), the Court used an "emanation" from the "penumbra" of this right to deny not just the humanity of the unborn child but to reject the notion that marriage gives a man any role in deciding the life or death of a child he fathered. In *Romer v. Evans* (1996), the Court applied this doctrine to erase the distinction between married sex and homosexual sex. The Court does not have to follow the logic any further to reduce marriage to one idiosyncrasy among others—a point made by Hillary Rodham Clinton and backed by the "Beliefs" column of the *New York Times*.[8] In 1997, the regime—from then Senate Republican majority leader Trent Lott to the Democratic secretary of defense to the *New York Times*—poured scorn on the military's practice of severely punishing members who had adulterous affairs. They were offended that the military sided with those who were faithful to their promises.

The *Times* condemned the prosecution of adultery as an offense against "current societal mores."[9] What mores, specifically? The authoritative ones, the ones belonging to those for whom personal choice trumps marriage.

Betty Friedan encapsulated their view when she described marriage as "a comfortable concentration camp." Hillary Rodham called it "a dependence relationship" and likened it to "slavery and the Indian reservation system." Quite as much as in Sweden, elite opinion in America despises the young woman, especially if she proves her talent with something like a Phi Beta Kappa, who chooses to stay at home and, in Hillary Rodham Clinton's derisive expression, "bake cookies." And so elite opinion has demanded of young women that they be so gender-liberated as to act precisely as sexually demanding men want them to, while paying half the rent.

In sum, the regime has demanded more effort and responsibility from women and less from men. It tells women to do the job of a man—while raising children, too—while telling men they no longer need even try to support their families by themselves. Nevertheless, three-fourths of married people agree with the proposition "If there is no financial necessity for her to work, a mother of small children should stay home full time to raise the children."[10] That means that the old American ethos is far from dead. Still, nowadays fewer and fewer American men include in their proposal of marriage the promise to support the woman and any children she may bear. Hence, when financial necessity comes, most often it means one more job for her rather than two jobs for him. David Gelertner aptly summed it up this way: "The typical husband would always have been happy to pack his wife off to work; he did not need Betty Friedan to convince him that better income in exchange for worse child care was a deal he could live with. Society used to restrain husbands from pressuring their wives (overtly or subtly) to leave the children and get a job. No more."[11] The regime, then, has devalued marriage for both sides. Men no longer need it to satisfy and legitimate their sexual urges. To women, it is increasingly a set of burdens uncompensated for by economic or social security.

The biggest change in the American way of marriage is, of course, no-fault divorce. Like so many other parts of the revolution in America's habits, it originated at the top. In 1966, only 13 percent of respondents thought that divorce should be made easier to obtain.[12] There was no popular pressure for granting divorce merely on the demand of both parties, never mind of either. Pollsters *did not even ask* about divorce requested by one party only. Yet this was the ideal for which judges, lawyers, psychologists—that is, the regime—strove. They got it, and divorce rates doubled. In some categories (divorce after long marriages), they quintupled. Perhaps changes in the law were not responsible. But the coincidence of changes in habits subsequent to changes in law is probably more significant than that of planetary alignments.

Among successful men no-fault divorce produced a kind of serial polygamy—one trophy wife after another. It also imposed injustices on people who thought they had entered into a lifetime commitment that could only be broken for exceptional cause, who had given no cause, and who found themselves dumped. And, of course, it brought tragedy on millions of still more innocent children. But the biggest impact of no-fault divorce may have been the changed expectations of married people in general. Marriage means living together. In the past, it differed from cohabitation in that one couldn't just walk away. But if one can walk away from it, why call it marriage? Naturally, the spreading realization that the ceremony had been emptied of legal standing, and that it had become legally (and soon, socially) acceptable to abandon a spouse, led people to act and think defensively to supplement the now unenforceable contract of marriage with enforceable prenuptial agreements, which the courts treat as ordinary contracts. Limited protection is better than none. But it is not marriage.

The fading of the expectation of lifetime unions has had a profound impact on the attitudes of young men and women. After spending nearly half a century around college campuses, I (and just about everyone else) have noticed a decline in romance. Nowadays, especially at elite colleges, it is bad form for couples to walk hand in hand. By all accounts, there is at least as much sexual activity as ever. But romance—a complex trial of emotions and judgment both wonderful and terrifying because its logical end is the irrevocable commitment of one's one and only life—is scarce. That is logical: With lifetime commitment legally impossible, politically incorrect, and even "corny," young people logically look on each other as short-term resources.

There is in America a reaction against no-fault divorce. The legislatures of several states considered bills to reinstate a limited concept of fault, especially when there are children involved, or at least to impose waiting periods.[13] Much as such proposals aim at correcting somewhat the balance between the modern passion for autonomy and the interests of innocent parties, they do not begin to question the regime's basic preference for consensual rather than natural relationships. To really strengthen the institution of marriage, one would have to go beyond recognizing its utility to appreciating its naturalness. But that is anathema to our regime.

There is also a reaction against girls who bear babies to whom they give perfunctory care, if any. In 1995, Congress passed a bill that would have required unmarried pregnant girls, on condition of receiving government benefits, to live in some kind of supervised environment—either in a privately run group home or with a relative's family, but pointedly not in their own apartments. President Clinton vetoed it, to the acclaim of most of the regime.

There has always been a strong consensus for forcing men to pay to support the children they have fathered. In the 1992 presidential campaign, both Bill Clinton and George H. W. Bush excoriated "deadbeat dads" as the bane of society. Some 38,000 officials and over $3 billion a year are devoted to enforcing child-support payments. But the very notion that "the major problem the children have in a single parent family is not the lack of a male image, but rather the lack of a male income," confuses child support with family support. Many middle-class divorces nowadays are initiated by women enticed by the prospect of getting most of the financial benefits of marriage without the troublesome guy. In such circumstances, men feel justified in evading payments. Hence, a tenfold increase in collection efforts has yielded little result.[14]

Moreover, the whole notion of forcing ex-husbands to pay for children is irrelevant to our time's biggest and fastest-growing phenomenon: men siring children out of wedlock knowing that avoiding marriage protects them from the responsibilities of paternity. Nothing short of imprisonment on a chain gang would have the slightest chance of making them pay, let alone of forcing them to perform the role of husband and father. Law might, however, prevent the siring of children out of wedlock by defining it as statutory rape.[15] That is what certain localities are trying. But such laws swim against the currents of the regime's axioms: First, the Good Family Man—that typically masculine combination of sacrifice and authority—is a dangerous, repressive, reactionary figure; second, sex is sport.

Thomas Hobbes described with characteristic bluntness the necessary consequences of these attitudes:

> If there be no Contract, the Dominion [over the child] is in the Mother. For in the condition of mere Nature, where there are no Matrimonial laws, it cannot be known who is the Father, unless it be declared by the Mother: and therefore the right of Dominion over the child dependeth on her will, and is consequently, hers.

Again, seeing the infant is first in the power of the Mother, she may either nourish it or expose it; if she nourish it, it oweth its life to the Mother; and is therefore obliged to obey her rather than any other; and by consequence the Dominion over it is hers.[16]

The Supreme Court would have done well to consider the social consequences portended by Hobbes before writing its opinion on *Roe v. Wade*. But our regime intellectuals don't read Hobbes any more than they read Aristotle.

SEX AND RESPONSIBILITY

The Supreme Court's imposition of abortion on demand of the mother only, at all times and for any reason or no reason, wholly precludes the logic of family. Predatory young men grasp this with a directness that surpasses even Hobbes's: *"Her choice, her kid,"* they say about the results of their sport. In so saying, these paragons of irresponsibility are truly the modern American regime's law-abiding citizens, following the letter of the law according to its spirit. Just as truly, any man who asserts his responsibility for the child he fathered and objects to a woman's decision to have the child killed is a hostile, disruptive stranger to the regime. So are the grandparents who might object to the killing of their grandchildren and the brothers and sisters who might object to siblings being killed. And, of course, any children who survive to the age of reason and wonder how close their mother came to having them killed are similarly out of tune with a regime that puts one person's choice above natural responsibilities. Families are about natural responsibilities. Abortion trains everyone to disregard the most fundamental responsibility of all.

Our regime made abortion into literally the most unqualified right in the land and pays for most abortions. Despite a legal ban on direct federal funding, the U.S. government funds them by directly paying some 30 percent of the budget of the nation's largest abortion provider, Planned Parenthood, which also runs some 33,000 of the public schools' sex education programs, paid for by federal, state, or local governments. This private organization, then, is paid for almost exclusively by public funds to advertise a service that the government then pays it to provide. Here is what the standard instruction book of this extension of government in the Rocky Mountain region has to say: "Sex is fun, and joyful and courting is fun and joyful, and it comes in all types and styles, all of which are OK. Relax about loving. Do what gives pleasure and ask for what gives pleasure. Don't rob yourself of joy by focusing on old fashioned ideas about what's 'normal' or 'nice.' Just communicate and enjoy."

Not all public school sex-education programs are run by Planned Parenthood. Most of the rest are run by the Sex Information and Education Council of the United States (SIECUS). Originally funded by the Playboy Foundation, it is now funded by the U.S. government as a contractor for the Centers for Disease Control and Prevention, whose officials wear pseudomilitary uniforms. Compared with the official SIECUS program, which includes condom distribution, the Planned Parenthood's semiofficial version seems family-friendly.

What the regime actually does with programs that push in opposite directions makes its thrust even more unmistakable. In 1985, Congress passed the Adolescent Family Act, specifically to encourage the teaching of sexual abstinence outside marriage. The federal district and circuit courts stayed the act's application for four years on the ground that it unconstitutionally established religion. After the Supreme Court vacated constitutional objections to the program, the bureaucracy of the Department of Health and Human Services and of the relevant congressional committees nevertheless kept its 1994 funding at a token $6 million per year, while at the same time funding "hard" sex education (Title X) at $199 million.

Therefore, if you are a local school official and you want to make money teaching that sex belongs in families, forget it. But if you want to make money teaching the joys of sex at will, and then shuttling girls to abortion clinics without their parents' knowledge, you can count on being able to keep up your payments on your BMW. And if you are on the local council and you want to regulate the sale of cigarettes and beer to minors, so be it. But don't even think of trying to regulate the sale of condoms to minors. That is strictly against national family policy, as is failure to make unmarried pregnant teenagers—or their impregnators—feel welcome in the new America. A 1972 federal law made sure they must be included in cheerleading, football, and all that.[17] Despite superficial presidential rhetoric to the contrary, adoption, too, is against family policy. Despite a surplus of couples so eager to adopt that thousands go overseas to do it, adoptions in America have fallen since 1970 because the courts and the various social service bureaucracies have thrown up barrier after barrier to adoption—chief among them the new doctrine that natural parents may assert legal rights to the child regardless of any prior renunciation on their part. In sum, if you live the kind of reproductive life Americans lived in Tocqueville's time, you will be doing so against family policy.

CHILDREN

Raising children as in Tocqueville's time is also against our regime's family policy. First of all, the regime does not want children raised by their mothers. Look closely at the instructions to IRS Form 1040. If you pay someone else to raise your two children, the IRS will let you take $6,000 off your tax bill. Thus, one-earner families subsidize two-earner couples, who typically earn 60 percent more than they do. If one adds to this equation the marriage penalty built into the earned-income credit, a couple with two children and earning $47,000 per year loses $9,142 by being married rather than cohabiting. In other words, the difference between living in accord with or against modern American family policy can add up to almost one-fourth of some couples' income.

If you raise your children yourself, you should know that although the law allows no interference in a mother's decision to abort a child, administrative practice forbids a mother from slapping a foul mouth, spanking a recalcitrant bottom, or punishing a character fault with a memorable beating. "The first thing a child learns here," complained a recent immigrant, "if you spank me, I'll call 911." Another immigrant was more specific: "The state comes between you and your children. Americans don't discipline their children well, and when you do it the right way, there's the danger your kids can call social services on you."[18] The difference, however, has nothing to do with geography. Americans used to take children "to the woodshed" regularly. Many still do. The difference now is that the administrative bureaucracy, often outside the framework of law, penalizes it.

This is not out of tenderness: Police and juvenile officers today handcuff, strip-search (including body cavities), and otherwise "process" preadolescent children as a routine part of taking charge of them—something they did not do a generation ago. Nor are the authorities simply enforcing ways of handling children that are known to produce good or even quiescent behavior. On the contrary, while serious criminal behavior by adults has decreased somewhat in recent years from the fearful peaks of 1970–1995, there is no argument about the fact that juvenile behavior in America has worsened to the point that the country is threatened by young people whom James Q. Wilson calls "feral presocial beings." His point is that they were never socialized and that no one is socializing them. The data are clear: Where families are in charge of their children, the authorities are not needed, and where families are not in charge, the authorities are powerless to ensure elementary safety.[19] The fact is, the authorities are trying to inculcate a certain way of raising children, not because it is known to produce good results, but because they value it for its own sake. The regime actually fears the results of its own prescriptions. But it despises the alternative to those prescriptions.

America's social service bureaucracies, well connected with police and prosecutors, lack neither power nor latitude. Good sense is what they lack. During the late 1980s, social service agencies in New Jersey, Massachusetts, California, and Florida mounted a series of high-profile prosecutions for sexual abuse of children based on testimony coached from toddlers. In these incidents the social service bureaucracies acted as combatants in the culture wars. In 1986 in Florida, after a jury acquitted one such falsely accused victim, Grant Snowden, a district attorney named Janet Reno, who was later President Clinton's attorney general, ordered a chain of new charges against him and kept the jury from knowing about the previous acquittal. He got five life terms.[20] He served twelve years before a federal court found the case against him bogus. In 1994–1995, the epidemic hit tiny Wenatchee, Washington. Dozens of innocent lives were wrecked. But in the end, almost all the convictions in these cases were reversed.[21] In 2008, Texas Child Protective Services seized 159 children from a polygamist sect's compound solely on the basis of an anonymous telephone call by a self-described sixteen-year-old girl (who turned out to be a fabricator) alleging that she had been forced to marry an older man (who was elsewhere). Under national scrutiny, judges could find no cause to abrogate parental rights. But they tried. Hundreds of defendants around the country who did not rate attention from the national press, however, were deeply victimized by charges of sexual molestation or for fitting the wrong "profile" in the social service agencies' operating manuals. Today, sexual molestation and "recovered memory" are yesterday's bureaucratic fads. But the social service bureaucracies are sure to invent new reasons for meddling.

What is the safe, politically correct method of disciplining children? What positive child-rearing habits are our regime's social service agencies pushing? How can one restrain an unruly child in America today without getting in trouble? Use the prescription drug Ritalin, sales of which have increased 600 percent since 1991. It is routinely prescribed for something called Attention Deficit Disorder (ADD), diagnosis of which has boomed to the point that 5 percent of American boys and 2 percent of American girls are now said to be afflicted with it. In the nation's trendy prestige suburbs, the percentage is several times that. Moreover, adults are being diagnosed with ADD at a rate that Dr. Alan Zametkin of the National Institutes of Mental Health, a major figure in the field, describes as "just chaos" and "a cottage industry."[22]

ADD is not an objective fact like a viral infection or a severed nerve. Rather, it is a label that some physicians have recently begun to use for behavioral traits known in children since time immemorial: short attention span, restlessness, distractibility, and impulsiveness. As Zametkin has noted, "Even procrastination is now said to be a sign of ADD."[23] Although Ritalin is a stimulant related to amphetamines, it undoubtedly has a calming effect and often improves performance. The schools are typically the first to point out that a child does not sit still, underperforms, or exhibits other "symptoms," but doctors diagnose ADD. Parents increasingly agree with the diagnosis and buy the Ritalin. A diagnosis of ADD or of "bipolar disorder" has become socially acceptable because it relieves schools, parents, and the children themselves of responsibility. Inattention was once thought to be caused by the boring nature of the material or by the child's ordinary disinterest in it. Nasty behavior was considered just that. Lack of discipline was once thought to be due to bad parenting, bad character, or both. Poor performance spoke for itself. But judgments about performance, whether the school's, the child's, or the parents', call for effort at self-improvement. Now, the relief from responsibility and effort for everyone comes in little bottles of value-free pills.

The issue of parental responsibility also divides those Americans who are in tune with the regime from those who are not. The legal struggle, however, is full of contradictions. About one-half of the states and many smaller jurisdictions have passed laws that hold parents liable to varying extents for the criminal acts of their minor children. The premise of such laws is that the parents must exercise control. But parental control, of course, is precisely what the public schools and the social service agencies have been working so hard to undermine. In a recent case of parental conviction, the prosecutor argued that the parents had failed to send a larcenous, violent, armed youth to counseling.[24] What good would that have done? What could have restrained such a youth? Ritalin? Nothing could have stood a chance short of memorable, awe-inspiring physical thrashings combined with strong incentives to religious conversion. But if the parents had inflicted such things on him, the social service agencies could well have prosecuted them for violating what they regard as the child's right to be free from religious compulsion and parental physical abuse. However, the secular priesthood of the state's counselors and the prison guards' invasive "procedures" are acceptable.

To be consistent, parental responsibility laws would have to be coupled with laws that establish parental rights over children. Had such laws been proposed in Tocqueville's America, they would have been regarded as superfluous, because the notion that anyone other than parents should be responsible for the upbringing of children would have been incomprehensible. Yet in 1996 Senator Charles Grassley of Iowa felt it necessary to propose a law (modeled after a dozen similar ones working their way through state legislatures) that would prohibit federal, state, or local governments from interfering with or usurping "the right of a parent to direct the upbringing of the child." Under the proposed law, parents could have sued governmental agencies to stop their interference with the family's social, religious, and disciplinary practices. Grassley's proposal was rightly described by its opponents as disruptive of the established order.[25]

Charges that such laws would allow parents to chase Shakespeare out of school curricula and make it impossible to protect children from murderous parents are smokescreens. In fact, children schooled at home are likelier to read Shakespeare than are public school attendees. But charges that parental rights laws would chase sex education and abortion counseling—indeed, all mandatory New Age counseling—out of the public schools, while reinstituting the rule of the rod in many homes, are right on the mark. That is what struggles for habits are all about: One man's civilization is another's barbarism.

The readiest evidence of objective differences between habits on either side of the struggle consists of scores on standardized tests. Although such scores are not comprehensive measures of human worth, they are the only widespread, objective measures of performance at the same task. The test scores' first lesson is that school funding and student-teacher ratios correlate negatively with performance. In 1959, when the student-teacher ratio in the public schools was 26:1 and per pupil expenditure was in real terms one-fourth what it is today, SAT scores were 90 points higher, on average.[26] The next lesson is that if socioeconomic background is controlled for, private and parochial schools perform better than public schools, but home schools do best of all.[27] This suggests that the greater the degree of parental control, the better the educational performance. This becomes even clearer when you consider that the highest average scores come from states like Iowa, Utah, and the Dakotas, even though private schools are rare in those states, student-teacher ratios are high, and per capita expenditures are among the lowest in the country.[28] That is because in these states, public schools are tiny, the bureaucracies relatively weak, and parents exercise much more control over school policy than in most other states. In urban areas, the clincher is the performance of recent Asian immigrants. Their socioeconomic status is very low. They attend schools where the average performance is extremely low, and where the modern American regime is giving its numbing, dumbing, coarsening cultural messages in their most undiluted, corrosive form. Yet the scores of these children on standardized tests typically lead the country. The one and only explanation is that the grip of their families is so tight that it overcomes all else.

The upshot is that the modern American regime's antifamily culture has an unbroken correlation with the dissipation of social capital in all its forms: the alienation of man from woman, of parent from child, of young people from the community through vice and crime, and, in the end, of young people from their own minds and souls. It is possible to make the case that escalating divorce rates, increased single-mother households, and even high rates of crime are the price we should be glad to pay for wider sexual and personal choices. It is somewhat more difficult to argue that the new postfamilial American way of life is a step up in civilization, given that the package includes fostering ever lower intellectual performance in and by the regime itself.

AGED PARENTS

No account of changing American family habits would be complete without reference to the new American way of aging and dying: in the tender bosom of government-regulated institutions.

Inspired and supported by the ideal of independence fostered by Social Security and Medicare, and pushed by an increasing desire among America's adult population for living without the hassle of taking care of elderly parents, aging Americans began to move into nursing homes en masse around

1970. By the 1990s, however, the *Wall Street Journal* reported: "The current crop of older Americans appears to be more averse to nursing homes than their parents were. They are the first generation to have seen their own parents in large numbers survive into their 70s. They anguished over sending parents to nursing homes 20 or 30 years ago and now facing a similar fate, are determined not to go."[29]

And in fact, stories of subhuman ends to human lives in factory-like nursing homes staffed by "slave drivers and lion tamers" have become *images d'Epinal,* goading symbols powerful enough to drive the elderly to search for just about any alternative. However, government regulations—driven, as always, by the private groups closest to the operating agencies, in this case operators of nursing homes and hospitals—are making it more difficult to avoid this fate. And so are many adult children, who feel ever less obligation to their families. In a nutshell, new regulations are forcing many small establishments for the elderly to close—places like the Swiss Home in Mount Kisco, New York, that cared for people unto death through all stages of debility. New regulations require such things as "team planning of patient care"[30] and other features characteristic of the large institutions people try to avoid. This is not surprising, because the rules were designed by large institutions. Similarly, when the Florida legislature passed an "aging in place" law that specifically permitted "assisted living" homes to keep frail residents there rather than turning them over to big nursing homes, the state health department—on the advice of such big homes—issued regulations to gut the intent of the law.[31]

Thus, on the one side, the elderly are finding that the government is not the family substitute it was cracked up to be, but on the other side, they are finding that their families have become less familial. In 2005, the U.S. National Center on Elder Abuse estimated that between 2 and 10 percent of disabled elderly persons are abused at any given time. The American Association of Retired Persons reported on the spreading phenomenon it calls "granny dumping"—the abandonment of frail elderly people by their adult children.[32] Although the case of John Kingery, an eighty-two-year-old suffering from Alzheimer's disease abandoned at an Idaho dog track in a wheelchair in 1992 with a note pinned to his chest, was an anomaly, perhaps 70,000 elderly each year are dumped onto hospitals or nursing homes, especially at vacation time.[33] No doubt, dumping such unwanted elderly people relieves the dumpers of an imposition on their constitutionally guaranteed right to privacy and of a restriction of their choices. One might say that such dumping amounts to aborting a family relationship—and constitutes an exercise of choice. Within the intellectual framework and habits fostered by the modern American regime, such treatment of the elderly is impeccable and even logically necessary.

STRUGGLING FOR AMERICA'S SOUL

Tocqueville's America had the kind of family, economic, and civil life it did because the souls of Americans were arranged mostly by biblical religion. American life today is the way it is because a significant part of the American people order their souls according to a remarkably seamless combination of the teachings of the Supreme Court and Hugh Hefner's *Playboy* philosophy. David Brooks labeled this synthesis "bourgeois bohemian," or "bobo."[34] The U.S. government is the prime combatant in a bitter war to establish—in the strict, old-fashioned European sense of the term—the bobos' religion, complete with government-paid priests and acolytes. The resulting clash, however, may strengthen contrary tendencies so much that the course of the war may resemble less the metamorphosis of Sweden in the twentieth century than America's internecine struggle in the middle of the nineteenth.

It is a commonplace that America's culture is up for grabs, that there is a "crisis of values" or a "culture war."[35] Some argue that this multiculturalism is the result of a wave of immigration almost as big as that which occurred at the turn of the twentieth century, a wave that has brought to America peoples much less in tune with the souls of the founders. The turbaned Sikhs and Hindus who run so many motels and Seven-Elevens, the varied Southeast Asians of Confucian background so prevalent in the computer business, the Mexican laborers who seem less the product of Spanish than of Aztec or Mayan traditions, and the generic Middle Easterners who seem to have taken over the country's taxicabs, so goes the argument, are not interested in biblical religion. Hence, the argument continues, it is impossible to impose traditional American moral standards upon them, "and because Americans cannot enforce them upon immigrants, they will tend to enforce them less on themselves."[36] The argument concludes that while monoethnic societies can survive multiculturalism, ethnically pluralistic ones must be ruined by it quickly. Hence, the proponents of this view call for a long pause in immigration to absorb such disparate cultures into the American *forma mentis*.

This conclusion, however, has more merit than the premises. That is because America's cultural war is very strictly an intramural affair—an ever less civil domestic war. Most of the new immigrants were drawn to America by a dim but essentially accurate understanding of its original culture. Almost none are hostile to it, and most are more or less eager to join it. By no means are they the ones who wage war on it.

THE PROTAGONISTS

In fact, neither Hinduism, nor Islam, nor Confucius, much less Quetzal-coatl, are contending for America's soul. What is preached in America's universities as the multicultural alternative to Judeo-Christian civilization has nothing to do with learning or affirming any foreign culture or language, let alone religion. It is neither more nor less than the denigration of Judeo-Christian civilization. The judges, bureaucrats, and bobos who are the principal aggressors in this war are hardly moved by love of foreign gods. Rather, they are moved by the vision of a good society ruled by themselves, by visceral antagonism toward biblical religion, and arguably far above all, by contempt for Americans whom they deem inferior.

Elected officials seem to be on both sides at once. Thus, even politicians who appoint the most antireligious judges extol the importance to America of religious practice.[37] Speaking well of religion is not only smart politics in a country where the majority are churchgoers and where, according to a major survey, the overwhelming majority pray regularly.[38] It is downright unavoidable in a country where all but a few believe that the decline in the overall quality of life—the increase in crime, the worsening relations between the sexes, between parents and children, and so on—is due to a decline in what just about everyone now calls "values."

Social science amply backs the popular perception and biblical teaching that love of neighbor as well as of self depends in practice on love of God. Survey after survey correlates churchgoing with every possible index of social and personal well-being, and estrangement from churches with the opposite.[39] There is little doubt that even politicians who lead personally dissolute lives and have the greatest contempt for the average God-fearing family find it convenient to preside over people who exhibit more, rather than fewer, of the behavioral characteristics associated with religion. If taxes for social services—police, welfare, and the rest—were assessed on the basis of statistical propensity to use the services—in short, if such taxes were re-garded as user fees and assessed on social groups proportionately to each group's use of the services—it would be child's play to make the case that non-churchgoers should be taxed at a higher rate than their churchgoing neighbors—a kind of infidel tax.

And yet surely the most remarkable feature of contemporary American public life is the unrelenting consistency of the regime's attacks on religion, even when the targets of the attacks are the very secular consequences that even antireligious politicians desire. Thus, in 1980 the Supreme Court for-bade the state of Kentucky from posting the Ten Commandments in schools and other public buildings, and in 1996 a federal district court in Alabama ordered a facsimile of the Ten Commandments removed from the court-room of an Alabama judge.[40] Kentucky argued that it had a secular interest in promoting the acts and forbearances on the list, and that by posting the list it was not thereby establishing any confession over any other. The Court agreed that the state had an interest in a population more likely to honor parents than to lie, kill, cheat, and steal. But it left no doubt that pursuit of such personal characteristics through a code said to have been promulgated by God was impermissible. The code may be good, but the divine origin of that code was horrid. Kentucky would have to find a way of teaching the same things that was wholly untainted by belief in God. Good luck! By the same token, the Court has branded as a violation of the First Amend-ment the use of Alcoholics Anonymous (AA) as a treatment for alcoholic prison inmates.[41] True, AA has proved to be the only successful cure for al-coholism. But since AA cures through daily, confessional prayer, the Court held that exposure to it violated the rights of convicted felons. Better that they keep their destructive habit than that they be exposed to the unconsti-tutional wiles of prayer.

Prayer and public observance have been the Court's most immediate targets. As recently as the 1960s, every day in almost every public school in America began with a reading, usually from the Old Testament, and with some nondenominational invocation to God. The Court outlawed these practices.[42] Society never voted on it. In addition, almost everywhere else in the world, parents who send their children to religious schools (thereby re-lieving the state of the cost of educating them) somehow have their tuition paid or their taxes remitted, but American parents who send their children to religious schools (mostly Catholics, Baptists, and Orthodox Jews) must pay taxes as well as tuition. Again, no vote has determined this, just court decisions. The Supreme Court has outlawed student references to God in graduation speeches, "moments of silence" during which students might pray, and even a teacher's habit of keeping a Bible—along with the Koran and the Bhagavad Gita—on the desk (the Court saw through that ruse, too). In a recent case, the Court struck down a Mississippi school's practice of turning over the public address system to students who would pray aloud through it, as well as the school's practice of providing classrooms for local clerics to conduct Bible studies for students who chose to attend.[43]

As one might expect, officials have acted mostly within the antireligious spirit of these judicial laws, going so far as to prohibit students from reading the Bible on school buses. Why, they should have been reading their Planned Parenthood guides to condom use instead, or maybe the Reverend Jeremiah Wright's reasons why God should damn America. In what may be the most extreme manifestation of all, police in southern Illinois handcuffed and threatened a fifteen-year-old girl with Mace because she had gathered with others around the school's flagpole to pray before the beginning of school.[44] Anyone who tries to practice religion more or less as it was practiced during the first 300 years of America's history is treated by the American regime as a subversive. Given our regime's character, such people are, indeed, subversives.

The U.S. government, indeed the regime, considers any public act contaminated to the extent that it is derived from Judeo-Christian religion. The regime allows nothing to happen in the public realm that lends the slightest support to such acts. This prohibition results in actions by lower officials that range from the awful to the ridiculous. In the latter category, consider a regulation promulgated by the county counsel of Monterey County, California, for public employees for the "holiday season" (née Christmas) of 1992. Typical of such pronouncements, it says: "Secular, or non-religious decorations and activities are appropriate decorative items in public buildings. Secular and permitted decorations include Christmas trees, and religious-neutral ornaments, tinsel, poinsettias, greenery and wreaths, reindeer, Santa Clauses, and snow-persons. Religious displays or symbols, including nativity scenes, however, are not appropriate for display in public buildings." The memo concludes with wishes for "a joyful Holiday season, a Merry Christmas, and a Happy New Year," as well as with a warning that "no employee or visiting member of the public be offended by the use of patently religious symbols, activities, music, language, or decorations in our workplace."[45] Never mind the offense inherent in prohibiting the expression of individual employees' religious sentiments and in delegitimizing the public's desire to see its own heart and soul expressed in its own buildings. Ironically, the counsel's own memo could have been used to take action against him for saying "Merry Christmas."

THE REGIME'S RELIGION

But why does the regime spread what Stephen Carter has called "a culture of disbelief"? Just as important, what are that culture's bedrock beliefs? The origin of these beliefs is social, not intellectual. American elites long ago proudly, very proudly, set themselves apart from the biblical religion of the common herd. When surveys of religious practices account for occupation, it becomes clear that the small percentage of Americans who reject the Bible is concentrated among *nonscientific* academics, lawyers, senior civil servants, and people working in the media, the arts, and the entertainment industry. Within these sectors of the population—largely coterminous with the regime—ignorance of and contempt for biblical religion are de rigueur. When American elites refer to people who actually believe the Christian Nicene Creed or the Jewish Halacha, they tend to use the adjectives "ultra" or "fundamentalist," implying that there are "moderate" modes of religion that they might not despise. They define moderation as not taking seriously the teachings of Christianity or Judaism. But they themselves adhere passionately to a this-worldly religion that defines itself largely in opposition to that of the Bible. *This* religion, not Hinduism or Zoroastrianism, is the true contender for American souls.

Whereas biblical religion requires believers to restrain their appetites and attune themselves to God's commandments, the American regime's religion demands that government—so long as it is in the proper hands, of course—manipulate society to whatever extent necessary to achieve good results. In short, the Establishment's secular humanism celebrates the indulgence of one's own desires and the control of others'. It subsidizes its priesthood with tax monies, requires reverence of its own icons (feminism, abortion, homosexuality, and so on), and punishes questions about the character of its saints (try mentioning the fact that Martin Luther King Jr. plagiarized his doctoral dissertation, cheated on his wife, and preyed on his movement's female interns). The regime's religion does not treat criticism of itself as legitimate.

Otherwise, the regime's religion celebrates the freedom to do what you want, to feel good about yourself while doing it, and to be free of responsibility for consequences to others. Most immediately, this is freedom from children, from parents, and from one's own conscience. Achieving that freedom from conscience requires abolishing the whole concept of innocence or guilt from discussions of what may be legitimately done with or to children and parents. To do this, the regime's religion deifies choice regarding anything that is yours. Children are a problem for the religion, because they are at once part of you, and whole individuals. The Supreme Court took care of that problem in *Roe v. Wade* by declaring the unborn to be mere parts of their mothers, just as in *Dred Scott* it had declared slaves to be their owners' mere appurtenances. Aging parents are no problem for this liberating, empowering religion because it does not contain any commandment about honoring parents. Divorce, abortion, and euthanasia, in addition to being convenient, are spiritual icons for the regime.

Nevertheless, in American society these are not icons but bones of contention. Hence the culture war. The term "war," however, misrepresents a struggle whose sides are matched so unevenly: One side has a monopoly on offense. The other side's war consists of resistance, evasion, and occasional local counterattacks. The Supreme Court, not public opinion, imposed abortion on America. Still, although, rhetoric aside, the Republican and Democratic parties both joined the regime consensus to keep the abortion issue out of the reach of the electorate, the American people have coupled practical acceptance of their political disenfranchisement about abortion with increasing practical rejection of it. In 1973, after centuries during which abortion was considered a heinous crime or "grave misprision," polls showed that some three-fourths of American citizens thought it was wrong; by 1996, only two-thirds thought it was wrong. But by 1999, only 28 percent of women thought abortion should be available in all circumstances. Support for abortion has dropped most significantly among young women, and it is confined more than ever to the highest and lowest socioeconomic groups. This is despite more than two decades during which abortion was promoted as a basic constitutional right.

But the regime and the law keep pushing: The American Medical Association, which once strenuously opposed abortion, now officially endorses it and has abolished the 2,400-year-old Hippocratic Oath (which forswears abortion and euthanasia and pledges the physician to work exclusively for the interest of the patient) as a requirement for entry into the profession.

This has made the American College of Obstetricians and Gynecologists, which is reluctant to train new abortionists, shy about stating its position and incurs the wrath of the Establishment's voice—the *New York Times*'s editorial page—for "avoid[ing] responsibility to train doctors in a legal procedure."[46] Still, most physicians and nurses will have nothing to do with it, which is why abortion is unavailable in 83 percent of America's counties—abortionists fly a lot and make a lot of money servicing narrow demographic constituencies—blacks and the upper middle class.

The regime has changed American public opinion more when it comes to euthanasia, the practice of taking terminally ill patients off of life support to allow them to die, or even helping them commit suicide. Whereas in 1973 the topic was unmentionable, ten years later Colorado's governor, Richard Lamm,[47] made it a constant theme that old people were burdening the younger generations and had a duty to get out of the way. By 1996, this concept had sunk so far into Americans' souls that no jury could be found to convict Dr. Jack Kevorkian of manslaughter for admitting to having helped to dispatch dozens of willing patients. Later, though Kevorkian was convicted and jailed, popular revulsion at the thought of people being kept in vegetative states for years, combined with the high cost of health care, led an increasing number of Americans to a growing, if silent, consensus that the dying should die. By 2008, Montana had joined Oregon and Washington in allowing physician-assisted suicide.

Given that most old people have accumulated property, the desire to hasten their death can be even more powerful and mercenary than the desire to keep a baby from being born. In one case as in the other, the regime's religion provides moral justification for bloody self-serving. This logic frightens even Dutch practitioners of euthanasia. One told an interviewer that "in view of the financial cost that the care of patients imposes on relatives and society under the U.S. health care system, the legalization of euthanasia in America would be 'an open door to get rid of these patients.'" Another said that when American doctors asked him how to introduce euthanasia into the United States, he always replied: "Don't . . . I wouldn't trust myself as a patient if your medical profession, with their commercial outlook, should have that power."[48]

Above all, the regime's religion requires adherents to vanquish the social manifestations of the faith of the uncouth American masses. The typical American elite's vision of hell is an "Ozzie and Harriet" lifestyle: distinct sex roles, no therapists, marital fidelity, child rearing without nannies, and church. The very pit of hell would be if this family ate red meat, smoked, and told ethnic jokes. Indeed, Hollywood repeatedly produces shows mocking this way of life. And yet many of the regime's members live very conventional, industrious lives. Much of their radicalism is a matter of chic symbolism, of cultural one-upmanship. Descended from ancestors who were "holier than thou," the adepts of today's secular religion now look down on lesser beings because they themselves are "trendier than thou."

One of the pillars of modern psychology, celebrated in high literature and sitcoms alike, is the desire to think well of oneself regardless of what one does. The serpent in this garden of self-esteem is the legacy of dysfunctional relationships with parents, spouses, and others. The specter haunting it all is the possibility that you may not be very different from those whom you despise. Thus, millions of people engage in "therapy" to overcome their legacies as "adult children," as "codependents," and so forth. In the new religion, "therapy groups" and even television talk shows replace confessionals. The first big step to self-esteem is to project onto others responsibility for your own imperfections. Confession of others' sins, apologizing for neighbors or ancestors, absolves you from the things apologized for and lets you look down on lesser men. Because this ritual is so inexpensive, its popularity is burgeoning. It is biblical religion turned upside-down.

THE TEMPLES AND THE PRIESTS

The temples and priesthoods of these cults, at universities and in the arts and humanities, are largely funded by the U.S. government, which fuels their powers over American culture. Even many private universities receive one-half of their funds from the U.S. government through various grants and federally guaranteed student loans. Since the government routinely uses its power over these temples to make them do a variety of things—for instance, transfer funds from men's wrestling and track teams to a variety of women's teams—it would be hard to argue that government is not extraneous to the universities' uniform hostility to religion, to Western culture, and to America in general.

That hostility is a consequence of the fact that, outside the hard sciences, universities, with few exceptions, have hired only political leftists and adepts of the elite religion ever since the 1960s. In 1984, Hoover Institution fellow George Marotta compared voter registration records in the vicinity of

Stanford University with the membership of the university's departments of humanities and social sciences. He found that only 11 percent of the faculty members in these departments were registered as Republicans, and most of those who were had been hired prior to the mid-1960s. Some departments had no Republicans at all. Significantly, at Stanford and elsewhere, faculty in math, physics, chemistry, engineering, and medicine are much more diverse. U.S. government does not worry about this kind of discrimination, because it approves.

The universities teach the nation's schoolteachers, who are the backbone of the Democratic Party. At the Party's 1992 convention, 13 percent of the delegates were members of teachers' unions, and many other delegates were spouses, parents, or children of members of the teachers' unions.[49] In 2008, the biggest of these unions, the National Education Association, claimed it alone had "a powerful bloc" of "more than 200" delegates to the convention.

Not least of the consequences of placing the commanding heights of American culture in partisan hands is that the nation's public schools teach almost exclusively a version of American and world history that amounts to a veritable antihistory—developed by university professors appointed by government[50]—the subtext of which is that the regime's religion gradually overcame America's original evils but has a ways to go to finish the job. While students at universities have access to original documents and alternative interpretations, schoolchildren are trapped by their textbooks. In 1996, Republican presidential candidate Bob Dole briefly touched on the relationship between the educational establishment, the U.S. government, and the Democratic Party. But he was quickly persuaded that to take note of such facts was to put himself outside the Establishment. Neither President George W. Bush nor any other prominent Republican has pointed out these obvious connections.

The U.S. government abets this near monopoly of the new secular religion with the $100 million it grants each year to artists through the National Endowment for the Arts (NEA). In their practical aspects, these endowments are straightforward patronage mills operated with taxpayer funds by cliques. The chance of an artist who is a realist and works on religious themes being supported by an NEA grant is worse even than the possibility of Harvard hiring a white conservative professor. President John F. Kennedy dedicated the NEA to "grace and beauty" and told Americans that their tax dollars would buy "contributions to the human spirit." Instead, the endowment has subsidized a class at war with the culture of the average American. Pictures of Christ and of the pope submerged in urine, artists whose performance consists of urinating on a picture of Christ, or of inter-active genital contact with the audience, of naked people covered with paint rolling on paper, of black masses, or of homoeroticism, pedophilia, and so on are the rule rather than the exception.[51] The endowment puts the government-approved stamp of high culture on things that were once crimes—and in many cases still are. They also shut nonconforming artists out of, say, the theater and art shows by enabling subsidized artists to tie up the schedules of theaters and galleries. In short, through the NEA, the U.S. government puts Gresham's law—which says that bad money drives out good—to work in American culture. The social consequences of bad soul-craft pale in comparison with the spiritual consequences.

THE CONSEQUENCES

It is not necessary to show that a causal relationship exists between the government-sponsored secular religion and the many and varied manifesta-tions of spiritual emptiness in America. It is easy enough to measure the dif-ferences in how citizens in general behaved before this religion made its inroads and how they have behaved since. Gross statistics on crime, child abuse, drug use, suicide, and even SAT scores do not identify the mentali-ties behind the figures. But the correlation is undeniable: Over the past gen-eration, as the new religion has claimed a greater and greater share of America's souls, the indices of nastiness have climbed (or dived) most steeply precisely in those sectors of the population most receptive of government guidance. As sociologist Myron Magnet has shown, the underclass—defined not by income but by a debilitating set of attitudes—resulted from the ac-ceptance by the poor in general and the black community in particular of the new secular religion's main tenets, which are very different from those that ministers had been preaching in the black churches.[52]

America's epidemic of drug use—roughly one-half of high school se-niors have at least tried marijuana—is the matrix of almost every kind of dys-function. But keep in mind that these all-too-familiar dysfunctions affect least of all people whose souls are filled by biblical religion and most of all those who follow the regime's religion. The sextupling of cases of child abuse that has accompanied the quintupling of abortions since 1973 cannot but be related to the idea that children are an incidental byproduct of the exercise of the inalienable right of self-fulfillment. Since post-birth babies are just as dependent and even more bothersome than pre-birth ones, it was inevitable that as the law habituated people to sacrificing the latter, they would learn quickly enough to rid themselves of the former. The elite media and public officials pushed this cultural train down its tracks: In November 1996, when a couple of high-born college students crushed their newborn's skull, the governor of New Jersey said that they should have considered their options more carefully. Indeed. Had they crushed that little skull while any part of their child was still inside the mother, they would have performed a partial-birth abortion, something endorsed by presidents of the United States, the Supreme Court, and any number of governors. For its part, the *New York Times* suggested that a charge of murder was unwarranted, because people in other times and places have been more tolerant of such things.[53] Indeed they have. That is the point: The regime is fostering quite another civilization among us.

Because America's culture wars are about two sets of separate and unequal beliefs and ways of life, they are leading Americans to sort themselves out according to religion. This does not mean separation between Protestants, Catholics, and Jews. Rather, in the face of challenges from the new religion, people who strive to live under the Ten Commandments—Protestants, Catholics, and Jews—are drawing together. The legalization of abortion, for example, has led to a natural sorting of marrying couples according to radically incompatible views on how to treat the products of their union. The trivialization of the marriage contract is also naturally separating those whose religion mandates permanent unions from those who pledge to be together only "so long as love shall last." Marriage, *and indeed friendship,* is possible only among people who share the things that are dearest to them, from art to personal habits, the things that make them what and who they are. Even music is inherently partisan.[54] As cultural differences widen, we are seeing two populations living out the increasingly different consequences of their cultures.

As the regime's culture takes in larger percentages of our population, keep James Q. Wilson in mind: "There are only two restraints on behavior—morality enforced by individual conscience or social rebuke, and law, enforced by the police and the courts. If society is to maintain a behavioral equilibrium, any decline in the former must be matched by a rise in the latter (or vice versa). If familial and traditional restraints on wrongful behavior are eroded, it becomes necessary to increase the legal restraints."[55] Machiavelli's teaching on these matters—"fear of the prince . . . may *temporarily* supply the want of religion"[56]—is even more to the point.

It seems never to have occurred to Machiavelli, who highly valued a polity's capacity to engineer internal peace, in part because it put that polity in a better position to face the dangers of foreign war, that a regime would be so stupid as to imagine it could make war against the religion on which it had been founded, and reap anything but the wind.

13

──▸

AMERICA'S DEFENDERS

[War is] the gravedigger of decadences.
—CHARLES DE GAULLE, *THE EDGE OF THE SWORD*

The ultimate test of any regime is its capacity to "summon up the blood"—to draw out of itself and its people the willingness to kill and be killed, to make the coherent preparations and carry out the wise operations that win wars. Especially in democracies, war and preparation for war test a people's character—its capacity to produce high-quality goods, its capacity for order and self-sacrifice, the authority by which families send their sons to fight, and the spiritual strength of fighters and leaders alike.

On the eve of World War II, Adolf Hitler fatally underestimated America's character. On the basis of static economic analysis, he judged the American people could spare little of their $100 billion GDP to affect the war in Europe. But the American people miraculously doubled their GDP and devoted one-half of it to the war, producing more armaments than the rest of the world combined. Hitler thought that the Americans were mongrels. Instead, as Lincoln had hoped, the American people had become "blood of the blood and flesh of the flesh" with the founders through the acceptance of the Declaration of Independence's "self-evident" truths. Their unity amazed the world. Hitler thought that American families would not give their sons and could not muster a fighting spirit because they were in the grip of a pacifist religion. But the American people mounted a crusade to kill him. When the war was over, the Americans fed their defeated enemies. This break with the custom of conquerors, which awed the world even further, also proceeded from a uniquely religious character. In sum, the American people of the mid–twentieth century were no less the world's wonders than their Tocquevillean forefathers had been.

No one can be sure how Americans today would react to a challenge of World War II's magnitude. But it is unlikely they would deal with the crisis as their grandparents did, because the regime has instilled in many Americans habits different from those of their grandparents, and even more different from those of their forebears of Washington's or Tocqueville's time.

Contemporary Americans are not as likely as their grandparents were to see a need and take charge of a project to fill that need. How could they be, after decades of training in making sure that "all the players are on board," especially the government regulators? Contemporary Americans know that to start a project without, say, an environmental impact statement could lead to jail. Much like Europeans or Japanese, they have reason to believe that certain contracts, jobs, roles, and activities are set aside for people specially designated from above. Although the storehouse of interpersonal trust is fuller in America than just about anywhere else, the very fact that the American legal profession has been mushrooming shows that decisions, agreements, and transactions are taking more time and have become more complex than ever before. Add to this the fact that the proportion of Americans doing useful work has declined, that for the upper middle class physical work is unknown—worse, unfashionable—and it is difficult to imagine countless new factories, new processes, and redoubled results springing up overnight as they did during World War II.

Contemporary Americans also lack their grandparents' experience in civic responsibility. As the number of school boards, companies of volunteer firemen, and all manner of local officials has shrunk, the percentage of the population habituated to exercising leadership and responsibility for others has also plummeted. In innumerable, irreducible personal ways, government has become something that "they" do rather than something that "we" do. One of the essential elements of military power, whether on the home front or the war front, is that as many individuals as possible must behave as if everything depended on them. Of all the advantages over other combatants that America enjoyed in World War II, perhaps the greatest was the tendency of individual American soldiers and sailors to take matters into their own hands. Contemporary Americans have become accustomed to the proposition that war is the business of those whom we hire to wage it.

As the years pass, American families are becoming less and less like the families for whom American soldiers fought in World War II. Nearly all who fought then had grown up with their mothers and fathers and did not want to shame them. Even more ominous than the fact that, as already noted, white children born nowadays stand only a 30 percent chance of growing up to age eighteen with both natural parents at home (and black children a 5 percent chance) is the near-total replacement of the concept of shame in the raising of children with that of a self-esteem not tied to behavior. Everybody gets a trophy, everybody passes. Military recruits raised without habituation in honor and shame could not be trained quickly and could not be expected to perform with as little supervision as the Americans of World War II. In circumstances where casualty rates are low, morally uncertain soldiers may be adequate. But for youths who lack faith in life after death to face mass casualties, something different would have to take place. They would have to be trained like the low-life recruits of Europe's *ancien régimes*—given artificial families and artificial courage.

But surely the greatest reason that the America of the 2000s could not duplicate America's feat in World War II is that its regime, in addition to inculcating habits that are not conducive to military efficiency, itself has a character less than fit for the ultimate test. Increasingly incompetent, obviously untrustworthy, it inspires distrust. In a nutshell, the modern American regime is constitutionally not oriented to generating military power and has substantially alienated itself from those in American society—to the remnants of yesteryear's America—who do produce military power.

REGIME OF LOSERS

The officials in charge of foreign and defense policy have diverged from the original American pattern no less radically than those in charge of the federal judiciary. In the twenty-first century, few, if any, senior staff members of the State Department, the Defense Department, or the Central Intelligence Agency, not to mention the major foundations concerned with these matters, ever served in the military. They share aversion to and ignorance of military matters as well as a social aversion to military people. Under

Republican and Democratic administrations alike, those who have risen to such positions since the 1970s either worked for or admired Senator J. William Fulbright, author of *The Arrogance of Power*. They made their careers helping to defeat the United States in Vietnam, worked to diminish and restrain American military power in the Cold War, and jeered Ronald Reagan's call to cast communism on the scrap heap of history. They made their careers delaying, denaturing, and denigrating programs to defend America against missiles. They came to power gradually through the government's front door, through the best schools, and through the patronage of elders who advanced them precisely to promote their ways. Hence, their accession to power amounted to a transmutation of the Establishment.[1]

People like Anthony Lake, who served Democrat President Bill Clinton and advised Barack Obama, set the regime's tone. They learned about America's role in the world from William Appleman Williams's *The Tragedy of American Diplomacy*. Like their mentors and patrons, the extreme Left of the 1950s and 1960s, the pillars of today's foreign policy establishment, regard the American people as ignorant, violence-prone jingoists. They believe that America has stood in the path of the world's progress toward peace, cooperation, and socialism. They believe that modernity, and especially nuclear weapons, dictate a new approach to international relations based on the widest possible collective security arrangements rather than on American military power.[2] They therefore think that the biggest threats to peace lie, first, in the belief among most Americans in their right to do as they think best without leave from the Establishment's favorite foreigners,[3] and second, in the tendency of American military leaders to cling to outdated notions about winning wars. They see themselves as the indispensable sophisticates who will *make the American people safe for the world by* restraining a trigger-happy military as well as by harnessing the energy of America's noxious culture. They believe themselves entitled to lead because they have weaned themselves from their fellow Americans' retrograde morality, militarism, and interestedness, because they are open to the socialist world and the Third World—and yes—because their differences from their fellow Americans make them morally superior.

In sum, our regime has been eager to manage America's wide involvement in the world, but it neither knows nor appreciates military things, and it has at heart the opposite of the country's grandeur. Hence, a gap has opened between the ends of American policy and the means by which those ends have been pursued. As a result, though the regime has sent Americans around the world to kill and be killed, it has preferred stating utopian goals to pointing out enemies whose destruction would end the war. Thus American soldiers have died losing wars undeniably, as in Vietnam; or in victories that were victories in name only, as in Korea or in the Battle of Kuwait in 1991; or in nation-building exercises in Bosnia, Afghanistan, and Iraq. *Our regime has done everything and anything with the U.S. armed forces except win.* As it plays one incompetent game of global chess after the other with American bodies, our regime corrodes the American people's capacity to defend itself.

INSOLVENCY

In the Korean War, American elites began the practice of sending their fellow citizens to kill and be killed, not to win wars for America's interest, righteousness, or glory but rather to pressure other governments to negotiate terms that would be in the best interest of the world community. That is, they began to use their fellow Americans' lives to try to realize such figments of the imagination as "collective security" and "stability." While both the troops and the professional military men of the age thought that the Korean War was worth winning if it was worth dying for, and that if it was not worth winning no one should die for it, the regime deemed these thoughts laughably unsophisticated. Ordinary Americans damned the Korean War with the label "no-win war." But while the Establishment and the American people each thought the other would not act that way again, neither understood how deeply the other was committed to its ways.

Americans did not want the Cold War to turn hot. And if it did, they wanted the fighting to be done as much as possible with nuclear weapons, as far away as possible, with as little damage to America as possible. But the growing consensus of elite opinion saw nukes as thaumaturgic instruments for transcending the human condition. Our regime, whether under the guidance of the Republican Henry Kissinger or the Democrat Robert McNamara, imagined that it could build an eternal U.S.-Soviet nuclear balance that would make the Soviet regime into a partner and banish major war forever. Pursuant to this illusion, it built and planned to use nuclear weapons to maximize civilian casualties in the Soviet Union while making sure that Soviet nuclear weapons would have unimpeded access to America. Since the Soviet Union's demise and the proliferation of missiles to the world's backwaters, Republican members of the regime as much as their Democratic counterparts, rhetoric aside, have continued to regard attempts to build American antimissile defenses as threats to peace. By contrast, polls of the American people have shown that they neither know nor believe that their government has neither the means nor the intention to defend their lives against missile attack. Consequently, when the first missile lands on a deliberately undefended America, it will tear the social contract just as surely as bodies.

In Vietnam, the American people came to learn that "limited war" meant that the Establishment would balance its incompetent foreign policy with American bodies. This is still very much the case in our time. Our best and brightest expected America's unwashed to lend themselves to their supposedly sophisticated maneuvers. Accordingly, they derided those who urged them to choose between victory and withdrawal, refused to declare a state of war, and vigorously upheld the legitimacy of those in their own political and social circles who were working to defeat the armed forces they were sending into battle.[4] In the end, the regime convinced itself that it was fighting on the wrong side of the war and that the real enemy was America's arrogant anticommunism. As then–Secretary of Defense Robert McNamara explained (much later) in his book *In Retrospect,* he and his colleagues were trying, above all, to forestall the majority of Americans who wanted victory, because they themselves wanted no such thing. They got what they wanted. But to deflect the onus of defeat, our regime promulgated the proposition that public opinion hampered its conduct of military operations and made victory impossible. Not so. In 1968, 70 percent of Americans opposed any cessation of bombing in North Vietnam, while only 23 percent identified themselves as "doves."[5] Alas, the regime's heart and mind was with the 23 percent.

In 1977—in a speech at the University of Notre Dame written by that paragon of the regime, Henry Kissinger's former assistant Anthony Lake, later to be President Clinton's national security adviser—President Jimmy Carter explained that it was only by losing the Vietnam War that we had been able to "find our way back to our own values." Thus convinced, the regime sent 50,000 men to die and six times that many to be wounded, until the American people forced the regime into political bankruptcy.

But the bankruptcy led to a complete takeover of the regime by precisely those elements of the Establishment—personified by Anthony Lake himself, replicated in high office throughout the foreign policy establishment, and carried over into the time of Barack Obama—that embodied the greatest discrepancy between the ends they sought, the means they could muster, and the willingness of the American people to lend themselves to either. What Americans and their leaders learned about themselves and one another in Vietnam caused wounds that have only widened.

THE SECESSION OF THE ELITE

In Vietnam, our Establishment learned that while it was okay for people like themselves to direct such wars, it was okay not to send their own children to fight in them. It was okay to send the sons of the middle and lower classes, but it was not okay to let them use whatever tools they had to annihilate the enemy. This has led to failures abroad and stored up worse at home.

By the early 1960s, Americans had become comfortable with the military draft. Knowing that the fittest stood a good chance of serving, college boys filled the Reserve Officers Training Corps (ROTC), and recent graduates who felt the draft's hot breath often signed up for Officer Candidate School. But beginning in 1965, the sentiment flowed down from the highest levels of American society to the lower ones that evading the draft was socially preferable to going to Vietnam. Trendy entertainers urged college girls to "say yes to the boys who say no." College deans released girls from the parietal arrangements that were then universal to attend all-night events that turned into giant parties celebrating the anti-American cause that had made them possible. Deferments for education (originally meant as postponements of service) became upper-middle-class exemptions. American elites tended to see the end of the draft as a release from the responsibility of conducting foreign policies that the American people would have to approve of. They remained almost as eager as ever to have a muscular foreign policy. But foreign policy became a spectator sport. The regime would play global chess with hired hands.

The end of the draft was only the beginning of the elite's secession from the military. Since 1973, the Pentagon and Congress have marshaled figures to argue that America's armed forces are not unrepresentative of society. Perhaps the most subtle of these efforts shows that (based on average family income within particular zip codes) the proportion of youth from any given income bracket in the general population differs from the proportion of the youth from those brackets in the armed forces by only a few percentage points—except for the top sixth of the income scale, which gives only about one-half its expected share of members.[6] Even leaving aside that the volunteers from high-income zip codes are likeliest to come from low-income enclaves therein where the servants live, the argument's basic proposition is refuted easily enough by ordinary observation of American society. At Stanford, Harvard, and similar ladders into the regime, perhaps 1 in 1,000 graduates enters the military. The professoriate, the legal profession, the media, finance, and even corporate bureaucracy (except for military contractors) are now almost exclusively without veterans younger than the age of sixty. Nor do their families serve. Seldom do they have friends who serve. So the policymaking class deliberates about what risks and burdens are acceptable for the U.S. military as if its members were what they are—strangers possessed of alien habits and mores.

Whereas prior to the Vietnam War streams of new veterans were flowing into country clubs and Congress as well as into blue-collar American Legion posts, today fewer than one-third of the members of Congress have ever served, and the proportion is dropping. This is not a matter of revocable policies. The young elites who do not enter the military are part of a regime culture that inculcates value-free nonviolence starting in preschool—sometimes even banning playing tag at recess—that frowns on toy guns for tots, treats hunting and smoking as semicriminal activities, and labels the very notion of citizen militias subversive. The members of today's American regime lack the capacity to serve as well as the moral authority to lead in things military. So war, which is too important to be left to the military—especially in democracies—is becoming the military's exclusive business.

The military has contributed to this separation by discouraging all but long-term enlistments and by nearly shutting down the sources of noncareer officers. Officer candidate schools function primarily to process physicians and lawyers. Scholarships have transformed ROTC into a source of commissions for young persons who intend to make the military a career or who just want their tuition paid for. Military pilots must now commit to serving for at least nine years. Even as the military downsizes, classes at the military academies are near all-time highs and seem to have more children of military officers than ever. The military has become accustomed to blaming the decadence of civilian society for problems in its own ranks. Thus when the U.S. Naval Academy discovered massive academic dishonesty among cadets in 1995, its spokesmen blamed civilian society rather than any shortcoming of the academy's.

Though the military would prefer not to be mixed up with civilian society any more than it has to be, it cannot resist as the regime pushes and pulls at its character. In 2006, the George W. Bush administration ordered the U.S. Air Force (and by implication the other services as well) to forbid anyone in uniform from giving "the reasonable perception that [the armed forces] support any religion over other religions or the idea of religion over the choice of no religious affiliation." "Public prayer," it continued, was banned—except in "extraordinary circumstances," such as when there are "mass casualties," or during "preparation for *imminent* combat, and natural disasters."[7] What is worse, the Bush team allowed prayer as part of "change of command, promotion ceremonies, or significant celebrations," but only if such "prayer" was emptied of "specific beliefs" and intended "to add a heightened sense of seriousness or solemnity." Letting servicemen invoke the name of God only as the equivalent of a shot of booze or of a mood-altering drug, or patently unseriously, was not part of a closely guarded formula for military success. Like forcing the military to keep homosexuals in the ranks, it was one more means of re-creating it in the regime's own image and likeness.

Arguably the most consequential of these means in the twentieth century was Secretary of Defense Robert McNamara's institution of new criteria for promoting officers beginning in 1961. Whereas the post–World War II military had sought to elevate men with the potential to become like admirals Arleigh Burke and Hyman Rickover or General George Patton—hard-charging types who would gain the love of their men, get the job done, and ask about regulations later—McNamara sought to weed such people out in favor of those who got advanced degrees, served in Washington, and competed for the favor of civilian officials. The Vietnam War helped McNamara sort out the officer corps by drawing a line between those who thought it unethical to hazard lives without seeking victory—who left—and those who came to regard the war as a chance to "punch tickets" for advancement in rank. McNamara and Vietnam morally emasculated the armed forces. Since then, Republican and Democratic administrations alike have appointed to the ranks that shape the culture below them such quintessential briefcase carriers as Alexander Haig and Colin Powell—men more at ease leaking to reporters than leaking in the woods. The new tone of the officer corps sharpened the contrast that had long existed between it and the senior enlisted ranks by reason of the fact that advancement among enlisted is by competitive examination rather than by competitive favor seeking.

The Reagan administration's encouragement of military seriousness and buildup of military force proved to be a five-year exception in the regime's reduction of American military power. Beginning with the administration of George H. W. Bush, the regime consensus came to be that American armed forces should be sent to the ends of the earth on nonwar, mostly constabulary missions that require unprecedented absences from home. In the 1990s, the U.S. government sent naval, ground, and air forces to the Middle East, to Africa, to Bosnia, and to Haiti. True, such troops suffered violent deaths at rates inferior to those of their cohorts in civilian life. But by undergoing unaccompanied deployments first for ten months, then twelve, then fifteen, in rapid succession, they were inconvenienced far more than the recruiting pitches led them to expect. By 1997, the Pentagon had concluded that one-third of the men and women serving in Bosnia had become "psychological casualties" as a result of privations suffered for no evident sufficient reason.[8]

U.S. military forces responded to the attacks of 9/11 with enthusiasm driven by the very traditional reaction of many Americans to "join up" to crush those who had attacked us. But our military leadership, responsive to the regime, quickly smothered that enthusiasm by occupying Iraq and Afghanistan, intending to "nation build" them. The entire structure of the U.S. armed forces, including the reserves and some of the National Guard, was occupied supporting fifteen-month-long unaccompanied tours of duty in Iraq and Afghanistan for army and Marines, while the navy's carriers and support ships were out nine months at a time. While Republicans and Democrats argued superficially whether there should be more Americans in Iraq or Afghanistan, the regime gave every indication that it would require this sort of activity indefinitely. For what? It does not take much intellect to grasp that driving around replenished minefields in Iraq while paying off sheiks in the hope that they will plant fewer bombs in their own cities is irrelevant to ensuring safety on America's streets. Moreover, even the slightest acquaintance with Afghanistan suggests that the notion of "nation building" the Afghans is a bad joke.

Soldiers and sailors of all ranks—unless they are mere jobbers, and mere jobbers are useful only to the extent that combat is not serious—live and die by the prospect of victory, of getting the job done and going home in peace. This is the prospect that our regime cannot give our military, because it mostly does not understand the concept of victory, and disagrees with it to the extent it does. Exemplar of our regime's mind on such matters is Philip Bobbitt, who served in the Clinton administration's National Security Council and was a member of the Columbia University law faculty and of the Hoover Institution's Task Force on National Security and Law. His 2008 book *Terror and Consent: The Wars for the 21st Century* argues that the proper, perpetual role of the U.S. armed forces is "constabulary" duty equally in America and around the world, forcefully to promote on the retail level what persons like himself consider "justice." In fact, our regime is restructuring our armed forces according to such views. Alas, real war will disabuse a military thus structured of many illusions, devastate its leadership, and further discredit our regime.

There is no doubt that members of the U.S. armed forces vote Republican as overwhelmingly as public schoolteachers vote Democratic. Nor could one miss the contempt with which, from private to general, the armed forces referred to President Clinton and to his civilian subordinates in general, sometimes to their faces. Soldiers and sailors surely did not regard them as fonts of wisdom or as having their best interests at heart. This, however, does not reflect any big differences between Republicans and Democrats within the regime when it comes to military policies. There are few. Rather, it reflects general dissatisfaction with the regime's sociopolitical substance and the sense—fundamentally correct—that Democrats are the ones who are setting the regime's tone. The members of our armed forces are conservative, demographically and ideologically. But nothing ties them to the Republican Party in the way that schoolteachers are tied to Democrats. The shallowness of the military's reservoirs of habitual respect for either party's regime representatives is evident in the reaction of American troops in Saudi Arabia to Secretary of State James A. Baker III on a 1990 pre-Thanksgiving visit during Operation Desert Shield. Troops who had been in hot tents for two months without prospect of an end or of a reasonable purpose greeted him with expletives and invited him to drink hot water with them.[9] The troops are not near mutiny. But then again, there is virtual unanimity among soldiers and sailors that back-to-back deployments without victory are unendurable.

Establishment authors often discuss how civilian control over the armed forces may be strengthened. Suggestions usually involve "rebuild[ing] the diversity of the officer corps, particularly with respect to prevailing attitudes and perspectives."[10] In practice, such suggestions mean inflicting yet more indoctrination sessions (all personnel are already required to attend "training" sessions on sexual etiquette, diversity, environmentalism, and the like) and perhaps establishing officers whose principal job would be to ensure that other officers do not deviate in word or perhaps even in thought from the regime line. One would not have to go far in this direction to step into territory foreign to America and to republics in general.

It is most significant that no member of the regime has gone so far as to suggest that citizen control (or even regime control) of the military can happen only when prominent members of the regime and their families are part of the military. That may be because, given what the American regime is in our time, it is inconceivable that its children, or students at Harvard, might decide to join the military en masse for any reason whatever. They just do not have that in them. In any event, history teaches that regimes that bemoan their armed forces' alienation while refusing to take part in them might as well bemoan the law of gravity.

THE GREAT DIVORCE

The modern American regime's fostering of habits not particularly conducive to military power will matter only when a serious military challenge arises. The belief that such a challenge will not arise in our lifetimes became de rigueur for the regime at the end of the Cold War. Terrorism does not rank as a serious military challenge. Note well, however, that any and all military challenges, like any and all fistfights, can turn deadly because they may uncover fatal weaknesses. In short, even such militarily insignificant challenges as we face from terrorists may leverage the many debilities we have fostered among ourselves by a regime we have raised up for ourselves.

Commerce, Montesquieu taught, is the profession of equals. As our regime lowers barriers between business and politics, it fosters unearned inequality and thus renders us less fit for the enriching economics our forefathers practiced. It trains us to get ahead by getting close to power and to seek security over self-reliance. We thus acquire some of the thirst for privilege that sank the Soviet economy, some of the reliance on bureaucracy that has robbed the Japanese of the fruits of their labors, some of the passion for security that has hardened Europe's economic arteries, and some of the craving for unearned money that makes the Third World what it is.

Ruling and being ruled in turn, taught Aristotle, is the essence of citizenship, and citizens are people who share equally the privileges of the regime. As our regime increases the number of rules and bureaucrats governing society and as it transfers power to the judiciary, it trains us to be subjects. The metal detectors that shield the entrances to federal buildings, like the security barriers that now close the streets around the White House against a domestic threat presumed to be greater than that of our enemies in World War II, teach civilians and government workers alike that they are each other's natural enemies.

As we let go of the old American view that law is somehow the expression of right, and get into the habit of thinking of it as a means of gaining advantage, we learn, like republican Romans, to argue about who ought to live off of whom and who should be treated as a human being and who should be proscribed. By getting out of the habit of running our own localities and ensuring our own safety and becoming consumers of government, some of us are gaining a taste for Singapore-style efficiency. Having learned that equality and modern government are incompatible, we focus on social mobility.

Nature and religion make family ties that bind and chafe. Our regime, like so many others in the modern world, teaches that those bonds are dysfunctional and offers help to those who want to loosen them or live without them. Hence, with our regime's help, men and women are learning that they do not have to marry and that they do not have to bear responsibility for the children they conceive. We are acquiring some aspects of the Swedish lifestyle, though laced with the bitterness that characterizes relations between the sexes in Russia.

George Washington and his colleagues taught that the American regime was built on the foundation of biblical religion. Our regime, by contrast, has sought to train us in the exercise of a new, secular religion. But like the citizens of the Roman republic, we are losing the old while not acquiring the new. Indeed, like the modern Israelis, we are dividing along religious lines.

The purpose of this long essay has been to explore the effects of regimes on the habits that most affect the quality of human lives. Nowhere is the regime anything like the sole influence on these habits. In America, resistance to the influences of the regime is particularly strong. Throughout American society, there is plentiful evidence of secession from the regime and of countercurrents against it. The computer industry has raised up a set of products that change too fast to be regulated. The government's postal system has been overwhelmed by undisciplined private initiatives. A passion for deregulation does battle with environmental pretexts for regulation. To regain control over their lives, people move to gated communities or to exurbs. More Americans are dealing with the tax system as if they were Italians. More and more families are opting out of public education, and networks of families are springing up to keep the official culture at bay. For some, Branson, Missouri, has replaced Hollywood as the standard for entertainment. And, of course, people are sorting themselves out according to religious practice. But secessions, however numerous, and the countercurrents, however powerful and ominous, are no more than that. Even in America, there is only one regime at a time.

NOTES

INTRODUCTION

1. U.S. Department of Commerce, Bureau of the Census, 1991.

2. Sophocles. *The Plays and Fragments,* vol. 3, trans. R. C. Jebb (Cambridge: Cambridge University Press, 1891), 126–127 (ll. 662–663 in Greek text).

3. Norman J. Ornstein, Thomas E. Mann, and Michael J. Malbin. *Vital Statistics of Congress, 1995–1996* (Washington, D.C.: Congressional Quarterly, 1996), 22, 28.

4. John Leo. "Bust Those Candy Cane Felons," *Newsweek,* December 30, 1996, 26.

5. 1 Sam. 8. The corruption begins with King David's appropriation of Bathsheba, extends to the civil wars between David and Saul and between David and Absalom, and is detailed in the Kings 1 and 2. This divine warning was the centerpiece of Thomas Paine's argument against monarchy in *Common Sense,* the most influential and least original piece of writing ever published in America. Less well known and more pervasive were countless similar references from America's pulpits. See Ellis Sandoz, ed., *Political Sermons of the American Revolution* (Indianapolis: Liberty Press, 1991).

6. In the modern world several of the categories of regimes mentioned by the classics— real monarchies and timocratic warrior regimes—hardly exist. In addition, while some might want to characterize the Islamic Republic of Iran as a theocracy, comparison with the real thing—ancient Egypt or pre-1950 Tibet—shows that modern Iran has a government well within the normal range of Muslim statecraft. As for the Aristotelian category of the mixed regime, I treat most actual regimes as belonging to that category broadly conceived.

7. This commonsense principle, known as the *via negativa,* is the basis of the structure of, among other works, Dante's *Divine Comedy.* The *Purgatorio's* discrimination of the mixture of evil and good, never mind the *Paradiso's* grasp at the sublime, was made possible by the *Inferno's* confrontation with unmasked evil. For a contemporary application, see George

Will, *Statecraft as Soulcraft* (New York: Simon and Schuster, 1983), 68: "Begin at the outer edges of the awful. Begin from circumstances that are so intolerable that they drive many persons to desperation. Then work in, by small inferences, toward an understanding of political excellence."

8. Gannett News Service. "Census Bureau Reports Rate of Out-of-Wedlock Births Holding Steady," November 7, 1995.

CHAPTER 1

1. Cf. Leo Strauss, *Natural Right and History* (Chicago: University of Chicago Press, 1950), 36–42. Contrast perhaps the urtext of modern social science methodology: Quincy Wright, *A Study of War* (Chicago: University of Chicago Press, 1964).

2. Thomas Sowell. *Race and Culture* (New York: Basic Books, 1994).

3. Robert D. Kaplan. "The Coming Anarchy," *Atlantic Monthly,* February 1994, 44–75. Also Jared Diamond, *How Societies Choose to Fail or Succeed* (New York: Viking, 2005).

4. Richard Herrnstein and Charles Murray. *The Bell Curve* (New York: Free Press, 1994).

5. Ralph Reed. Op-ed, *Wall Street Journal,* December 15, 1994.

6. In February 1992, Prime Minister Kiichi Miyazawa of Japan remarked that Americans' lack of a work ethic contributed to the nation's economic slump. *Boston Globe,* February 4, 1992.

7. Xenophon. *Oeconomicus,* vol. 4, Loeb Classical Library (Boston: Harvard University Press, 1923), 168. Language and style aside, Xenophon's argument is very close to that of Gary Becker in *A Treatise on the Family* (Cambridge: Harvard University Press, 1981).

8. Jonathan Rauch. *Demosclerosis* (New York: Times Books, 1994).

9. Scott Shane. *Dismantling Utopia: How Information Ended the Soviet Union* (Chicago: Ivan R. Dye, 1994).

10. T. S. Eliot. *Christianity and Culture: The Idea of a Christian Society and Notes towards the Definition of Culture* (New York: Harcourt Brace, 1968).

11. Myron Magnet. *The Dream and the Nightmare: The Sixties' Legacy to the Underclass* (New York: W. Morrow, 1993).

12. St. Augustine. *City of God,* vol. 19, Loeb Classical Library (Boston: Harvard University Press, 1957), 24, 411–417.

13. William Shakespeare. *Henry V,* Act 5, scene 2 (Oxford: Clarendon Press, 1971).

14. Norman Cohn. *Pursuit of the Millennium* (Cambridge: Harvard University Press, 1970).

15. See Edward Goerner, *Peter and Caesar* (New York: Herder and Herder, 1965).

16. Plato. *Republic,* trans. Allan Bloom (New York: Basic Books, 1968), 368c–369b, 544e.

17. Thucydides. *The Peloponnesian War* (Ann Arbor: University of Michigan Press, 1959), bk. 3, chaps. 81–85.

18. Aristotle. *Politics,* trans. Carnes Lord (Chicago: University of Chicago Press, 1984), 1290a.7–11.

19. Ibid., 1279a.26–31.

20. George Will. *Statecraft as Soulcraft* (New York: Simon and Schuster, 1983).

21. Plato, *Republic,* 553e–555a.

22. Ibid., 547d–548d.

23. Ibid., 539c–541b.

24. See Harvey Mansfield, *America's Constitutional Soul* (Baltimore: Johns Hopkins University Press, 1991).

25. Charles de Gaulle. *Le Fil de l'épee* (Paris: Union Générale d'Editions, 1962), 96.

26. Angelo Codevilla. "A Second Italian Republic," *Foreign Affairs* 71 (Summer 1992).

27. Harry V. Jaffa. *Crisis of the House Divided* (Chicago: University of Chicago Press, 1958).

CHAPTER 2

1. Edward Banfield. *The Moral Basis of a Backward Society* (Glencoe, Ill.: Free Press, 1958).

2. Needless to say, these battles take place in every culture, hence rulers know that a society's literary appetites make a difference. For a discussion of this phenomenon in the American context, see Allan Bloom's *The Closing of the American Mind* (New York: Simon and Schuster, 1987), 55–60.

3. See Chris Black, "GOP Senator Denounces Fan Pier as 'Taj Mahal' and 'Obscene Waste,'" *Boston Globe,* November 9, 1995. According to this article, Senator John McCain denounced the planned $220 million federal courthouse in Boston as a "Taj Mahal" and a "shrine." In response, General Services Administration officials (the construction arm of the federal government) argued that they "were attempting to strike a balance between budgetary constraints and construction of long-lasting buildings that convey the dignity and majesty of the law."

4. Comic strip heroes such as Batman and Superman recall the ingrained American preference for people who fight crime at their own peril, following standards of common decency rather than statutes or (possibly corrupt) officials.

5. Alan Erenhalt. *The Lost City: Discovering the Forgotten Virtues of Community in the Chicago of the 1950s* (New York: Basic Books, 1995).

6. James Q. Wilson and George L. Kelling. "Broken Windows," *Atlantic Monthly,* March 1982, 29–36.

7. Samuel Huntington. "Clash of Civilizations?" *Foreign Affairs* 72 (Summer 1993).

8. See Leo Strauss's *Natural Right and History* (Chicago: University of Chicago Press, 1950), 1.

9. John Rawls. *Theory of Justice* (Cambridge: Harvard University Press, 1971).

10. Aristotle. *Politics,* trans. Carnes Lord (Chicago: University of Chicago Press, 1984), 1294b.14–16.

11. See Xenophon's *Hiero* (London: Macmillan, 1935), 5.3–4.

12. Niccolò Machiavelli. *The Prince,* trans. Angelo Codevilla (New Haven, Conn.: Yale University Press, 1997), chap. 7. Stalin took note of Borgia's use of Messer Remirro d'Orco. See Paul Johnson, *Modern Times* (New York: Harper Perennial, 1991), 300–304.

13. Machiavelli, *Prince,* chap. 17: "Men forget the death of a father more quickly than the loss of patrimony." In most regimes, there must be at least a seeming respect for the property of one's subjects.

14. See Stephen Handelman, *Comrade Criminal* (New Haven, Conn.: Yale University Press, 1995).

15. See N. S. Timasheff, *Religion in Soviet Russia, 1917–1942* (New York: Sheed and Ward, 1942); see also Daniela Deane, "Chinese Army, Police Overshadow Tibetan Monks: Decaying Monasteries, Once Revered Religious Centers, House Fear and Divisiveness," *Washington Post,* July 3, 1991.

16. James L. Payne. *Why Nations Arm* (New York: Basil Blackwell, 1989).

CHAPTER 3

1. Francis Fukuyama. *The End of History and the Last Man* (New York: Free Press, 1992).

2. Cf. Aristotle, *Politics,* trans. Carnes Lord (Chicago: University of Chicago Press, 1984), 1305a.28–36. Also, for the best-known prescriptive document against the danger of this tendency, see *The Federalist Papers,* no. 10 (Boston: University of New England Press, 1982), 51.

3. "A Nationwide Study of Home Education," The National Home Education Research Institute, Salem, Oregon, 1990. The average scores of home-schooled students showed that the national percentile mean for home-schooled students was 84 for reading, 80 for language, 81 for math, and 84 for science. See also press release by Home School Legal Defense Association, December 7, 1994, citing a study by Dr. Brian Ray of student performance in the Iowa Test of Basic Skills. The national average for home-schooled students is at the seventy-seventh percentile. The "grand mean percentile in language and math" is 73 percent.

4. In the *Politics* (1337a.11–22), Aristotle assumes this is the case.

5. "Home School Germans Flee to UK," *Guardian,* February 24, 2008.

6. Cf. *The Federalist Papers.* Hamilton attributes the idea of federalism to Montesquieu, whom he cites as the author of "the new science of politics." Burke is justly famous for his reference to "the little platoons" of society that hold the whole together.

7. Alexis de Tocqueville. *Democracy in America,* vol. 1 (New York: Alfred A. Knopf, 1945), 91–92.

8. Cf. David Hume, "Of the Parties of Great Britain," in *Essays: Moral, Political, and Literary,* ed. Eugene Miller (Indianapolis, Ind.: Liberty Press, 1985). Hume's discussion of the

Tory and Whig parties is pertinent here. Also see Harvey Mansfield, *Statesmanship and Party Government* (Chicago: University of Chicago Press, 1974).

9. Cf. Plato, *Republic,* trans. Allan Bloom (New York: Basic Books, 1968), 488a–489c.

10. However, if they had looked at the Roman republic, they would have seen how quickly shifting economic policies change a people's way of life. Cf. David Hume, "Of Taxes," in *Essays: Moral, Political, Literary,* ed. Eugene Miller. See also Edward Gibbon, *The Decline and Fall of the Roman Empire* (New York: Heritage Press, 1946), chap. 17.

11. Cf. Aristotle, *Politics,* 1259b.18–21. Also see John Locke, "Of Paternal Power," in the *Second Treatise of Government* (Buffalo: Prometheus Books, 1986), as well as Xenophon's *Oeconomicus.*

12. One can see the roots of this conceptual transformation in the writings of Karl Marx and Friedrich Engels. But even they, to a certain extent, accepted the natural basis of gender differences. Their followers, on the contrary, take a different approach. While Eleanor Marx (Marx's daughter) could write that Shakespeare was the Bible in their home, Jonathan Dollimore, a modern Marxist Shakespearean scholar, calls for a rewriting of *Antony and Cleopatra*—in which gender roles are switched and Cleopatra has a "same-sex" and "cross-class" relationship with one of her attendants (Dollimore, "Shakespeare, Cultural Materialism, Feminism, and Marxist Humanism," *New Literary History* 21 [Spring 1990]: 471–493).

CHAPTER 4

1. This is most obvious in Karl Marx's *The Economic and Philosophical Manuscripts of 1844, The Communist Manifesto,* and *Critique of the Gotha Programme,* as well as in Karl Marx and Friedrich Engels, *The Origins of Family, Private Property, and the State.*

2. B. P. Pockney. *Soviet Statistics since 1950* (New York: St. Martin's Press, 1991), 101.

3. Mikhail Bernstam. "Economic Systems, Demographic Change and Global Conflict," in *Population Change and European Security,* ed. Lawrence Freedman and John Saunders (London: Brassey's, 1991), 169. I am deeply indebted to Mr. Bernstam, a former colleague at the Hoover Institution, for many insights into the Soviet economy drawn from this seminal article and from countless conversations over many years.

4. Ibid., 165–167.

5. Mikhail Voslensky. *The Nomenklatura* (New York: Doubleday, 1984).

6. Stephen Handelman. *Comrade Criminal: Russia's New Mafiya* (New Haven, Conn.: Yale University Press, 1995), 110.

7. Ibid., 104.

8. Georgii Arbatov. *The System* (New York: Random House, 1992).

9. In an instance that shows the peculiar viciousness of Russian criminals, Sherry Jones, in an op-ed piece (*New York Times,* November 25, 1995), tells about a businessman friend who was being extorted by two officially connected gangs. He tried to give up his business

when the payments got too high, but was forced to continue paying lest his family be killed. Having exhausted loans from friends, he committed suicide (which was reported as an apparent heart attack).

10. "Smuggling Raw Materials to West Creates Huge Fortunes," *Washington Post,* February 2, 1993.

11. Steven Erlanger. "Corrupt Tide in Russia from State-Business Ties," *New York Times,* January 3, 1995.

12. Andrei Amalrik. *Will the Soviet Union Survive until 1984?* (New York: Harper and Row, 1970).

13. See Erik Von Kuhnhelt-Ledihn's *Liberty or Equality* (Front Royal, Wash.: Christendom Press, 1993 [1953]) for a full exposition of this argument.

14. Robert Putnam. *Making Democracy Work: Civic Traditions in Modern Italy* (Princeton, N.J.: Princeton University Press, 1993).

15. Abdurakman Avtorkanov's *The Communist Party Apparatus* (Chicago: Regnery, 1964), 49, 60–61, 73, 84.

16. From Josef Stalin's *Works,* as cited in ibid.

17. This is the point of vol. 3 of Aleksandr Solzhenitsyn's *The Gulag Archipelago* (New York: Harper and Row, 1976), pt. 7, chaps. 1 and 2.

18. Solzhenitsyn. *Gulag Archipelago,* vol. 3, 524.

19. Hedrick Smith. *The Russians* (New York: Ballantine Books, 1976), 352.

20. Ibid.

21. Robert Conquest. "The Importance of Historical Truth," *Freedom Review* (November-December 1992): 36.

22. Alessandra Stanley. "Russian Mothers, from All Walks, Walk Alone," *New York Times,* October 21, 1995.

23. Francine Duplessix Gray. *Soviet Women* (New York: Doubleday, 1989), 45–48.

24. See "Loyal Wives, Virtuous Mothers: Women's Day and Russian Women of the '90s," *Russian Life* 39 (March 1996): 4.

25. Mikhail Gorbachev. *Perestroika: New Thinking for Our Country and the World* (New York: Harper and Row, 1987), 117.

26. See Katherine P. Henry, "Registration of Churches in Soviet Union," *Religious and Communist Dominated Areas* 1 (Winter 1987): 14. See also Radio Liberty Research Bulletin RL 171/88 (April 22, 1988), and Dmitry V. Pospielovsky, *A History of Marxist-Leninist Atheism and Soviet Anti-Religious Policies,* vol. 1 (London: Macmillan, 1987).

27. Smith, *The Russians,* 434.

28. Ibid., 580–581.

29. Niccolò Machiavelli. *Discorso o dialogo interno alla nostra lingua,* ed. Bortolo Tommaso Sozzi (Torino: G. Einaudi, 1976).

30. *Le Monde,* March 28, 1995.

31. This is also the opinion expressed by Condoleezza Rice, provost of Stanford University, later secretary of state, who followed Soviet military affairs for the National Security Council between 1989 and 1992, as expressed in an address to the Hoover Institution, Stanford University, June 21, 1993.

32. J. Michael Waller. *Secret Empire: The KGB in Russia Today* (Boulder: Westview Press, 1994), 113.

33. Bill Keller. "Cry of 'Won't Give My Son!' and Soviets End Call-Up," *New York Times,* January 20, 1990.

CHAPTER 5

1. Lester Theroux, Chalmers Johnson, and James Fallows. "Head to Head Containing Japan," *Atlantic Monthly,* May 1989; Clyde Prestowitz, Ronald Morse, and Alan Tonelson. *Powernomics: Economics and Strategy after the Cold War* (Washington, D.C.: Economic Strategy Institute, 1981).

2. Kenneth A. Schultz and Barry Weingast. *The Democratic Advantage* (Stanford: Hoover Institution Press, 1996).

3. See John Locke, "Of Property," chap. 5, in the *Second Treatise of Government* (Buffalo: Prometheus Books, 1986). In this chapter, Locke bases lawful government and property rights on the fact that all people mix their labor with nature. Because all people have an equal interest in their property, all property must be treated equally.

4. See Plato, *Republic,* trans. Allan Bloom (New York: Basic Books, 1968), 367b–372c.

5. Paul Kennedy. *The Rise and Fall of the Great Powers* (New York: Random House, 1986). This oversight reminds one of André Malraux's lines in *Man's Fate:* "Europeans never understand anything of China that does not resemble themselves" (New York: Vintage, 1934), 111.

6. This is the theme of John Kenneth Galbraith's *The Affluent Society* (Boston: Houghton Mifflin, 1960).

7. *Wall Street Journal,* July 23, 2008.

8. See *1997 Index of Economic Freedom* (Washington, D.C.: Heritage Foundation, 1997).

9. In *The Immoralist,* André Gide wrote: "The honest Swiss! All their prosperity is worthless. Without crimes, without history, without literature, without art, what are they but an overgrown rosebush that bears neither thorns nor bloom!" (Paris: Mercure de France, 1921), 146–147. Gide understood, like many before and after him, that the prosperity of a people and the relative success of government depends more on the quality of the souls composing a state than on quantifiable economic factors. Indeed, the authors of the "Third World" concept and the managers of the programs meant to uplift it included in that category countries

that had never been Western colonies (for example, Taiwan, South Korea, and Latin American countries). They even included Argentina, a country that had once been among the world's richest but had fallen on hard times. For a moving account of the character of Third World leaders and what they have wrought, see Paul Johnson, *Modern Times* (New York: Harper and Row, 1983), especially the chapters entitled "The Bandung Generation" and "Caliban's Kingdoms."

10. David Landes. "Rich Country, Poor Country," *New Republic,* November 20, 1989.

11. John H. Coatsworth. "Obstacles to Economic Growth in Nineteenth-Century Mexico," *American Historical Review* 83 (1978): 94.

12. See Hilton Root, "Institutional Foundations for a Market Economy in Tropical Africa," Stanford University, Hoover Institution, March 1994. I am indebted to Hilton Root for countless insights on the relationship between power and money.

13. In this regard, note the intriguing suggestion by R. Emmet Tyrell in *Boy Clinton: The Political Biography* (Washington, D.C.: Regnery, 1996) that under Governor Bill Clinton, the state of Arkansas effectively franchised Donald Lasater to import drugs and a variety of other well-connected people to loot its banks, much as happens in the Third World.

14. Edward A. Gargan. "Family Ties That Bind Growth," *New York Times,* April 9, 1996.

15. Dan A. Cothran. *Political Stability and Democracy in Mexico: The "Perfect Dictatorship"?* (Westport, Conn.: Praeger, 1994), 193–198. Arrested ostensibly for murder, La Quina has never been tried.

16. Steven Greenhouse. "Comparing Wealth as Money Fluctuates," *New York Times,* August 23, 1987.

17. See E. H. Norman, *Origins of the Modern Japanese State* (New York: Pantheon Books, 1975), 233; and Walter McDougall, *Let the Sea Make a Noise* (New York: Basic Books, 1994), 353–362, 531–539, 663–673.

18. In a 1991 Mainichi Press poll, 62 percent of Japanese respondents believed that "it was strange" that products manufactured in Japan were less expensive in other countries than in their own. See *Index to International Public Opinion, 1990–1991* (New York: Greenwood Press, 1992), 69.

19. Nicolas Kristoff and Sheryl WuDunn. *China Wakes* (New York: Times Books, 1990).

20. See, for example, the lead article in the March 1997 *National Geographic,* "China's Gold Coast."

21. Ramon H. Myers. "The Socialist Market Economy in the People's Republic of China," *Fifty-fifth Morrison Lecture,* Australian National University, November 8, 1994, 11. "Shared Cooperative Systems" is from Gao Lu, "Call for Reform of Ownership, Property Rights—Brief Account of Seventh, Eighth Symposiums at 'Forum on China's Market Economy,'" *Jingji Ribao,* November 2, 1993, in *JPRS Report: China,* January 21, 1993.

22. Hilton L. Root. "Has China Lost Its Way? Political Risk and Financial Intermediation in the PRC," Hoover Institution, Stanford University, 1995. I am indebted to Hilton

Root in general and to this paper in particular for insight into the systemic importance of China's *guanxi* (4, 13–15).

23. Ibid.

24. Sheryl WuDunn. "China's Rush to Riches," *New York Times Magazine,* September 4, 1994, 39.

25. Ibid., 41.

26. "China, the Art of the (Raw) Deal," *New York Times,* February 12, 1995.

27. See *New York Times,* December 22, 1993. Costs average under $1,000 per (good) worker per year. See also "China, the Art of the (Raw) Deal," *New York Times,* February 12, 1995.

28. Here is how the *Economic Daily* described it: "'Leaping into the sea' is to march into the central battlefield of economic construction. . . . If it had not been for the Party Central Committee Third Plenum and Eleventh Meeting and Deng Xiaoping's southern tour, leaping into the sea would never have been possible." See also Ruhying Chen, ed., *The Mania for Leaping into the Sea* (Beijing: University of Beijing Press, 1993), 47.

29. Alternatively, some hypothesize that a new contest is taking place in China to see which regime can be friendliest to business. Barry Weingast has called this "market-preserving federalism." See Yingyi Quian and Barry Weingast, *China's Transition to Markets* (Stanford: Hoover Institution Press, 1995).

30. World Bank. *World Development Report, 1992* (New York: Oxford University Press, 1992).

31. In one of the more clamorous cases of discovery, an armed robber, caught in the Rome suburbs after a high-speed chase by car and on foot, was found to have been on the disability rolls for total blindness. See *Il Tempo* (Rome), September 4, 1994.

32. Wilfried Prewo. "Germany Is Not a Model," *Wall Street Journal,* February 1, 1994.

33. Tocqueville wrote, "In fact, the nobility was regarded in the age of feudalism much as the government is regarded by everyone today; its exactions were tolerated in view of the protection and security it provided." *The Old Regime and the French Revolution,* trans. Stuart Gilbert (Garden City, N.Y.: Doubleday, 1955), pt. 2, chap. 1, 30.

34. *Sweden's Prosperity in Comparison with Other Countries* (Stockholm: Ekonomipakta, 1989), 9.

35. George Melloan. "Looted Banks, One-Eared Cows, and Moral Fog," *Wall Street Journal,* August 15, 1994.

36. See chap. 6 in this work for a discussion of the relationship between the welfare state and demographic trends.

37. Francisco Orrgeo Vicuna. *Chile: The Balanced View* (Santiago: University of Chile, 1975), 185, table 18.

38. Between 1965 and 1970, food imports averaged $100 million per year. By 1972, the figure had risen to $450 million, and in 1973, it hit $600 million (Sergio de Castro, ed., *El Ladrillo* [Santiago: Centro de Estudios Publicos, 1992], 36–37).

39. Figures from Banco Central de Chile, quoted in Jorge Rodriguez Grossi, ed., *Perspectivas economicas para la democracia* (Santiago: Instituto Chileno de Estudios Humanisticos, 1984), 32.

40. Official Chilean government figures cited in James R. Whelan, *Out of the Ashes* (Washington, D.C.: Regnery Gateway, 1989), 308.

41. *El Ladrillo,* 32.

42. Declaration of the Supreme Court of Chile, May 26, 1973, quoted in Whelan, *Out of the Ashes,* 413.

43. Angelo M. Codevilla. "Is Pinochet the Model?" *Foreign Affairs* (November-December 1993): 129.

44. Ibid., 30.

45. In 1988, the government and opposition established a commission under Raul Rettig Guissen, a respected jurist, to compile a report on the actions of all sides in the civil war. According to the Rettig Report, published in March 1991 and accepted by all sides as definitive, 2,115 people had been killed. See *The Report of the Chilean National Commission on Truth and Reconciliation* (London: Notre Dame Press, 1993).

CHAPTER 6

1. John Fortescue. *De laudibus legum Angliae* (Cambridge: Cambridge University Press, 1942).

2. Robert William Fogel and Stanley L. Engerman. *Time on the Cross: The Economics of American Negro Slavery* (Boston: Little, Brown, 1974).

3. Aristotle. *Politics,* trans. Carnes Lord (Chicago: University of Chicago Press, 1984), 1277b.7–15.

4. Tocqueville remarks in *Democracy in America* (New York: Alfred A. Knopf, 1945), vol. 2, bk. 4, chap. 6, 435: "It is vain to summon a people who have been rendered so dependent on the central power to choose from time to time the representatives of that power; this rare and brief exercise of their free choice, however important it may be, will not prevent them from gradually losing the faculties of thinking, feeling, and acting for themselves, and thus gradually falling below the level of humanity."

5. Plato. *Republic,* trans. Allan Bloom (New York: Basic Books, 1968), 388c.

6. "The Notion of a Living Constitution," *Texas Law Review,* 54 (1976): 693. This is the revised text of the ninth annual Will E. Orgain Lecture, delivered at the University of Texas Law School, March 12, 1976.

7. José Pedroni, quoted in William Ratliff and Roger Fontaine, *Changing Course: The Capitalist Revolution in Argentina* (Stanford: Hoover Institution Press, 1990), 19. See also Carlos Weisman, "Argentina, Autarkic Industrialization and Illegitimacy," in *Democracy in*

Developing Countries, ed. Larry Diamond, Juan Lunz, and Martin Lipset (Boulder: Lynne Rienner, 1988).

8. Homer. *The Odyssey,* bk. 23, ll. 208–230. Upon returning home, Odysseus objects to Penelope's test of his identity—the suggested moving of their bed away from the trunk of an olive tree—by stating: "Woman, by heaven you have stung me now! Who dared to move my bed? No builder had the skill for that—unless a god came down to turn the trick. No mortal in his best days could budge it with a crowbar. There is our pact and pledge, our secret sign, built into that bed—my handiwork and no one else's!" Homer shows us the suitors as worthy of death because they had been eating Odysseus's property.

9. Plato, *Republic,* 553d–556a.

10. Cf. Jean-Jacques Rousseau, *The Social Contract,* trans. Charles Frankel (New York: Hafner, 1947), bk. 4. See also Montesquieu, *Considerations on the Causes of the Greatness of the Romans and Their Decline,* trans. David Lowenthal (New York: Free Press, 1965).

11. Titus Livius. *Ab Urbe Condita Libri,* trans. B. O. Foster (Cambridge: Harvard University Press, 1970).

12. Fragment (August 1, 1858). From Roy P. Basler, *The Collected Works of Abraham Lincoln,* vol. 2 (New Brunswick, N.J.: Rutgers University Press, 1953), 532.

13. The finest summary account of this is in Norman Cohn, *Pursuit of the Millennium* (New York: Harper and Row, 1960).

14. See John Stuart Mill, *Considerations on Representative Government* (Buffalo: Prometheus Books, 1991), especially the chapter titled "Of True and False Democracy; Representation of All and Representation of the Majority Only."

15. The classic discussion of how proportional representation destroys democracy at all levels in the organization of parties is in Ferdinand A. Hermens, *Democracy or Anarchy* (South Bend, Ind.: Notre Dame University Press, 1941), 51–58. Hermens's discussion of the role of proportional representation in the rise of fascism and Nazism is on 178–246.

16. C. P. Snow. *Science and Government* (New York: New American Library, 1960), 9.

17. Ibid., 71.

18. *Public Papers of the Presidents,* January 17, 1961, 1034–1040. Emphasis mine.

19. Chris Mooney. *The Republican War on Science* (New York: Basic Books, 2005), 11.

20. Ibid., 4.

21. Ibid., 11.

22. Simon Schama. *Citizens: A Chronicle of the French Revolution* (New York: Knopf, 1989).

23. Charles de Gaulle. *La France et Son Armée* (Paris: Plon, 1938), 271.

24. Ralf Dahrendorf. *Society and Democracy in Germany* (Garden City, N.Y.: Doubleday, 1969), 397–411. As the late Lewis Gann used to say, every German truck driver, every cleaning

lady, knew that the German Democratic Republic was a fraud. But few of the elites did, and after 1970 none said so publicly.

25. Nicholas D. Kristof. "A Lesson in Heroics Is Lost on Many," *New York Times,* November 2, 1990. Such campaigns are indistinguishable from countless similar Soviet efforts (for example, the glorification of Pavel Morozov) to teach unnatural morality. The Chinese seem to "buy" such teachings even less than the Russians. Kristof reported a Chinese teacher's comment: "Nobody believes that rubbish."

26. Zhisui Li. *The Private Life of Chairman Mao,* trans. Tai Hung-Chao (New York: Random House, 1994).

27. John Byron and Robert Pack. *The Claws of the Dragon: Kang Sheng, the Evil Genius behind Mao and His Legacy of Terror in People's China* (New York: Simon and Schuster, 1992).

28. Kenneth Lieberthal. *Governing China* (New York: W. W. Norton, 1996).

29. Hu Chang. "Impressions of Mainland China Carried Back by Mainland Visitors," in *Two Societies in Opposition,* ed. Ramon H. Myers (Stanford: Hoover Institution Press, 1991), 144–153.

30. Thomas A. Metzger et al. "Understanding the Taiwan Experience, an Historical Perspective," *Pacific Review* 2, no. 4 (1989): 300. Estimates of the number of Taiwanese killed in the repression of the anti-Kuomintang riots of 1947 range between 8,000 and 10,000. This great bloodshed is to be compared with that of the Communists on the mainland, who killed uncountable millions.

31. Sidney H. Chang and Leonard H. D. Gordon, eds. *All under Heaven: Sun Yat-sen and His Revolutionary Thought* (Stanford: Hoover Institution Press, 1991).

32. Ed Campos and Hilton Root. "Rethinking the Asian Miracle," Stanford University, Hoover Institution, June 1994, 71.

33. "Taiwan's Prosperity Is Exacting a Heavy Toll," *Los Angeles Times,* May 14, 1995. Note that mainland Chinese officials do not worry about divorce rates—which makes sense for officials who three decades ago forced the physical separation of hundreds of millions of Chinese couples. However, in an increase similar to that of the Taiwanese, the Chinese divorce rate between 1982 and 1990 rose 42 percent (*Los Angeles Times,* July 18, 1995). For a comprehensive discussion of this development in Asia, see Ken Davies and Graham Richards, "Asian Values Myth Debunked," *Plain Dealer,* December 24, 1995.

34. Seth Mydans. "Good Life Guide: To Five Cs, Add Clout," *New York Times,* June 5, 1996.

35. Philip Shenon. "Models for China: Either Filthy and Free or Clean and Mean," *New York Times,* February 6, 1995.

36. The positivist movement, founded by the French founder of sociology, Auguste Comte (1798–1857), preached the scientific management of society. Its motto, "Order and Progress"; its philosophical premise, that reality consists only of measurable data; and its mil-

itant secularism became the foundations of modern social science. Only Brazil has "Order and Progress" written on its flag. But most modern regimes have the premises of positivism in their bones.

37. The government's typical response to the exposure of a bureaucrat caught red-handed in corruption or violence is simply to transfer him laterally and geographically. See Alicia Ely-Yamin, *Justice Corrupted, Justice Denied* (New York: Mexico Project, World Policy Institute, 1992).

38. "*La mordida es institucion nacional,*" or "graft is a national institution," is a popular saying in Mexico. But note that while more money can buy some elbow room within the system in Mexico, in honest social democracies like Sweden, nothing can substitute for connections.

39. See Javier Livas, *Confesion de un ingenier electoral* (Monterrey, Mexico, 1992). This is an account of how Francisco Loredo Valdes fixed elections for the PRI in Monterrey between 1976 and 1991. Note that the electorate's "pride in Mexico" is about triple its "pride in the Mexican political system." Cf. Jorge I. Dominguez and James McCann, *Democratizing Mexico: Public Opinion and Electoral Choices* (Baltimore: Johns Hopkins University Press, 1996), 38–39.

40. See Brian Latell, *Mexico at the Crossroads* (Stanford: Hoover Institution Press, 1986). Latell, a senior analyst at the Central Intelligence Agency, was the author of a highly regarded national intelligence estimate on Mexico in 1985. This unclassified version retains all the author's insights into the revolutionary significance of changing attitudes in Mexico. In northern Mexico there is probably a majority in favor of joining the United States.

41. George Washington. "First Inaugural Address," in *Writings,* ed. John Rhodehames (New York: Library of America, 1997), 732–733. Note the parallel with the theme of Aristotle's *Nicomachean Ethics.*

42. Thomas Jefferson. *Thomas Jefferson, Writings,* ed. Merrill D. Peterson (New York: Library of America, 1984), 492–493.

CHAPTER 7

1. Aristotle. *Politics,* trans. Carnes Lord (Chicago: University of Chicago Press, 1984), 1252a.37–38.

2. Ibid., 1259a.37–1259b.10, 1260b.8–1260b.19.

3. Thomas Jefferson. *Notes on Virginia* (New York: Library of America, 1984), 186. See also Francis Parkman, *France, England, and North America,* vol. 1, ed. David Levin (New York: Viking Press, 1983). Writing a half century after the founding, Parkman described the life of Huron women as beginning with "a youth of license" followed by "an age of drudgery." "Female life among the Hurons," he wrote, "has no bright side" (358). I am indebted

to Thomas G. West for pointing me to Parkman's judgment on the Indians' treatment of women.

4. *Cleveland v. United States* 329 US 14 (1946). The Court ruled that the Mann Act—which made it illegal to transport women across state lines "for the purpose of prostitution or for any other immoral purpose"—also included polygamous practices. In essence, it affirmed the decision of *Reynolds v. United States* 98 US 145 (1878), in which the court ruled that "from the earliest history of England polygamy has been treated as an offense against society."

5. *Time,* July 18, 1994. Emphasis mine.

6. Fustel de Coulanges. *The Ancient City* (New York: Doubleday, 1965), bk. 2, chap. 2. In this chapter, de Coulanges stresses the aspect of rebirth. The custom of carrying the bride across the threshold dates to these times and symbolizes that the wife did not walk into the husband's house but rather was born there.

7. Take, for example, Sophocles' Antigone, whose tragedy consists precisely in refusing the process of alienation and rebirth implicit in marriage. She tells the chorus: "O, but I would not have done the forbidden thing for any husband or for any son. For why? I could have had another husband and by him other sons, if one were lost; But father and mother lost, where would I get another brother? For thus preferring you, My brother, Creon condemns me and hales me away, never a bride, never a mother, unfriended, condemned alive a solitary death." In *The Theban Plays* (New York: Penguin, 1947), 150.

8. A recent survey—albeit a summary one—by *Reader's Digest* (July 1992, 48–54) shows that Americans who are married with children tend to have substantially different and much more conservative opinions on social and political matters than other Americans do. This is non-news. Practical politicians realized long ago that married people with children vote conservative by margins of at least 20 points. Even among the animals, those with young behave very differently than those who do not have them.

9. Cf. "Ireland Should Vote No," *Daily Telegraph,* November 23, 1995.

10. "Family Values to Shift; Divorce Rate to Climb," *Trends Research Institute* 5 (Summer 1996): 4. Anyone frequenting an expensive restaurant can observe the prevalence of couples consisting of men middle-aged or older and women half their age.

11. Deut. 22:28–29.

12. "More Men in Prime Not Working," *New York Times,* December 1, 1994. In the United States since the end of the 1960s, the share of prime-age men who are not in school, on the job, or looking for work has tripled, moving from 3 percent to 9 percent, according to Robert H. Haverman, an economist at the University of Wisconsin: "The decline in men's work is concentrated at the bottom of socioeconomic scales." Note Myron Magnet's thesis that upper-class ideas have had devastating effects on the lower classes. See Myron Magnet, *The Dream and the Nightmare: The Sixties' Legacy to the Underclass* (New York: W. Morrow, 1993).

13. Even those who favor these recent developments—for example, see Jane Wheelock, *Husbands at Home: The Domestic Economy in Post-Industrial Society* (New York: Routledge, 1990)—admit these tendencies, although their slogan is "give it time."

14. Gary Becker. *A Treatise on the Family* (Cambridge: Harvard University Press, 1981). See *The Family Wage: Work, Gender and Children in the Modern Economy* (Rockford, Ill.: Rockford Institute, 1988). The domestic division of labor is efficient in part because mothers will agonize over the best ways to care for their own, while a day-care worker will not, while husbands will care for their homes as hired maintenance workers will not.

15. From *Taxpayer* (Winter 1992), as quoted by William Gairdner, *The War against the Family* (Toronto: Stoddart, 1992), 178.

16. Tamar Lewin. "The Decay of Families Is Global, Study Says," *New York Times,* May 30, 1995.

17. Ibid.

18. "Fings Ain't Wot They Used to Be," *The Economist,* May 28, 1994, 31.

19. The idea that "the best trained practitioners of both sexes," namely, scientifically trained government employees, know better about children than parents has been popularized by such authors as Kate Millet, who wrote *Sexual Politics* (Garden City, N.Y.: Doubleday, 1970).

20. T. S. Eliot. *The Rock* (London: Faber and Faber, 1934), 42.

21. Hillary Rodham. "Children under the Law," *Harvard Educational Review* 43 (November 1973): 508. The full statement reads: "If the law were to abolish the status of minority and to reverse its underlying presumption of children's incompetency, the result would be an implicit presumption that children, like other persons, are capable of exercising rights and assuming responsibilities until proven otherwise. Empirical differences among children would then serve as the grounds for making exemptions to the presumption and for justifying rational state restrictions."

22. Erick Eckholm. "Parents Give Up Youths under Law Meant for Babies," *New York Times,* October 2, 2008.

23. The litany is just about the same, regardless of where one gets the statistics. In the United States, some 70 percent of men in state and federal prisons come from homes where no husband was ever present. One can argue that children of criminals or children who live in criminal-infested neighborhoods have a higher tendency to commit crimes than those who do not. But that only pushes the correlation back one logical step. Most impressive is the consistency of the phenomenon around the world.

24. Aristotle, *Politics,* 1259b.12–17.

25. Sheila B. Kamerman and Alfred J. Kahn, eds. *Child Care, Parental Leave, and the Under 3's: Policy Innovation in Europe* (New York: Auburn House, 1991), 173–176.

26. David Popenoe. *Disturbing the Nest: Family Change and Decline in Modern Societies* (New York: Aldine de Gruyter, 1988), 175.

27. Alexis de Tocqueville. *Democracy in America,* vol. 2 (New York: Alfred A. Knopf, 1945), chap. 12, n. 3. Tocqueville thought that this can only "degrade both" and "produce nothing but feeble men and unseemly women."

28. Linda Haas. "Family Policy in Sweden," *Journal of Family and Economic Issues* 113 (Spring 1996): 75.

29. Ibid., 78. The quality is so high that according to one of Sweden's admirers, the Swedes have achieved something that intuitively appears to be physically impossible: "The amount of time parents spend directly interacting with their children is not lessened by Swedish children's time spent in day care."

30. Roland Huntford. *The New Totalitarians* (New York: Stein and Day, 1992), 84.

31. See *Basic Statistics of the Community: Comparison with Some European Countries, Canada, the USA, Japan, and Russia* (Luxembourg: Office for Official Publication of the European Community, 1993).

32. "A Change of Course: The Model Starts to Show Her Age," *The Economist,* March 3, 1990, 5.

33. One craze was a drug named "Special K," or Ketamin—a veterinary anesthetic given to dogs and cats ("Party Craze for Cats' Drug," *Guardian,* July 7, 1996).

34. Mary Nourse. "Women's Work in Japan," *National Geographic,* January 1938, 99.

35. Robert C. Christopher. *The Japanese Mind* (New York: Random House, 1983), 114.

36. Nicholas D. Kristof. "Baby May Make 3, but in Japan That's Not Enough," *New York Times,* October 6, 1996.

37. Christopher, *The Japanese Mind,* 115.

CHAPTER 8

1. Jean Bodin, *Dix Livres de la Republique* (1576) states this, the thesis of the *politiques,* and became the template for modern secular government.

2. Edward Gibbon. *Decline and Fall of the Roman Empire,* vol. 1 (Chicago: Encyclopedia Brittanica, 1955), chap. 2, 12.

3. *National Longitudinal Survey of Youth* (Washington, D.C.: U.S. Department of Labor, 1993).

4. This old story in social science applies even to "black male inner-city youths." See National Bureau of Economic Research, Working Paper Series no. 1656 (Cambridge, Mass.: NBER, 1985).

5. "Incentive Pay, Information and Earnings Evidence from the *National Longitudinal Survey of Youth*" (Washington, D.C.: U.S. Department of Labor, 1995).

6. Howard M. Bahr and Bruce A. Chadwick. "Religion and Family in Middletown, U.S.A.," *Journal of Marriage and the Family* 47 (May 1985): 407–414.

7. It is not appropriate to say the faithful practice of religion of any sort predicts this because, after all, the Thuggees (from which the word "thug" derives) worshiped Siva, the Hindu god of violent death, at least according to the Thuggees' testimony-in-deed. The murderous followers of the medieval heresiarchs described by Norman Cohn and the suicidal followers of the Reverend James Jones in the 1970s are among many examples of the sad consequences of bad theology.

8. The Turkish government of Mustafa Kemal (1923–1938) waged a war against Islam almost as violent as that which the Soviet regime waged against Russia's religions. Turkey appeared to have won that war with relatively few ill effects. Then, in 1995, Turkey's Islamic Welfare Party won a plurality in parliamentary elections, and the Turkish regime began to ask how ready the army was to wage another civil war on behalf of secularism.

9. Dante. *Il Purgatorio,* canto 32: 129. The translation is mine.

10. Ibid.

11. The Mughal emperor Akhbar's attempt to confuse himself with Allah is interestingly described in Douglas E. Streusand, *The Formation of the Mughal Empire* (Delhi: Oxford University Press, 1989).

12. In Sweden, a 1990 poll showed that only 38 percent of the people trusted in the church (lower than in any other Western European country). Correspondingly, trust in the police force was twice as high. See Hans-Dieter Klingemann and Dieter Fuchs, eds., *Citizens and the State* (New York: Oxford University Press, 1991).

13. On the effects of the German church tax, see Dennis L. Bark and David Gress-Wright, *A History of the Federal Republic* (London: Basil Blackwell, 1990).

14. Edward G. Shirely. "Is Iran's Present Algeria's Future?" *Foreign Affairs* 74, no. 3 (May-June 1995): 38.

15. Bill Broadway. "Poll Finds America 'As Churched as Ever,'" *Washington Post,* May 31, 1997. See also Larry Witham, "Europeans Forge New Religious Paths; Boomers Tilt Traditions to Fit Their Needs," *Washington Times,* March 11, 1996.

16. Plutarch. *Lives,* vol. 1, trans. John Dryden et al. (Philadelphia: Henry T. Coates, 1896), 113.

17. Titus Livius. *Ab Urbe Condita Libri,* trans. B. O. Foster (Cambridge: Harvard University Press, 1970), bk. 3, chap. 20, para. 5.

18. Benito Mussolini. *Fascism* (Rome: Arditi, 1932).

19. Stephen Kinzer. "Coming of Age, Unideologically," *New York Times* (international edition), June 11, 1994. Kinzer describes the Jugendweihe's being revived "to promote good citizenship."

20. "The Counterattack of God," *The Economist,* July 8, 1995, 19.

21. Jean-Marie Guehenno. *The End of the Nation-State* (St. Paul: University of Minnesota Press, 1996).

22. Poll conducted by *Yediot Ahronot,* December 2, 1996. Significantly, 51 percent of the secularists thought so, but only 38 percent of the religious did. Eighty-three percent of the respondents thought the best way to avoid such a war was for secularists and the religious to study the Torah together.

CHAPTER 9

1. Thucydides. *The Peloponnesian War* (Ann Arbor: University of Michigan Press, 1959), bk. 1, 140–144.

2. Ibid., bk. 6, 8–31.

3. Niccolò Machiavelli. *The Prince,* trans. Angelo Codevilla (New Haven, Conn.: Yale University Press, 1997), chaps. 20, 24.

4. See also William McNeill, *The Pursuit of Power* (Chicago: University of Chicago Press, 1982), for a discussion of how the changing technology of weapons affects those who use them.

5. Machiavelli, *Prince,* chaps. 6, 8, 13, 24.

6. Rudyard Kipling. "Pharaoh and the Sergeant," in *Rudyard Kipling's Verse, Inclusive Edition, 1885–1926* (Garden City, N.Y.: Doubleday, 1929), 227.

7. Charles de Gaulle. *La France et Son Armée* (Paris: Plon, 1938), 138. My account of the Napoleonic regime owes much to de Gaulle's admirable chapter.

CHAPTER 10

1. John Allen. "An Oration upon the Beauties of Liberty," preached in Boston, December 3, 1772, and widely circulated, in *Political Sermons of the American Revolution,* ed. Ellis Sandoz (Indianapolis, Ind.: Liberty Press, 1991), 305.

2. Thomas Paine. *Common Sense* (New York: Knopf, 1994).

3. Samuel Cooper, October 25, 1788, in Sandoz, ed., *Political Sermons,* 639.

4. Alexis de Tocqueville. *Democracy in America,* vol. 2 (New York: Alfred A. Knopf, 1945), pt. 2, chap. 4, 482–483.

5. Ibid.

6. Ibid., vol. 1, pt. 1, chap. 5, 61.

7. Ibid., 86.

8. See James Thomas Flexner, *Washington, the Indispensable Man* (Boston: Little, Brown, 1974), parts of chaps. 11–13, 16, and 17.

9. Tocqueville, *Democracy in America,* vol. 1, pt. 2, chap. 6, 221–222.

10. Ibid., chap. 7, 234.

11. Ibid., chap. 4, 179. Note Tocqueville's foreshadowing of the Leninist practice of "democratic centralism."

12. Ibid., vol. 2, pt. 2, chap. 21, 487.

13. Ibid., vol. 1, pt. 1, chap. 5, 79.

14. See Alexis de Tocqueville, *The Ancien Régime and the French Revolution,* trans. Stuart Gilbert (Garden City, N.Y.: Doubleday, 1955), for a broader analysis of this phenomenon.

15. Eph. 6:22–24.

16. 1 Cor. 7:4.

17. Matt. 19:6.

18. Aristotle. *Nicomachean Ethics,* trans. W. D Ross (New York: Random House, 1941), 1162.

19. Memorandum on a tour from Paris to Amsterdam (1778). See chapter on "Women and the Family" in *Vindicating the Founders: Race, Sex, Class, and Justice in the Origins of America,* ed. Thomas G. West (Lanham, Md.: Rowman and Littlefield, 1997). I am indebted to Professor West for numerous insights on the American founding generation's family ways.

20. John Adams. *The Works of John Adams, Second President of the United States, with a Life of the Author, Notes and Illustrations by His Grandson Charles Francis Adams,* vol. 3 (Boston: Little, Brown, 1850–1856), 171.

21. Thomas G. West, *Vindicating the Founders: Race, Class, and Justice in the Origins of America* (Lanham, Md.: Rowman and Littlefield, 1997), 74.

22. Tocqueville, *Democracy in America,* vol. 2, pt. 3, chap. 12, 576–577.

23. Ibid.

24. Ibid., 578.

25. Ibid., 564.

26. Ibid., 568.

27. Ibid., 571.

28. Tocqueville, *Democracy in America,* vol. 1, pt. 2, chap. 9, 271.

29. Ibid., 268.

30. Paul Johnson. "God and the Americans," *Commentary,* January 1995, 25–45.

31. Ibid., 28.

32. Ibid., 29.

33. Tocqueville, *Democracy in America,* vol. 2, pt. 1, chap. 1, 396.

34. Tocqueville, *Democracy in America,* vol. 1, pt. 2, chap. 9, 266–270.

35. Ibid., 272.

36. Johnson, "God and the Americans," 31.

37. Tocqueville, *Democracy in America,* vol. 1, pt. 2, chap. 9, 269.

38. Tocqueville, *Democracy in America,* vol. 2, pt. 2, chap. 15, 517.

39. Saxe Comins, ed. *Basic Writings of George Washington* (New York: Random House, 1948).

40. Thanksgiving proclamation, October 3, 1789, in *George Washington: A Collection,* ed. W. B. Allen (Indianapolis: Liberty Classics, 1988), 534.

41. John Adams. *A Defense of the Constitutions of Government of the United States of America: Against the Attack of M. Turgot in His Letter to Dr. Price, Dated 22nd March, 1778* (Philadelphia: Budd and Bartram, 1797).

42. See Werner Jaeger, *Paideia: The Ideals of Greek Culture* (New York: Oxford University Press, 1939).

CHAPTER 11

1. Elizabeth Bumiller. "The Elephant's Ecstasy and Washington in Wait; Now Get Ready for the Country Club Presidency," *Washington Post,* November 6, 1980. See also Henry Allen, "The Fifties Are Coming; Say Hello to Reagan Retro, So Long to Liberal Chic," *Washington Post,* November 12, 1980.

2. Quoted in editorial, "Review and Outlook: Vacuum of Justice," *Wall Street Journal,* April 30, 1997, 14.

3. The United States supposedly became the world's largest debtor in 1986. That year, however, Americans netted $20.8 billion from overseas investments. See Charles Wolf and Sarah Hooker, "Who Owes Whom, and How Much," *Wall Street Journal,* January 6, 1988.

4. Jason DeParle. "Social Investment Programs: Comparing the Past with the Promised Payoff," *New York Times,* March 2, 1993.

5. Gary Becker. "The Best Reason to Get People off the Dole," *Business Week,* May 1, 1995.

6. Paul Gigot. "The Fine Art of Helping Political Friends," *Wall Street Journal,* March 28, 1997.

7. See Mancur Olson, *The Logic of Collective Action: Public Goods and the Theory of Groups* (Cambridge: Harvard University Press, 1971), and Jonathan Rauch, *Demosclerosis* (New York: New York Times Books, 1994).

8. Ibid., 30.

9. Niccolò Machiavelli. *The Prince,* trans. Angelo Codevilla (New Haven, Conn.: Yale University Press, 1997), chap. 16. The recipients of benefits cannot possibly be satisfied. As their demands grow, the government is compelled to become more tax prone and to alienate society's producers, who retreat into sullen passivity or worse.

10. Rauch, *Demosclerosis,* 67.

11. James L. Payne. *The Culture of Spending* (San Francisco: Institute for Contemporary Studies, 1991), 13. See also "Where Experience Doesn't Count: Arguments for Limiting Congressional Terms," *Across the Board* 28, no. 9 (September 1991): 21.

12. See *New York Times,* March 31, 2008. Also Jason DeParle, "Social Investment Programs: Comparing the Past with the Promised Payoff," *New York Times,* March 2, 1993.

13. See Heather MacDonald's report entitled "Welfare's Next Vietnam" from Manhattan Institute's *City Journal,* cited in *Wall Street Journal,* January 20, 1995.

14. Charles Murray. "The Coming White Underclass," *Wall Street Journal,* October 29, 1993.

15. In "Welfare's Next Vietnam," MacDonald reported: "Stories abound of parents coaching their kids to misbehave in school or fail their tests. A child in Wynne, Arkansas, asked his teacher if doing well on an exam would affect his 'crazy check.' According to Morton Gold of the Social Security Administration's Savannah, Georgia, office, parents sometimes hold their children out of school to ensure that they will fall back several grades and thus fail the age appropriate test."

16. Kimberly Amadeo. "U.S. Federal Budget 2008," About.com. See also Carolyn L. Weaver, "Social Security's Infirmity," *American Enterprise* 4, no. 2 (March-April 1993): 30.

17. See Sylvester J. Schieber, "Your Retirement, Your Social Security," *Wall Street Journal,* January 8, 1997, for one proposal for transitioning from the current social security system to something closer to the Chilean model.

18. Lisa Belkin. "Under New Health Plans Patients Change Habits," *New York Times,* January 6, 1993.

19. During the Thomas confirmation, Senator Joseph Biden and other liberal senators on the Judiciary Committee, following counsel by Harvard law professor Laurence H. Tribe—who had argued for "natural" rights to privacy during the Bork proceedings—attacked Thomas's position that the Constitution is an expansion of natural law. See Jacob Weisberg, "Supreme Courtier: Larry Tribe's Hopeless Quest," in *The New Republic,* September 30, 1991, 16. Biden could not understand how it would be possible for Thomas to serve on the Supreme Court if he held the position that natural law arguments against the institution of slavery—embodied in the Declaration of Independence—were true. Confused, Biden argued, "I find it hard to understand how you can say what you're now saying, that natural law was only . . . , you were only talking about the philosophy in a general philosophic sense, and not how it informed or impacted upon Constitutional interpretation" (as stated in a recording of the confirmation hearings by the *MacNeil/Lehrer News Hour* on September 10, 1991). Like many others, Biden fails to recognize that humans comprehend truth through reason. That is why truth is "self-evident." Also see "'Lord Biden'—Font of Natural Law," *Washington Times,* September 22, 1991.

20. See the debate between Lino A. Graglia and Harry V. Jaffa in *National Review,* August 14, 1995, 27, 31.

21. Philip K. Howard. *The Death of Common Sense* (New York: Basic Books, 1995), 10.

22. Internal Revenue Service. *Annual Report, 1992,* 42.

23. James Bovard. *Lost Rights* (New York: St. Martin's Press, 1994), 268, 270.

24. Ibid., 65.

25. Cf. Gene Wirges's *Conflict of Interest: The Gene Wirges Story* (North Little Rock, Ark.: Riverboat, 1992). To a lesser extent, the lessons apply elsewhere. Also see Kevin Sachs, "The Great Incumbency Machine," *New York Times Magazine,* September 27, 1992.

26. *Moore v. Valder,* 314 US App. D.C. 209 (1995).

27. Note that Cokie Roberts of ABC News reported that members of a test audience responded most passionately when speakers at the 1996 Republican National Convention called for the abolition of the IRS. See transcript, *This Week with David Brinkley,* August 18, 1996.

28. Lance Morrow. "A Nation of Finger Pointers," *Time,* August 12, 1991, 18–22.

29. Mary Ann Glendon. *Rights Talk: The Impoverishment of Political Discourse* (New York: Free Press, 1991).

30. See the case of Diane Joyce versus Paul Johnson, the subject of *Johnson v. Santa Clara County* (1987), in Melvin Urovsky, *A Conflict of Rights* (New York: Charles Scribner's Sons, 1994). At stake was a road dispatcher's job.

31. See, for example, Dan Levy, "San Jose Coaches Upset by Spoof of Sexual Harassment," *San Francisco Chronicle,* November 22, 1990.

32. Ellis Cose. *The Rage of the Privileged Class* (New York: HarperCollins, 1993).

33. Tom Brune. "Washington State: Want Your Check? Draft a Growth Plan," *Christian Science Monitor,* August 5, 1996.

34. Two of the landmark cases were *Plessy v. Ferguson* (1896), in which the Supreme Court allowed government-mandated racial separation in public transportation, and *Brown v. Board of Education* (1954), in which it ruled for government-mandated integration of schools. In both cases the Court rejected Justice John Marshall Harlan's argument that "our Constitution is color blind" and that rights inhere in individuals rather than in groups.

35. Richard Raymer. "Wanted, a Kinder, Gentler Cop," *New York Times Magazine,* January 22, 1995, 26.

36. Jeffrey Snyder. "A Nation of Cowards," *Public Interest* (Fall 1993): 42.

37. David Kopel. "The Untold Triumph of Concealed Carry Permits," *Policy Review,* July-August 1996, 9.

38. Samuel Francis. "Elites Are Prosperous amid the Slaughter," *Washington Times,* December 17, 1993.

39. Mark Melcher. *Potomac Perspectives* (Washington, D.C.: Prudential Securities, 1995).

CHAPTER 12

1. Inter-University Consortium for Political and Social Research. *American National Election Studies, 1948–1994* (Ann Arbor: University of Michigan Press, 1994).

2. U.S. Bureau of the Census. *Marital Status and Living Arrangements: March 1990.* Current Population Report Series, 15–25. See also www.libraryindex.com/pages/795/Marital-Status-Family-Living-Arrangements.

3. Barbara Bennett Woodhouse. "Who Owns the Child? Meyer and Pierce and the Child as Property," *William and Mary Law Review* 33, no. 4 (Summer 1992): 1051.

4. "Advance Data from Vital and Health Statistics," no. 51, December 15, 2004, U.S. Department of Health and Human Services, Centers for Disease Control.

5. Steven A. Holmes. "Quality of Life Is Up," *New York Times,* November 18, 1996.

6. "The Marriage Gap," *Wall Street Journal,* November 15, 1996; "The Family—A Reader's Digest Poll," *Reader's Digest,* July 1992, 48–54.

7. I am much indebted for this insight to David Wagner, "The Family and the Constitution," *First Things* (August-September 1994).

8. Peter Steinfels. "Unmarried Couples, Single-Sex Couples, Triads and Quintets: Why Marriage Norms?" *New York Times,* May 14, 1994, "Beliefs."

9. Editorial, *New York Times,* June 6, 1997.

10. Reader's Digest poll on "The Family Gap," *Reader's Digest,* July 1992, 52.

11. David Gelertner. "Why Mothers Should Stay at Home," *Commentary,* February 1996, 28.

12. Herbert Jacob. *Silent Revolution: The Transformation of Divorce Law in the United States* (Chicago: University of Chicago Press, 1988), 28.

13. William A. Galston. "Needed, a Not So Fast Divorce Law," *New York Times,* December 27, 1995.

14. See testimony by Andrew J. Cherlin before the House Select Committee on Children, Youth, and Families, cited in David Blankenhorn, *Fatherless America* (New York: Basic Books, 1995).

15. See Bill Callahan, "DA Gives Priority to Statutory Rape Law; Case against Man, 19, Launches Offensive," *San Diego Union-Tribune,* February 5, 1996.

16. See Thomas Hobbes, "Of Dominion Paternall, and Despoticall," in *Leviathan* (New York: Penguin, 1968), chap. 20, 254.

17. Lena Williams. "Pregnant Teens Are Outcasts No Longer," *New York Times,* December 2, 1993.

18. Celia W. Dugger. "A Cultural Reluctance to Spare the Rod," *New York Times,* March 1, 1996.

19. Patrick Fagan. "The Real Root Causes of Violent Crime: The Breakdown of Marriage, Family, and Community," *Heritage Foundation,* March 17, 1995.

20. Dorothy Rabinowitz. "Justice in Dade County," *Wall Street Journal,* October 26, 1996.

21. Timothy Egan. "Child Sex Abuse Charges Tear at Scandal-Shaken Community," *Houston Chronicle,* April 19, 1995.

22. Gina Kolata. "Boom in Ritalin Sales Raises Ethical Issues," *New York Times,* May 16, 1996.

23. Ibid.

24. See, for example, Robyn Meredith, "Parents Convicted for a Youth's Misconduct," *New York Times,* May 10, 1995.

25. Editorial, *New York Times,* May 5, 1996.

26. "After surveying 65 studies on the influence of expenditures per pupil, Professor Eric A. Hanushek of the University of Rochester reported in the *Journal of Economic Literature* that 49 showed no statistical significance and that of the 16 that showed significance, 3 indicated a negative relationship. Of 112 studies on the influence of changing teacher-pupil ratios, only 23 were statistically significant, 9 in the positive direction, and 14 in the negative direction" (Edwin G. West, "Restoring Family Autonomy in Education," *Chronicles,* October 1990, 17).

27. On the performance of private and Catholic schools, see the classic work by James S. Coleman and Thomas Hoffer, *Public and Private High Schools: The Impact of Community* (New York: Basic Books, 1987).

28. Dirk Johnson. "Study Says Small Schools Are Key to Learning," *New York Times,* September 21, 1994.

29. Michael J. McCarthy. "Grim Prospect: Aged Try Mightily to Avoid the Nursing Home," *Wall Street Journal,* December 3, 1992.

30. Melinda Herneberger. "Losing the 'Home' in 'Nursing Home,'" *New York Times,* December 17, 1992.

31. Michael J. McCarthy. "Many States Await Result of Florida Attempt to Support 'Aging in Place,'" *Wall Street Journal,* March 4, 1992.

32. See James Thorsen, *Aging in a Changing Society* (New York: Psychology Press, 2000), 333–337.

33. Timothy Egan. "When Children Can't Afford Parents," *New York Times,* March 29, 1992.

34. David Brooks. *Bobos in Paradise: The New Class and How They Got There* (New York: Simon and Schuster, 2000).

35. Richard Grenier. "The America You Don't Know," *Washington Times,* October 31, 1995. See also Edward Rothstein, "As Culture Wars Go On, Battle Lines Blur a Bit," *New York Times,* May 27, 1997; and Clifford D. May, "America's Culture Wars, Society Engaged in an Intellectual Battle over the Country's Moral Direction," *Rocky Mountain News,* May 7, 1995. But above all, see the debate between the magazine *First Things* (October-November 1996) and *Commentary* (February 1997) on whether and to what extent the American Establishment's hostility to the mores and religion of most Americans is depriving the regime of its legitimacy.

36. Peter Brimelow. "America's Identity Crisis: On the Importance of Immigration; Why Kemp and Bennett Are Wrong," *National Review,* November 21, 1994.

37. Thus, Bill Clinton has delivered several moving speeches on the subject. See, for example, his speech in the *New York Times,* July 12, 1995.

38. Kenneth Woodward. "Talking to God," *Newsweek,* January 6, 1992. Apparently, some 78 percent of Americans pray at least weekly, and 57 percent do so at least once per day. Ninety-one percent of women and 85 percent of men report that they "pray regularly."

39. See Allen E. Bergin, "Values and Religious Issues in Psychotherapy and Mental Health," *American Psychologist* 46 (1991): 394–403; David B. Larsen et al., "Dimensions and Valences of Religious Commitment," *American Journal of Psychiatry* 149 (1978).

40. *Stone v. Graham,* 449 US 39 (1980). For the confrontation in Alabama, see Katherine Q. Seelye, "House Republicans Back Judge on Display of 10 Commandments," *New York Times,* March 5, 1997.

41. *Jones v. North Carolina Prisoners' Labor Union,* 433 US 119 (1977).

42. *Wallace v. Jaffree,* 472 US 38 (1985), is the latest significant case.

43. "*Herndahl v. Pontontoc Co.,*" *New York Times,* June 4, 1996.

44. As retold in a speech by Ralph Reed, Laguna Beach, Calif., January 21, 1995. See the prepared testimony of Jay Alan Sekulow, chief counsel, American Center for Law and Justice, before the House Committee on the Judiciary, Subcommittee on the Constitution, July 23, 1996.

45. Douglas C. Holland, county counsel, Monterey County, Calif., memo dated December 8, 1992.

46. Editorial, *New York Times,* October 13, 1994.

47. "Lamm Dispenses Bitter Pills Not Likely Swallowed," *Palm Beach Post,* August 10, 1996.

48. John Keown. "Dutch Slide Down Euthanasia's Slippery Slope," *Wall Street Journal,* November 5, 1991.

49. Editorial, "Educators or Lobbyists," *Washington Times,* September 1, 1996. Moreover, the *Times* reports "Half of all unionized delegates were teachers. The NEA delegation, about the size of California's, again represented the largest special-interest block, a distinction it has prized for each of the last six Democratic conventions."

50. *National Standards for United States History: Exploring the American Experience* (Los Angeles: National Center for History in the Schools/University of California at Los Angeles, 1994).

51. James F. Cooper. "Art Censors: A Closer Look at the NEA," *New Dimensions,* June 1991, 26–29. See also Robert Knight, "The NEA," *Heritage Foundation,* January 18, 1991; and Mark Lasswell, "Not All AIDS Dramas Are on Broadway," *Wall Street Journal,* April 29, 1996.

52. Myron Magnet. *The Dream and the Nightmare: The Sixties' Legacy to the Underclass* (New York: W. Morrow, 1993).

53. *New York Times,* December 22, 1996, "News of the Week in Review."

54. Terry Teachout. "Abortion, Set to Music," *First Things* 65 (August-September 1996): 42.

55. James Q. Wilson. "Tales of Virtue: Moral Development and Children," *Current* 365 (September 1994): 4.

56. Niccolò Machiavelli. *Discorso o dialogo interno alla nostra lingua,* ed. Bortolo Tommaso Sozzi (Torino: Einaudi, 1976), bk. 1, 11–15. Emphasis mine.

CHAPTER 13

1. See Angelo M. Codevilla, "Birds of a Feather," *National Interest* 35 (Spring 1994).

2. See John Lewis Gaddis, "The Tragedy of Cold War History," *Diplomatic History* 17, no. 1 (January/February 1993): 1–16, for a friendly acknowledgment of the Establishment's orthodoxy.

3. See Anthony Lake, ed., *The Vietnam Legacy: The War, American Society, and the Future of American Foreign Policy* (New York: New York University Press, 1976), xxi.

4. Perhaps the most poignant document is Robert McNamara's memoir, *In Retrospect: The Tragedy and Lessons of Vietnam* (New York: Times Books, 1995), in which the former secretary of defense explains how family and friends persuaded him that he was on the wrong side of the war but that he nevertheless continued to order men to fight and die in it.

5. Polls cited in Arthur M. Schlesinger Jr., *Robert Kennedy and His Times* (Boston: Houghton Mifflin, 1978), 843.

6. *Social Representation in the U.S. Military* (Washington, D.C.: Congressional Budget Office, 1989), 41.

7. Found at www.af.mil/library/guidelines2005.pdf. Emphasis mine.

8. Chris Hedges. "Studying Bosnia's Prisoners of Peace." *New York Times,* March 30, 1997.

9. *New York Times,* November 4, 1990. See also Owen Ullman, "Baker's Vagueness Does Little to Relieve Frustration of Troops," *Orange County Register,* November 5, 1990.

10. See Richard H. Kohn, "The Crisis in Civil-Military Relations," *National Interest* 36 (Spring 1994); and Colin Powell, John Lehman, William Odom, and Samuel Huntington, "Civil-Military Relations Debated," *National Interest* 36 (Summer 1994).

INDEX